MORAL COMMERCE

MORAL COMMERCE

QUAKERS AND THE TRANSATLANTIC BOYCOTT OF THE SLAVE LABOR ECONOMY

JULIE L. HOLCOMB

CORNELL UNIVERSITY PRESS
Ithaca and London

First published 2016 by Cornell University Press
First paperback printing 2020

Library of Congress Cataloging-in-Publication Data

Names: Holcomb, Julie L., author.
Title: Moral commerce : Quakers and the Transatlantic
    boycott of the slave labor economy / Julie L. Holcomb.
Description: Ithaca ; London : Cornell University Press
    2016. | Includes bibliographical references and index.
Identifiers: LCCN 2016017620 | ISBN 9780801452086
    (cloth)
Subjects: LCSH: Antislavery movements—United
    States—History. | Antislavery movements—Great
    Britain—History. | Quaker abolitionists—United
    States. | Quaker abolitionists—Great Britain.
Classification: LCC E441 .H69 2016 | DDC
    326/.80973—dc23
LC record available at https://lccn.loc.gov/2016017620

ISBN 978-1-5017-4849-3 (pbk.)

For Stan

Contents

ILLUSTRATIONS

ACKNOWLEDGMENTS

As a history major at Pacific University, I anticipated a career that would combine my interests in public and academic history with a desire to study American labor history, particularly the activism of women like the Progressive Era labor reformer Florence Kelley. Although my intellectual interests have changed in the last fifteen years, I have, in many ways, come full circle because it was in writing about Kelley, the niece of Quaker free-produce activist and abolitionist Sarah Pugh, that I first encountered the American free-produce movement. Pugh and the other activists who boycotted slave-labor goods have engaged my deepest intellectual interests for more than ten years. In researching and writing the story of the boycott of slave labor, I have had the opportunity to work with many individuals and institutions. It is a pleasure to acknowledge the many ways in which they have supported and shaped this work.

This book began as a research project under the direction of Sam W. Haynes at the University of Texas at Arlington. He along with Stephanie Cole helped shepherd me through both the exam and the dissertation process. Their generous feedback and their critical reading of my research helped clarify my ideas, and their influence remains although the book bears little resemblance to that research. I also benefited from the knowledge and advice of several other historians at UTA, including Robert Fairbanks, Stephen Maizlish, Christopher Morris, and Steven Reinhardt.

At Cornell University Press, Michael McGandy worked hard to help me to transform an academic document into a book. I appreciate his support and his patience as well as the assistance of the various editors, especially my copy editor, and staff members who helped bring this project through to publication. I also thank Richard Huzzey and Beth Salerno for their incisive comments on various drafts of the manuscript. Their suggestions, comments, and questions have made this a much better work.

I appreciate the many scholars who have commented on conference papers and chapter drafts, including Winifred Connerton, A. Glenn Crothers,

Seymour Drescher, Carol Faulkner, Lynne Getz, Natalie Joy, Bonnie Laughlin-Schultz, Bruce Laurie, Seth Offenbach, Stacey Robertson, Srividhya Swaminathan, Julie Turner, and Michael Woods. I also thank Caleb Mc-Daniel, Edward Rugemer, and Beverly Tomek.

For the past eight years, Baylor University has been my academic home. In the department of museum studies and in the larger university community I have found a supportive, collegial group of colleagues, including Eric Ames, Ellie Caston, Trey Crumpton, Kenneth Hafertepe, Heidi Hornick, T. Michael Parrish, Stephen Sloan, Gary Smith, Joy Summar-Smith, Stephanie Turnham, and Lenore Wright. Lisa Rieger, administrative associate for the department of museum studies, has assisted in ways both large and small as has the amazing staff of the Mayborn Museum Complex. I am indeed quite fortunate to work with such a generous and talented group of people.

The knowledge, skills, and guidance of numerous archivists and librarians were invaluable to this project. I relied in particular on the amazing Quaker collections at Swarthmore and Haverford Colleges. At Swarthmore, Christopher Densmore, director of the Friends Historical Library, along with Patricia O'Donnell and Susanna Morikawa, provided valuable assistance and advice. At Haverford, I thank Sarah Horowitz, head of special collections, as well as past staff members, Diana Franzusoff Peterson and Ann Upton. I am grateful to the staff members of the Chester County Historical Society and the Boston Public Library. At Baylor University and at the University of Texas at Arlington, the staff members of the interlibrary loan departments were remarkably intrepid, tracking down even the most obscure of sources.

The Office of the Vice Provost for Research at Baylor University supported this project with grants from the University Research Committee and the Arts and Humanities Research Program. Financial support came also from the American Historical Association in the form of an Albert J. Beveridge grant. As a doctoral student, I received funding from the National Society of the Colonial Dames of America in Texas, Ft. Worth Town Chapter; the Trudy and Ben Termini Graduate Student Research Grant fund; and the history department, University of Texas at Arlington.

No project of this magnitude happens without the support of friends and family. For more than fifteen years, my life has been enriched by the friendship of Sarah Canby Jackson. I also thank Mary Hayes, Michael and Alice Mattick, Rosalie Meier, Amanda Morrison, Sue Sanders, and Hugh and Bonnie Reynolds. At St. Joseph Catholic Church, I have found a warm, welcoming community of friends who have sustained me. Their friendship and their faith is a much needed reprieve from teaching, research, and writing. I know that I could not have finished this project without the support of my extended family: Mark Holcomb and Sara Eckel, David Holcomb, Steven and Debra Holcomb, as well as my son-in-law Eric Sfetku and his parents Bob and Joyce Sfetku. My daughter Jennifer Holcomb Sfetku has been an amazing force for good in my life. She continues to inspire me. My grandchildren Noah and Paige remind me that my most important title, my most important role is to be their Grams. I hope Noah will not be too disappointed that the cover does not say "Grams Holcomb."

More than anyone, my husband Stan Holcomb has felt the stress of this particular project, which has occupied me for a full one-third of our time as husband and wife. For more than thirty years, his unwavering, unconditional love has kept me centered. Words cannot sufficiently express my appreciation for his laughter, his faith, his patience, and his reassurance throughout this process. Only he can understand what I mean when I say this book is, like its author, his.

Introduction
A Principle Both Moral and Commercial

> To live means to buy, to buy means to have power, to have power means to have responsibility.
>
> —*Florence Kelley*, Founder, National Consumers League, c. 1914

In May 1840, New York businessmen Thomas McClintock and Richard P. Hunt presented American abolitionist William Lloyd Garrison with four yards of olive wool suiting that had been manufactured at Hunt's Waterloo woolen mill. The gift to the publisher of the *Liberator* was intended to publicize the free-produce cause. McClintock and Hunt were antislavery Quakers who boycotted the products of slave labor: McClintock helped establish the Free Produce Society of Pennsylvania, while Hunt chose to manufacture free-labor wool rather than slave-grown cotton.[1] In separate letters of appreciation to McClintock and Hunt, Garrison wrote of his plans to have the fabric made into a "free suit" to wear at the upcoming World Anti-Slavery Convention in London. The free-labor wool, he noted, would "be regarded with interest and pleasure on the other side of the Atlantic, as well as on this."[2]

Like many abolitionists in the 1820s and 1830s, Garrison supported free produce, describing it as "the most comprehensive mode that can be adopted to destroy the growth of slavery." Although he did not believe the boycott should be the "sole weapon" in the fight against slavery, Garrison did call for "the multiplication of free produce societies."[3] By the mid-1830s, however, Garrison began to withdraw his support for the boycott, claiming free produce suffered from significant economic and moral shortcomings. As an economic measure, the boycott was misguided, targeting slaveholders who were motivated "not [by] the love of gain, but the possession of absolute power, unlimited sovereignty." As a moral principle, the boycott gave supporters a "pretext to do nothing more for the slave because they do so much" in their efforts to locate free-labor goods. Supporters of the boycott, Garrison claimed, found "it much easier to pursue" free produce than "to engage in any 'fanatical agitation' of society, after the manner of the 'ultra abolitionists.'" By 1840, despite his remarks to McClintock and Hunt, Garrison had come to believe free produce was "an extraneous issue" of "comparatively small importance."[4]

Throughout the late 1830s and 1840s, McClintock, Hunt, and other supporters of the boycott tried in vain to change Garrison's mind. Among those supporters was Sarah Pugh, a Philadelphia Quaker and an officer of the American Free Produce Association (AFPA). A petite woman, she was characterized as "conscience incarnate" by her niece, the Progressive Era labor reformer Florence Kelley. Pugh joined the abolitionist movement in 1835, after hearing a speech by British abolitionist George Thompson. A member of the Philadelphia Female Anti-Slavery Society (PFASS) as well as the AFPA, Pugh represented both organizations at the World Anti-Slavery Convention in 1840. She lamented abolitionists' apathy toward the boycott of slave labor: "The great mass of abolitionists need an abstinence baptism." In a direct reference to Garrison's dismissal of free produce, she claimed many abolitionists had "sacrificed political party and religious sect for the cause of freedom, yet the taint of slavery still clings to them, and they need to be pointed to the stain that dims their otherwise consistent testimony." Pugh emphasized both the economic principle and the moral commitment of free produce. Although she recognized the practical limits of the boycott of slave labor, she still believed it possible for abolitionists "to cease from *direct* support" of slavery by refusing to consume slave-labor goods such as sugar and cotton. If all consumers were to end their direct support of slavery, Pugh reasoned, "the slave [would] be a slave no longer." More importantly, abstention from slave-labor products served as evidence of abolitionists' ideological consistency. "I can never know that any slave was personally helped," Pugh later told her niece, "but I had to live with my own conscience."[5]

Garrison's dismissal of free produce has had a long afterlife, overshadowing the efforts of abolitionists like Pugh to situate the boycott at the heart of the abolitionist movement. Arguably the most prominent of American abolitionists, Garrison was an important supporter of the boycott. When he gave up the boycott in the 1830s, his defection reverberated throughout the abolitionist community. Rowland T. Robinson, a Quaker from Vermont, urged Garrison to give "more than a mere recommendation" to abstention, while

Angelina Grimké of the PFASS described herself as "grieved" by the loss of Garrison's support for the movement. "The weight of his example & his influence are very extensive," Grimké noted. If Garrison had "continued, as he began, to earnestly and powerfully advocate the disuse of slave products," Quaker Samuel Rhoads wrote in 1850, "the downfall of slavery would at this moment be nearer than it is."[6] Often this debate played out in public, as it did in the spring of 1847, when Garrison and the editors of the *Non-Slaveholder*, including Rhoads, argued about Garrison's inconsistent testimony against slavery.[7] In 1850, in one of the last mentions of free produce to appear in the *Liberator*, Garrison accused supporters of the boycott of "giv[ing] to an inch the importance of a mile."[8] In 1868, when Wendell Phillips Garrison, son of the abolitionist, wrote the first historical account of the movement, he like his father dismissed the movement: "The Abolitionists proper . . . although always stigmatized as impracticable, never mounted this hobby as if the battle-horse of victory." Supporters of free produce, wrote the younger Garrison, were inconsistent and irrelevant "sentimentalists" whose only value lay in "the conspicuousness of their testimony against slavery."[9]

Historical scholarship of the free-produce movement has until recently been quite limited. Wendell Garrison's article was the only historical account of free produce for more than seventy years until 1942 when Ruth Ketring Nuermberger published *The Free Produce Movement: A Quaker Protest against Slavery*. Like Garrison, she dismisses free produce as simply a Quaker movement: free produce as an idea was "not compelling enough to attract outsiders." As Nuermberger concludes, "Whether it is viewed as just another crackbrained scheme or as the sincere effort of earnest people, it could scarcely be called a success."[10] In the last thirty years, however, historians have begun to redirect our attention to free produce, noting in particular the support the movement had among women and black abolitionists as well as Quakers. Focusing on discrete temporal moments within the British or American movements, scholars such as Clare Midgley, Carol Faulkner, and Stacey Robertson have deepened our historical understanding of the slave-labor boycott. As important as these accounts are in recovering the history of free produce, they are focused on a particular national context.[11]

This book, in contrast, embraces a global framework to uncover the breadth as well as the depth of the free-produce movement. Tracing the genealogy of the boycott of slave labor from its seventeenth-century Quaker origins through its late nineteenth-century decline reveals the possibilities and the limitations of consumer activism. Free produce was the first consumer movement to transcend the boundaries of nation, gender, and race in an effort by reformers to change the conditions of production.[12] Even when they acted locally, supporters embraced a global vision, mobilizing the boycott as a powerful material force that could transform the transatlantic marketplace. Although the boycott often failed to overcome the power structures that kept slave labor in place, it still "could literally move people, move goods, and move possibilities for freedom around the world."[13] Understanding the movement's historic successes and failures has important implications for us as we continue to use the power of commodity consumption to solve political problems.[14]

Not every abolitionist abstained from slave-labor goods, but abstention attracted every kind of abolitionist: conservative and radical, Quaker and non-Quaker, male and female, white and black. Among the more conservative, boycotting slave-labor goods was a principled response to slavery that did not require a comparable commitment to Garrisonian-style immediatism.[15] Among the more radical, the boycott was "an act of racial rebellion," encouraging adherents to view slave-labor goods "as the fruits of the labor of our own children, brothers and sisters."[16] Abstention appealed especially to the politically marginalized: Quakers, women, and black abolitionists. Since these three themes—religion, gender, and race—guide our discussion, it is worth considering them here briefly.

Quaker opposition to slavery began with a condemnation of the trade and of slavery itself before it advanced to include the products of slave labor. The first advocate of abstention was the Quaker zealot Benjamin Lay, a man whose outward appearance was as startling as his actions. Standing less than five feet tall with a long white beard, Lay was infamous for a series of antislavery protests that included splattering Quakers with fake blood and kidnapping the child of a slaveholder. Lay lived simply, adopting a vegetarian diet, wearing coarse clothes, and, on occasion, living in a cave as part of his campaign to avoid anything produced by slave labor. He was disowned in 1738 after publishing a fiery antislavery tract without the permission of the Quaker elders. Inheriting this tradition of individual dissent against slavery, mid-eighteenth-century Quaker reformers like John Woolman transformed the "guerilla theater" of Lay into a sectarian critique of slavery and slave-labor goods.[17] Woolman developed a powerful moral argument against the products of slave labor, claiming the commerce in slaves and the products of their labor were both cause and consequence of a human desire for wealth. That desire for wealth perverted God's plans, Woolman wrote, forcing men "to labour harder than was intended by our gracious Creator." For Woolman, abstention was part of larger program of moral reform that would, with the help of God, remake the world.[18] The moral arguments against slave-labor goods put forth by Woolman continued to resonate with Quakers even after the rise of radical abolitionism in the 1830s led many conservative Quakers to disavow the organized abolitionist movement.

The continuity of the moral argument against the products of slave labor has led some scholars to assume that the boycott was simply a sectarian protest with little appeal beyond its Quaker proponents. One of the key questions this book seeks to address is to what extent the boycott was indeed a Quaker movement. The answer to that question has important implications for our understanding of Quakers' relationship to the broader antislavery movement. In the eighteenth century, Quaker activists were deeply involved in the antislavery activities of the period, even using, as historian Kirsten Sword argues, "Quaker saintliness" to mask their "cosmopolitanism." As she concludes, "a small but extraordinarily committed and well-connected group of Quakers" pushed antislavery onto the imperial stage, creating a mass movement.[19] In contrast, in the nineteenth century, Quakers were seemingly disconnected from antislavery, retreating as opposition to abolitionism strengthened. While most Quakers left the secular antislavery movement, many continued to abstain from slave-labor goods. Quaker support for free produce reminds us that, even after 1830, Friends continued to play a significant role in the fight for social justice in the United States. Whether conservative or radical, Quakers never wavered from their commitment to slavery's demise even if they rejected Garrisonian abolitionism.

More recent scholarship of the slave-labor boycott emphasizes the role of women and black abolitionists. Among women, abstention was one of the most popular and consistent forms of activism. Quaker and non-Quaker alike, British and American women asserted the moral commitment of abstention. The eighteenth-century slave-sugar boycott unfolded concurrently with two cultural processes that impacted women's participation in the boycott. The first was the ideological development of the domestic sphere. The ideology of "separate spheres" described men as rational, competitive, and independent. In contrast, "true womanhood" was based on the qualities of piety, purity, submissiveness, and domesticity. Women were considered morally superior to men and, therefore, expected to wield virtuous influence over husbands, brothers, and sons through their guidance and example.[20] This cultural ideal associated women with the domestic sphere, an association that later provided the basis for naturalizing the boycott as a female concern. The second cultural process was the proliferation of consumer goods, the so-called consumer revolution.[21] As opportunities to consume material goods expanded in the Atlantic world in this period, critics questioned the impact such changes had on society and, in particular, on women. The female consumer was a "powerfully paradoxical presence" in society, at times "supremely disciplined" while at other times "disruptive or disorderly." As literary scholar Elizabeth Kowaleski-Wallace argues, "British culture projected onto the female subject both its fondest wishes for the transforming power of consumerism and its deepest anxieties about the corrupting influences of goods."[22] During the British slave-sugar boycott, these cultural concerns about female commerce became entangled in abstention rhetoric as supporters and opponents alike questioned women's motivation and morality.

In contrast, in the nineteenth century, the expansion of evangelical Christianity with its emphasis on individual action, perfectibility, and female morality made it seem self-evident that women would support the boycott. Many women did just that and more, organizing antislavery and free-produce societies, petitioning political leaders, and canvassing neighborhoods. Once again questions were raised about women's participation in the movement; only this time the questions focused on what constituted appropriate female behavior. Many of the women who participated in the boycott accepted a gendered view of the world and women's moral responsibility, but they often blurred the distinction between private and public spheres. The boycott, with its dual emphasis on individual and collective action, aided the creation of competing visions of gender and political action among women and men, reinforcing women's domestic role while supporting the development of a more radical, activist role for women. As a result, the pliable rhetoric of abstention attracted both conservative and radical women who used the movement to reinforce their particular ideals of womanhood.[23]

For black abolitionists, the boycott was a practical antislavery tactic, one that was critical to racial uplift because it reinforced black abolitionists' efforts to establish an economic foundation for the free black community. Free and enslaved blacks challenged racial stereotypes, asserted their political rights, and demanded the fruits of their labor. In early national America free blacks engaged in community building, developing a power base in a time and place when blacks were stripped of "every vestige of power." According to historian Richard S. Newman, these "black founders created the social and economic infrastructure that defined free black life through much of the late eighteenth and all of the nineteenth century, developing autonomous black churches, insurance and self-help organizations, and early abolitionist strategies."[24] The presence of black businessmen in eighteenth-century Philadelphia and elsewhere contradicted white stereotypes. Through their individual and collective actions, black activists demanded a place in the transatlantic economy, one based on their right to the fruits of their labor.

Black activism influenced the boycott in vital ways, challenging early abstention rhetoric that emphasized African contamination of white domestic goods. In his famous anticolonization letter of 1827, the former slave and founder of the Bethel African Methodist Episcopal Church, Richard Allen, used the language of white abstention writers to claim American citizenship: "This land, which we have watered with our tears and blood, is now our mother country and we are well satisfied to stay where wisdom abounds and the gospel is free."[25] During the slave-sugar boycott, white writers claimed African bodily fluids had contaminated the goods produced by slave labor. Allen turned that argument around, claiming that African blood, sweat, and tears were the means by which blacks would demand civil and political rights. In the 1830s, black and white abolitionists formed integrated societies such as the PFASS and the AFPA. While racism and division persisted in the relationship between white and black abolitionists, these integrated communities played a critical role in raising activists' awareness of the connection between free-labor goods and racial equality. In the 1850s the boycott contributed to the development of black nationalism. Abolitionist Henry Highland Garnet claimed African colonization provided an opportunity to gain civil and political rights for American blacks and to provide a source for free-labor commodities such as cotton and sugar. Black supporters of the boycott used consumer activism to test, contest, and transcend the limits placed on them by white society.[26]

Bringing together in a single narrative these three groups—Quakers, women, and black abolitionists—complicates the conventional story of a Quaker free-produce movement. It also complicates recent free-produce scholarship that highlights the activism of women and black abolitionists. The men and women who boycotted slave labor created diverse, biracial networks that simultaneously divided and united their efforts as they worked to reorganize the transatlantic economy on an ethical basis. This book recovers these multivocal networks, positioning them within the global context of the movement.

The men and women who boycotted slave-labor goods faced a formidable task. They had to first convince consumers that the immorality of slavery tainted all goods produced by slave labor. Then they had to convince consumers to take action against such tainted goods. This was no easy task in an era when "freedom, not slavery, was the peculiar institution."[27] Still, supporters of the boycott persisted, describing African bodies and the productions of those laboring bodies as stolen goods. In his *Twenty Reasons for Total Abstinence from the Products of Slave Labor* (c. 1852), American abolitionist Elihu Burritt began by describing slave-labor goods as "the fruits of an aggravated robbery perpetrated upon [the slave] daily." For Burritt, all other reasons for abstinence followed from this simple fact: the theft of the slave's labor was both sinful and criminal. Such language reinforced the moral argument against slave-labor goods first articulated by Quakers in the eighteenth century. It also challenged slaveholders' belief that the goods produced by their slaves were simply the result of a well-managed business. Recognizing the immorality of slave-labor goods was not in itself sufficient, however, and boycotters like Burritt urged consumers to take practical action against such goods by refusing to consume anything produced by slave labor. Abstention was an act of ideological consistency, multiplying abolitionists' efforts and giving "force and emphasis" to all other antislavery activities. Moreover, Burritt believed abstention was "a mode of anti-slavery activism in which every man, woman, and child may take a part every day, at every meal, in every article of dress they wear and enjoy. And this silent, daily testimony would tend to keep their anti-slavery sentiments active, out-spoke, and ever working in their spheres of influence."[28]

In addition to abstention, Burritt advocated the substitution of free-labor goods. Like many supporters of the boycott, Burritt believed free produce could combine moral and commercial principles to stimulate the free-labor production of cotton, sugar, rice, and other goods, thus forcing slaveholders to free their slaves when the market for slave-labor goods disappeared. The idea of free-labor substitutes was not a new one. Eighteenth-century Quaker reformer Joshua Evans, for example, believed home-grown herbal drinks were better than "East India tea."[29] Not only was tea consumption habit forming, it also relied on slave-grown sugar. During the sugar boycott of the 1790s, activists encouraged consumers to use maple sugar or East India sugar rather than slave-grown West Indian sugar. Despite these similarities, free produce in the nineteenth century was more complicated and more activist in its outlook than its eighteenth-century predecessor.

The development of free produce in the nineteenth century reflected both the greater availability of free-labor goods, especially after Britain abolished slavery in the 1830s, and the efforts of boycotters to create a free-labor economy. Supporters of free produce explored free-labor alternatives in British India, Haiti, Africa, Texas, and Massachusetts. Unfortunately, these alternatives were often plagued by questionable labor conditions and poor financial support as well as having problems with distribution and quality. Quaker George W. Taylor, who operated a free-labor store in Philadelphia from 1847 to 1867, struggled to maintain a steady flow of free-labor goods. Often his supplies were sporadic, out-of-season, of poor quality, and more costly than slave-labor alternatives. His correspondence in the 1840s and 1850s suggests a man in perpetual motion, attempting to secure goods for his customers.[30] The actions of merchants like Taylor led Boston abolitionist Samuel J. May to quip that free-produce activists "fritter[ed] away great energies & respectable powers in controversies about yards of cotton-cloth & pounds of sugar."[31] Frustrated with irregular supplies, Taylor attempted to manufacture his own cotton cloth, leasing a small mill in Chester County, Pennsylvania, in the 1850s. Manufacturing free-labor goods tied moral commitments to economic principles. Supporters continued to expect that an increase in the production of free-labor goods, combined with concomitant increase in consumer demand for such goods, would force slave-labor goods from the market.[32]

Boycotters believed that if slavery were rendered unprofitable, slaveholders would be forced to free their slaves. However, economic boycotts were (and remain) an imperfect political weapon. Critics of free produce were quick to point out the difficulties of maintaining a total boycott of slave labor. Consider the transatlantic economy in this period. From international trade to local commerce, slave- and free-labor goods comingled, if only by proximity. Ships used slave-produced cotton and hemp for their sails and ropes. Sailors on those ships were clothed in cotton while slave-produced sugar and rum provided essential calories and offered diversion from the long voyage. Once in port, those ships and sailors delivered cotton, sugar, and other goods produced by both slave and free labor, for sale and consumption in the local market. And the profits produced by all of those commercial exchanges assured a continual flow of goods and people throughout the Atlantic world.[33] As Garrison concluded in 1847, slave-labor products were "so mixed up with the commerce, manufactures and agriculture of the world—so modified or augmented in value by the industry of other nations,—so indissolubly connected with the credit and currency of the country" that abstaining from them was "preposterous and unjust."[34]

Many abolitionists, including Garrison, opposed the boycott of slave labor. Abolitionist opponents maintained that taken to its logical extreme, the boycott would bring the abolitionist movement to a halt. American abolitionist Elizur Wright, for example, claimed that boycotting slave-grown cotton would force abolitionists to avoid travel by stage or steamboat and to suspend all publications because such activities led abolitionists to consume—directly or indirectly—cotton and other slave-labor goods. Complete abstinence, he said, would force "merchants and manufactures [to] throw perhaps half their stock and their capital into the fire," significantly weakening the transatlantic economy.[35] Other abolitionists like William Goodell claimed the boycott of slave-labor goods did not go far enough. Rather, to be consistent, abolitionist consumers should boycott *all* goods produced under oppressive conditions.[36]

Abolitionist opposition to free produce, however, was the least of the boycotters' worries even though, at times, it seemed to occupy much of their energy. In the first half of the nineteenth century, the exponential expansion of the slave economy, particularly in the production of cotton, proved to be the boycott's most formidable obstacle. Tracing "the march from seed to mill to consumer," historian Edward E. Baptist measures what he describes as the first-, second-, and third-order effects of slave-grown cotton. The first-order effect was the cotton crop itself. Cotton sales in 1836, for example, totaled 5 percent of the entire U.S. domestic product, constituting the single-largest source of value in the American economy. Second-order effects resulted from the goods and services necessary to produce cotton and included financial transactions such as slave sales, land sales, and lines of credit as well as provisions such as pork, corn, and cloth. Third-order effects included the money spent by individuals as diverse as textile workers in New England and hog farmers in Illinois whose labor provided goods for slaveholders. The purchases made by these millworkers and hog farmers fueled local economies throughout the so-called free-labor North. As Baptist concludes, "All told, more than $600 million, or almost half of the economic activity in the United States in 1836, derived directly or indirectly from cotton produced by the million-odd slaves—6 percent of the total US population—who toiled in labor camps on slavery's frontier."[37] Such sobering statistics reveal the sheer audacity of the free-produce movement. Slave labor infiltrated every aspect of the American economy and was as historian Seth Rockman notes, "indispensable to the American economy as it rose to global importance in the nineteenth century." The global reach of the American economy ensured that it influenced commercial transactions in the Atlantic world and beyond.[38] Indeed, Elihu Burritt described American slavery as an "international evil [that] feeds itself at the markets of nations and communities that have abolished or repudiated the inhuman institution."[39] Still, for every Garrison who rejected the boycott of slave labor as "impracticable," there could be found a Sarah Pugh who believed success "will come in good time if we faint not."[40]

The men and women who boycotted slave-labor goods forced abolitionists to confront the connection between consumers and slaves. Supporters of abstention and free produce demonstrated incredible resilience and persistence, living their antislavery principles, publicly and privately, to an extent rarely seen in the abolitionist movement. Contrary to Garrison's view, supporters of the boycott did indeed engage in a "'fanatical agitation' of society, after the manner of the 'ultra abolitionists.'" Long before Garrison initiated the radical abolitionist movement of the 1830s, boycotters demanded the immediate abolition of slavery and challenged the racial inequality that defined the transatlantic economy. Boycotters called for nothing less than a thorough transformation of the global economy. That such a change was impractical mattered not. Boycotters believed that when consumers aligned their daily lives with their morals they would in time make the world a better place.

Using a global framework and the themes of religion, gender, and race, this book recovers the networks, identities, and processes of the boycott of slave labor. Its eight chapters proceed in roughly chronological order, from the seventeenth century through the American Civil War. Of necessity, some chapters overlap in chronology. Chapters 1 and 2 focus on the eighteenth-century abstention movement. Chapter 1 examines the development of Quaker antislavery, which was critical to the establishment of the religious and intellectual foundation of the abstention movement, whereas chapter 2 details the first popular campaign against slave-labor goods, the boycott of West Indian slave-grown sugar in the 1790s. Chapter 3 considers the abstention movement after the abolition of the international slave trade by Britain (1807) and the United States (1808), focusing particularly on the impact of Quaker abstention on the developing crisis among American Quakers. This chapter culminates with the 1827–28 schism among American Quakers, a split many contemporaries and historians have attributed to conflicts over the boycott of slave labor. Chapters 4 and 5 examine the popular revival of the boycott in the 1820s. The British movement is the focus of chapter 4, whereas the American movement is detailed in chapter 5. In Britain, the publication of Elizabeth Heyrick's *Immediate, Not Gradual Abolition*, in 1824, initiated a renewal of the antislavery movement, including the boycott against slave-labor goods, and culminated in Parliament's passage of the Emancipation Act in 1833. Heyrick's tract was reprinted in the United States in Benjamin Lundy's abolitionist publication, *Genius of Universal Emancipation*. As in Britain, Heyrick's tract influenced the expansion of the boycott and the antislavery movement; however, the outcome was quite different in the United States. Chapters 6 and 7 focus on organizational efforts in the United States and Britain in the 1830s and 1840s. The final chapter considers the movement from the 1840s through the 1860s, as Quakers, women, and black abolitionists, individually and collectively, attempted to keep the boycott alive despite numerous setbacks.

The history of the boycott of slave labor highlights the protracted and complicated transatlantic battle for emancipation. For more than one hundred years, antislavery consumers asserted the moral imperative of supporting an economy that measured its success by humanity and justice rather than its traditional narrative of profit and loss. They highlighted consumers' complicity in sustaining slavery and claimed economic principles did not justify enslavement. Ultimately, the boycott failed to achieve its goal: the abolition of slavery. However, that failure does not reflect a lack of commitment among supporters of the boycott; instead, that failure reveals just how thoroughly slavery had infiltrated the transatlantic economy in the antebellum era. Boycotters like Sarah Pugh recognized that challenge and still continued to make the daily commitment to boycott slave labor. "Active benevolence among evil-doers does not require us to support their iniquity," she claimed in 1844. "I go into a tavern and mingle with its inmates, but I need not buy a glass of rum to help in its support."[41] Pugh, like other supporters of the boycott, made slavery an inescapable national and international moral, economic, and political question. For supporters of the boycott, the abolition of slavery was a step, albeit a significant step, toward a broader goal of a just and humane economy. In their failures and in their successes, in their resilience and in their persistence, antislavery consumers help us understand the possibilities and the limitations of moral commerce.

CHAPTER 1

Prize Goods: The Quaker Origins of the Slave-Labor Boycott

In her history of the American free-produce movement, Ruth Nuermberger describes abstention from slave-labor goods as the "the most advanced" form of Quaker antislavery, identifying Benjamin Lay as "the first abstainer on record" and John Woolman as "the first to impress the idea" upon other Quakers. Framing abstention in this way, however, limits its genesis to the more eccentric (Lay) or the more saintly (Woolman).[1] Lay, a former sailor, settled in Philadelphia in 1731, after living in the British sugar colony of Barbados.[2] Lay later documented the horrors of plantation life in *All Slave-keepers That Keep the Innocent in Bondage, Apostates*, which he published in 1737 without the permission of the Overseers of the Press of Philadelphia Yearly Meeting. In addition to violating the unity of Friends by publishing outside the meeting, Lay also staged a series of dramatic public protests against slavery: splattering Friends with fake blood, smashing his wife's china, and kidnapping the child of a neighboring slaveholder. These actions contributed to Lay's disownment in 1738. He also refused to eat with slaveholders, or to be served by slaves; he dressed in coarse clothes and abstained from sugar because he refused to use anything produced by slave labor.[3] Woolman likewise rejected sugar and adopted a singular mode of dress, wearing simply tailored, undyed garments. When addressing the issue of slaveholding, however, Woolman chose a more moderate approach. Woolman's personal struggle with slavery began in 1742 when his employer requested he write a bill of sale for a woman sold as a slave. Although uncomfortable with the transaction, Woolman executed the document, choosing to share his misgivings privately with his employer and the buyer of the slave woman. Four years later, Woolman began to compose what would become his first antislavery tract. In 1752 six new members were appointed to the Overseers of the Press, an action that had "the effect of making the group, as a whole, more receptive to antislavery arguments."[4] The Quakers' response to the activism of Lay and Woolman reflected broader political, religious, and social changes in the eighteenth-century Atlantic world.

Two processes—one religious and one cultural and commercial—unfolded in the eighteenth century. Both were critical to the development of Quaker abstention. The first process, which was religious and focused inward, began with the efforts of individual Quakers to end slaveholding among members of the Society of Friends. While Lay was perhaps the most confrontational of these early reformers, he was not the only one to challenge Quakers' participation in slaveholding. Beginning in the 1750s, reformers like Woolman began to transform these individual arguments against Quaker slaveholding into a collective sectarian argument. The second process was the cultural and commercial transformation of the Atlantic world as a result of the consumer revolution. In this period men and women were presented with unprecedented opportunities to acquire a variety of material goods. However, these new consumer goods challenged Quaker conceptions of luxury and vice in ways more insidious than merely engaging in vain displays of wealth by purchasing superfluities such as china tea ware. Rather, "It was the ambiguity that confounded elders, reformers, and others concerned about moral and spiritual purity within the Society," Quaker scholar Ross Eiler explains. "The primary threat of luxury came not from 'unlawful things,' but from the new danger of the unlawful *use* of *lawful* things." Quaker reformers, like Lay and Woolman, reacted to "a changing ethos" of luxury—"not actual violations of luxury"—that undermined traditional Quaker "safeguards" against the world. The widespread availability of consumer goods allowed Quakers to purchase that which was deemed necessary and lawful, according to Quaker discipline, and yet still be recognized by others as wealthy.[5] In the second half of the eighteenth century, these two processes combined in a movement to abstain from slave-labor goods. As Quakers struggled to reconcile religious beliefs with commercial expansion, reformers like Woolman claimed antislavery principles should apply not only to African bodies but also to the products of those laboring bodies. Rather than a movement of the eccentric or the saintly, abstention was instead the result of ordinary Quakers' attempts to align their Christian principles with the newly expansive commercial society.

Early Quaker Antislavery

To understand the products of slave labor as stolen goods, Quakers had to first understand the enslavement of Africans as a form of theft. For many Quakers in this period, the slave trade and slavery were simply standard business practice: "God-fearing men going about their godless business," as historian James Walvin argues. In the late seventeenth century, when individual Quakers began to question Friends' relationship with slavery, their unease about the slave trade and slavery triggered "tiny shifts in the tectonic plates of British political life."[6] Early Quaker antislavery described the theft of African bodies and the appropriation of African labor. Although these early protests did not articulate an argument against the goods produced by those laboring bodies, they did provide the intellectual foundation for the abstention movement that developed in the late eighteenth century. To understand the origin of abstention from slave-labor goods, we need to begin with the organization of the Society of Friends and their first attempts to define the relationship between their religious beliefs and the social practice of the enslavement of Africans.

The Society of Friends was a product of the political turmoil of the English Civil War and the disruption of monarchical rule in the mid-seventeenth century. In the 1640s, itinerant preacher George Fox began an extended period of religious wandering that led him to conclude that the answers he sought came not from church teaching or the scriptures, but rather from his direct experience of God. "When all my hopes in them [preachers] and in all men were gone, so that I had nothing *outwardly* to help me, nor could tell me what to do," Fox wrote in 1647, "then, oh, then, I heard a voice which said, 'There is one, even Christ Jesus, that can speak to thy condition.'" This experience of direct revelation, coming at a time when Fox was discouraged and unable to find answers from those around him, led him to conclude that wisdom and guidance came from God rather than man. Fox's experience of individual, direct "intimacy with Christ" is "foundational and definitional" of Quakerism.[7] While the theological origins of Quakerism may be dated to 1647, the formal organization of the sect did not occur until 1652 when Fox traveled to the north of England. It was there that Fox attracted followers from the Seekers, a small sect that had rejected the established church and sought a return to primitive Christianity. Fox also received support from

Margaret Fell, the wife of a wealthy and prominent judge. After 1652 Quakerism spread rapidly throughout England and its North American colonies despite persecution from English authorities.[8]

The Quaker experience of intimacy with Christ led Friends to develop distinct spiritual beliefs and patterns of worship. Friends believed each individual, even those who had not been exposed to Christianity, possessed a divinely inspired "light within" that if followed would allow them to become "children of the light." Spiritual beliefs and patterns of worship flowed from this central idea. Worshipping in silence encouraged Friends to spiritually prostrate themselves before God and to wait for divine inspiration. The silence of the meeting was broken only when someone felt led by God to offer ministry. Rather than a trained or "hireling" ministry, Friends emphasized the universal priesthood of believers. This view led Friends to recognize women as spiritual leaders and ministers, a practice that distinguished Friends from other religious groups. The presence of the divine in each individual also led Friends to espouse the Golden Rule—"Whatsoever ye would that men should do to you, do ye even so to them." While Quakers' belief in the Golden Rule did not distinguish them from other Christian or even religious groups, their emphasis on the Golden Rule as a fundamental guiding principle did. The Golden Rule along with Quakers' pacifism, or peace testimony, served as the foundation of Quaker antislavery.[9]

Quakers also developed a network of communication that aided the growth of antislavery sentiment long before the corporate body of Friends took an active stand against slavery. This network was supported by Quakers' hierarchical structure of meetings that Friends established to facilitate worship and to direct the business of the sect. Meetings for worship met twice weekly. Preparative, monthly, quarterly, and yearly meetings were established to ensure doctrinal unity, to regulate Friends' behavior, and to provide mutual aid and encouragement. For most Friends, the preparative and monthly meetings were the most visible sign of the Quaker community. Monthly meetings represented the primary governing structure within the Society of Friends, assuming responsibility for defining membership, supervising marriages, recording births and deaths, overseeing transfers to other meetings, and identifying and recognizing ministers. Much of the work of the monthly meeting was conducted by elders and overseers who were selected by the preparative meeting and approved by the monthly, quarterly, and yearly meetings. Clerks, who were appointed by each monthly meeting, recorded the consensus of each meeting, keeping careful records so the minutes could be agreed upon by all present. This system of meetings allowed Friends to remain connected to the broader Quaker community, maintaining "a continuity of Quaker spiritual values and behavior across geographic space and sparsely settled regions."[10]

Friends' spiritual beliefs also led them to adopt distinct cultural principles. "Plain dress, plain speech and plain living" separated Friends from "a corrupt and corrupting world." Plain clothing, without superfluities such as buckles and collars, kept Friends focused on the inward light. They also rejected social customs that implied deference, believing traditions such as removing one's hat or using the singular "you" highlighted superficial distinctions of social class and hid the divine light within each person. Friends were to tell the truth at all times; thus, Quakers refused to swear an oath in court and only bought and sold goods at a fixed price rather than haggling. The Golden Rule and the Quaker peace testimony encouraged Friends to avoid war making by refusing to serve in the military, to pay military taxes, or to take sides in times of conflict. Such cultural principles distinguished Quakers from the world around them, allowing Quakers instead to emphasize the experience of God and reject the apostasy (the falling away from faith) of the outward life.[11]

Quaker religious beliefs did not align with the cultural ideas that encouraged the enslavement of Africans. Beginning in the late seventeenth century, in a series of protests against slavery, colonial Quakers began to question the legitimacy of slavery. The earliest of these statements, the Germantown Protest, was presented by four Pennsylvania Quakers to their monthly meeting in 1688. The authors of the Germantown Protest emphasized the relationship between the commerce in slaves and the consumers of those slaves: the slave trade would continue so long as Quakers purchased slaves. The Germantown statement described the slave trade as a violation of biblical sanctions against man stealing, as promulgated in Exodus, Leviticus, and Deuteronomy.[12] Quakers believed it was wrong to steal; therefore, they should avoid the purchase of stolen goods, removing any incentive for theft. Furthermore, slaves should "be delivered out of the hands of the Robbers & made free." The protestors contrasted the oppression of Quakers in Europe against the enslavement of Africans. Whereas Quakers had come to Pennsylvania to find "liberty of conscience," Africans had been forcibly transported to the colony to labor for life because they were "of a black colour." Race, the protestors claimed, did not justify enslavement: where there was "liberty of conscience" there "ought to be likewise liberty of the body."[13] The monthly meeting referred the Germantown appeal to the quarterly meeting, who in turn referred the petition to the yearly meeting. The leaders of the yearly meeting refused to take action, citing the number of Quakers who owned slaves.[14]

Subsequent protests in 1693 and 1698 reinforced the argument that slaves were stolen goods. In 1693, followers of Quaker schismatic George Keith wrote *An Exhortation and Caution to Friends Concerning Buying or Keeping of Negroes*. After Keith joined the Friends in 1662 in Scotland, he traveled widely in the British Isles and Ireland, which brought him into contact with many early Quaker leaders including George Fox, George Whitehead, William Penn, and Robert Barclay. Keith's move to the colonies in 1684 also brought him into contact and, ultimately, conflict with leading Pennsylvania Quakers. He believed Quakers had lost touch with the fundamental Christian nature of their faith; therefore, he sought to construct a more ecclesial structure among the Society of Friends, creating a scriptural and theological style of Quakerism. Keith's efforts were rebuffed by Pennsylvania's Quaker leadership. The subsequent dispute resulted in Keith becoming the head of a separatist group of "Christian Quakers." He was condemned by Pennsylvania Quakers in 1692. He appealed his subsequent disownment to London Yearly Meeting, which upheld the decision. In 1700 Keith joined the Church of England and was ordained an Anglican priest two years later.[15]

Keith's *Exhortation* was printed in New York in 1693 by William Bradford, a follower of Keith. Like the Germantown Quakers, Keith and his followers cited the biblical sanctions against man stealing and reiterated Quaker teachings against theft and the commerce in stolen goods. "Stollen Slaves" were "accounted a far greater Crime under *Moses's* Law than the stealing of Goods . . . *he that stealeth a Man and selleth him, if he be found in his hand, he shall surely be put to Death*"; therefore, "as we are not to buy stollen Goods . . . no more are we to buy stollen slaves." Slavery violated the Golden Rule and Quakers' peace testimony. Africans were captives of "War, Violence, Cruelty and Oppression, and Theft & Robbery of the highest Nature"; they were "stollen away or robbed from their Kindred" and "sold to white men." Enslavement subjected Africans to "continual hard Labour" with few "Provisions" to sustain life. Thus taken and held by violence, slaves were "Prize or stollen goods." The Keithians urged their readers to exercise the "Fruits of the Spirit of Christ" (i.e., "*Love, Mercy, Goodness, and Compassion*") and to recognize that the doctrine of the atonement applied to Africans as well as to Christians: "*Negroes, Blacks* and *Taunies* are a real part of Mankind, for whom Christ hath shed his precious Blood, and capable of Salvation, as well as White Men."[16]

The third protest was written in 1698 by Robert Piles of Concord, Pennsylvania. Piles had debated for some time whether to "buy a negro, or negroes." He considered Christ's message of the Golden Rule and realized that he would not willingly become a slave for life; he also recognized that slaves might rise in rebellion. As Piles weighed his decision, he fell asleep and had the dream he later recounted. In his dream, as Piles and his friend were walking down a road, they came across a black pot. Piles picked it up. As soon as he did, he "saw a great ladder standing exact upright, reaching up to heaven." Piles began to climb the ladder with the pot in hand. He soon realized that he would need both hands to climb the ladder because it was standing so upright. Placing the pot on the ground, he saw a man and asked him about the ladder. It is the "light of Christ," the man responded, "and whoever it bee that his faith be strong in the lord, God will uphold that it shall not fall." Suddenly Piles woke from his dream, resolving "to lett black negroes or pots alone." Piles's narrative mirrored the structure of the Germantown Protest: citing the Golden Rule, describing the slave trade as man stealing, and emphasizing the danger of slave rebellion. Of particular interest in the dream narrative is the depiction of slaves as the material culture of the pot. The materiality of the pot prevented Piles from climbing the ladder to receive "the light of Christ," suggesting that slave ownership led Quakers to focus on the outward accumulation of wealth and goods rather than focus on the inward experience of God.[17] The pot reinforced the idea, expressed by the Germantown Quakers and the Keithians, that slaves were corrupt goods whose consumption separated Quakers from God.

These early arguments emphasized the illicit commerce in African men, women, and children. The slave trade violated biblical sanctions against man stealing, a crime that was punishable by death under Mosaic law. Significantly, slavery and the slave trade infringed the Golden Rule and contravened Quakers' peace testimony. Although early Quaker antislavery highlighted the theft of Africans from their families and from God, these early statements did not specifically address the theft of African labor or the benefits Quakers derived from the theft of that labor. As a consequence, early Quaker antislavery statements did not specifically characterize the consumer of African slaves. In the early eighteenth century, with the expansion of the trade in global consumer goods such as coffee, tea, chocolate, sugar, silk, cotton, and china, Quaker antislavery writers began to explicitly link the consumption of slaves to the consumption of material goods.[18]

Quaker Antislavery and Consumer Goods

Like their predecessors, eighteenth-century Quakers described slaves as stolen goods and denounced the slave trade as man stealing. Their arguments also reflected the contemporaneous growth in the transatlantic trade in consumer goods. Quakers like John Hepburn and Ralph Sandiford described the trade in more explicitly commercial terms, connecting the slave trade to consumer desire for new luxury goods. As a result, Hepburn and Sandiford laid the foundation for later Quaker arguments that claimed the trade in slaves was driven by the consumption of slave-labor goods.

John Hepburn, a Quaker from Middletown, New Jersey, published *The American Defence of the Christian Golden Rule* in 1714. Hepburn's background is largely unknown. In his text, Hepburn claimed to have opposed slavery for thirty years before publicly expressing his opposition. There is evidence to suggest that Hepburn migrated to New Jersey around 1684 as an indentured servant. He is not listed in any meeting records; however, in attesting to his will in 1721, he identified himself as a Quaker. Historian J. William Frost suggests that Hepburn was a "backbencher," that is, a Friend who attended meetings "but was neither minister nor elder nor 'weighty Friend.'"[19]

Hepburn claimed the trade in African slaves and the theft of slaves' labor was driven by consumer desire for wealth, luxury, and ease. To emphasize his point, Hepburn introduced three archetypes that would, in time, become stock figures in antislavery literature: the greedy, blood-soaked slaveholder; the vain, self-absorbed slaveholder's wife; and the degraded slave. The slaveholder robbed the slave of his freedom and his labor and enriched himself in the "Bargain." Further emphasizing slaveholders' wealth and vanity, Hepburn described slaveholders' "*fine powdered Perriwigs*, and great *bunched Coats*." He then introduced slaveholders' wives, who were kept "*Jezebel-like*" with leisure time "to *paint their Faces*, and *Puff*, and *powder their Hair*, and to bring up their Sons and Daughters in *Idleness* and *Wantonness*, and in all manner of *Pride* and *Prodigality*, in *decking* and *adorning* their Carkasses with pufft and powdered Hair, with *Ruffles* and *Top-knots*, *Ribbands* and *Lace*, and *gay Cloathing*, and what not." This wealth of material goods was "produced by the Slavery of Negroes," who were dressed in the "vilest of *Raggs*, much ado to cover their nakedness, and many of them not a *Shirt* upon their Backs, some of them not a *Shoe* upon their Foot in *cold Frosts* and *Snow* in the Winter Time." Seeking wealth and luxury, as well as respite from labor, the slaveholder extorted the slave's labor. The slaveholder maintained "white hands, except at some Times they chance to be besparkled with the Blood of those poor Slaves, when they fall to beating them with their *twisted Hides* and *Horse-whips*, and other *Instruments of Cruelty*." The slave's labor produced the wealth that purchased the ribbons, lace, and other finery worn by the slaveholder and his family, a point which is further emphasized by the stark contrast between the slave's ragged clothing and the "puff and powder" of the slaveholding family. Hepburn denounced slaveholders as robbers who

"*Beat-Men*, and sometimes kill them to take their Money from them." Rather than money, the slaveholder stole the slave's labor: slaveholders "*beat* the Negros, and *take them Captives*, and *banish* them from their Country forever, and take their *Wives* and *Children* from them, and sometimes Cause their *Death*, and all to get their Labour from them; which is as much worth as their Money."[20]

The *American Defence of the Christian Golden Rule* marked a significant shift in Quaker antislavery. Hepburn cataloged, as no other Quaker had done, the evils of slavery: forced labor without pay, violence, and cruelty. He described the effect slavery had on slaveholders, encouraging idleness, indolence, vanity, and greed and "establish[ed] an image of the slaveholding household as one that [was] both corrupt and corrupting."[21] Significantly, Hepburn described the slave's labor as a tangible commodity that was stolen from the slave to benefit the slaveholder. Slaves were unique commodities, producing, by their labor, additional wealth for the slaveholder, as evidenced by his fine clothes and luxurious wigs. Thus the ease of slaveholding families depended upon the continued theft of Africans and their labor. As Hepburn concluded, the slaveholder had robbed Africans of the most basic provisions— their families, their labor, and, often, their lives—and, as a result, the slaveholder would receive God's judgment.

Publication of The *American Defence of the Christian Golden Rule* coincided with statements, issued by London Yearly Meeting, warning Quakers of the "pernicious effects" of vanity. Parents were cautioned to "be exemplary to their children in keeping out off the vain fashions, customs and pride of the world."[22] Quaker men, women, and children (through the example of their parents) had adorned themselves with "extravagancies, as those who are not of our profession observe as marks of declension from our primitive plainness." Rather than the "meek and quiet spirit" of godliness, Quakers had instead become "unseemly and immodest" in appearance.[23] Young Quaker men were reported to "have cut off their good heads of hair, and put on long extravagant and gay wiggs" while young Quaker women were apparently wearing their hair high and wearing gowns "like the proud fashion mongers of the world." Parents should avoid dressing their children in "Gaudy Apparel" because children "led into such Vanities and Fineries, Come gradually to be in Love with them."[24] Outward displays of fashion and vanity distracted Quakers from the inward experience of God. Hepburn connected these Quaker admonitions against luxury goods to slavery, calling on Quakers to reject both slavery and luxurious material goods.

Like Hepburn, Ralph Sandiford claimed the slave trade was caused and perpetuated by the desire for luxury goods and ease from labor and by greed.

A Quaker convert from Liverpool, England, Sandiford had settled in Philadelphia at a young age. He wrote *A Brief Examination of the Times* in response to the Pennsylvania Assembly's dramatic reduction in the duty on slave imports in 1729, which, as Sandiford noted, made "a revenue of the evil instead of removing it."[25] Frustrated by Quakers' inaction against slavery, Sandiford decided to speak out. Quakers had argued against slavery since the late seventeenth century; still, Friends continued to purchase slaves and Quaker meetings' cautionary statements against slavery had brought no disciplinary action. If leading Quakers could be convinced to emancipate their slaves, Sandiford believed the meeting could also be cleared of the sin of slavery. Acting without the permission of the Overseers of the Press of Philadelphia Yearly Meeting, Sandiford convinced Benjamin Franklin to print his tract.[26]

In Britain and her American colonies, the African slave trade had altered the national and the local economy in fundamental ways, according to Sandiford. Africans transformed forts into markets and sold their neighbors "for the least Bawbles."[27] Sandiford believed the slave trade reflected a lack of trust in God's providence: "Has not the Lord, by his extraordinary Providence, opened this *America* before the *Europeans*, and given us Peace and Plenty among the Natives? And shall we go to *Africa* for Bread, and lay the Burden which appertains to our Bodily Support on their Shoulders?" Instead, Sandiford claimed, God's bounty had been "Crucified by this Trade." Slaveholders had forsaken the "*Providence of God, to feed upon the Flesh and Blood of Slaves instead of Christ.*"[28] In *The Mystery of the Iniquity*, the second edition of Sandiford's tract, which was published in 1730, he described the Caribbean slave market: "They are a naked figure at their first landing in the *West Indies*, that the buyer may inspect even their secret parts, lest they should be corrupted in their passage by the debaucheries of those that are called Christians . . . under such circumstances the poor creatures easily transgressing, are whipped naked to common view, until their secret pores are shamefully extended beyond what may be rehearsed, unto chaste ears; and also for seeking their liberty, racked and burned to death, as lately at the *West Indies.*" Lest his readers believe such brutal treatment of slaves was limited to the markets in the West Indies, Sandiford then linked the Caribbean slave market to "the churches of Philadelphia" that had been "defiled" with the horrors of the slave trade. Philadelphians, "tho' they meet in sundry places of worship, can all agree to shake hands with man-stealers, the worst of thieves."[29] Sandiford's graphic text emphasized the ways in which the slave trade had perverted transatlantic commerce and corrupted Christians all for the sake of wealth.

Sandiford's book was not well received by the weighty Friends of Philadelphia Yearly Meeting who denounced the author and his publication. In his second edition, he appealed unsuccessfully to London Yearly Meeting for support. In the end, Sandiford was disowned. Afterward, he purchased a small farm outside Philadelphia where he built a log cabin and lived in "patriarchal simplicity," as Quaker biographer Roberts Vaux noted in 1815. Here Sandiford lived out his conscious opposition to the habits of luxury: "His clothing was made in the most simple manner, and was of natural colour of the material of which it was composed." Sandiford died in 1733.[30]

Hepburn and Sandiford made clear the link between slavery and the consumption of luxury goods. Slavery and the slave trade catalyzed the expansion of the transatlantic economy in the eighteenth century. Slaves were among the most profitable and most consistently demanded and consumed goods in the Atlantic world in this period. In the British Empire alone, between 1700 and 1780, more than four times as many Africans as Europeans landed in the American colonies. In turn, the slave trade made possible a second tier of goods. Among other commodities, enslaved labor produced sugar, coffee, rice, and tobacco. Slaves labored in agriculture, maritime trades, military service, and skilled professions, in urban and in plantation settings. In addition to the goods and services produced by slaves' labor, entire industries in North America and Europe, such as salt cod, pork, and certain textiles, were developed to provide goods to slave owners for their slaves.[31] Hepburn and Sandiford's protests against slavery are best understood within this growing consumer economy. As anthropologist Grant McCracken notes, in this period, the consumption of consumer goods "was beginning to take place more often, in more places, under new influences, by new groups, in pursuit of new goods, for new social and cultural purposes." From 1720 on, men and women came to expect that certain consumer goods could be theirs. Moreover, an individual's relationship to those goods changed as consumer goods, such as tea and sugar, became important signifiers of identity as well as necessities of daily life.[32] For Quaker reformers like Lay and Woolman, tea and especially sugar came to symbolize the apostasy that afflicted Friends.

"Sugar Is Made with Blood"

By the mid-eighteenth century, tea had become, as historian T. H. Breen observes, "the master symbol of the new consumer economy."[33] Of the three stimulant beverages introduced into Europe in the seventeenth century—tea, coffee, and chocolate—tea quickly outpaced the other two in consumption.

Between 1725 and 1800, annual tea imports into Britain increased from £250,000 to £24 million. A pamphlet, printed at the request of tea dealers in 1744, estimated Britons consumed an average of two million pounds of tea annually.[34] Colonial consumption of tea experienced similar increases. In 1773, for example, a Philadelphia businessman estimated that Americans purchased six million pounds of tea annually.[35] Tea benefited from its intrinsic qualities; it was easily enhanced with sugar, cream, or milk and was tolerable even when served weak. Tea was also more economical than coffee or chocolate. Aided by government protection and the monopoly held by the East India Company, supplies of tea increased and prices declined throughout the eighteenth century. Significantly, tea created and sustained a substantial market in related goods: tea ware and specialized brewing equipment made from porcelain and silver, furniture made from exotic woods such as mahogany, and, of course, sugar.[36]

Tea and sugar were inextricably linked in the eighteenth century. Like tea, sugar consumption was influenced by an increase in supply and a decline in cost. Sugar consumption in Britain rose 400 percent, from four to eighteen pounds per capita per year, during this period.[37] The increased consumption of tea and sugar "demonstrated the new accessibility of luxury goods and evidenced a new degree of purchasing power" while registering a "decline in nutritional values occasioned by the shift from agricultural to industrial labor, as workers gave up the time-consuming preparation of nutritious oat porridge and vegetable stock." Tea and sugar were both objects of mercantile trade, benefiting from preferential trade duties and supporting the monopolies held by the East India Company (tea) and the West India Company (sugar). Yet, the trade in these two commodities differed in important ways. Tea was imported into Britain from China; therefore, as an import, tea did not rely on the "direct exploitation of colonial labor."[38] Sugar, however, was made possible by and contributed to Britain's stake in the African slave trade.

Sugar production was a complex combination of agriculture and manufacture that required substantial capital and a large workforce. By the late seventeenth century, in the sugar colonies, large plantations had replaced small farms and the number of African slaves rose sharply. Sugar plantations were, as anthropologist and historian Sidney Mintz notes, "a synthesis of field and factory . . . quite unlike anything known in mainland Europe at the time." Sugar production required careful timing: the "cane must be cut when ready so as not to lose its juice or the proportion of sucrose in this juice; and once it is cut, the juice must be rapidly extracted to avoid rot, dessication, inversion, or fermentation." Once the sugar cane had been cut, it was transported to the mill, where it was crushed and the juices of the pith extracted. The extracted juice was then taken to a boiling house where it was crystallized for consumption. Molasses, the uncrystallized portion of the sugar, was often taken to the distillery to be rendered into rum. Sugar production required both "brute field labor and skilled artisanal knowledge," according to Mintz.[39]

The sweetness of the final product did not reveal the violence of its production. Slave mortality rates on sugar plantations were very high. In Barbados, one out of three slaves died within three years of arrival; in Jamaica, the death toll was 50 percent higher on sugar plantations than on coffee plantations. Overall, the West Indian slave population declined about 5 percent per year in the eighteenth century unless new slaves were bought to replace those that had died.[40] The high rate of mortality was the consequence of deficiencies in diet, shelter, and clothing; brutal working conditions; and tropical disease. In *Five Years' Expedition against the Revolted Negroes of Surinam*, Dutch soldier John Stedman described the dangers of producing sugar in the eighteenth century:

> So very dangerous is the work of those negroes who attend the rollers [through which the cane passes twice to extract the liquefied pith], that should one of their fingers be caught between them, which frequently happens through inadvertency, the whole arm is instantly shattered to pieces, if not part of the body. A hatchet is generally ready to chop off the limb, before the working of the mill can be stopped. Another danger is, that should a poor slave dare to taste that sugar which he produces by the sweat of his brow, he runs the risk of receiving some hundred lashes, or having all his teeth knocked out by the overseer.— Such are the hardships and dangers to which the sugar-making negroes are exposed.[41]

The brutality of sugar production remained a constant well into the nineteenth century. For example, in Jamaica, for the period 1829–1832, the slave mortality rate averaged 35.1 deaths per 1,000 enslaved.[42] Cuban planters perhaps said it most succinctly: "Con sangre se hace azúcar"—"Sugar is made with blood."[43]

The exponential increase in the consumption of sugar-sweetened tea generated widespread debate. Poets and authors lauded, mocked, and criticized consumers' new obsession with tea and its accoutrements. In one of the earliest poems on tea, *Poem in Praise of Tea*, also published as *A Poem upon Tea*, Peter Motteux claimed tea both humanized and civilized Britons.[44] In another poem, published in 1749, a woman defended her tea habit against her husband's charge that she had devoted too much time and too much expense to her tea table.[45] Social critic Jonas Hanway, best known for his charitable interest in London's chimney sweeps, published "An Essay on Tea" in 1756, refuting the salutary effects of tea and claiming that tea drained Britain's economic and military resources.[46] Minister and Methodist founder John Wesley, writing in 1748, claimed tea consumption jeopardized the individual's relationship with God.[47] Tea consumption generated similar debate among Quakers. Unlike the fine clothes and powdered wigs discussed earlier, tea is noticeably absent from the collected statements issued by London Yearly Meeting in the early eighteenth century; however, references to tea can be found in meeting minutes and in other sources, suggesting that tea consumption was for many Quakers a concern. For example, in 1714, the Yorkshire Women's Quarterly Meeting called on Friends to "refrane from haveing fine Tea Tables sett with Fine Chenae being it is more for Sight then Service, & that Friends keep Cleare of the superfluous part in Drinking Tea." In 1724, the Men's Meeting at Cork described tea consumption as "too much a Worldly custome" and "a hurtfull thing creeping into Friends familys and Earnestly recommend it to the care of concerned Friends to put a stop to it."[48] Many Friends believed the consumption of tea led Quakers to emphasize the outward life rather than the inward journey toward God.

In the North American colonies, many Quakers refused to consume tea. Woolman and Lay as well as Joshua Evans were among those Quakers who refused to consume the beverage. Colonial Quakers' rejection of tea, in general, was not the result of the political crisis of the 1760s and early 1770s; indeed, many colonial Quakers, like Woolman, stopped using tea much earlier because tea was customarily sweetened with slave-grown sugar. Tea was also closely associated with the superfluous consumption of other goods. Evans, for example, believed "East India tea" to be unnecessarily expensive and habit forming. A contemporary of Woolman, Evans lamented how customary tea consumption had become "even amongst those who know not where to get the next meal." Instead, Evans consumed home-grown herbal drinks, which he believed were better suited to the colonial constitution. Tea consumption, Evans lamented, "blinded, and bound [Friends] to prevailing customs." He noted the "tea-tables set, conformably to fashion, with curious cups, saucers, tongs of bright metal, etc., etc. Are not needless eating and drinking sometimes encouraged through this custom?"[49] For Evans and Woolman, consumer goods led men and women to support "prevailing customs" such as the consumption of tea or the use of slave labor. In the second half of the nineteenth century, Woolman became the foremost proponent of a new form of antislavery, anticonsumer testimony targeting slave-labor goods.

John Woolman

Born into a New Jersey Quaker family in 1720, Woolman belonged to a younger generation of Quakers raised in a period of shifting attitudes toward slavery. In the 1730s Sandiford and Lay were disowned for their dramatic actions against slavery. Less than twenty years later, Woolman published his antislavery tract with the approval of the Yearly Meeting. The changes that allowed Woolman to speak out against slavery, with the permission of the Quaker elders, were rooted in the preliminary efforts of the 1680s and 1690s, which laid the foundation for the attacks of Sandiford and Lay in the 1720s and 1730s. That in turn supported the final assault on slavery beginning in the 1750s and led by Woolman.[50] Changes in Quaker antislavery rhetoric occurred in dynamic relationship with changes in slave ownership among leading Philadelphia Quakers. Between 1706 and 1730, more than three-quarters of leading Philadelphia Quakers owned slaves; between 1731 and 1751, that number dropped slightly to two-thirds. After 1750, however, the number of leading Quakers who owned slaves dropped steeply to less than one in three. Of these changes, scholar Brycchan Carey concludes, "All things considered, the most likely explanation [for the decline in slave ownership] is that a younger generation of Friends, brought up in a climate where antislavery discourse was current, were asserting the values of their generation by choosing not to replace the slaves that they inherited from their parents when they died, or choosing not to replace the slaves that their parents manumitted in their wills."[51]

Woolman's antislavery activism began in 1742 when his employer requested he write a bill of sale for a woman sold as a slave. He did not speak out publicly against the sale or against slaveholding among Quakers; he did, however, begin writing an antislavery essay. While the momentum of Quaker antislavery had begun to accelerate in the 1740s, it was still not an opportune time for Woolman to publish his antislavery tract. As a birthright Quaker, Woolman understood Quaker bureaucracy. He knew that a frontal attack on Quaker slaveholders, or publishing without the consent of the meeting, as Lay and Sandiford had done, would be unproductive. As Quaker historian J. William Frost observes, "Being moral for Woolman did not require being foolish, tilting at windmills." Woolman waited to go public until after six new members were appointed to the Yearly Meeting's Overseers of the

Press, essentially reconstituting the group and creating an atmosphere more receptive to antislavery. The following year Woolman submitted *Some Considerations on the Keeping of Negroes* to the overseers, who published it in 1754. Woolman published an even more forceful antislavery essay, *Considerations on Keeping Negroes, Part Second*, in 1762. In all, Woolman wrote five major essays between 1746 and 1772, two of which were published posthumously. *A Plea for the Poor*, most likely written in 1763 and 1764 and published in 1793, is the fullest expression of Woolman's economic views. Woolman also kept a journal that was published by Friends after his death in York, England, in 1772.[52]

Developing a broad critique of slave trading, slavery, slave-labor goods, and the transatlantic economy, Woolman highlighted the inextricable link between slavery and the emerging consumer society. The trade in African slaves and the products of slaves' labor were the most visible signs of an oppressive, global economy driven by the greed of Quakers and non-Quakers alike, an evil that threatened the current generation as well as future generations. Woolman abstained from slave-labor goods, such as sugar, for motives that went beyond opposition to the slave trade and slavery. Rather abstention from slave-labor goods was part of a comprehensive plan to reform the transatlantic economy, one based on what he described as "the right use of the Lord's outward gifts." Woolman imagined a just and simple economy that would benefit everyone, freeing men and women to "walk in that pure light in which all their *works are wrought in God*."[53]

That just economy was based on the principle that "Man is born to labor." Labor is a "proper part" of life, Woolman wrote, and when "directed by the wisdom from above, tends to our health, and adds to our happiness in this life." Labor opened the pores, improved the circulation of the blood, and prepared the individual "to enjoy the sweetness of rest."[54] The fruits of labor should be received as "a trust committed to us, by HIM who formed and supports the world."[55] "The right use" of labor and the fruits of labor created the moral economy Woolman envisioned. Woolman advocated that the hours of labor be reduced so that toil and income might be more equitably shared; however, he did not imagine an equal distribution of wealth or of labor. He recognized that men had varying capacities for labor and different needs, so he called on the wealthy to set an example by paying a just wage and living a plain and frugal life. Thus material prosperity included moral responsibility toward others who were not as blessed. Laying aside the desire for "outward greatness" and instead seeking "the right use of things," Woolman wrote, would lead people to "be employed in things useful that moderate labour with the blessing of heaven would answer all good purposes relating to people and their animals, and sufficient number have leisure to attend on proper affairs of society." If individual labor was guided by the inward light of Christ, receiving the fruits of that labor as a trust from God, social and economic inequities would be moderated and all men and women would be able to enjoy "the blessing of heaven."[56] As Woolman wrote, "If one suffer by the unfaithfulness of another, the mind, the most noble part of him that occasions the discord, is thereby alienated from its true and real happiness." The "neglect and misuse" of talents separated men and women "from the heavenly fellowship and are in the way to the greatest of evils" while the "true medium" of labor led Christians to wait with humility on "the inward teaching of Christ."[57] In this way, "the right use" of labor and the fruits of labor restored mankind to "the true harmony of life."[58]

Woolman lauded the benefits of labor; yet, he also recognized that selfish individuals would use the principle that "man is born to labor" to exploit men. The abuse of labor led to an array of evils: indolence and vanity, immoderate consumption of alcohol and other consumer goods, and violence and cruelty toward others. Idleness caused men to neglect their families while too much labor made "understanding dull" and "intrude[d] upon the harmony of the body." Excessive labor was contrary to "divine order," Woolman observed. "To labour too hard or cause others to do so . . . is to manure a soil for propagating an evil seed in the earth." Slavery represented the worst abuse of labor because slaveholders neglected "the true medium" of labor, forcing slaves to labor for others without benefit.[59] Contrasting African village life to African slavery, Woolman noted that in Africa men and women "with a little labour raise grain, roots, and pulse to eat, spin and weave cotton, and fasten together the large feathers of fowls to cover their nakedness, many of whom in much simplicity live inoffensive in their cottages and take great comfort in raising up their children." Captured and enslaved, African men and women were "put to labour in a manner more servile and wearisome than what they were used to, with many sorrowful circumstances attending their slavery." Slavery disrupted the divine order of labor; thus, the violence of slavery "belongs not to the followers of Christ."[60]

Some Considerations on the Keeping of Negroes reflected Woolman's firsthand experience with southern slavery, which he encountered for the first time in 1746 when he traveled through Maryland, Virginia, and North Carolina. Quaker traveling ministers often relied on their hosts for lodging and meals as well as the feeding and care of their horses. On this trip, Woolman struggled to reconcile his developing antislavery views with his dependence on the hospitality of slaveholders. Slaveholders, Woolman wrote in his journal, "lived in ease on the hard labour of their slaves." Although Woolman felt "more easy" in households where slaves were "well provided for and their labour moderate," he continued to feel uneasy about the benefits he received from slavery. Woolman was also disturbed by the effect slaveholding had on southern society. "White people and their children so generally living without much labour," he wrote, "so many vices and corruptions increased by this trade, and this way of life that it appeared to me as a dark gloominess hanging over the land."[61] Still, Woolman kept his misgivings to himself.

Eleven years later, on a second visit to Quakers in the South, Woolman was not so reticent. By 1757 Woolman's views of slavery and consumerism had had time to develop and mature. Among Quakers, the pace of antislavery had experienced a similar maturation. Quakers, individually and collectively, were discussing the morality of the slave trade and slaveholding, discussions that were intensified by the political and religious crisis of the Seven Years' War. Still, Woolman felt quite alone: "Soon after I entered [Maryland] a deep and painful exercise came upon me," he wrote in his journal. "The people in this and the southern provinces live much on the labour of slaves, many of whom are used hardly."[62] This second visit among southern Quakers made clear to Woolman the connection between luxury and violence. One could not love God and mammon; nor could one love God and simultaneously "exercise cruelty toward the least creature moving."[63] Woolman concluded that if he accepted hospitality from slaveholders, he would, in effect, contribute to the evil of slavery and benefit from the "gain of oppression": "As it is common for Friends on such a visit to have entertainment free of cost, a difficulty arose in my mind with respect to saving my own money by kindness received, which to me appeared to be the gain of oppression. Receiving a gift, considered as a gift, brings the receiver under obligations to the benefactor and has a natural tendency to draw the obliged into a party with the giver."[64] Woolman worried that his slaveholding hosts offered hospitality to him out of respect for his reputation as a Quaker minister rather than in a spirit of unity with his antislavery views. Thus by accepting the hospitality of slaveholders, Woolman believed he would encourage Quaker slaveholders to feel at ease with slaveholding. After an intense period of reflection, Woolman decided on a course of action: "When I expected soon to leave a Friend's house where I had entertainment, if I believed that I should not keep clear from the gain of oppression without leaving money, I spoke to one of the heads of the family privately and desired them to accept of them pieces of silver and give them to such of their Negroes as they believed would make the best use of them; and at other times I gave them to the Negroes myself, as the way looked clearest to me."[65] By the mid-eighteenth century, many Quakers described the commerce in African slaves as a "gain of oppression," a reference to the prophet Isaiah's exhortation to the faithful to reject everything related to evil commerce.[66] Woolman broadened the definition of a "gain of oppression" to include all "social and economic benefits that free people derived from slavery."[67]

The journey into Maryland in 1757 marked a transitional moment for Woolman as he began a "lifelong, rigorous struggle to distance himself from the operations of the slave economy."[68] In his journal, he described the lives of slaves in greater detail than in the past. Woolman noted the tattered clothing of slaves: "Men and women have many times scarce clothes enough to hide their nakedness, and boys and girls ten and twelve years old are often stark naked amongst their master's children."[69] The rags worn by African slaves were used to fix in white minds that slaves were "a sort of people below us in nature." Slaves had "little else to eat but one peck of Indian corn and salt for one week with some few potatoes." Slaveholders destroyed slaves' humanity and claimed their actions were justified by slaves' miserable living conditions. The labor of slaves supported their masters, "many of them in the luxuries of life"; yet, slaves had "made no agreement to serve us and [had] not forfeited their liberty." Woolman warned that all would face divine judgment for the treatment of enslaved Africans: "These are souls for whom Christ died, and for our conduct toward them we must answer."[70]

Woolman's trip deepened his understanding of the ways in which slavery violated the morality of labor and the divine order of the economy. He does not indicate exactly when he decided to reject slave-labor goods as a "gain of oppression"; still, his decision was likely influenced by this second trip to the South. In 1769 Woolman noted in his journal that he had "some years ago, retailed rum, sugar, and molasses," but having learned of the "oppressions too generally exercised" in the West Indies, decided to forgo such products.[71] In the 1760s Woolman began to criticize other aspects of the transatlantic economy, "associating transatlantic commerce with warfare, economic inequality, godlessness, intemperance, and cruelty to animals" as well as the enslavement of Africans. Increasingly, Woolman associated his economic choices with a sense of prophetic calling. As his biographer Geoffrey Plank observes, "By the end of his life he believed that the clothes he wore, his manner of speaking, the gifts he accepted and refused, the way he traveled, where he slept, the food he ate and his choice of spoons were freighted with moral significance."[72] Woolman recognized the interdependent character of transatlantic commerce. Using his economic choices, Woolman chose to serve as an example of how to engage in moral commerce.

In the most visible sign of his new calling, Woolman adopted a unique style of dress in 1762. As one contemporary noted, "His shoes were of uncurried

leather, tied with leather strings, his stockings of white yarn, his coat, waist-
coat, and breeches of a strong kind of cloth undyed, the natural colour of
the wool, the buttons of wood with brass shanks; his shirt of cotton un-
bleached, about 14d. pr yard, fastened at the neck with three large buttons
of the same stuff, without either cravat or handkerchief about his neck; his
hat a very good one was white." Another said simply, "he was all white."[73]
In *A Plea for the Poor,* Woolman discussed his objections to dyed cloth and
"fine-wrought, costly apparel." Such goods were rooted in a self-pleasing
spirit that separated men and women from universal love. The desire for such
goods constituted a "gain of oppression," encouraging consumers to purchase
goods for reasons of fashion rather than necessity. Dyes damaged cotton,
linen, and wool, shortening the life of the fabric; additionally, dyes served
no purpose other than "to please the eye and partly hide the dirt," Woolman claimed.[74] Instead, Woolman encouraged men and women to "lay
aside curious, costly attire, and use that only which is plain and serviceable"
and thus "contribute toward lessening, that business which hath its foundation in a wrong spirit."[75]

By adopting simply tailored attire, Woolman affirmed traditional Quaker
tenets about plain clothing; however, he was also part of a tradition that was
gaining traction in the American colonies. In the late seventeenth century,
antislavery activist Thomas Tryon encouraged Quakers in Pennsylvania and
New Jersey "to dress only in locally made textiles, with natural, locally produced colors, as part of his broad scheme to promote a just and simple economy."[76] Likewise, Ralph Sandiford and Benjamin Lay wore coarse, simple
clothes in protest against slavery.[77] By the 1760s, other Quaker opponents
of slavery were adopting similar forms of dress. Joseph Nichols, founder of
the "New Quakers," or Nicholites, urged his followers to "keep from making
or buying any dyed, striped, flowered, corded or mixed stuff" and to avoid
"all needless cuts and fashions in their clothes." In 1780 a visitor to the
Nicholites noted that they dressed only in white.[78] Joshua Evans made a
similar commitment to avoid dyes, opting for a utilitarian form of dress as
part of a "broader project for economic and spiritual reform."[79] Fashionable
dyed clothing, like East India tea, was inconsistent with "the dictates of the
blessed Truth," Evans observed. He longed for the day when this "pure influence may spread more and more" so that the "hungry would be fed, and
the naked, clothed."[80] Woolman and Evans had been neighbors and had attended the same Quaker meeting. Likely, the two men discussed cloth dyes
in 1761 or 1762 because both men decided almost simultaneously to reject
dyed clothing. Woolman likely influenced Joseph Nichols, too, having visited Nichols and his followers in 1766. These connections suggest that

Woolman's arguments against slavery "resonated within a vibrant, if small, American tradition."[81] For this small group of reformers, simply tailored, undyed clothing became an important statement of anticonsumer, antislavery identity.

The desire for consumer goods led men and women to engage in habits that disrupted God's divinely ordered economy. Woolman believed that oppressive practices, such as the enslavement of African men and women or the pursuit of fashionable clothing, impacted the entirety of the Atlantic economy. He was not the first to recognize the interdependent nature of transatlantic commerce. In 1713 novelist and economic journalist Daniel DeFoe argued for the importance of the African slave trade: "The case is as plain as cause and consequence: Mark the climax. No African trade, no negroes; no negroes no sugars, gingers, indicoes, etc; no sugars etc no island, no islands no continent; no continent no trade."[82] DeFoe recognized the interconnected nature of transatlantic commerce and concluded that the slave trade, regardless of the violence done to African men and women, was vital to that commerce. Woolman, however, reached a different conclusion. In his journal, he recounted a dream he had in the spring of 1770, a dream that seemingly collapsed the global economy into a single horrific vision of violent consumption:

> I dreamed a man had been hunting and brought a living creature to Mount Holly of a mixed breed, part fox and part cat. It appeared active in various motions, especially with its claws and teeth. I beheld and lo! many people gathering in the house where it was talked one to another, and after some time I perceived by their talk that an old Negro man was just now dead, and that his death was on this wise: They wanted flesh to feed this creature, and they wanted to be quit of the expense of keeping a man who through great age was unable to labour; so raising a long ladder against the house, they hanged the old man.

> One woman spake lightly of it and signified she was sitting at the tea table when they hung him up, and though neither she nor any present said anything against their proceedings, yet she said at the sight of the old man a dying, she could not go on with tea drinking.

> I stood silent all this time and was filled with extreme sorrow at so horrible an action . . . but none mourned with me.[83]

The central action of this dream is the execution of the old slave and the consumption of his body. In the marginalia of his manuscript, Woolman noted the cunning of the fox and the leisure of the cat and the connection between tea and sugar and African slavery. The slave's execution and the sub-sequent consumption of his corpse by the creature suggests the literal con-sumption of slaves in the agriculture and manufacture of sugar. The tea drinking woman witnessed the execution of the slave and experienced first-hand the process by which her use of tea and sugar was made possible and, as a result, she was unable to continue the tea ritual.[84]

Woolman believed the slave trade and slavery encouraged the consump-tion of African slaves as well as consumer goods. The more consumers traded in goods produced by the oppressive labor of slaves, the more at ease slave traders and slaveholders became in the immoral traffic. That ease with slav-ery also made men and women much more comfortable with other oppres-sive economic habits such as the consumption of fashionable clothes or the relentless pursuit of wealth. Although Woolman worked within the struc-ture of the Society of Friends, he consistently challenged Quakers to recon-sider their relationship with the transatlantic economy. It was important for Quakers to realize how thoroughly the "gain of oppression" had infiltrated the Atlantic world. Woolman's unique clothing served as a visible statement of his disengagement with the status quo. Using his words, his social inter-actions, and his appearance to protest the oppression of the Atlantic econ-omy and to demonstrate to others the benefits of moral commerce, Woolman sought to "make the world better by living well, trusting God, and serving as an example to others."[85] For Woolman, the restoration of "the true har-mony of life" required fundamental changes in the social and economic basis of the global economy, including but not limited to the abolition of slavery.

Quaker abstention from slave-labor goods focused on the ascetics of the boycott, urging Friends to disengage from the marketplace and, in particu-lar, from slavery by refusing to benefit from the "gain of oppression." While such rhetoric provided the ideological basis for the boycott of slave-labor goods, it had limited appeal beyond the Society of Friends. For many con-sumers in Britain and the United States, the source of their goods mattered little. Indeed, many agreed with DeFoe, believing the commerce in slaves and the products of their labor were critical to success of the nation. "The . . . motives of commercial policy [require] that the claims of religion and mo-rality ought to be subservient to those of avarice and luxury," British Quaker Joseph Woods observed in 1784. "It is better a thousand poor unoffending people should be degraded and destroyed [than] the inhabitants of Europe should pay a higher price for their rum, rice, and sugar." The slave trade, he claimed, had corrupted British commerce, implicating the government, merchants, and consumers in the "disgraceful commerce."[86] Woods, like Woolman, worried about the impact of the consumer revolution on Friends;

yet, Woods did not connect his call for the abolition of the slave trade to a specific religious creed. Rather, he gave abolition a nonsectarian voice. *Thoughts on the Slavery of Negroes* is an important transitional moment, emphasizing both the beginning of British Quaker involvement in the abolition campaign and broader consumer activism against slavery and the slave trade. Seven years after Woods published his tract, London Baptist printer William Fox published his own tract on the slave trade and slavery, sparking a national boycott of slave-grown sugar.

CHAPTER 2

Blood-Stained Sugar:
The Eighteenth-Century British
Abstention Campaign

By the early 1770s, in the North American colonies, the simultaneous expansion of Quaker antislavery and consumer society had influenced the development of a small, but committed, community of Friends who abstained from a variety of consumer goods, including the products of slave labor. Quaker abstention linked the processes of sectarian reform and consumption, disciplining men and women to avoid the immorality of slavery and commerce. Quaker abstention was therefore both antislavery and anticommerce. Colonial Quakers like John Woolman carried the idea of abstention to Britain where it garnered little interest until the late 1780s when abolitionists, many of them Quakers, began to suggest that a boycott of slave labor might force Parliament to take action against the slave trade.

One of the more striking features of eighteenth-century British abstention was its popularity—nearly one-half million consumers abstained from slave-grown sugar, an unprecedented level of participation. It is also striking that many of these consumers were not Quakers, though their activism also originated in protests against slavery and the growth of the market economy. On both sides of the Atlantic, Quakers and non-Quakers alike worried about the effects of consumer society. The so-called consumer revolution allowed more men and women than ever to participate in the marketplace regardless of race, class, or gender. New social and cultural customs, such as the ritualized consumption of tea contributed to the development of an increasingly elaborate array of specialized material goods. Presented with this dazzling selection of new wares, consumers ascribed cultural narratives to consumer goods to convey social status, personal identity, political alliance, gender, and religious ideals.[1] While Quakers like Woolman described consumer goods as contrary to Christian principles, other men and women claimed consumer goods were necessary signifiers of class and gender. As historian Ellen Hartigan-O'Connor concludes, the language of "commerce was shot through with other concerns, including affection, family obligation, and ideas about appropriate 'masculine' or 'feminine' interests. . . . If a market ethos permeated social and emotional lives, so, too, did social and emotional concerns influence commercial decisions."[2] It is within these social and emotional concerns that we may find the explanation for the popularity of the British abstention movement.

In Britain attempts to define consumption and the practices of modern consumerism unfolded with efforts to define the female subject. These two cultural processes intersected most powerfully at the tea table where tea sweetened with slave-grown sugar was most frequently consumed. Tea's association with the domestic sphere naturalized its consumption as feminine even though both men and women consumed tea and participated in the tea ritual. Frenchman Ferdinand Bayard, touring the United States in the late eighteenth century, described the various tea parties he attended. In one example he described the equipment used for the tea party, the ritualistic behavior of the participants, and the confounding sign language used to indicate the desire for more tea. At another party Bayard contrasted the luxurious tea equipage with the otherwise primitive conditions of the home in rural Virginia.[3] Commenting on the women he met, he claimed that American women's "mania for luxury [had] reach[ed] such an extent that the wife of the laboring man wishes to vie in dress with the wife of the merchant, and the latter does not wish to be inferior to the wealthy women of Europe." Yet earlier in his narrative Bayard had lauded the patriotic behavior of American women who during the political crisis with Britain had used homespun rather than purchase British goods.[4] These seemingly contradictory descriptions of female economic behavior highlight how the language of commerce and consumption became entangled with other social, political, and cultural concerns. Poets lauded the civilizing influence of tea-drinking women, thus the tea table could reflect the disciplined female consumption made possible by the wealth of empire. However, the protean nature of the tea table could suggest an opposite reading: uncontrolled, narcissistic female consumption. As one scholar notes, in the eighteenth century, women simultaneously embodied society's "fondest wishes for the transforming power of consumerism and its deepest anxieties about the corrupting influences of goods." The female consumer was "a powerfully paradoxical presence" at the tea table, at times "supremely disciplined" while at other times "disruptive or disorderly."[5]

These changes in gender ideals as well as the increase in consumer goods helped transform Quakers' sectarian arguments against slavery into a political movement against slave-labor goods in Britain in 1791.[6] The boycott originated in Quaker protests against slavery and slave-labor goods and gained momentum as it engaged contemporary debates about female consumption. Urging British women to ban slave-grown sugar from their tea tables, supporters of the boycott shifted the focus of the slave-trade debate from the political realm to the domestic sphere. In doing so, abolitionists opened up the slave-trade debate to larger questions about feminine consumption and colonial expansion, creating in the process a broader base of support for the boycott of slave labor.

British Quakers and Antislavery in the 1780s

The transformation of Quaker abstention began in the early 1780s as British Quakers launched an extensive and unprecedented propaganda campaign that utilized the extensive connections of British and American Friends. In 1783 London Yearly Meeting's Meeting for Sufferings appointed twenty-three men to form the Committee on the Slave Trade. This organizational activity followed an abolition petition, the first of its kind, presented to the House of Commons on June 16 by London Yearly Meeting and signed by 273 Quakers. Although the petition had no impact on the government's stance toward the slave trade, its generally positive reception by members of Parliament encouraged British Quakers to accelerate their efforts. William Dillwyn and John Lloyd, members of the committee, prepared a short pamphlet that was published in December of that year and distributed to each member of Parliament.

In addition to the Committee on the Slave Trade, Quakers organized a smaller, informal group that included Dillwyn and Lloyd as well as Joseph Woods, Samuel Hoare, George Harrison, and Thomas Knowles. This group of men had extensive transatlantic connections that were critical to the work of the group. Dillwyn, a Quaker businessman from Pennsylvania, had been a student of Anthony Benezet in Philadelphia before quietly relocating to England in 1774, citing business and family interests rather than political loyalties. Woods was a woolen merchant. Hoare, the younger brother of Wood's wife, and Harrison were bankers. By 1783, Woods, Harrison, and Hoare, as well as James Phillips, were deeply engaged in commerce in England and North America, cultivating a wide range of contacts among Quakers and non-Quakers. Dillwyn, for example, served as an important connection between Benezet and the Anglican Granville Sharp in England. Additionally, in 1783, Dillwyn and Woods were asked to serve as purchasing agents for the Library Company of Philadelphia, placing many of their orders through the printer Phillips. John Lloyd, son of a wealthy merchant and banker, was involved in the tobacco business and had observed American slavery while traveling in the American colonies between 1775 and 1777. Knowles had been an apothecary before taking up the study of medicine. He was a member of the Royal College of Physicians, which placed Knowles in the highest ranks of the English medical profession. His wife, Mary Morris Knowles, was a poet and an artist whose needlework won her the friendship of the royal family. Of the six men, only Woods was not a member of the formal Committee on the Slave Trade.[7]

Operating independent from London Yearly Meeting, the informal group used its members' extensive connections to arrange the distribution of articles and pamphlets about the slave trade. The autonomy of the group allowed it to publish works without subjecting them to review by London Yearly Meeting, which was the standard process for Quaker publications. As a result, the informal association published works by both Quakers and non-Quakers. Their independence also freed individuals to publish their antislavery views anonymously, thereby gaining a broader audience by remaining unaligned with any particular religious sect. Thus the informal group could distribute antislavery literature throughout Britain and America without regard for denominational lines.[8]

The informal group was responsible for the publication and distribution of Woods's thirty-two-page essay, *Thoughts on the Slavery of Negroes*, which was published anonymously in 1784. Woods's essay was the first ecumenical argument for abstention from slave-labor goods. In his essay, Woods defended the humanity of Africans: "They cannot be denied to be *men*." He admitted the economic value of slavery and the slave trade, noting that the "very sufferings" of African slaves were "the source of public revenue and private wealth." Still, the slave trade was "a disgraceful commerce" that exceeded humanitarian limits. "No subsequent purchase can convert the wrong into right, the receiver of the stolen goods, knowing them to be so, is equally culpable with the thief," he asserted. Woods demanded that humanitarianism be used as the standard to judge what goods could be bought and sold in the marketplace. Although his arguments originated in Quaker abstention, Woods appealed to a nonsectarian audience, broadening the scope of moral commerce and aligning abolitionism and humanitarianism with the duties and privileges of merchants and consumers.[9]

In addition to Woods's pamphlet, the informal group arranged for the publication and distribution of other antislavery works. Together the informal and formal groups arranged for the distribution of tens of thousands of antislavery articles and pamphlets in the 1780s. Woods, Lloyd, and the other committee members arranged to place items about the slave trade in newspapers throughout England. The Quakers selected materials from a variety of sources: writings by Anthony Benezet, histories by the French writer and propagandist Abbé Raynal, and excerpts from Adam Smith's *The Wealth of Nations*. Additionally, they published travel accounts from North America, Africa, and the East Indies; letters from Philadelphia Yearly Meeting; and selections from Blackstone's *Commentaries*. The Quakers also arranged the publication of numerous tracts including a reprint of Benezet's *Caution and Warning to Great Britain and Her Colonies*, James Ramsay's landmark antislavery tract, *Essay on the Treatment and Conversion of African Slaves in the Sugar Colonies*, and Anglican Thomas Clarkson's prize-winning essay on the slave trade, *An Essay on the Slavery and Commerce of the Human Species, Particularly the African* (1786), written while Clarkson was at Cambridge in 1785. The diversity of material disseminated by the committee and the informal group gave the impression that a nonsectarian, ecumenical movement against the slave trade was gaining momentum.[10] It also allowed the Quakers to disguise the sectarian origins of the antislavery sentiment that had suddenly started to appear in print. "British newspapers and periodicals published from the summer of 1783 to the spring of 1787 need to be read with caution," historian Christopher Brown notes. "Historians will never know how many of the antislavery statements that appear in the British press in this period resulted from [the] sponsorship [of the informal group]." Significantly, the Quakers "tried to create the appearance of an emerging public consensus on behalf of abolition more than two years before that support materialized in full."[11]

Quaker antislavery efforts between 1783 and 1787 did not create a movement, but those efforts did make a difference. The Quakers' campaign, according to Brown, "profoundly affected the political and cultural landscape" of England. By the 1780s, antislavery had gained "moral capital." As Brown explains, "To condemn slavery in principle and colonial institutions in practice had become . . . the mark of an enlightened, humane Christian." Quaker antislavery took hold in part, because antislavery could bestow moral prestige on the individuals who sustained the movement and generate moral capital for other movements. For example, antislavery gained support from the activists who sought parliamentary reform because they believed association with antislavery would bring credit to their movement. Moreover, the example of the American colonists who sought liberation from British sovereignty brought into public discussion the subject of imperial reform. In the 1780s, Quakers rebranded antislavery by aligning it with the national projects of the period, ultimately transforming sectarian antislavery into a genuine mass movement.[12]

The momentum of the early and mid 1780s culminated in the organization of the Society for Effecting the Abolition of the Slave Trade (SEAST), which was organized in 1787 by Quakers and their allies. The establishment of the SEAST coincided with the reorganization of the Pennsylvania Abolition Society (PAS) and the founding of the Free African Society (FAS) in Philadelphia. The simultaneous establishment of the three associations led activists to hope that competition between the two nations would lead both to abolish slavery. British supporters of abolition made the strategic decision to focus on the slave trade rather than the larger, more complicated issue of slavery. The Quakers who helped establish the SEAST recruited prominent Anglicans to the organization, including Clarkson, Sharp, and Phillip Sansom. Between 1787 and 1794, Clarkson traveled more than 30,000 miles, gathering evidence against the slave trade to be used in parliamentary proceedings. Sharp had gained fame for his role in *Somerset v. Stewart* (1772), which was widely albeit erroneously interpreted as freeing all slaves on English soil. Sansom was an Anglican businessman with American ties. Additionally, William Wilberforce, a member of Parliament, pledged his support as did pottery manufacturer Josiah Wedgwood. The SEAST initiated a nationwide petition campaign and began to collect subscriptions. Wedgwood designed a cameo of a kneeling slave framed by the words "Am I Not a Man and a Brother?" The society also arranged for the publication of numerous antislavery publications, enlisting, for example, the aid of evangelical Hannah More, who produced the didactic poem *Slavery* to coincide with the renewed debate in the House of Commons in 1788. From 1789 to 1791, the SEAST gathered and disseminated information about the slave trade and the parliamentary debates about the trade, all in an effort to generate support for its abolition. In April 1791, Wilberforce's bill against the slave trade came up for vote, just as news of the massive slave rebellion in Saint Domingue began to reach England. Opponents of abolitionism blamed the situation in the Caribbean on the agitation for abolition. When the votes were tallied, Wilberforce's bill was resoundingly defeated.[13]

In the wake of parliamentary defeat, the formal Committee on the Slave Trade broadened its membership and began to align itself more with the abstention movement. In the weeks following Parliament's action, the committee added new members, many of them evangelicals, and issued a report questioning for the first time, whether "the luxuries of Rum and Sugar can only be obtained by tearing asunder those ties of affection which unite our species and exalt our nature." Describing parliamentary action "a delay rather than a defeat," the committee urged supporters to join in "asserting the claims of Humanity" and to continue to fight for the abolition of the trade until "the commercial intercourse with Africa shall cease to be polluted with the blood of its inhabitants." The committee ordered one thousand copies of the report printed and distributed to local correspondents.[14]

Outside the Committee on the Slave Trade, others also responded to parliamentary defeat. In July 1791, the Baptist printer William Fox composed and published anonymously *An Address to the People of Great Britain on the Utility of Refraining from the Use of West India Sugar and Rum*.[15] The first four editions of Fox's pamphlet were printed and sold by the Quaker James Phillips and Fox's business partner Martha Gurney, London's only female dissenting printer, in a partnership of abolitionist elite (Phillips) and radical outsider (Gurney and Fox). Gurney was the only daughter of Thomas Gurney, a high Calvinist Baptist and a shorthand writer at the Old Bailey, and the sister of Joseph Gurney, who became the leading court stenographer in the late eighteenth century. Before their partnership in 1782, Fox had been a minor bookseller while Gurney had been an active printer and bookseller. Between 1770 and 1813, Gurney's name appeared on more than one hundred titles, thirty-four of which were political pamphlets, published between 1788 and 1802, on various topics including abstention, abolition of the slave trade, and Britain's war with France. With Fox, between 1791 and 1794, Gurney produced thirteen abolitionist pamphlets, many of them promoting abstention from slave-grown sugar.[16] Gurney, along with the Quaker Phillips, dominated the printing and selling of abolitionist works in London in this period; with the publication of Fox's tract, Gurney found herself at the center of the strident pamphlet wars of the 1790s.[17] Fox's *Address* quickly came to symbolize the eighteenth-century rejection of slave-grown sugar. Clarkson credited Fox's tract with helping to start a boycott of slave-grown sugar that garnered support from an estimated 300,000 Britons.[18] In January 1792, Clarkson wrote and circulated a private letter acknowledging the influence of Fox's tract and requesting Wedgwood arrange for the printing of another 1,000 copies of the pamphlet. "I have seen the effects of the work in the

course of my travels, and I am so convinced that the like effects will be produced upon others if it still be more circulated," he told Wedgwood. Clarkson also suggested that abstention might lead to more signatures on petitions.[19]
Even Fox's critics noted the rapid dissemination of the *Address*. As one
author wrote, "this pamphlet claims particular attention [for] the rapid and
extraordinary manner in which it has been circulated in all parts of the
kingdom."[20]

The partnership of Fox, Gurney, and Phillips aided the wide distribution
of the *Address* in England and the United States. A note in the tenth edition
indicated 50,000 copies had been printed in the first four months. Likely,
Gurney alone printed 130,000 copies by the twenty-sixth edition. Gurney
was not the only printer to produce copies of the *Address*, however. Approved
and bootleg copies were published throughout Great Britain and the
United States in the early 1790s, as well as private printings such as the one
requested by Clarkson. In his analysis of the Fox-Gurney partnership, literary scholar Timothy Whelan estimates at least 250,000 copies were printed
by Gurney and others during 1791–1792, eclipsing Thomas Paine's *Rights of
Man* as "the most widely distributed pamphlet of the eighteenth century."[21]
Fox's pamphlet outsold every other antislave-trade pamphlet up to that
time and caused a veritable war of words in the months following its initial
publication. More than twenty pamphlets were printed either challenging
or supporting Fox's contention that consumers should reject the produce
of slavery.[22]

Fox's argument for abstention resonated with supporters in large part
because it engaged with contemporary ideas about gender and commerce
as well as slavery. In his *Address*, he made three arguments that together emphasized the moral potential of commerce if individual consumers, especially
women, would demand more ethically produced goods. First, he argued the
slave trade had corrupted commerce. Sugar, according to Fox, was produced
by a corrupt system of manufacture, which produced only "human woe"
and "poison." The trade in slaves and in slave-grown sugar surpassed, in
brutality and injustice, even "the most barbarous ages."[23] Second, consumer
desire sustained the slave trade. The traffic in slaves was driven by domestic
desire for luxury items, which habit had transformed into essential household
goods. Fox reasoned that if one family consuming five pounds of sugar per
week abstained from sugar for twenty-one months, that family "would prevent the slavery or murder of one fellow-creature."[24] Finally, Fox argued that
regardless of parliamentary action, consumers could accept or reject the products of slavery. Criticizing the mercantile system that had protected West

Indian sugar, Fox warned that while British law might only provide slave-grown sugar for the domestic market, consumers could choose not to purchase such tainted goods.[25]

Fox did not appeal specifically to female consumers. He did, however, make explicit the connection between domestic consumption and colonial slave labor. In the months following publication of Fox's *Address*, the rhetoric of the abstention movement changed as writers responded to contemporary debates about female commerce and slave labor. Increasingly, writers appealed to female consumers using both economic and gendered language.[26] In doing so, activists shifted the focus of the slave-trade debate from Parliament to the tea table. The tea table symbolized the promises and the costs of consumption, thus the tea table acted as a centripetal force in private and public debates about commerce, gender, and the slave trade. Cultural anxieties about female consumption, particularly at the tea table, became enmeshed in political debates about the blood-stained commerce of the African slave trade.

Gender and Consumption at the Tea Table

The association of tea and women dated to the late seventeenth century. Edmund Waller, for example, linked tea consumption to Queen Catherine in his poem "Of Tea, Commended by Her Majesty" (1690), thus describing tea as an essentially upper-class female activity.[27] In the eighteenth century, poets celebrated the virtuous properties of tea, particularly when compared to wine. In *A Poem on Tea* (1712), Peter Motteux claimed tea banished brutish male behavior, which had been caused by the consumption of wine:

> I drink, and lo the kindly Streams arise,
> Wine's vapour flags, and soon subsides and dies.
> The friendly Spirits brighten mine again,
> Repel the Brute, and re-inthrone the Man.
> The rising Charmer with a pleasing Ray
> Dawns on the Mind, and introduces Day.[28]

Wine led to excess and dissipation while tea calmed and civilized. When tea was served by a British woman, she participated in this process of civilization. "The Task" by William Cowper described the classic tea-table scene, emphasizing the civilizing characteristics of British tea consumption:

> Now stir the fire, and close the shutters fast,
> Let fall the curtains, wheel the sofa round,

And, while the bubbling and loud-hissing urn
Throws up a steamy column, and the cups,
That cheer but not inebriate, wait on each,
So let us welcome peaceful ev'ning in.

The feminine architect of this harmonious scene is unidentified yet understood as essential to its creation. Shutters and curtains enclose the scene, shut-
ting out "The grand debate, / The popular harangue, the tart reply" of the
public sphere though the man and the material culture of the tea ritual were
reminders "of a noisy world."[29] Cowper's poem emphasized the dual benefits of tea consumption, which simultaneously civilized Britons and expanded the British economy.

As opportunities to consume material goods increased, critics questioned
the impact such changes had on society and, in particular, on women. In a
letter in Eliza Haywood's *Female Spectator*, published in 1775, John Careful
described the tea table as "the Bane of good housewifery." Women, according to Careful, believed a well-equipped tea table as important as a wedding
ring. Female commerce turned British households upside down.[30] Politician
Joseph Addison, for example, lamented his wife's obsession with collecting
china: "The common way of purchasing such trifles, if I may believe my
female informers, is by exchanging old suits of cloaths for this brittle ware. . . .
I have known an old petticoat metamorphosed into a punch-bowl, and a
pair of trousers into a tea pot."[31] Similarly, in a rather wistful look back, the
poet Charles Jenner wrote in 1773:

Time was, when tradesmen laid up what they gain'd,
And frugally a family maintain'd;
When they took stirring housewives for their spouses,
To keep up prudent order in their houses;
Who thought no scorn, at night to sit them down,
And make their childrens cloaths, or mend their own;
Would *Polly's* coat to younger *Bess* transfer,
And make their caps, without a milliner:
But now, a -shopping half the day they're gone,
To buy five hundred things, and pay for none.

Commerce preyed on the worst of female behavior. "Miss despises all
domestick rules," Jenner wrote, preferring to "spend their precious time in
hackney-coaches."[32] "Whilst mine is the Labour and you have the Gains,"
wrote an anonymous poet in 1749, "I have but ill Words and worse Looks for
my Pains."[33] Yet something is amiss, as scholar Karen Harvey argues: "The

horror and inappropriateness of exchanging clothes for china is made all the more outrageous by the transformation of a woman's petticoat into a punchbowl and a man's breeches into a teapot." Rather than a description of male impotence when confronted by female consumption, these narratives suggest instead that the benefits and costs of modern consumerism were far from settled. Like Quakers on either side of the Atlantic, non-Quakers worried about the effects of the new consumer society. For many Britons, as evidenced by these examples, men were just as culpable as women. The men in Jenner's poem, for example, despised "laborious trade" as "too slow a way" to gain wealth. Instead, "Fortunes must rise, like mushrooms, in a day."[34]

Questions about male and female commerce assumed that consumption had a cultural narrative as well as its traditional explanation of profit and loss. Faced with a dazzling new array of goods, consumers often assigned cultural narratives to material goods that conveyed social status, reflected individual values, and even conditions of production. Moreover, those cultural narratives were contextual and often influenced by social class, gender, and politics. Consider, for example, how social class could blur definitions of appropriate female commerce. Among the upper class, the tea ritual could be the epitome of ladylike sociability. British diarist Elizabeth Shackleton served tea to exclusively female company, often using tea as a forum for her business dealings with haberdashers, mantua makers, and other tradeswomen.[35] In contrast, tea drinking among the "common sort" led some critics to claim that tea consumption encouraged the poor to squander money and time in an attempt to mimic their betters. In 1761, Englishman John Galt described the new habit of tea drinking among the elderly women of the parish, who would sneak off to "out-houses and by-places," consuming their tea in "cups and luggies [a wooden dish or bowl] for there were but few that had cups and saucers." The women, Galt noted, gathered in hedges, "cackling like pea-hens" until they were scattered by passersby. In the first example, the tea ritual creates an amiable atmosphere in which to conduct business; in the second example, the tea ritual creates instead an atmosphere of superfluity, which is further emphasized by the raucous laughter of the old women.[36]

As the habit of tea drinking spread through all the social classes of England, some critics linked the breakdown in class relations to the disintegration of British national identity. In "An Essay on Tea" (1756), social critic Jonas Hanway claimed tea consumption drained Britain's economic and military resources. "It is the curse of this nation, that the laborer and the mechanic will ape the lord," Hanway observed. Describing tea drinking as an "infection" and a "disease," Hanway believed consuming the food of another culture would somehow transform England into that culture. Tea consumption "took its rise from EXAMPLE; by EXAMPLE it is supported; and EXAMPLE only can abolish it." Hanway urged "ladies of rank" to abstain from the habit of drinking tea, claiming the "welfare" of the nation depended on female virtue. Leisured women had contributed to the spread of the habit of tea drinking, and leisured women must be the ones to put an end to the practice.[37]

Motteux and Cowper lauded the civilizing effects of conversation with a virtuous woman over a cup of tea; yet, their descriptions contrast sharply with contemporaneous complaints about excessive female speech at the tea table. Haywood, for example, asked, "Where have the Curious an Opportunity of informing themselves of the Intrigues of the Town, like that they enjoy over a TEA-TABLE, on a Lady's *Visiting Day?*"[38] Male and female behavior is contrasted in *The Tea Drinking Wife, and Drunken Husband* (1749). The husband claimed his wife spent too much time and money on tea:

Until ten or eleven o'Clock you seldom will rise;
And then when you're up you must have your desire,
And straight get the Tea-kettle Clapton the Fire.
Then in comes her Gossips to prate and to Chat,
Here is this that and t'other and the Devil knows what,
There is prattling and tatling until it be Noon
. . . And if I find Fault your Tongue it will run
So fast one would think you would never have done,
For such is your Humour; if ever controul'd;
I'm certain to hear a most damnable Scold.

Not only is the tea table the site for gossip and idleness, it also becomes the source of tension between husband and wife. Criticized by her husband, the wife responded with harsh words, "a most damnable Scold." Asserting the innocence of tea, the wife lamented her husband's habit of drinking ale and returning home late and unable to work. Poet Edward Young described "Scandal" as "the sweet'ner of a female feast" while Haywood noted that at the tea table, "Scandal, and Ridicule seem here to reign with uncontented sway, but rarely suffer the intrusion of any other themes."[39]

Women's rights advocate Mary Wollstonecraft claimed the consumer revolution had made objects of women much as slavery had made property of Africans. Women, according to Wollstonecraft, were "rendered weak and luxurious by the relaxing pleasures which wealth procures." Enslaved by a commercial culture that transformed women into "alluring" objects, women

FIGURE 1.   James Gillray. "Anti-Saccharites; or, John Bull and His Family Leaving Off the Use of Sugar," 1792. Courtesy of the Trustees of the British Museum, London.

were forced to rely on man to "lend them his reason to guide their tottering steps aright."[40] Consumerism transformed women's lives, creating in them "an immoderate fondness for dress, for pleasure, and for sway." Moreover, commercial society made such pursuits possible for women of all classes. "Women all want to be ladies," Wollstonecraft noted. "The blessed effect of civilization," according to Wollstonecraft, rendered "the most respectable women [into] the most oppressed." Thus "treated like contemptible beings," women "become contemptible." Men and women alike were to blame for the current state of gender relations, preferring "slavish obedience" from women rather than "rational fellowship" between the sexes.[41]

Two political caricatures, produced in 1792, reflect women's ambiguous place at the tea table and in the slave-trade debate. James Gillray's "Anti-Saccharites; or, John Bull and his Family Leaving Off the Use of Sugar" reflects the intertwining of contemporary debates about slavery, gender, and domestic consumption. Focusing on Queen Charlotte, Gillray highlighted the importance of women in the boycott. In the caricature, the Queen attempts to convince the recalcitrant princesses to accept unsweetened tea, re-

FIGURE 2.   Isaac Cruikshank. "The Gradual Abolition off [sic] the Slave Trade; or, Leaving of Sugar by Degrees," 1792. Courtesy of the Trustees of the British Museum, London.

minding them that abstention from sugar-sweetened tea would save both money and "the poor Blackamoors." Yet the question remains: Is the royal family's "Noble Example of Oeconomy" influenced by compassion for enslaved Africans, or concern over the high cost of sugar?[42] Likewise, Isaac Cruikshank's "The Gradual Abolition off [sic] the Slave Trade; or, leaving of Sugar by Degrees" focuses on Queen Charlotte at the tea table. Carefully weighing the sugar, the Queen tells Mrs. Schwellenberg, Keeper of the Robes, to take "only an ickle Bit" and to reflect on "de Negro Girl dat Captain Kimber treated so Cruelly."[43] Once again, the viewer is reminded of the connection between sugar and slavery. The luxury of sugar-sweetened tea is made possible at a high cost in both African bodies and English currency. On the left side of the image, Princess Elizabeth refuses to give up sugar, claiming that she cannot forgo a "good thing." Her sister, however, turns away in disgust, emphasizing her rejection of slave-grown sugar with a dramatic facial expression and hand gestures. Again, we are left to wonder what motivates the royal family's boycott of slave-grown sugar: economics or morals.

Consumer goods created a political and moral crisis that threatened British domesticity and rendered virtuous English womanhood a novel construct. The boycott provided supporters the opportunity to challenge these unflattering images of English womanhood, constructing instead an ideal of an activist feminine sympathy for the oppressed. After publication of Fox's *Address*, boycotters increasingly appealed to female compassion. Pamphleteer William Allen, for example, described Englishwomen as "MODELS of every just and virtuous *sentiment*." Another author hoped to capitalize on the popularity of the new Duchess of York, seeking to draw her attention to the abstention movement and to obtain her support through a public appeal to her "heart of sensibility."[44] Men were not alone in their appeals to women. Dublin Quaker Mary Birkett, for example, called upon women to adopt an activist sensibility:

> Yes, sisters, yes, to us the task belongs
> 'Tis we increase or mitigate their wrongs,
> If we the produce of their toils refuse,
> If we no more the blood-stain'd lux'ry choose;

Birkett rejected the notion of a limited, distinct female sphere of influence:

> Say not that small's the sphere in which we move,
> And our attempts would vain and fruitless prove;
> Not so—we hold a most important share,
> In all the evils—all the wrongs they bear,
> And tho' their woes *entire* we can't remove,
> We may th' *increasing* mis'ries which they prove,
> Push far away the plant for which they die,
> And in this one small thing our taste deny,
> We must, we ought, 'tis Justice points the way;
> Mercy and Charity loudly call—"obey."

Birkett called on women to reject slave-grown sugar and to adopt an activist sensibility, responding to the wrongs of slavery by refusing to consume "the plant for which they die."[45]

Much of this rhetoric used the language of sensibility, which as Brycchan Carey argues, served "as a site for the working out of changing gender relationships" in the eighteenth century.[46] The rhetoric of sensibility positioned feminine sympathy apart from the marketplace, defining abolition as a moral question. Female behavior represented "authoritative moral consistency."[47] For example, an anonymous letter published in the *Manchester Mercury* in 1787 called on women to use "the qualities of Humanity, Benevolence, and Compassion" to draw public attention to the slave trade. Men were too "much involved in the cares of the world, the bustle of trade" to have time to consider "the Humanity of our Commerce."[48] Yet the distinction between the humanity of the private sphere and the calculating commerce of the public sphere was unstable. In a letter to the *Gentleman's Magazine* in 1788, "Polinus" claimed that the fashion "of the present day is HUMANITY, or as it was well called by a great minister, the *Philanthropy of five days.*"[49] Indeed abolitionism seemed ubiquitous (partly because of the abolitionists' extensive propaganda campaign), resulting in the "mammoth overproduction" of antislavery poetry and abolitionist artifacts. Wedgwood's iconic image of the kneeling slave was reproduced widely on cameos, tea ware, snuff boxes, and other domestic goods. "The ladies," author Hester Thrale wrote in 1788, "now wear the Figure of a Negro in Wedgwood's Ware round their Necks."[50] The consumption of abolitionist artifacts and prose led many critics and supporters of slavery to question female motivation. Were women motivated by genuine benevolence, or were they simply responding to the fashion of the moment? Polinus, for one, believed that fashion prevailed: "Our poetesses who can oppress and abuse one another when opportunity offers, unite in opposition to oppression with . . . ill . . . grace."[51]

Abolitionists who struggled to define the appropriate role for female sensibility in the slave-trade debates focused their arguments on the distinction between false and true sensibility. In her poems *Sensibility* and *Slavery*, evangelical Hannah More distinguished between false and true sensibility. The former, according to More, was superficial and feigned while the latter was natural and active. More rejected false sentiment and insisted her readers weep and then act when confronted by suffering.[52] In his lecture on the slave trade, Samuel Taylor Coleridge noted that "true Benevolence is a rare Quality among us. Sensibility indeed we have to spare—what novel-reading Lady does not over flow with it to the great annoyance of her Friends and Family."[53] More and Coleridge, as well as Wollstonecraft, criticized false sensibility but did not renounce the use of feminine sympathy altogether. These critiques of false sensibility were an attempt by writers to use sentimental rhetoric to garner support for abolition while simultaneously countering proslavery authors who argued that abolitionist prose was based on emotion rather than reason.[54]

Proslavery literature suggested that women's sensibility rendered them susceptible to the arguments of abolitionists and supporters of the boycott. "No Planter," a widely quoted essay first published in the *Gentleman's Magazine* in 1789, satirized abolitionist sentiment: "The vulgar are influenced by names and titles. Instead of SLAVES, let the Negroes be called ASSISTANT PLANTERS; and we shall not then hear such violent outcries against the slave trade by pious divines, tender-hearted poetesses, and short-sighted

politicians."[55] Writing at the height of the boycott, the proslavery author of
Strictures on an Address to the People of Great Britain suggested that Fox's argument was successful because he worked on "the passions." According to the
anonymous author, Fox owed his success to the patronage of his female readers who were "pierced to the heart with the sufferings of the oppressed Africans."[56] Another critic of the boycott suggested that women had been duped
by "hypocrites who make fortunes by using cotton and other things provided by Negroes labor."[57] Such arguments reflected contemporary ideas that
women's commercial behavior was based on fashion rather than economics.
In a review of Fox's *Address*, one author criticized the pamphlet as the "effu-
sion of some fond zealot" who hoped to destroy the slave trade "by a serious
dissuasion of our wives and daughters from the use of sugar!" Contrasting
male and female consumption, the anonymous reviewer warned readers
against "what uproars [Fox] may occasion, should his reasons prevail with any
masters of families to enforce such a decree, while the females remain uncon-
vinced and contumacious?"[58]

The rhetoric of sensibility thus became a battleground for pro- and
antislave-trade writers. False sensibility made women particularly vulnerable
to the passionate arguments of the abolitionists; yet that same false sensibility rendered women unable to take an active role in response to abolitionist
rhetoric. Proslavery supporters used false sensibility to dismiss the popularity of the abolitionist movement as just another example of overwrought female sensibility. In this view, the horrors of slavery and the slave trade were
fabricated by abolitionists in much the same way novelists and poets created
works meant to generate an emotional response, usually in female readers.
Abolitionists did not deny the presence of false sensibility; instead, abolitionists
sought to transform false sentiment into true benevolent action. The implications of this debate were the same: women were unreliable abolitionists.
For both pro- and antislave-trade writers, questions remained about the true
character of female sensibility.[59]

Blood-Stained Sugar

Anxieties about female commerce intensified with the publication of sensa-
tional stories of white female cruelty, which were presented to the House
of Commons during the slave-trade debates of 1790 and 1791. According to
testimony, colonial women of all ranks were responsible for ordering, supervising, and even inflicting punishment on their slaves; one colonial woman
was accused of routinely prostituting her female slave.[60] Wollstonecraft ques-

tioned the integrity of female sensibility in light of the evidence: "Where is the dignity, the infallibility of sensibility, in the fair ladies, whom, if the voice of rumour is to be credited, the captive negroes curse in all the agony of bodily pain, for the unheard of tortures they invent?" She criticized colonial women who "after the sight of a flagellation, compose[d] their ruffled spirits and exercise[d] their tender feelings by the perusal of the latest imported novel."[61] Parliamentary testimony indicated that the political crisis was also a gender crisis. Writing in 1792, radical political writer Benjamin Flower urged British women "to attend to the conduct of some of the West India Ladies toward their slaves." Flower's *The French Constitution*, inspired by a six-month visit to France a year earlier, criticized the British more than it considered the French political system. In the appendix to the second edition, Flower reviewed the progress of slave-trade legislation. Flower recommended Fox's *Address* to "the LADIES. They are formed to feel *more* than men are." Yet, Flower warned readers that emotions were little more than "pretensions" if women continued to "sweeten their tea, and the tea of their families and visitors, with the blood of their fellow creatures." Slavery, according to Flower, stripped women "of their peculiar glory; their amiableness, their sensibility, "transform[ing] the loveliest part of God's creation into savages and brutes!"[62] Beneath Flower's chivalrous appeal to virtuous English women lay the fear that women needed abolitionist tracts more than men because ultimately women were the real savages. In this way, the world of the white English woman and the West Indian colonial woman collided, and the "English woman is advised to look into the mirror of her own barbarity."[63]

Such criticism of Englishwomen reflected the anxiety of many that slavery had contaminated British society. British writer Anna Laetitia Barbauld, for example, claimed that both the colonial and metropolitan space had been corrupted by their commercial connection with slavery. In her poem *Epistle to William Wilberforce*, written after parliamentary defeat of the abolition bill in the spring of 1791, Barbauld denounced an indifferent British public, which had been influenced by "the artful gloss, that moral sense confounds." The "contagion," she wrote, was a "monstrous fellowship" of female virtue and corruption:

Lo! Where reclin'd, pale Beauty courts the breeze,
Diffus'd on sofas of voluptuous ease;
With anxious awe, her menial train around,
Catch her faint whispers of half-utter'd sound

. . . .

See her, with indolence to fierceness join'd,
Of body delicate, infirm of mind,
With languid tones imperious mandates urge;
With arm recumbent wield the household scourge;
And with unruffled mien, and placid sounds,
Contriving torture, and inflicting wounds.

In Barbauld's narrative, "voluptuous ease" slid easily from civilized to savage. Under the influence of the "seasoned tools of Avarice," manners melted and hearts hardened until the "spreading leprosy taints ev'ry part."[64]

For opponents of slavery, the contaminating effect of slavery was most visible in the blood-stained sugar served at ladies' tea tables. "Is sugar always to be produced by vital blood?" asked Wollstonecraft.[65] Abstention rhetoric claimed the bodily fluids of African slaves were active agents in the production of colonial produce, nourishing the produce of slave labor and contaminating the tea consumed by British women. In Cowper's "The Negro's Complaint," one of the most popular poems of the period, water is replaced by the tears and sweat of the slave:

Why did all-creating Nature
Make the plant for which we toil?
Sighs must fan it, Tears must water,
Sweat of ours must dress the soil.

Cowper's poem was reprinted on the cover of many editions of Fox's *Address* and was included in a small privately circulated publication, *A Subject for Conversation and Reflection at the Tea Table*.[66] African blood, sweat, and tears were frequent tropes in abstention rhetoric. While such rhetoric intensified in the early 1790s, particularly after the revolutions in Saint Domingue and in France, such bloody rhetoric actually began to appear in the late 1780s.[67] For example, a poem published in the *Scots Magazine* in 1788 claimed the luscious juice of the sugar cane resulted from African blood: "Are drops of blood the horrible manure / That fills with luscious juice the teeming cane?" Thus, the "keen sorrows" of the slave "are the sweets we blend / with the green bev'rage of our morning meal."[68]

The rhetoric of the boycott of slave labor linked the consumption of slave-grown sugar to the cannibalistic consumption of slave bodies. In a series of "bloody vignettes," abolitionists described the slave's passage from freedom to enslavement, from Africa to the West Indies. Abstention completed the triangle of trade, explaining the slave's transformation from producer of consumer goods to that which is consumed.[69] This blood-stained rhetoric had been used to describe the production of slave-labor goods as early as the seventeenth century as both Quakers and non-Quakers connected the violence of slavery to the products of slave labor. London merchant Thomas Tryon, writing in 1684, described the evils of slavery from the slave's viewpoint. Slaveholders, the slave lamented, had "grow[n] fat with our Blood and Sweat, gormandizing with the fruits procured by our *Slavery* and sore *Labour*." The slaveholder reclined by his "*Rum-Pots, Punch-Bowls, Brandy-Bottles,* [and other] *Intoxicating Enchantments*."[70] In 1729, colonial Quaker Ralph Sandiford condemned slaveholders who fed on "the flesh and Blood of Slaves instead of Christ," a claim later adopted by William Fox who suggested that each pound of West Indian sugar contained two ounces of African flesh.[71] British political reformer Thomas Cooper claimed "the infernal voracity of European avarice" had consumed an estimated 180 million slaves so "*That the Gentlefolk of Europe, (my friend) may drink Sugar in their Tea!*"[72] Samuel Taylor Coleridge mocked Christians who sought divine blessing for a meal sweetened by African blood: "Gracious Heaven! . . . A part of that Food among most of you is sweetened with the Blood of the Murdered . . . O Blasphemy! Did God give Food mingled with Brothers blood! Will the Father of all men bless the Food of Cannibals—the food which is polluted with the blood of his own innocent children?"[73] However, none were as graphic as pamphleteer Andrew Burn, whose *A Second Address to the People of Great Britain* has been described as the "paranoid double" of Fox's *Address*. Appeals to sentiment, he believed, were not strong enough. Rather he hoped to disgust consumers into abstention by convincing his readers that "either in Puddings, Pies, Tarts, Tea, or otherwise, that they literally, and most certainly in so-doing, eat large quantities of that last mentioned Fluid [blood], as it flows copiously from the Body of the laborious slave." Burn went beyond the standard trope of blood-stained sugar, however, as he described in great detail the physical conditions of slavery in the sugar colonies. Sweat, lice, and jiggers all contaminated the sugar produced by African slaves in the West Indies and were in turn consumed by Britons. After piling horror on horror, Burn concluded with the story of a British wine merchant who opened a cask of West Indian rum and discovered inside "the whole body of a roasted Negro."[74]

Contaminated sugar was most dramatically depicted by the caricaturist James Gillray in April 1791. "Barbarities in the West Indias" invoked the horror of cannibalism: as an overseer stirs a steaming vat of sugar cane juice, the flailing arms and legs are all that is seen of the slave who has been tossed into

Figure 3. James Gillray. "Barbarities in the West Indias," 1791. Courtesy of the Trustees of the British Museum, London.

the pot. In the background, a bird, a fox, some rats, two black cats as well as two black ears, and a black arm have been pinned to the wall. As he works, the overseer sneers, "B—t your black Eyes! what you can't work because you're not well?—but I'll give you a warm bath to cure your Ague, and a Curry-combing afterwards to put Spunk into you." Gillray's image is made all the more horrible because it was based on testimony given to the House of Commons by "Mr. Frances." In his *History*, Clarkson noted that Phillip Francis reported the case of an overseer who punished a slave by throwing him into a pot of boiling cane juice. Gillray, however, embellished the story Francis reported, which casts doubt on the veracity of the source and renders Gillray's political cartoon an ambiguous commentary on slavery and the slave trade.[75]

Opponents of abolitionism criticized the bloody rhetoric of abstention, suggesting that boycotters' emphasis on blood-stained sugar overlooked other products that had been contaminated by slave labor. One critic asked, "How anybody who will not eat Sugar because it is eating Negro flesh, can handle gold or silver, or feed themselves with silver spoons or forks; for if eating Sugar is eating Negroes flesh, sure every time anybody puts a fork or spoon in their mouths, it is putting a poor dead Negro's finger or toe there."[76] Such criticism mocked abstention rhetoric that saw blood and flesh in every bowl of sugar; yet, such criticism used the very rhetorical devices of the antislave-trade writing it mocked.

The graphic violence of abstention rhetoric served both to repel and to remind consumers of the bloody connection between colonial production and domestic consumption. By depicting ladies' sugar bowls as dripping with the blood of slaves, supporters of abstention suggested that metropolitan women who did not support the boycott were no better than their counter-parts in the colonies. Women who did support the slave trade were forced to defend not only their support of slavery but their femininity as well.

Debating Gender and Commerce

Of the dozens of tracts about the slave-trade debate that were produced in 1791 and 1792, none is as unusual as the one sold by W. Moon of Whi-techapel. Bearing the title *An Answer to a Pamphlet Intituled [sic] An Address to the People of England against the Use of West India Produce*, this piece was pur-portedly written by a female apologist for slavery. While it was one of many proslavery tracts written in this period in response to Fox's *Address*, it was the only one allegedly composed by a woman. The apologist's arguments caught the attention of Richard Hillier, who had for a time worked as a sailor in the West Indies. Compelled to challenge the female apologist and to de-fend Fox, Hillier published *A Vindication of an Address to the People of Great Britain, on the Use of West India Produce* in late 1791.[77] Read together, these three tracts—*An Address to the People of Great Britain, An Answer to a Pamphlet,* and *A Vindication of an Address*—highlight the importance of the domestic world to the political campaign against the slave trade.

In her *Answer*, the female apologist defended her femininity, outlined the economic benefits of the slave trade, and suggested that activists alleviate the suffering of the working men of Britain. The female apologist made a careful distinction between support of slave-produced goods and the slave trade. Aligning herself with the ascribed female qualities of "humanity" and "Christian principles," she denied that she supported the slave trade just because she did not support the boycott. If the boycott were successful, it would have a devastating effect on Britons, the apologist argued. The British trade in slave-grown sugar was a "vast and extensive branch of commerce"; thus, abstention would force West Indian planters to find another market for their sugar and force thousands of British businessmen into bankruptcy or prison. The end of the market for slave-grown sugar would "effectually cramp the spirit of industry and enterprise." Indeed, in a rather tortured discussion of scriptural authority, the female apologist suggested that the availability of slave-produced goods in the marketplace indicated a divine sanction of the consumption of such goods. The female apologist further suggested that activists should focus first on the suffering of workingmen at home rather than Africans in the colonies. She denied Fox's claim for a high rate of death among African slaves in the Caribbean and instead argued that more working-class men in Britain died young "either by hazardous employments, by working in infectious trades, or by extreme labor." Calling English miners "underground slaves," she argued that if the labor conditions of these workingmen were examined, their situation would be found "unenviable, even by the West Indian slave."[78]

Comparing African slaves to the workingmen of Britain demonstrated that the female apologist had a clear understanding of pro- and antislave-trade rhetoric. By diverting attention to miners, she placed her tract within an established rhetorical tradition. Emphasizing the importance of slave-goods, proslave-trade writers created what literary scholar Brycchan Carey has described as a "hierarchy of suffering." Child chimney sweeps and miners were most often singled out for comparison with slaves, Carey argues, because all three groups shared harsh labor conditions, child labor, high mortality, and "black faces." Relief for child chimney sweeps was supported by abolitionists and proslavery supporters alike; however, proslavery supporters used their concern for child chimney sweeps to argue, like the female apologist, that "charity" should begin at home.[79]

Hillier's *Vindication* challenged the female apologist on gendered terms, focusing in particular on her lack of feminine sympathy. "*Your* charity, my good Lady, may *begin* at home, and *end* at home, *and stay at home* for ever," he asserted.[80] Hillier referred to the now-familiar testimony in the House of Commons about the cruelty of colonial women and suggested that with a little practice the female apologist could become just like those colonial women. "The ladies in the West-Indies have a happy dexterity in flipping off their shoes, and beating the heels of them about the heads of their negroes," he wrote. "Now, with a very little practice upon your bed-post or dressing table, you will make a tolerable proficiency in the art." To further emphasize her lack of feminine sympathy, Hillier contrasted the apologist with more notable women such as antislavery author Helen Maria Williams, who linked support for abolitionism with the moralization of politics and commerce.[81]

The use of gender in this debate reveals just how important feminine ideals had become in the slave-trade debate and in the boycott. In *An Answer*, the author identifies herself as female on the first page though she chooses to remain anonymous.[82] Anonymity was common among political authors in the eighteenth century. Many pieces of pro- and antislave-trade rhetoric were published anonymously or pseudonymously. Generally, women adopted a male identity; however, by the late eighteenth century, women's experience increasingly held an authority that tempted men to appropriate it.[83] If the female apologist was a man appropriating a female identity, it is significant that the author did not emphasize gender more. Hillier, in contrast, emphasized the author's gender in his title and in his argument, claiming she had violated appropriate gender ideals by rejecting the boycott of slave-grown sugar. Criticizing the female apologist allowed Hillier to implicitly censure other women who failed to support the boycott. If An Answer was authored by a man using a female identity, it suggests the power of sentimental rhetoric in the slave-trade debates. For example, when the female apologist and Hillier debated the relative situation of West Indian slaves and British miners, the two authors suggested divergent responses to suffering: one focused on distant pain, and the other focused on nearby distress. The anonymous author consciously created a "hierarchy of suffering" and may well have decided to use a feminine authorial identity to strengthen the argument privileging white laborers over black slaves. In the second edition of A Vindication, Hillier revealed his knowledge of the apologist's identity and, in refusing to identify the author, suggested again that the author was indeed female. Hillier also noted that the author "retail[ed] a commodity," which might well be affected by the boycott, thus implying her arguments against the boycott might be more self-interested than she admitted.[84] Whether authored by a man or a woman, the anti-boycott argument of An Answer suggests growing awareness of the importance of gender and sentiment as well as commerce in the slave-trade debates. The gender of the female apologist might have escaped the notice of the careless reader had Hillier not given it such prominence in his tracts. This along with the apparent relationship between the anonymous author and Hillier raises questions about this particular debate. An Answer to a Pamphlet—regardless of the author's gender—may have been written in conjunction with Hillier's pamphlet in an attempt to use gender to bring attention to the abstention campaign. As writers on either side of the slave-trade debate addressed arguments from the opposition, the authorship and form of pro- and anti-slavery appeals changed, using complex ideological shifts to more effectively petition their audience. In the process, ideologies of gender and sentiment and commerce and trade intertwined within the slave-trade debates to create competing ideas of British national identity.[85]

Eighteenth-century abstention rhetoric developed within this oppositional interchange, as subsequent editions of Fox's *Address* illustrate. In mid-1791, the title of Fox's pamphlet changed. The first six editions were published as *An Address to the People of Great Britain on the Utility of Refraining from the Use of West India Sugar and Rum*. Beginning with the seventh edition, the tract was published as *An Address to the People of Great Britain on the Propriety of Abstaining from the Use of West India Sugar and Rum*. Replacing "utility" with "propriety" and "refraining" with "abstaining," the new title emphasized the morality of the abstention campaign rather than its more utilitarian aspects. Shifting the emphasis to the morality of abstention also reinforced the gendered nature of the abstention campaign.

The Decline of the Boycott

Throughout the winter of 1791–1792, supporters and opponents of the slave trade publicly debated the future of colonial slavery with perhaps as many as one-half million consumers agreeing to boycott slave-grown sugar until Parliament took action. In the spring of 1792, hoping to build on the momentum of the boycott, abolitionists once again brought the issue of the slave trade before the House of Commons. In a matter of weeks, 519 antislave-trade petitions bearing at least 390,000 names were presented to Parliament. In contrast, Parliament received just four petitions supporting the trade. Abolitionists' hopes were high when the debate began on April 2. To their dismay, however, home secretary Henry Dundas inserted the word "gradually" into Wilberforce's bill. Ultimately, the House of Commons passed the gradualist proposal postponing debate about the slave trade until 1796 when the trade was supposed to end. When the slave-trade abolition bill came before the House of Lords, the Lords insisted on holding their own hearings about the trade. The hearings were monopolized by proslavery interests until Parliament adjourned, effectively ending any hopes of passing the bill.[86]

As British abolitionists regrouped after this latest defeat, events in France took a violent turn. King Louis XVI was taken prisoner. Then in September, two thousand French royalists, clergy, and aristocrats were killed. Conservatives in Britain were horrified by the events. On January 21, 1793, as British abolitionists were attempting to schedule another hearing on the abolition of the slave trade, the French king was executed. "Every bosom burns with indignation in this kingdom against the ferocious savages of Paris," declared the London *Times*. The French ambassador was expelled from Britain, and relations between Britain and France spiraled downward, ending in

France's declaration of war against Britain on February 1.[87] The abstention writer Fox took a strong antiwar stance, claiming Britain was the aggressor and wished to destroy the new French republic because the revolution held dangerous possibilities for Great Britain. He criticized a British government that worried about the affairs of other European nations while neglecting British issues such as the slave trade. It was, Fox noted, easier "to express the warmest emotions, and the most indignant feelings against *them*, . . . than to pursue the thorny path of virtue, and steadily resist the temptations to which we are exposed." Britons wept for the French king and sobbed at the tragedy of Oronooko (Aphra Behn's tale of an enslaved African prince), yet failed to act against the slave trade, a crime supported daily by British consumers.[88] Noting that Britons sympathized with the victims of the very crimes they committed, Fox raised uncomfortable questions about the nature of sympathy and the pleasure that the spectacle of death could invoke.[89] Nonetheless, events in Saint Domingue and France had a chilling effect on the boycott and the slave-trade debate. Many leading abolitionists, including Clarkson, distanced themselves from the boycott, which waned significantly after 1792. In 1793 the SEAST made an abortive attempt to continue the boycott after the House of Commons refused to revive the slave-trade debate. By 1797 the SEAST had suspended all operations and the slave-sugar boycott was a distant memory.[90]

It is likely that more than half a million Britons participated in the boycott of slave-grown sugar. Grocers reported decreases in sugar sales, dropping as much as "a third to a half in just a few months' time," while "the sale of sugar from India increased more than tenfold." That grocers began to stock East rather than West Indian sugar suggests that female consumers, who were responsible for most of the household purchases, had had an influence. Yet the success of abstention was tempered by declining supplies, rising prices, and increased demand elsewhere. In January 1792, for example, sugar riots broke out in the streets of Paris. Moreover, the narrow scope of the boycott, targeting only slave-grown sugar, limited its economic impact on slaveholders. Clarkson, for example, was unwilling to extend the boycott to cotton, which he believed "might take away the bread of a million of our fellow subjects, the innocent poor of this country." Nonetheless, the British boycott of slave-grown sugar highlights the possibilities of consumer activism. When abstention merged with contemporary anxieties about the slave trade and female commerce, the boycott gained support from outside the Society of Friends. For these new supporters of the boycott, more was at stake than Britain's support of the slave trade. Nowhere is this more evident than in the debates surrounding women's participation in the boycott. Critics on either side of the boycott were uncertain whether women were appropriate ac-tivists in the movement. Supporters of slavery believed women were too easily swayed by the sentimental rhetoric of abolitionists, whereas anti-slavery writers worried that women were too driven by their insatiable appetites to make the moral choice. For the women who abstained from slave-grown sugar, the boycott provided an opportunity to actively partici-pate in the abolitionist movement. Women who did so rejected cultural con-structions of gender that described women as apolitical and interested only in fashion and consumption. Abstention transformed the landscape of ladies' tea tables into a liminal zone where conversations about gender, commerce, and abolitionism blended into one another. In addition to cultural debates about gender and commerce, the British boycott of slave-grown sugar ben-efited from the large-scale political movement against the slave trade that developed in the late 1780s. The idea of abstention was drawn into and in-fluenced by these debates and, in turn, abstention shaped discussions of the slave trade and gender and commerce. As a result, the boycott benefited from a much broader base of support than it might otherwise have had if it had remained tied solely to the antislavery movement.

CHAPTER 3

Striking at the Root of Corruption: American Quakers and the Boycott in the Early National Period

American opponents of slavery followed the progress of the British boycott of slave-grown sugar. Reprints of William Fox's *Address to the People of Great Britain* were published in New York, Boston, and Philadelphia, while excerpts of Fox's *Address* appeared in various American newspapers, including *Dunlap's Daily American Advertiser* (Philadelphia). On May 14, 1792, *Dunlap's* reported that "upwards of 12,000 persons" in Limerick, Ireland, had "discontinued the use of sugar." Later that same month, the *New York Journal and Patriotic Register* reprinted a British news item that three hundred families in Worcester, southwest of Birmingham, were abstaining from sugar. These same papers also reported on Americans' growing interest in domestically produced maple sugar. Supporters of maple sugar celebrated the connection between moral responsibility and economic self-interest. The author of a letter to the editor of New York City's *Daily Advertiser* claimed consumers could support the moral principles of the boycott and help America "save" close to $1.5 million each year by consuming maple sugar.[1] In another account, maple sugar was described as a safe alternative to slave-grown sugar after reports surfaced that West Indian slaves, "skilled in [the] fatal science of poisoning people," had contaminated sugar and molasses.[2] Nonetheless, a large-scale sugar boycott never materialized in the United States in the 1790s.

It is instructive to compare the popularity of the British boycott with the limited scope of the American abstention movement even if doing so risks supporting a historiography that is, as one scholar notes, "invested in the seemingly inevitable failure of eighteenth-century American antislavery."[3] The absence of a widespread slave-sugar boycott in the United States in the 1790s reveals the highly contextual nature of consumer activism. As we have seen, British Quakers successfully transformed the boycott of slave-grown sugar into a popular, ecumenical movement by using current political and cultural debates about the slave trade and the rise of consumer society. The most popular pamphlet of the boycott was written not by a Quaker but by the Baptist printer Fox, a testament to the success of Quakers' disappearing act. British Quakers gained the support of leading political and civil leaders, including Clarkson and Wedgwood, as well as thousands of British consumers. As it developed in the 1790s, the British boycott reinforced abolitionists' attitude toward slavery, treating slavery as a discrete issue that was most effectively addressed through judicial or parliamentary means.[4] Consumers believed the boycott could be used to pressure Parliament into taking action against slavery, using parliamentary reform to end slavery and to alter the marketplace.

In contrast, the American movement lacked the vigor of political and cultural debates about slavery and female commerce. Although abstention developed in dynamic relationship with other cultural forces—the advent of new ideas about labor, the ongoing debate among Quakers about slavery, the expansion of evangelical Christianity, and an increase in black activism—these cultural influences tended to reinforce rather than transform the fundamental Quaker character of abstention. During his lifetime, John Woolman's example influenced the development of a committed group of Quakers who abstained from slave labor. After his death in 1772, London and Philadelphia Yearly Meetings each published an edition of Woolman's journal.[5] Thus Woolman's economic and social critique continued to influence Quakers, including the Americans Warner Mifflin, Elias Hicks, Jesse Kersey, and Enoch Lewis. Woolman and other American Quakers had become disillusioned with politics after the Seven Years' War; consequently, they shunned political action when it came to slavery. Instead, Quakers sought to strike at "the root of corruption," resolving to "make the world better by living well, trusting God, and serving as examples to others."[6] Abstention from slave-labor goods was integral to this approach. Quaker abstention was more audacious, as a result, seeking deep-rooted moral change that would in time transform the fundamental premise of transatlantic economic and social life. This vision of abstention influenced the American movement through the 1820s.

Abstention and Free Labor

Quaker arguments against slave labor asserted the morality of free labor, or the labor of free men and women. Woolman, as we have seen, believed the right use of labor to be the foundation of a moral economy. He praised the African subsistence economy, contrasting the benefits of such an economy where the labor of all sustained all, to the immoral economy of slavery, where the abuse of labor promoted violence and greed.[7] Woolman and like-minded Quakers claimed slave labor degraded all aspects of life. Even the landscape reflected the ruinous effect of slavery. Traveling in North Carolina in 1796, Woolman's contemporary Joshua Evans observed, "The country looks poor, barren, and desolate." Slaveholders "fare sumptuously every day, and waste that which might be a comfort to those poor, oppressed slaves." Slavery caused both physical and spiritual poverty. According to Evans, "Religion is in the talking, the country is poor [and] barren as are the people, and the land is poorly cultivated." Slavery seemed "to hang over the land" like "a thick cloud of darkness."[8] For Woolman and Evans, the morality of free labor was more important than its efficiency. Morality rather than economy was the goal.

Indeed, in the mid and late eighteenth century few individuals argued for the economic efficiency of free labor. Conventional wisdom defined slave labor as more productive than free labor. Thus, when individuals such as Benjamin Franklin and Benjamin Rush argued for the moral and the economic superiority of free labor, they helped create a new understanding of labor. Franklin and Rush, like Woolman, contrasted the honor of labor against the dissipation of luxury. Writing in 1751, Franklin framed his argument for free labor in terms of population growth, claiming slavery diminished productivity by limiting slave owners' ability to support many children. Free labor encouraged men to "Frugality and Industry," he noted. Whereas the slave would neglect his "Business," the free man would tend more closely to it because he would reap the benefits of his labor: "Neglect is natural to the man who is not to be benefited by his own care or diligence." Rush made similar arguments about the productivity of free labor, citing as evidence Monsieur Le Poivre's observations of sugar cultivation by free labor in Cochin China (present-day southern Vietnam). "Liberty and property form the basis of abundance and good agriculture," Le Poivre observed. "The earth, which multiplies her productions with a kind profusion, under the hands of the free-born labourer, seems to shrink into barrenness under the sweat of the slave." In addition to the productivity of labor, Rush emphasized the ways in which free labor suppressed luxury and vice and promoted the equal distribution of property for the good of society.[9]

Arguments for the economic superiority of free labor often appeared alongside traditional arguments that slave labor was the source of wealth, suggesting that in this period ideas about labor were in transition. For example, an essay by "Rusticus," which appeared in the *New York Daily Advertiser* in 1790, argued for the efficiency of free labor while emphasizing slaveholders' claims that slave labor was cheaper, in other words, more efficient. Such contradictions reflect the variable and protean nature of ideas about free labor. Outlining the transition of ideas about free labor from the 1750s to the 1810s, historian Eva Sheppard Wolf argues that Franklin and Rush were at "the leading edge of a new intellectual and cultural wave." Although free-labor ideals such as those put forth by Franklin and Rush were unusual in the mid-eighteenth century, by the 1790s those ideas assumed "a more frequent and central place in antislavery writing."[10]

As a result in 1790, when William Cooper sought support for maple sugar as an alternative to slave-grown cane sugar, he and his supporters were able to deploy multiple arguments in favor of maple sugar, including an explicitly moral-economic argument that included free labor. Cooper, who founded Cooperstown, New York, and was the father of the writer James Fenimore Cooper, had acquired a patent on a large tract of heavily forested land on New York's Lake Otsego in the late 1780s. He then sold parcels of land to farmers for commercial development.[11] In 1789 Cooper partnered with Philadelphia Quaker and dry goods merchant Henry Drinker, who had purchased 24,000 acres along the Delaware River. Drinker had his agent establish Stockport on the Pennsylvania side of the river and invited Cooper to sell and settle his frontier lands. At the same time, Cooper drew Drinker into his maple sugar enterprise.[12] Drinker also provided Cooper with important links to antislavery Philadelphians, including Rush, who along with Tench Coxe, James Pemberton, John Parrish, and Jeremiah Parker, agreed to organize an association to purchase annually a quantity of maple sugar to encourage its manufacture, thus reducing American dependence on slave-grown West Indian sugar. The group attracted seventy-two subscribers, primarily in Philadelphia. For the Quaker Drinker, maple sugar promised the ideal combination of morals and economics. No longer would his sugar kettles support the "polluted and wicked" sugar industry of the British Indies.[13]

Rather than invest large amounts of capital to start the maple sugar manufacturing operation, Cooper and Drinker relied on farmers motivated by promotional literature. Drinker and Rush each produced pamphlets promoting the benefits of maple sugar. In 1790, Drinker assisted in the publication of a tract titled, *Remarks on the Manufacturing of Maple Sugar: With Directions for Its Further Improvement.*[14] It was subsequently reprinted in New York and London along with reprints in British and American newspapers such as the *New-York Magazine, or Literary Repository.*[15] Rush's *An Account of the Sugar Maple-Tree of the United States, and of the Methods of Obtaining Sugar from It* was published in 1792. Although Rush claimed his *Account* had been written as a letter to Thomas Jefferson, the work was actually created as an address to the American Philosophical Society, which counted Drinker, Rush, and Jefferson among its members. This publication was also reprinted in London.[16] Drinker's and Rush's efforts were further bolstered by the French abolitionist Jacques Brissot de Warville, founder of the French abolitionist society, the Société des Amis des Noirs, who also lauded sugar made from the maple tree. Although not directly involved in the efforts to manufacture maple sugar, Brissot nonetheless praised the morality of maple sugar. Brissot had encountered the commodity during his 1788 trip to the United States. When he published his *New Travels in the United States of America* three years later, he celebrated the moral benefits of maple sugar. "Providence," he observed, had placed on the North American continent a "powerful and infallible means of destroying" the evil of slavery: the sugar maple. According to Brissot, "Since the Quakers have discerned in [maple sugar cultivation] the means of destroying slavery, they have felt the necessity of carrying it to perfection; and success has crowned their endeavors." Brissot also called for the cultivation of great orchards of sugar maples in France in an effort to reduce European dependence on slave-grown sugar.[17]

Advocates of maple sugar emphasized both its economic and its moral benefits. Maple sugar production required little labor while generating great wealth. As one optimistic supporter enthused, "a farmer . . . could raise nothing on his farm with less labor, nothing from which he would derive more emolument, than the sugar maple tree."[18] Supporters often borrowed liberally from the rhetoric of the British boycott of slave-grown sugar to highlight the morality of maple sugar. One writer contrasted the "buxom health and voluntary labor" of American girls in gathering and processing maple sap to the dismal West Indian "scene" of "the famished mother on the parched mountain with her child tied to her back."[19] The editors of the *Daily Advertiser* noted that maple sugar was "obtained by the willing labor of freemen" whereas West Indian sugar "cost four lives" for every hogshead, and was therefore "stained with blood."[20] The editors of the *New Jersey Journal* calculated the human cost of West Indian slave-grown sugar: "One hundred and eighty millions of human beings have been deprived of life, to gratify the palates of those who consume the produce of their labour—that Europeans might be supplied with sugar!" The editors also published reports from "Philadelphia, New-York, and Hudson" that consumers who used slave-produced molasses had been purposely poisoned. "Why should we risk the poison and filth of the West-India negroes in our sugar and molasses," the author asked, "when we can have the pure juice of the maple for nothing?"[21] Supporters also appropriated the free-labor arguments that were gaining traction in the late eighteenth century, which resulted in interesting promotional experiments. For example, activists organized an association to encourage the manufacture of maple sugar, offering premiums of up to seventy-five silver dollars to the top three producers of maple sugar. To qualify, applicants for the premiums had to sign an affidavit that only they or their family and no more than five "persons exclusive of the said family" had manufactured the sugar.[22] As historian David Gellman concludes, the cultivation of maple sugar "demonstrated the benefits of household prerogative, speculative landownership, and nature's well-managed bounty."[23]

Still, these efforts failed to overcome some pragmatic problems, in particular, that maple sugar was an imperfect substitute for cane sugar. Sugar maples, although indigenous to North America, grew only in certain areas and produced limited quantities of sugar. Moreover, maple sugar lacked the versatility of cane sugar; among other problems, it was too moist for some purposes such as most types of candy making, and its distinctive taste meant it could not function as an anonymous sweetener like cane sugar.[24] Although activists continued to laud maple sugar as an ethical alternative to slave-grown sugar well into the nineteenth century, the consumption of maple-sweetened goods never caught on with consumers. Writing in 1884, Anna Davis Hallowell, granddaughter of Quakers James and Lucretia Mott, described maple sugar candies as "an abomination," noting that "free sugar was not always as free from other taints as from that of slavery."[25]

However, the lack of an American boycott of slave-grown sugar in the 1790s cannot be blamed on the shortcomings of the maple sugar enterprise. Instead, we must look to the American political and economic context. Where British Quakers were successful in generating support for antislavery sentiment, American Quakers were thwarted by political compromise. When American reformers reorganized the Pennsylvania Abolition Society in 1787, they consciously timed the group's new founding with the organization of the British Society for Establishing the Abolition of the Slave Trade. Supporters of the PAS and the SEAST hoped the concurrent founding of the two groups would stimulate competition between the two nations to see which would be the first to rid itself of the slave trade. This shift in strategy is evident in the number of non-Quakers associated with both groups. Franklin and Rush helped write the PAS's new constitution, and Franklin served as president of the organization.[26] However, supporters found their efforts derailed by the compromises of the Constitutional Convention. In addition to delaying action against the international slave trade for twenty years, the delegates to the convention agreed to the Three-Fifths Compromise, which counted slaves as three-fifths of a person for purposes of representation. One result of the Three-Fifths Compromise was southern dominance of the presidency over the next seventy years. As historian Edward Baptist concludes, the compromises of the Constitutional Convention assured that "the upper and lower South would get to expand slavery through both the Atlantic trade and the internal trade" while "the Northeast would earn profits by transporting the commodities generated by slavery's growth." The compromises of the convention stalled the antislavery movement and with it the boycott of slave labor. Those compromises also made boycotters' task more difficult because it "helped to imprint an economy founded on the export of slave-made commodities onto a steadily widening swath of the continent."[27]

While the political compromises of 1787 and the subsequent expansion of slavery forestalled the development of a widespread, ecumenical boycott of slave labor in the United States, many American Quakers continued to encourage abstention from slave-labor goods. Increasingly, these arguments incorporated new ideas about the superiority of free labor. By the early nineteenth century, more Americans were beginning to share Franklin's assumptions about free labor even as consumers became more dependent on slave-labor goods. Discussions of the future of Louisiana, for example, suggested that westward development would prove a boon for free labor. Newspaper editor William Duane claimed that in Louisiana "three or four hundred white farmers with their families will produce more sugar than a negro estate with two thousand slaves." According to Alan Magruder, "The free white man who owns the soil he works, will double the quantity [produced by a Negro slave]."[28] As Quakers such as Enoch Lewis, Elihu Embree, and Benjamin Lundy asserted a moral-economic argument in support of abstention from slave-labor goods, they helped create new connections between abstention and free labor that aided the development of the free-produce movement in the 1820s.

Quakers and Free Produce

The promotion of maple sugar and the boycott of slave-grown sugar by Britons signaled an important shift in the abstention movement. In the mid and late eighteenth century, the majority of Quakers, including Woolman and Evans, opposed both the products of slave labor and the growing market economy. Indeed, these Quakers believed slavery and commerce functioned in dynamic relationship, each fueling an expansion of the other. In the 1790s advocates of maple sugar in America and boycotters in Britain introduced into the movement two key ideas. First, supporters on both sides of the Atlantic made clear the connection between domestic purchases and slave-labor goods. Slavery would continue so long as consumers continued to purchase its products. Thus, consumers could use their economic power to promote socially responsible commerce and to bring about the end of slavery. Second, the maple sugar debates, in particular, "helped introduce into public dialogue the notion that certain types of labor harmonized better than others with the standards of a just and economically healthy society," as Gellman notes. "They indicated free labor's superiority to slave labor."[29] Because this shift in the intellectual understanding of abstention was critical to the development of the free-produce movement in the 1820s, it is worth examining more closely the Quaker community influenced by Woolman's example before turning to the impact of free-labor ideas on Quaker abstention.

Quakers who were at the origins of the abstention movement protested "the systemic oppression produced by war, greed, and slavery." Motivated by a vision of a new and universal society premised on the Golden Rule, "to do unto others," these reformers adopted the practice of abstention as part of what historian Ellen Ross describes as "a theologically connected network of commitments." Abstention was one of several practices, or habits, adopted by reformers who were committed "to cultivating a society that recognized the equality of all people."[30] For example, Woolman and Evans eschewed most consumer goods, not just those made by slave labor, because such goods hindered the individual's relationship with God and contributed to the oppression of others. Both men protested the expansion of the market economy. Woolman, in particular, believed the commercialization of agriculture had led to the abuse of animals. "Near large towns there are many beasts slain to supply the market, and from their blood, etc., ariseth that which mixeth in the air," Woolman observed. "This, with the cleaning of the stables and other scents, the air in cities in a calm, wettish time is so opposite to the clear pure country air that I believe even the minds of the people are in some degree hindered from the pure operation of the Holy Spirit."[31] According to Evans, consumers had become too dependent on imported goods, which he believed contributed to creating a warlike economy. "I believe the vast extensive trade that has and now is carried on in this once favored land," he remarked, "has and will prove a curse instead of a blessing." Instead, he claimed time should be spent raising crops to provide food for local consumptions because such goods were healthier for American constitutions. Woolman, Evans, and other Quakers, such as Anthony Benezet, also adopted a vegetarian diet. As Evans's testimony became more nuanced, he assumed an even more austere diet, forgoing salt, for example, because the tax on salt was used to retire revolutionary war debt. Eventually, he consumed only bread and water so that he could live more consistently with his spiritual values.[32]

In adopting such "singularities," Evans recognized that his commitment to live in full accord with his spiritual values was a "a way different from [his] dear brethren."[33] In 1779 New Jersey Quaker David Cooper observed that many Friends had made a "Religion" of "disusing all Spirits, Cider, Wine, &c., all Sweets that came over tea, wearing coloured Clothing, Eating Flesh, wearing, or Eating out of Silver, &c." Cooper made this observation after witnessing Evans's unsuccessful attempt to gain permission from his meeting to visit in ministry Friends in Long Island. When Evans told his meeting that he planned to travel on foot "without Money" as a "Pilgrim in a Strange Land," his meeting refused to grant him a certificate. Though sympathetic with Evans's desire to travel in ministry, Cooper worried that his "singularities," which by that time had included wearing a beard, had not come from "the Life," that is, from God.[34] Still, Evans and Quakers like him persisted believing their example would make visible God's love and encourage others to seek personal transformation.

Among Quakers who sought personal transformation through such singularities, there were those who sought religious and political changes as well as personal change. Like their co-religionists, these Quakers abstained from slave-labor goods as one aspect of a larger program of reform. For example, Delaware Quaker Warner Mifflin abstained from foreign imports, slave-labor goods, and salt. A former slaveholder, Mifflin liberated twenty-one slaves he had received as a gift. In 1785 he prepared a petition to the Delaware state legislature. After receiving approval from the Meeting for Sufferings in Philadelphia, Mifflin gathered more than one hundred signatures on the petition, which he then forwarded to the state legislature in early 1786. The petition was introduced along with a bill calling for the gradual abolition of slavery. The legislature passed instead a milder bill encouraging voluntary emancipation. In 1792 Mifflin submitted an individual petition to Congress asking that action be taken to limit the slave trade and to ameliorate the condition of slaves. Southern legislators objected. Representative William Smith of South Carolina claimed the right of petition did not justify the "mere rant and rhapsody of a meddling fanatic."[35]

While Mifflin sought political change, Long Island Quaker Elias Hicks sought sectarian change. Like his "beloved friend" Evans, Hicks was critical of the growing market economy. As a Quaker minister, Hicks had been actively involved in ending slave trading and slaveholding among Friends. In 1776, under the authority of New York Yearly Meeting, which had three years earlier directed that Friends be disowned if they continued to buy and sell slaves, Hicks and his fellow committee members visited slaveholding Friends. Although the committee found "a great unwillingness in most of [the slave owners] to set their slaves free," the committee did succeed in drawing up papers of manumission for eighty-five slaves owned by the members of Westbury Monthly Meeting. Seven years later Hicks visited families in Westbury and Jericho warning Friends about the dangers of debt, which he believed was the result of Quakers' growing worldliness. For Hicks, as it was for Woolman and Evans, the enslavement of Africans and the expansion of the market economy were symptomatic of a general decline in society caused by selfish desire for wealth.[36]

All members of New York Yearly Meeting had freed their slaves by 1787; yet, they remained dependent on slavery through their consumption of slave-labor goods. To be truly antislavery, to live fully the principles of Quakerism, Hicks believed Friends should also abstain from the products of slave labor. In 1793 Hicks influenced Jericho Preparative Meeting to endorse his opinion that Friends should abstain from slave-labor goods. The Monthly and Quarterly Meetings approved the minute, or record of the decision, from the Preparative Meeting. The following year New York Yearly Meeting approved the minute and amended the ninth query of the discipline to include a statement asking whether members were implicated in slaveholding through the use of slave-labor goods. Queries, which consist of a question or a series of questions, were meant to provide a framework for prayerful reflection rather than a set of outward rules. While the content of queries has varied, the queries consistently reflect Quaker testimony such as simplicity, peace, and community. By adopting the change to the ninth query, New York Yearly Meeting urged Friends to prayerfully consider their use of slave-labor goods. From 1797 through 1810, New York Yearly Meeting discussed abstinence and, at the annual query, several Quarterly Meetings reported that some members regretted using slave-labor products. In 1810 members of New York Yearly Meeting approved a revision of the discipline, omitting the reference to slave-labor goods. The change came as many New York Friends decided that it had become impossible to distinguish between free- and slave-labor goods.[37]

Returning home after the yearly meeting had concluded, Hicks wrote *Observations on the Slavery of Africans and Their Descendants, and on the Use of the Produce of Their Labour*, a vigorous protest against Quakers' continued use of the products of slave labor. Slavery, according to Hicks, was established and continued by tradition and normalized as consistent with justice and social order. In a series of queries, Hicks asserted the traditional Quaker argument that slaves were prize goods and, as a result, the products of their labor were also prize goods and contrary to Quaker discipline. Slaves were captured in a state of war, a war caused by "an avaricious thirst after gain," Hicks argued, for the express purpose of "profit[ing] by the slave's labour." Thus, slave-labor goods were "the highest grade of prize goods, next to his person." Those who claimed to oppose slavery yet continued to use the products of slave labor "strengthen[ed] the hands of the oppressor." While Hicks emphasized abstention from slave-labor goods, he did not limit his critique to those goods. Like Woolman, his argument was both antislavery and anti-commerce. The Meeting for Sufferings approved Hicks's publication, which was widely circulated among American and British Friends after its publication in 1811. It was reprinted in 1814 and 1823.[38]

Although Hicks was arguably the most visible proponent of abstention in the early nineteenth century, his support for the boycott more closely resembled eighteenth-century Quaker abstention than it did nineteenth-century free produce. Hicks, like Woolman and Evans before him, opposed the growing market economy, believing it was fueled in part by the oppression of Indians and Africans, by the export and import of goods such as grain and rum, and by the purchase of slave-labor and luxury goods. As Ross concludes, "For Evans and others such as Hicks, objections to slavery arose out of an overarching concern for 'reformation' that included a critique of a spectrum of human interactions that were 'warlike' and a commitment to cultivating a society that recognized the equality of all people." Although the later movement shared with the earlier movement a concern for social justice, the earlier movement had a distinctly antimarket ethos. In contrast, Quakers such as Elihu Embree, Enoch Lewis, and Benjamin Lundy, who helped propel the abstention movement forward in the 1810s and 1820s, argued for moral commerce out of contempt for slavery and not as part of a broader critique of the market. The market-orientated arguments of Embree, Lewis, and Lundy helped transform the abstention movement of the eighteenth century into the free-produce movement of the 1820s.[39]

The three men—Embree, Lewis, and Lundy—were born in the last quarter of the eighteenth century: Lewis in Pennsylvania in 1776, Embree in

Tennessee in 1782, and Lundy in New Jersey in 1789. Lewis worked as an educator, surveyor, editor, and writer. He taught at Quaker schools in Radnor, Westtown, and New Garden, Pennsylvania, and in Wilmington, Delaware. Embree, who was a distant relative of Woolman, was an iron manufacturer and a former slaveholder before he became an editor. A saddler by trade, Lundy embraced abolitionism at a young age after seeing slave coffles (a line of slaves tied together) on the streets of Wheeling, Virginia. All three men were influenced by Quaker arguments for abstention, by the spread of free-labor ideas, and by the congressional debates preceding the Missouri Compromise of 1820, and all three used the pages of their respective publications to promote antislavery and free produce.[40]

Of the three men, Embree had the shortest career in free produce. In 1819 Embree established the *Manumission Intelligencer*, which was renamed the *Emancipator* a year later. In his paper, Embree combined traditional Quaker arguments against slavery, British abstention rhetoric, and free-labor ideas. Slaves and the products of their labor were prize goods, he asserted. Describing slave traders and consumers as the alpha and the omega of the slave trade, Embree claimed consumers who used slave-labor goods had become cannibals in their quest for luxury. "The feast of the luxurious may be called banquets of human flesh and blood; and the partakers thereof considered as cannibals devouring their own species," according to Embree, adopting the rhetoric of the 1790s. He called on his readers to abstain from slave-labor goods, believing the trade in slaves would cease if demand for slave-labor goods ceased. After Embree's premature death in 1820, Lundy acquired Embree's printing equipment.[41]

Lundy had apprenticed with Charles Osborn, publisher of the *Philanthropist*, before leaving for the Missouri territory in 1818. In Missouri he came into contact with ambitious proslavery men who wanted to expand slavery beyond the South. Lundy's experience in Missouri led him to conclude that journalism could be a potent weapon in the fight against slavery. In the early 1820s Lundy established his own antislavery paper, the *Genius of Universal Emancipation*. Published from the 1820s to the 1830s, sometimes irregularly, the *Genius* was the first white-run abolitionist paper to last for more than a few issues. Although Lundy has been described by some as a gradualist, often in contrast to the immediatism of William Lloyd Garrison, Lundy believed slaves should be freed regardless of the consequences. As he wrote in the pages of the *Genius*, "*Let justice be done*, and the God of nature will do the rest."[42] By mid-1820s, Lundy's support of abstention began to reflect the influence of the emerging ideas about free labor. "How different it is with the man of freedom;—though he may be black, he enjoys the fruit of his labor, and labors with animation, spurred by ambition, incited by the hope of one day enjoying the fruits of his industry," Lundy wrote. "With such incitements to emulation, how can it be otherwise expected, than that the freeman should excel the slave in industry and enterprise, who, without one single ray of hope, is doomed to perpetual bondage."[43]

Lundy's support for colonization of freed slaves originated in the conviction that free labor was more efficient than slave labor and in the desire to hasten the abolition of slavery. In the 1820s and 1830s, he explored colonization opportunities in Haiti and Mexico and Texas. Haiti's proximity to the United States made it an attractive alternative for Lundy, whose Haitian plan would make possible the transport of thousands of free blacks and freed slaves. In the summer of 1824, Lundy held a series of antislavery lectures among Quakers in North Carolina and Virginia. Quakers in Goose Creek, Virginia, were convinced to establish the Loudoun Manumission and Emigration Society, which hoped to abolish slavery as well as "aid and encourage . . . the emigration of our colored population to Hayti." The following year Lundy announced that he had opened an office in Baltimore to transact business for the Haitian Emigration Society, which had organized in Philadelphia in 1824. In 1826 he reported that North Carolina Quakers had agreed to send seven hundred freed slaves to Haiti. Seven northern Virginia antislavery societies met in Loudoun County in 1827 and adopted a Constitution of the Virginia Convention for the Abolition of Slavery. This group also supported the voluntary colonization of free and enslaved blacks to Africa or Haiti. Lundy's Haitian plan ran into considerable opposition, however, including opposition from the supporters of the American Colonization Society (ACS), which had organized in 1816 to support the transport of free blacks to Africa. In 1825 the Haitian government withdrew its financial support of the venture. As support for the Haitian plan began to deteriorate, Lundy sought out alternatives for a colony somewhere in the South, believing the establishment of a free-labor colony of free blacks and freed slaves would place economic pressure on slaveholders to free their slaves. Lundy's plan called for the purchase of slaves from their owners. Those freed slaves would then raise cotton on a cooperative system in which each slave would have returned their purchase price and expenses through their labor after a period of years. Having fulfilled their obligation, they would then settle elsewhere, potentially Haiti or Texas, which was at the time a part of Mexico. This plan would demonstrate the superiority of free labor and would provide a means for the speedy abolition of slavery. Lundy believed slaveholders could be convinced to free their slaves if economic motives were applied. As part of his plan to apply economic pressure on slaveholders, Lundy joined with Michael Lamb to establish a free-labor store in Baltimore in 1826, only the third such store to open. (Charles Collins opened the first free-produce store in New York City in 1817, and Jane Webb the second in Wilmington, Delaware, in 1825.) Opposition to Lundy's free-labor colony and to Haitian emigration continued to build. In 1827 he and Lamb closed their free-labor store. That same year articles about Haiti in the *Genius* peaked, dropping significantly the following year.[44]

In the late 1820s and early 1830s, Lundy turned his attention to Mexico, specifically Texas, as a possible site for a free-labor colony. Lundy had read H.G. Ward's *Mexico in 1827*, which included an account of sugar and cotton production in Mexico. Vera Cruz alone could supply all of Europe with sugar, Ward claimed, while American colonists in Texas had experienced success growing cotton. Coffee, tobacco, and indigo were also successfully grown in Mexico.[45] The fecundity of Mexico coupled with the Mexican government's abolition of slavery in 1829 made the country an ideal location for Lundy's colony. In 1832, Lundy traveled to Texas to explore the possibility of locating a free-labor colony in Mexico. This was the first of several trips Lundy would make to Texas and Mexico. At the beginning of 1836, prospects for Lundy's colony in Texas looked promising. That spring Texans forced Mexican troops to move south of the Rio Grande. As a result of the Texas Revolution, the land for Lundy's colony lay within the boundaries of Texas, not Mexico, effectively dooming the free-labor experiment.[46]

As the eldest of the three men, Lewis had a much longer history of antislavery activism. His antislavery views urged compassion for both the enslaved and the enslaver. "While it is our duty to bear a faithful testimony against African slavery, and against the laws that support it," Lewis wrote in 1850, "we are not to forget that righteous ends are to be attained by means compatible with the spirit and precepts of the gospel." Lewis encouraged an open, frank discussion of slavery by its opponents and supporters. Such well-reasoned arguments rather than impassioned denunciations would bring the two sides together and would in time lead slaveholders to realize the truth of slavery. "Denunciation was not the means by which [slaveholders] were to be persuaded, convinced or conciliated," Lewis believed. "The truth has nothing to fear from the most rigid examination," Lewis wrote. "It is error, not truth that seeks concealment." In addition to discussion, he also urged three other antislavery tactics: compensated emancipation, eradication of proslavery laws, and abstention.[47] Together these tactics would reform the American political and economic system, ending all support of slavery.

Lewis continued to promote a reasoned discussion of slavery even as he was forced to confront its shortcomings. In an incident that resonated long afterward, the Quaker teacher experienced firsthand the limits placed on ab-olitionists by slaveholding laws. While teaching at Westtown in 1803, Lewis learned that one of the black residents of the village had been seized as a fugitive slave. "Now it happened that this man told me, some time before, that he had escaped from slavery," Lewis later recalled. Setting out with an-other neighbor, Lewis located the party of slave catchers and demanded "the most rigorous proof on the part of the claimant." When the slave catcher provided "overpowering" evidence of ownership, Lewis realized he was "re-duced to the alternative of abandoning the poor victim of an unrighteous law, to the mercy of a master who did not seem to be overcharged with humanity, or of trying what could be done by way of purchase." When he "tried the effect of moral reasoning on the subject," Lewis "was answered by derisive laugh." Finally, he negotiated a reduced price for the slave, pay-ing four hundred dollars for the man. Lewis and others raised one hundred dollars. He advanced the fugitive the remaining three hundred dollars at con-siderable sacrifice to himself because he made only five hundred dollars annually as a teacher at the time. Fifty years later, reflecting on the incident, Lewis defended his action as a moral expedient: "The practice has long and extensively prevailed, of contributing to the purchase of slaves in cases of unusual hardship, not as an acknowledgement of any right in the possessor but as the only method which the laws and usages of our country have left within our power."[48]

Lewis supported abstention from slave-labor goods as an economic and a moral tactic. Abstention appealed to the slaveholder's sense of pragmatism: render slavery unprofitable and emancipation would follow.[49] Much of Lew-is's discussion of abstention focused on the ways in which the economics of the movement supported the morals. As editor of the short-lived *African Ob-server*, Lewis lauded the efforts of the "industrious families and religious societies [of the upper counties of Virginia] who have for a length of time depended on voluntary labor." In language reminiscent of Evans and other eighteenth-century Quakers, Lewis compared the slaveholding South and the free-labor North. While New England was characterized by "populous towns" and "prosperous villages," the South was marked by "large tracts of land ruined by bad cultivation" and "the cabins of the slaves, [which] ex-hibit the extreme of wretchedness." Free labor promoted "public enterprise, general intelligence, and virtuous habits." If the products of free labor were brought into competition with the products of slave labor, the products of slavery would be forced from the market.[50]

The use of an economic as well as moral argument by Lewis and Lundy in support of abstention reflects changes in the broader antislavery movement in the late eighteenth and early nineteenth centuries. This change is particularly evident in the actions of the American Convention for Promoting the Abolition of Slavery and Improving the Condition of the African Race, the annual meeting of antislavery delegates which began in 1794. The presence of Quaker delegates at the convention influenced the group's support of abstention, which was articulated in 1796 and again in 1816. However, by the mid-1820s, delegates were linking abstention to ideas about free labor, taking more concrete action to promote their view that free labor was more efficient than slave labor. In 1823, for example, the convention agreed to purchase two hundred copies of Adam Hodgson's *A Letter to M. Jean-Baptiste Say, on the Comparative Expense of Free and Slave Labour* that was being reprinted by the New York Manumission Society that year. Two years later, convention delegates offered a premium to the inhabitant of the United States who could give "an accurate statement of the nett profits arising from the employment of his slaves, and the nett profits arising from the same number and description of persons when manumitted, or employed as freemen in his service, and in the same species of labour."[51] This emphasis on the superiority of free labor was driven by new intellectual understandings about labor. It was also influenced by the growth of black activism.

Black Founders and Abstention

As Quakers and non-Quakers asserted the moral and economic superiority of free labor in the late eighteenth and early nineteenth century, black activists asserted their right to life, liberty, and the pursuit of happiness, arguing that the theft of their labor had denied them of these fundamental rights. In the 1770s and 1780s, in a series of freedom petitions, African Americans described the losses they had incurred as the result of whites' theft of their labor. A Petition of Many Slaves, submitted to the Massachusetts legislature in January 1773, emphasized this loss, stating that "neither they, nor their Children to all Generations, shall ever be able to do, or to possess and enjoy any Thing, no not even *Life itself*, but in a Manner as the *Beasts that perish.* We have no Property! We have no Wives! No Children! We have no City! No Country!" A Connecticut petition made a similar argument, describing how enslaved African fathers and mothers "not only groan under our own burdens, but with concern & Horror, look forward & contemplate, the miserable Condition of our Children, who are training up, and kept in Preparation for a like State of Bondage, and Servitude." A petition by four slaves from Boston compared English and Spanish treatment of slaves. While "the

Spaniards . . . have not those sublime ideas of freedom that English men have," they were still "conscious that they have no right to all the services of their fellow-men. . . . [thus] the *Africans*, whom they have purchased with their money [were] allow[ed] one day in a week to work for themselves, to enable them to earn money to purchase the residue of their time." Slaves of the English were granted no such opportunity to purchase their freedom. The Boston petition emphasized the value of Africans' stolen labor, claiming it "would be highly detrimental to our present masters, if we were allowed to demand all that of *right* belongs to us for past services." Despite its deferential tone, the petition asserted both the value of African American labor and the right of blacks to receive that value. Even after emancipation, blacks suffered from the theft of the labor. In protest against taxation, a group of free blacks from Massachusetts claimed their earlier service as slaves had denied them the opportunity to accumulate property, and if forced to pay taxes they would be reduced to a state of "beggary": "by reason of long bondage and hard slavery we have been deprived of enjoying the profits of our labour . . . and . . . we have been & now are taxed both in our polls and that small pittance of estate which through much hard labour and industry we have got together to sustain ourselves & families withal."[52] These early statements from enslaved and free blacks emphasized Quakers' arguments that white slaveholders had robbed African Americans of their labor.

The late eighteenth century witnessed the rise of black institutions and black print production. The slave population doubled, increasing from about five hundred thousand to nearly one million. Emancipation in the North gave way to segregation. While many whites remained silent, black activists did not. African Americans organized independent churches, Masonic lodges, insurance organizations, and mutual aid societies. Focused on community building and racial uplift, these groups provided important support for the free black communities that were developing and expanding in this period. Black print production supported the efforts of these African American institutions. Creating a distinct tradition of publication—a "counterpublic," as scholar Joanna Brooks argues—black authors' texts were "informed by black experiences of slavery and post-slavery, premised on principles of self-determination and structured by black criticism of white political and economic dominance." These early black texts expressed for the first time a corporate consciousness.[53] Men like Richard Allen and Prince Hall provided vital leadership for the developing black communities in Boston, Philadelphia, New York, and Baltimore. These so-called Black Founders shaped civil rights activism well into the nineteenth century.[54]

Black activists organized numerous independent black institutions to provide valuable support to free blacks and freed slaves. The exponential growth in slavery in the South took place at the same time as the North and the Midwest experienced substantial growth and maturation of free black communities. While the slave population doubled, the free black population quadrupled.[55] In Boston, in 1775, Prince Hall, a freed slave, started the first black Masonic lodge in the world. Two years later Hall and seven other African Americans petitioned the Massachusetts state legislature for the abolition of slavery. Hall was a leader in the Boston black community in the 1780s and 1790s. The African Masonic lodge stood at the center of this community, serving as a place of education, political organization, and equality. In Philadelphia, newly freed slaves Richard Allen and Absalom Jones organized the Free African Society in 1787, the same year that white activists established the Society for Establishing the Abolition of the Slave Trade and the newly reorganized Pennsylvania Abolition Society. Modeled on white benevolent societies, the FAS organized "without regard to religious tenets . . . to support one another in sickness, and for the benefit of their widows and fatherless children."[56] Allen established the African Methodist Episcopal Church (AME) in the 1790s. The AME Church grew from several dozen congregants in the 1790s to nearly fifteen hundred in the 1820s. In the 1820s Allen supported Haitian emigration, and in the 1830s joined the free-produce movement.[57] The FAS, the AME Church, and the African Masonic lodges were among the dozens of the institutions organized as part of the growing free black community.

The Black Founders of the late eighteenth and early nineteenth century were critical to the development of black opposition to colonization in the 1810s. In 1816, white activists organized the American Colonization Society to promote the establishment of an American colony in Africa for freed slaves and free blacks. Procolonizationists linked the potential for slave revolt to the presence of a large free black population, claiming slaveholders would be encouraged to free their slaves if those freed slaves were sent to Africa. Emigration would reduce the population of free blacks in the United States, especially in the South. Moreover, colonizationists claimed emigration to Africa would resolve racial problems and provide racial uplift. African Americans, colonizationists argued, could never attain equality in a white society. Initially, some black abolitionists supported the ACS; however, many abolitionists regardless of race came to believe the ACS was antiblack rather than antislavery.[58] African Americans used the language of Quaker abstention and the slave-sugar boycott to protest colonization. In 1817, at a gathering at Allen's church in Philadelphia, black activists asserted their right to citizenship:

"Whereas our ancestors (not of choice) were the first successful cultivators of the wilds of America, we their descendants feel ourselves entitled to participate in the blessings of her luxuriant soil, which their blood and sweat manured; and that any measure or system of measures, having a tendency to banish us from her bosom, would not only be cruel, but in direct violation of those principles, which have been the boast of this republic." William Lloyd Garrison later reprinted the text in his *Thoughts on African Colonization*, published in 1831, repudiating the colonization movement and embracing the immediate abolition of slavery.[59]

In the late eighteenth and early nineteenth centuries, black activism focused on building and sustaining an independent black community. Although African Americans did not explicitly articulate support for abstention, as the Quakers did, they used language reminiscent of the boycott of slave labor to describe their oppression. In 1811, speaking on the anniversary of the abolition of the slave trade, Adam Carman attacked the economic basis of slavery, the slave trade, and the system of European commerce. The slave trade had reduced African Americans to "commercial commodities." Blacks had become "interwoven into the system of commerce, and the revenue of nations," Carman remarked, thus "the merchant, the planter, the mortgagee, the manufacturer, the politician, the legislators, and the cabinet minister" were all implicated in the trade in African slaves. Rendered a "vendible article," blacks were sold to the "highest bidder."[60] Black activism transformed Quaker abstention rhetoric, informing traditional sectarian ideas about the theft of black labor with the lived black experience of slavery and postslavery.

The Quaker Schism and Abstention

Of the cultural forces that influenced Quakers' understanding of abstention from slave-labor goods—the ongoing debate about the relationship between slavery and religious beliefs, the advent of new ideas about labor, the rise of black activism, and the expansion of evangelical Christianity—none was so influential as the growth of evangelicalism in the late eighteenth and early nineteenth centuries. Evangelicalism affected Quakers' understanding of abstention; more importantly, evangelicalism shaped Quakers' participation in the boycott of slave labor as they found their support for abstention tested by the strong current of revivalism that had begun to infiltrate the quietism of British and American Friends. Quietism emphasized a personal, mystical knowledge of God through the experience of the inward light or the still, small voice of God within each individual. The experience of the inward light could be contaminated by "any involvement of the human will, reason, emotions, and intellect."[61] Thus, intermediaries such as priests, sacraments, and offerings were unnecessary and interfered with the experience of the inward light. Evangelicalism, in contrast, emphasized external rules and behaviors such as Bible reading, settled ministry, temperance, and restraint as a means to instill moral discipline. Rather than relying on individual interpretation of correct faith, such outward rules placed authority to weigh scriptural truth in the hands of a select few individuals.[62] Quietist Quakers emphasized gradual, individual growth into salvation whereas evangelicals emphasized conversion, the "profoundly emotional" experience of rebirth that established a relationship between the individual and God.[63]

In the early nineteenth century, in response to the spread of evangelicalism, some Quakers sought to create more uniformity among Friends. In the 1810s, American yearly meetings, including Philadelphia, Baltimore, and New York, considered plans to create a uniform discipline, uniting all of the yearly meetings into some central organization. Ohio Yearly Meeting considered a similar proposal in 1821.[64] Although these efforts failed, other efforts for evangelical orthodoxy did succeed. In 1806, both Philadelphia and Baltimore Yearly Meetings wrote into their discipline that any person who denied "the divinity of our Lord and Saviour Jesus Christ, the immediate revelation of the Holy Spirit, or authenticity of the Scriptures" should be disowned.[65] The revisions to the discipline of the Philadelphia and Baltimore Yearly Meetings marked the first time Quakers had set a doctrinal standard. While Friends had never denied these beliefs, they had never found it necessary for Quakers to affirm them.[66] In 1810, New York Yearly Meeting also modified its discipline in ways that reflected the growing influence of evangelicalism. In 1783, when Hicks had been a member of the committee that drafted the New York discipline, the only mention of the Scriptures was found in the Query, "Are Friends careful . . . in the practice of frequent reading of the holy Scriptures?"[67] By 1810, however, Friends, "especially parents and heads of families," were advised to impress on the minds of the young, a "due regard and esteem for those excellent writings, the Scriptures of the Old and New Testaments." Friends were advised to "frequently . . . read and meditate therein." Such "pious care" to "youthful minds" would lead them "into a firm belief of the christian religion . . . Particularly in those parts which related to the miraculous birth, holy life, blessed example, doctrine and precepts, of our Lord and Saviour Jesus Christ."[68]

Hicks and other like-minded Quakers opposed these evangelical tendencies. While Hicks acknowledged the importance of the Scriptures among

Christians, he continued to assert his belief in the inward light, claiming the scriptures must be interpreted by the Spirit and not by human effort.[69] Hicks worried that the reform activities of evangelicals were not guided by the Holy Spirit, believing that such activities had originated in "man-made ministry."[70] In the 1810s and 1820s, the conflict deepened between Hicks and his supporters, on the one side, and evangelical Quakers on the other. Increasingly, evangelical Quakers questioned Hicks's theological views, fearing Hicks's attempts to lessen the authority of the Bible. French émigré Stephen Grellet, for example, claimed Hicks had attempted "to lessen the authority of the Holy Scriptures, to undervalue the sacred offices of our holy and blessed Redeemer, and to promote a disregard for the right observance of the first day of the week."[71] In 1818, Phebe Willis, an evangelical elder from Jericho (New York) Monthly Meeting, asked Hicks to clarify his views on the Bible. In a hastily composed letter, Hicks claimed the Scriptures, as interpreted, "have been the cause of four-fold more harm than good to Christendom." Hicks believed "the light and spirit of truth in the hearts and consciences of men and women, [was] the only sure rule of faith and practice, both in relation to religious and moral things." He urged Friends to remain "close to the leading and inspiration of the spirit of truth" and to allow nothing "whether books or men, to turn them aside from their ever-present and ever-blessed guide." Hicks's letter was published without his consent and was, as one historian notes, "like a bombshell" among Quakers, going "to the very heart of the conflict developing among Friends" in the early nineteenth century.[72]

Historians, as well as Friends at the time, disagree on what caused the schism among American Quakers in the 1820s. In the United States, the revivalism of the Second Great Awakening coincided with religious disestablishment, creating the sense that the country was in the midst of what historian Robert Abzug describes as a "spiritual free-for-all." As a result of disestablishment, Americans were free to select their church, or to create a new church, or to forgo church altogether. Dissenting religious groups, such as the Baptists and Methodists, competed with previously state-supported religions for potential converts. Revivalism encouraged the growth of voluntary associations, often staffed by paid agents. Voluntary associations, such as Bible and Sunday School associations, were seen as the means by which the world would be made a better place. The expansion of religious benevolence led Quakers to make more explicit their definition of appropriate religious activism. There were many Quakers who, in opposition to Hicks, welcomed the opportunity to join with other evangelicals in various forms of benevolent activity, including abstention and antislavery societies. Often, though not exclusively, these evangelical Quakers were also more likely to have benefited from the spectacular growth in the nation's economy, becoming successful businessmen and merchants, including Philadelphia elder, Jonathan Evans, who was one of the more vocal critics of Hicks.[73]

The conflict between Evans and Hicks came to symbolize both the Hicksite schism and the role of free produce in the separation. Writing in 1801 to his wife, Evans claimed he no longer felt the need to abstain as it had become too difficult to distinguish between free- and slave-labor goods.[74] Described by one contemporary as "sound as a bell, and firm as a rock," Jonathan Evans was a formidable opponent. Evans's family roots dated to the early days of Pennsylvania. A lumberman, Evans had also speculated in landownership in Delaware County, just outside Philadelphia, amassing a substantial fortune. In 1817, when he retired from the lumber business, Evans had accumulated a fortune worth nearly $43,000. (In 2015 dollars, Evans's net worth would be near three-quarters of a million dollars.) During the American Revolution, he had been jailed for refusing to serve in the militia. At the center of Orthodox power in Philadelphia, Evans held appointments in his monthly meeting as well as the powerful and influential Meeting for Sufferings of Philadelphia Yearly Meeting.[75] The complete "breech of unity" between Evans and Hicks occurred in 1819 at Pine Street Meetinghouse in Philadelphia.[76] Hicks arrived in Philadelphia in late October to attend several meetings. On October 27, Hicks visited Pine Street meeting where he preached against the products of slave labor and noted that some Friends who had previously abstained from these products had taken a "retrograde course," as his testimony was later described, making a rather pointed reference to the lapsed abstinence practice of Evans.[77] After Hicks finished his testimony, he asked permission of the meeting to attend the women's business meeting at the other end of the building. All of the members except Evans agreed to Hicks's request. After Hicks's departure, Evans called for an adjournment of the meeting, suggesting members could finish their business at a later time. Though some members opposed the move, Evans was successful in adjourning the meeting. When Hicks returned to the men's meeting, he was surprised to find the meeting dismissed. Picking up his coat, Hicks observed that it was kind of the men to leave his coat for him. At the time, Hicks was traveling with certificates from his monthly and quarterly meetings. The incident, for Hicks's followers, demonstrated the hostility Evans and his supporters had toward Hicks. For many Quakers, Evans's behavior was "a mark of great disrespect and public hostility to that dignified minister of the Gospel."

The incident at Pine Street became "almost legendary among Hicks's followers," as historian H. Larry Ingle argues.[78] Evans attempted to make amends, visiting Hicks at the home of Samuel Fisher where he was staying. Evans objected to Hicks's appeal to the youth to disregard their elders' authority, and Hicks reminded Evans that the elders had objected to John Woolman's testimony. Evans responded that Woolman "bore his testimony in simplicity, but never called his friends thieves and murderers" as Hicks had described those who used the products of slave labor. The two men then began to discuss whether Hicks had misquoted the Bible when Hicks called for an end to the conversation until Evans had apologized. Evans refused.[79] Evans's biographer denied that the "rift" between Evans and Hicks had any connection to Hicks's free-produce testimony. The breech between the two Quakers, William Bacon Evans remarked, "occurred at least on the part of Jonathan Evans because of a difference in doctrine."[80]

Between 1819 and 1827, tensions increased between supporters and opponents of Hicks. The causes of those tensions were complex. The economic success of Orthodox Friends, such as Evans, contributed to the growing divide between Hicks's opponents and supporters. Likewise, questions of authority and power, particularly as it was wielded by Quaker elders and members of the Meeting for Sufferings, became entwined with theological debates, as well as personalities, heightening tensions among American Quakers. Hicks's support for free produce exacerbated these debates among Quakers. Philadelphia elders like Evans were correct in their belief that Hicks's sermons on free produce attacked their religious and business practices. Hicks emphasized the ascetic character of abstention and challenged Quakers' continued dependence on slavery through the consumption of slave-labor goods. Renunciation of slave-labor products was a visible sign that an individual upheld the traditional Quaker testimony on plainness and simplicity and had rejected the temptations of the emerging market economy, an economy based in large part on slave labor. As American abolitionist author Lydia Maria Child later claimed, Hicks's "zeal on the subject" of abstention caused in some Quakers, like Evans, "a disposition to find fault with him."[81] Still, it is important to emphasize that in April 1827, when supporters of Hicks walked out of the yearly meeting and set up a reformed yearly meeting, supporters of abstention were aligned on either side of the schism.

Hicks's opponents cited his testimony against slave-labor products as evidence of the unsoundness of his theological views. Elisha Bates, a member of Ohio Yearly Meeting and an opponent of Hicks, denied in 1819 that the use of slave produce was sinful. Bates outlined four reasons why the boycott of slave-labor was misguided. First, the boycott was an act of coercion rather than persuasion. Describing the boycott as "*a non intercourse act*," Bates argued that it applied a physical rather than a moral solution "to the evil."

Second, God provided for the good and the evil. "The bounties of Providence," he claimed, were "to be received with meekness, and with gratitude to the Divine Giver." Third, slaveholders should be the object of Christian charity. According to Bates, "we are taught to *believe* that there is still in [the slaveholder's] heart a principle of good, and we are prompted to *hope* that *this* may be reached and raised by the language of Gospel Love." Finally, Bates claimed, it was impossible to avoid the taint of slave labor: "The blood and the tears of the victims of cruelty may be showered on the soil from which my bread is drawn . . . the sighs of anguish, may mix with the air that I breathe."[82] Bates questioned Hicks's soundness and reasoning. Hicks "tells [Friends] that he never dares lay his head down to rest till he has consulted respecting the actions of the day, and feels *approved of God*," Bates claimed. "But how a *fallible* being is to be always able to feel the divine approbation at stated times, is not easy to be conceived."[83] For Bates and other like-minded Orthodox Quakers, Hicks's free-produce testimony provided more evidence of the minister's unsound theology.

Those Orthodox Quakers who supported free produce took refuge in the testimony of eighteenth-century Quaker ministers, most notably John Woolman. Philadelphia Quaker George W. Taylor, for example, focused his criticism of Hicks on theological questions rather than Hicks's support for free produce. Taylor "became in boyhood thoroughly antislavery." Reading Woolman's *Journal* convinced Taylor "that if slavery was wrong, it was wrong to assist in the wrong by giving the motive to perpetuate the wrong." Taylor described abstention as a practical antislavery activity and "not merely [a] speculative notion" such as colonization.[84] For Taylor, the decision to join with the Orthodox Quakers against Hicks was distinct from his decision to support free produce.

Among Hicksites, support for abstention and free produce was not as universal as might be expected given Hicks's support for abstention and free produce. For example, Hicksite John Comly no longer practiced abstinence, citing reasons that were similar to those given by Orthodox Quaker Jonathan Evans. In his *Journal*, Comly described his early participation in the boycott as a means of spiritual discipline rather than a political statement against the slave trade. During the eighteenth-century boycott of slave-grown sugar, Comly had been influenced by Thomas Clarkson (and perhaps William Fox) to abstain from the use of West Indian produce. Motivated by a desire to remain "clear of innocent blood" and to avoid "upholding the cruelties of the African slave trade," Comly maintained his testimony "against the injustice, cruelty, and oppression" of the trade for "a considerable number of years" until the slave trade was abolished in the United States and Britain.

Comly realized that "the habit of not using sugar" had become well established, yet the ground on which his testimony stood had been removed with
the abolition of the international slave trade. "I had nothing left to support
it," he observed, "unless slavery itself should seem to require it." Comly concluded that the way had appeared for him to resume "the moderate and
temperate use of 'whatever is sold in the shambles, (or stores) asking no questions for conscience' sake.'" In examining his years of abstinence, Comly
questioned the purpose of his boycott of West Indian produce. He believed
his individual abstinence had had no effect on the eventual abolition of the
slave trade. Comly concluded that the benefit of abstinence had been in the
disciplining of his own mind: "Even though no good had been done to any
other, to my own mind it had been of incalculable benefit. It had been a
school of discipline to me—a discipline that led to obedience to the light of
truth on many subjects to which my attention had been directed, and to
which it might yet be called."[85] For Comly, as it was for many Quakers on
either side of the schism, abstention from slave-labor goods was an individual decision, a matter of spiritual discipline, rather than a political statement
against slavery.

In the early nineteenth century, as Quakers weighed theological questions such as the authority of the Scriptures, abstention and free produce
became for many a powerful means with which to discredit the opposition.
That supporters and opponents of free produce could be found on either
side of the Hicksite schism suggests the protean meanings of abstention for
Quakers. For some, including Hicks, abstention from slave-labor goods was
an essential aspect of Christian identity whereas others, including Comly and
Evans, believed abstention had little relevance in spiritual matters. The spread
of evangelicalism deepened the theological fracture lines that had first appeared among Friends in the late eighteenth century. Abstention became entwined in these debates, emphasizing, in particular, Friends' varied responses
to the religious, economic, and social changes of the period.

Despite Quaker discussions of abstention, the boycott of slave-labor goods
waned significantly in the early nineteenth century in the United States and
Britain. After the abolition of the international slave trade by Britain (1807)
and the United States (1808), attention shifted to enforcing the ban on the
slave trade. The abolition of slavery remained the goal; yet, it hovered in
the distance, coming no closer to fruition than before the abolition of the
slave trade. Absent an active antislavery movement, there was little need or
interest in continuing to promote the boycott of slave labor. What support
remained was found primarily among the Quakers, who were preoccupied
with other religious matters, and among other individuals, who like the

Quakers emphasized the moral commitment of avoiding the tainted products of slave labor. That changed by the early 1820s. Several key events contributed to a renewal of interest in abolitionism and abstention. These events included the continued fight to enforce the ban on the international slave trade, the organization of the American Colonization Society in 1816, and the debates surrounding the admission of Missouri in 1820. Massive slave rebellions in Barbados (1816) and Demerara (1823) and the exposure of plots in Charleston, South Carolina (1822), and Jamaica (1823) also emphasized the danger in allowing slavery to continue.[86] The 1820s witnessed the revival of antislavery agitation in Britain and the United States. That agitation breathed new life into the abstention movement, particularly through the efforts of two Quaker women, one British and one American.

These two women are the focus of the next two chapters. The first woman, Elizabeth Heyrick of Leicester, England, had witnessed the slave-sugar boycott of the 1790s. Connected to two dissenting religious groups—the Unitarians and the Quakers—Heyrick had been active in social reform and radical politics since the early 1800s. In 1824 she turned her attention to the abolition of slavery, claiming the boycott of slave-labor goods was the safest and most effectual means of bringing about emancipation. The second woman, Elizabeth Margaret Chandler, had been raised in the Quaker community of Philadelphia, Pennsylvania. Nearly forty years younger than Heyrick, Chandler began writing as a teenager, composing romantic verses about nature. In 1825, her poem, "The Slave Ship," brought her to the attention of Quaker editor Lundy. She shared Heyrick's emphasis on the morality of the boycott of slave labor. Chandler believed that women who boycotted slave-labor goods could influence political change through the power of their virtuous example. After Chandler was hired by Lundy in 1829 to edit a woman's column in his abolitionist paper, she reprinted and often commented on the work of Heyrick. Together these two women reinvigorated interest in the boycott of slave labor in the 1820s and early 1830s. Yet, both women worked within very different social and political contexts that shaped their understanding of activism. Comparing Heyrick and Chandler highlights the differences between the British and the American social and political milieu. Such a comparison reveals the ways in which religion, gender, and race influenced the transformation of abstention and the subsequent development of the free-produce movement.

CHAPTER 4

I Am a Man, Your Brother: Elizabeth Heyrick, Abstention, and Immediatism

The abolition of the slave trade by Britain in 1807 and the United States in 1808 did not lead to the abolition of slavery as many had hoped. By 1823 opponents of slavery in Britain realized that merely enforcing the ban on the international slave trade was not enough. In January of that year, British abolitionists organized the London Anti-Slavery Society with the goal of gradual emancipation. Following the establishment of the Anti-Slavery Society, an aging Thomas Clarkson once again toured Great Britain to generate support for the cause. More than two hundred auxiliaries were established and nearly eight hundred petitions were sent to Parliament by the time the Anti-Slavery Society held its first meeting in 1824. Politicians also renewed their antislavery efforts. In May 1823, Thomas Fowell Buxton, who replaced William Wilberforce as the antislavery leader in Parliament, introduced a resolution calling for the immediate emancipation of the children of slaves and the implementation of a series of ameliorative measures for those who remained enslaved. Foreign Secretary George Canning offered an alternative resolution that emphasized the need to prepare West Indian slaves for emancipation and the importance of maintaining property rights and civil order in the colonies. Canning's resolutions called for religious instruction for slaves, prohibited work on Sundays, and abolished the flogging of female slaves. Canning opposed as unfeasible Buxton's resolution to free on birth the children of slaves. In an attempt to shape parliamentary action, the West Indian interest introduced their own measures to ameliorate the conditions of slavery. After much debate, several resolutions were passed. These resolutions, which were statements of good intentions rather than enactments with the force of law, were forwarded to the colonies in July 1823.[1] When news reached the West Indies that Parliament had passed measures improving the treatment of slaves, planters reacted with their usual resentment of interference in the affairs of the colonies. Slaves overheard planters' discussion of these measures, and soon the rumor spread that the King of England had freed the slaves. When no information was forthcoming from the planters, the slaves assumed their masters were withholding their freedom. On August 18, 1823, nearly twelve thousand slaves in the British colony of Demerara rose in rebellion.[2]

The uprising in Demerara framed popular and parliamentary debates about the future of slavery and led British Quaker convert Elizabeth Heyrick to write her first antislavery tract, *Immediate, Not Gradual Abolition*. This tract signaled an important shift in the abstention movement as Heyrick linked the boycott of slave labor to the immediate abolition of slavery and the granting of civil rights to freed slaves. Significantly, Heyrick emphasized economic strategy, "formulat[ing] an immediatism that went beyond the conversion of the heart to demand that feelings be put into the service of practical market manipulation," as historian Carol Lasser argues. Heyrick described consumption as a social act with consequences that resonated throughout the Atlantic world. Consumers who boycotted slave-labor goods would influence friends and neighbors; ultimately, the example would, as Heyrick wrote, "spread from house to house . . . city to city,—till, *among those who have any claim to humanity*, there will be but one heart, and one mind,— one resolution, one uniform practice."[3] This dramatic shift in emphasis was reinforced visually: the cover of the first British edition of Heyrick's tract featured an illustration of a muscular African slave with a broken chain and a discarded whip at his feet. Framed by the words, "I am a man, your brother," the man faced forward looking directly at the reader. The illustration reminded readers of the earlier campaign against the slave trade while clearly subverting Josiah Wedgwood's iconic profile of the kneeling chained slave that had symbolized that earlier movement.[4]

The revival of boycott activity in Britain reveals once again the importance of political context in garnering support for consumer activism. Heyrick's efforts helped spark another popular boycott of slave-labor goods in Britain. Estimates suggest that this second boycott was even more popular than the first.[5] Taking a cue from the earlier movement, activists such as Heyrick linked the boycott to a broad agenda of social reform, including the

1093

IMMEDIATE,

NOT GRADUAL

ABOLITION;

OR,

AN INQUIRY

INTO THE SHORTEST, SAFEST, AND MOST EFFECTUAL MEANS OF

GETTING RID OF

West=Indian Slavery.

I AM A MAN, YOUR BROTHER.

" He hath made of one blood all nations of men."—*Acts* xvii. 26.

A NEW EDITION.

LONDON:

Printed by R. Clay, Devonshire-street, Bishopsgate.

SOLD BY

F. WESTLEY, 10, STATIONERS' COURT; & S. BURTON, 156, LEADENHALL
STREET;

AND BY ALL BOOKSELLERS AND NEWSMEN.

[*Price Twopence, or* 1s. 6d. *per dozen.*]

FIGURE 4. Cover of *Immediate, Not Gradual Abolition,* written by Elizabeth Heyrick. Courtesy of Friends Historical Library, Swarthmore College, Swarthmore, Pennsylvania.

abolition of slavery, the implementation of reforms for the working class, and the expansion of women's organizational activity. Heyrick reinvigorated and radicalized the movement, contributing to the polarization of antislavery sentiment in Britain. In doing so, she helped the boycott gain attention from a broad cross-section of Britons. Ultimately, the boycott helped create a cultural climate that supported political efforts to abolish slavery in the empire, culminating in the 1833 passage of the Emancipation Act.

Abstention, Working-Class Radicalism, and Slave Rebellion

Heyrick's family background influenced her antislavery activism. She was born in 1769 to John and Elizabeth Coltman in Leicester in the English Midlands. Elizabeth's family belonged to the Presbyterian (later Unitarian) Great Meeting in East Bond Street, which was the center of Leicester's Protestant dissenting community. Her father was a successful worsted hosiery manufacturer, a radical political reformer, and a supporter of the campaign to end the slave trade. Likely, her family participated in the first slave-sugar boycott, which received widespread support in Leicester, where the residents were "nearly unanimous in rejecting the use of sugar and rum." In 1789 Elizabeth married the Anglican John Heyrick. Despite their tempestuous marriage, she was grief-stricken when John died suddenly in 1797. Forced to sell off her furniture to pay her husband's debts, Elizabeth opened a boarding school to support herself.[6] It was around this same time that she joined the Society of Friends and began to write, anonymously authoring more than twenty radical and reformist pamphlets that "oppos[ed] war, animal cruelty, poor prison conditions, corporal and capital punishment, low wages, and the oppression of the poor." In addition to writing about social issues, she took action. She stopped a bull-baiting contest by buying the bull and hiding it until the angry crowd dispersed. Heyrick also lived for a time in a shepherd's cottage to better understand the life of Irish migrant workers, visited prisons and paid fines to gain prisoners' release, called for laws limiting the workday, and supported workers' strikes.[7] While these early experiences were crucial to the development of Heyrick's antislavery activism, gender was equally important. As a young woman, Heyrick was introduced to a complex mix of female role models. Her mother emphasized women's domestic role and conformed to restrictive ideas of femininity. In contrast, other women in Heyrick's circle of family and friends challenged, implicitly or explicitly, the restrictions placed on women. These women included the poet Anna Laetitita Barbauld, who published works on controversial topics such as slavery, and Priscilla Hannah Gurney, who was a Quaker minister and cousin of the prison reformer Elizabeth Gurney Fry. Although Heyrick did not argue explicitly for women's rights, she did believe in women's spiritual equality and intellectual worth.[8]

These influences—religious dissent, political radicalism, and gender—framed Heyrick's activism, which intensified in the 1810s when she became involved in the fight for the economic rights of the poor. The end of the wars with France triggered an economic crisis in Britain that severely impacted the working class. Between 1815 and 1819, wages for framework knitters dropped steadily, reaching a low of four shillings a week for sixteen to eighteen hours of daily labor. Knitters and leading working-class radicals were unsuccessful in their attempts to set a minimum wage. Radical agitation increased as critics denounced Parliament for maintaining the price of corn but not the price of labor.[9] In 1819, at St. Peter's Field in Manchester, eleven people were killed and more than four hundred wounded when the militia and the cavalry broke up a gathering of more than sixty thousand men, women, and children who were demanding parliamentary reform, particularly universal male suffrage. The notorious Peterloo Massacre has been described as "one of the defining events of its age."[10] It was within this environment of working-class reform that Heyrick demanded the rights of the poor. In two pamphlets, published in 1817 and 1819, Heyrick rejected the philanthropic approach to poverty within which middle-class women engaged with the poor. She claimed that more was required than simply "humanity and benevolence." Instead, she insisted that justice had been denied. "We may discover," she wrote, "that, so far from having obeyed the requisitions of *charity*, we have not yet discharged the demands of *justice*." Heyrick used analogies with slavery to describe the plight of the working class. The declining value of human labor, as evidenced by the poor and the enslaved, reflected larger political problems in the British Empire. Comparing the two, Heyrick claimed both lived and worked in a "state of wretchedness and despair" because the "*spirit* of the slave-trade"—"the lust of wealth"—continued to frame the relationship between laborer and employer.[11] "The Rights of Man—The Rights of Woman—The Rights of Brutes—have been boldly advanced; but the *Rights of the Poor* still remain unadvocated," she observed.[12]

The comparison of the poor laborer and the enslaved African was an established trope in antislavery rhetoric. In the late eighteenth century, child chimney sweeps and coal miners were singled out for comparison with slaves to divert attention away from the slave trade and West Indian slavery and to instead focus public attention on the laboring poor.[13] In the early nineteenth century, such rhetoric increased as working-class activists and abolitionists sought parliamentary reforms. Working-class radical William Cobbett invoked the image of a happy group of "fat and lazy and laughing and singing and dancing negroes" in the West Indies. The "wage slaves" of England, he claimed, would be happy to lick the bowls of such well-fed slaves. Likewise the spinners of Stockport claimed to endure "all the horrors of a sullen and hapless slavery."[14] Abolitionists, on the other hand, worried that planters might use working-class conditions to deflect attention away from slavery; thus, some abolitionists privileged the British laborer. In an 1824 article in the *Christian Observer*, Clarkson reviewed the comparisons made between the enslaved and the laborer. To support his argument, he used examples culled from the colonial publication the *Jamaica Royal Gazette*. The poor would be so shocked by the slaves' sufferings, Clarkson concluded, *"they would absolutely lose sight of their own."*[15]

What set Heyrick's argument apart from comparisons like those put forth by Cobbett and Clarkson was her claim that because the two problems were so deeply intertwined, they had to be resolved simultaneously. The laborer was only nominally free, she argued; thus, to suggest, as some abolitionists did, that working-class reform should wait until slavery had been abolished was misguided. Yet to argue that the abolition of slavery should wait until working-class reform had been enacted was also wrong. The oppression of the working class and the oppression of the slave came from the same source, greed. The condition of the working class and the oppression of the slave were both *"directly contrary to the Divine will."*[16] She challenged waged labor as little better than slavery for British laborers who received a starvation wage. Heyrick believed consumers must apply economic pressure to bring about change and to free both the enslaved and the laborer.[17]

The working-class radicalism of the early nineteenth century coincided with massive slave rebellions in the British colonies of Barbados (1816) and Demerara (1823); both of these events influenced British antislavery in general and Heyrick's activism in particular. In Barbados, on Easter Sunday 1816, slaves on seventy plantations revolted after hearing rumors that "Mr. Wilberforce" had freed the slaves. More than two hundred slaves were killed or executed. In Demerara, the conditions of revolt were similar. On August 18, 1823, an estimated nine to twelve thousand slaves from at least sixty plantations in the East Coast region rebelled after hearing rumors that the King of England had freed the slaves. During the three-day uprising, only two or three whites were killed while colonial troops killed or wounded more than 255 slaves. After white West Indians regained control, mock trials and summary executions on various plantations claimed the lives of more than twenty slaves. The official trials that followed claimed another thirty-three slaves. Ten were decapitated and their heads displayed as a warning to other slaves.[18]

Supporters of slavery blamed abolitionists for the rebellions, which they saw as further evidence that Bryan Edwards was correct: abolitionist agitation caused slave rebellion. A West Indian planter, member of Parliament, and historian of the Caribbean, Edwards published his *Historical Survey of the French Colony of St. Domingo* in 1797, after the revolt in Saint Domingue. According to Edwards, the French abolitionist society, the Amis des Noirs, was responsible for the slave insurrection in Saint Domingue. Edwards's work quickly became the standard proslavery account of the Haitian Revolution. It was widely disseminated in Britain and the United States and went through several reprints well into the nineteenth century. Supporters of slavery transformed Edwards's argument into a general theory about the relationship between abolitionist agitation and slave insurrection.[19] For many white West Indians, missionaries were closely associated with abolitionists; therefore, they too were suspect. After the rebellion in Demerara, missionary John Smith was arrested for his alleged role in the rebellion. Smith and his wife had lived in the sugar colony since 1817 when he was sent there by the London Missionary Society. While Smith remained loyal to the goals of the society to not endanger public safety and to teach slaves to obey their masters, Smith was nonetheless horrified by the plight of West Indian slaves. His popularity with the slave population and his advocacy on behalf of slaves, as well as his private journal entries denouncing slavery, were all used as evidence against him in his trial. Smith was tried by court martial, found guilty, and sentenced to death. While awaiting word from England regarding his appeal, Smith died of consumption in jail in early 1824. As soon as word reached England of Smith's conviction and subsequent death, the London Missionary Society and their co-religionists inundated the religious press with evidence of Smith's innocence. Smith quickly became a martyr for the abolitionist cause.[20]

In *Immediate, Not Gradual Abolition*, Heyrick challenged the Edwards thesis and supported the defense of Smith that had appeared in the press. Slavery was a sin against God, thus the slave "has a natural *right* to his liberty, a right which it is a crime to withhold," Heyrick argued. As a result, both slaveholders and abolitionists were to blame for the rebellion. The conditions of enslavement and the protracted discussions of emancipation had left slaves frustrated. Heyrick recounted the story of a slave named "Respectable

Billy," who had been married for eighteen years and had fathered ten children and who had been forcibly separated from his family. Another couple had been separated when the wife was forced to become the mistress of the overseer. Both men sought redress through rebellion. Other slaves were refused passes to attend church or had been punished for attending services. Under these conditions, the spread of rumors of freedom denied had taken on powerful meaning. Yet, Heyrick claimed that the slaves had not resorted to violence, but instead had refused to work until news of their future was given to them. Instead, she suggested that the planters were responsible for the violent outcome. Heyrick also emphasized the guilt of abolitionists, who had been timid, cold-hearted, and exceedingly polite in their dealings with slaveholders.[21]

Heyrick linked slave rebellion and abstention from slave-labor goods, claiming that abstention would end slave rebellion by ending slavery. Frustrated with the inaction of Parliament and the abolitionists, she called for direction action against slavery by boycotting slave-labor goods, specifically sugar. "Too much time has already been lost in declamation and argument,—in petitions and remonstrances against *British* slavery," she wrote. "Why petition Parliament at all, to do that for us, which . . . we can do more speedily and more effectually for ourselves?" she asked. Emphasizing the effect of the "combined exertion" of individual consumers, Heyrick claimed their targeted economic choices would accomplish a "greater moral revolution" than could ever be accomplished by parliamentary action. At the heart of this moral revolution stood thousands of British women who once mobilized could render slavery unprofitable by simply changing their habits of consumption. Recognizing the connection between morals and economics, Heyrick appealed to women and their emotions, asking them to use their sympathy for the slave to change the market. As she wrote, "What rational hope is there left of the extinction of slavery but by rendering it unprofitable? And how can we render it unprofitable but by rejecting its produce? And how can such an extensive rejection of its produce be obtained *as shall render it unprofitable*, without direct appeals to the hearts and understandings, to the feelings and principles of individuals, on the folly, danger, and wickedness of upholding such a system of iniquity?" Heyrick believed that even if the planters did not experience a similar conversion of heart, their economic self-interest would lead them to make the morally right decision.[22] Such arguments encouraged female participation in the antislavery and abstention movements and resulted in the organization of dozens of ladies' antislavery associations in Britain in the 1820s.

Abstention and Women's Antislavery Activism

Heyrick identified "two very important branches of action" uniquely suited to women: the boycott of slave labor and the distribution of information about slavery.[23] To coordinate these efforts, Heyrick and other women organized an extensive network of ladies' antislavery associations. In April 1825, the Female Society for Birmingham (later renamed the Birmingham Ladies' Negro's Friends Society) was established by women from Birmingham and its surrounding communities. The society established a network of committees, district treasurers, visitors, and collectors. It also identified three primary goals: distribute information about slavery, provide direct aid to female slaves in the West Indies, and encourage the boycott of slave labor.[24] Functioning as an unofficial national antislavery organization for women, the group influenced the formation of other ladies' associations. Its vast organization of officers and committees, as well as the extensive correspondence maintained by society founder Lucy Townsend, enabled the Birmingham women to communicate with other like-minded women in Great Britain, the United States, and beyond.[25] The group's network of district treasurers grew from ten women in 1825 to forty-nine by 1830 spread throughout England as well as Wales, Ireland, France, Sierra Leone, and Calcutta. Often local antislavery associations were established by district treasurers. For example, as district treasurer for Leicester, Heyrick helped establish that city's local ladies' antislavery society. The network of women's associations expanded as a result of the system of treasurers. Though not directly affiliated with the Birmingham group, other associations such as the Sheffield Female Anti-Slavery Society (1825), the Colchester Ladies' Anti-Slavery Association (1825), and the Liverpool Ladies' Anti-Slavery Society (1827) also relied on the Birmingham women for information and support. Between 1825 and 1833, at least seventy-three ladies' associations were established. Of those, twenty were organized under the direction of the Female Society for Birmingham.[26]

The women's groups relied on direct action; thus, the visitors and collectors of the women's associations were essential to the arduous work of canvassing entire communities to spread the antislavery message and to encourage the boycott of slave labor. Door-to-door canvassing was a uniquely female method for distributing abstention and antislavery tracts, most likely adopted from the system of female district visitors to the poor used by benevolent associations in this period. In 1827 the Birmingham women reported that more than half of the households in the area had been visited; in 1828 the number of households visited in Birmingham rose to 83 percent. By 1829 they had completed their canvass of the entire Birmingham area. On her own, Sophia Sturge, sister of the abolitionist Joseph Sturge, visited more than three thousand Birmingham households while Heyrick and Susanna Watts, who together coedited the antislavery publication, *The Hummingbird*, were credited with canvassing most of Leicester.[27]

Women's canvassing efforts were supported by the use of print material, including a variety of pamphlets printed by the various associations for use with specific audiences. The Birmingham women issued five thousand copies of *What Does Your Sugar Cost? A Cottage Conversation on the Subject of British Negro Slavery*. The tract, which was intended for distribution among the poor, featured a conversation among three characters: "Woman," "Daughter," and "Lady." The lady is a visitor from the local antislavery society, who has come to call on the woman and her daughter to convince them to abstain from slave-grown sugar. In the dialogue that follows, the lady explains how slaves produced the sugar the woman and her daughter consume, and she urges the woman and her daughter to substitute East Indian sugar for that produced by the labor of slaves. By the end of the short tract, the woman is convinced, agreeing to abstain from slave-grown sugar. The conversational nature of the tract provided a model for visiting antislavery women to adopt.[28] While *What Does Your Sugar Cost?* targeted the poor, *Reasons for Substituting East Indian Sugar* was directed to the "higher classes." Without a dialogue, this tract emphasized parliamentary shortcomings and called on readers to bring the question of slavery "home to our own bosoms." Borrowing liberally from Heyrick's texts, the tract encouraged consumers to abstain from West Indian sugar. Four thousand copies of *Reasons* were printed for distribution.[29] The women also reached out to children. Charlotte Townsend, whose mother Lucy had participated in the first slave-sugar boycott, produced a pamphlet for children titled *Pity the Negro; or, An Address to the Children on the Subject of Slavery*. At least seven editions of two thousand copies each were published. During their canvasses, women also handed out cards that claimed that for every "six families using East India sugar[,] one slave less is required."[30] Although the use of print culture to support the boycott of slave-labor goods was not a new tactic in the nineteenth century, antislavery women introduced a novel twist. For the first time women were actively selecting materials to disseminate that could be used to appeal to particular individuals that they met during their door-to-door canvass. In the eighteenth century, women gathered in family groups around the tea table to read and discuss tracts such as William Fox's *Address to the People of Great Britain*; in

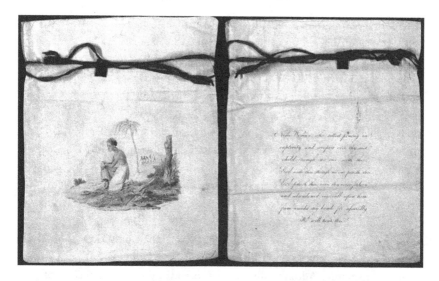

FIGURE 5.   Workbag with image of kneeling slave. Courtesy of Friends Historical Library, Swarthmore College, Swarthmore, Pennsylvania.

contrast, nineteenth-century women instead went into the neighborhoods to call on strangers to encourage them to join the boycott of slave labor. Their systematic canvass along with their strategic use of print media suggests a practical, focused consumer campaign against slave-labor goods. Unlike their predecessors, nineteenth-century women sought to convert entire communities regardless of traditional boundaries such as class.

These women did not limit their distribution of print materials to their neighborhood canvasses, however. British antislavery women included tracts in the workbags that were made for sale to "the affluent and influential classes of the community."[31] Workbags, which were generally used to store embroidery and other needlework, were made from free-labor East India cotton, silk, or satin by the women of organizations such as the Birmingham group. One side of the bag featured an image of a slave woman; on the reverse, a label admonished the slave woman to "call upon [God] from amidst thy bonds, for assuredly he will hear thee." The bags were filled with antislavery literature along with a note explaining the contents. The workbags were a significant fund-raiser and form of outreach for women's associations; indeed, the workbags produced by British women drew the attention of American editor Benjamin Lundy, who noted in the pages of the *Genius of Universal Emancipation* that the project was worthy of "particular notice."[32] In 1826 the Birmingham society reported that nearly two thousand bags had been distributed throughout England, Wales, and Ireland. In 1827 the group reported that during the preceding two years, the association had spent nearly £400 printing antislavery literature. Nearly all of that cost, they noted, had been covered with proceeds from the sale of workbags. The workbags were also an effective means of disseminating information about slavery and the boycott of slave-grown sugar, countering the numerous "misrepresentations" carried in the press. While the bags were an important fund-raiser, the bags were also distributed by the women to influential women and, on occasion, men.[33]

In addition to print literature and workbags, women exerted economic pressure in other ways. Relying on the various district treasurers, women in Dublin and Birmingham compiled registers of families that had agreed to abstain from slave-grown sugar. These lists were then published regularly in local newspapers, giving the impression that the numbers of boycotters were large and growing. Additionally, women organized general boycotts of grocers and confectioners who sold or used West Indian sugar and published lists of retailers who used only free-grown sugar. The systematic neighborhood canvasses conducted by the women allowed them to identify supporters and to disseminate information about tradesmen who supported the boycott. These coordinated efforts were critical to the successful expansion of the boycott in the mid and late 1820s. While exact numbers are not available, it is likely that the number of boycotters exceeded that of the eighteenth-century campaign.[34]

The direct economic action taken by British women drew on ideas of female sympathy, liberal political economy, and profitability. Women like Heyrick engaged women's hearts *and* heads, using an appeal to women's emotions that also relied on the economic arguments of Adam Smith, the eighteenth-century Scottish philosopher who authored *The Theory of Moral Sentiments* and *The Wealth of Nations*. For Heyrick, immediatism was "direct action undertaken without delay by individuals making particular and targeted economic choices." As Carol Lasser concludes, "Heyrick had a clear vision of the course to emancipation: Guide people to buy correctly; this involved appeals to the heart; with regenerate hearts, good people would pressure planters into making morally right decisions, even if the planters did not experience the sympathy that could produce a conversion of their hardened, economically driven hearts." In the marketplace, where men and women were equal, women could operate the levers of economic change, rendering slavery unprofitable.[35] Although women's antislavery work reinforced the political change sought by antislavery men, some men were embarrassed by such "unwanted allies."[36]

Abstention and Gender

In his history of the British antislavery movement, journalist Adam Hochschild describes ladies' antislavery associations as "almost always bolder than those of men." Hochschild's description points out the fundamental difference between the associations of women and the associations of men. While antislavery women called for the immediate abolition of slavery through direct tactics like abstention from slave-grown sugar, antislavery men emphasized amelioration and gradual abolition through political change.[37] Women rejected gradualism, defining their opposition in terms of Christian responsibility: women "ought to obey God rather than man," asserted the women of the Sheffield Female Anti-Slavery Society.[38] Christian principles required immediate action against the immorality of slavery. Significantly, antislavery women used direct economic action to bring about change not only in the marketplace but also in the abolitionist movement. In 1830 the antislavery women of Birmingham, frustrated with the gradualist polices of the national antislavery society, passed a resolution to withhold their annual contribution to the group unless "they are willing to give up the word *gradual* in their title." The network of women's associations accounted for more than one-fifth of the national society's annual income in 1829, so women were an important economic force in the antislavery movement. Seven weeks after the Birmingham women passed their resolution, the London Anti-Slavery Society resolved to drop "mitigation and gradual abolition" from the society's title. Although pressure from male provincial delegates likely had some influence on the change of title, the financial pressure from the women's networks surely had an impact as well.[39]

Gender differences were also critical to the debates about the equalization of sugar duties in the 1820s. The discussion of sugar duties reveals the ways in which the activism of women and men could simultaneously align and diverge. Heyrick described the revision of the tariff on sugar as more of the "slow and solemn process of parliamentary discussion."[40] Women recognized the financial impact such a change might bring. For example, the Ladies' Association for Liverpool and Its Neighborhoods estimated that local residents paid £5,000 annually in duties and bounties to support West Indian slavery.[41] Still, the revision of the tariff on sugar lacked the immediate impact of abstention and relied on the cumbersome process of political change. Although the London Anti-Slavery Society supported women's efforts by proposing an experiment to market East Indian sugar, many other men worried that the withdrawal of economic support for slave-labor goods might devastate the British economy. British Quaker James Cropper admired

the moral scruples of those who avoided the products of slave labor; however, as a businessman, he understood how dependent British commerce was
on the products of slavery. Instead, Cropper called for the opportunity for
slave-labor goods to compete equally with free-labor goods by revising the
protective duties that had made slave-grown sugar artificially profitable. Convinced of the superiority of free labor, Cropper believed that free labor
would ultimately prevail and West Indian planters would be forced to emancipate their slaves.[42]

Cropper's involvement in the antislavery movement began in response
to an attempt by the West Indian interest in Parliament to increase duties on
East Indian sugar. Cropper believed free labor and free trade in legitimate
commodities were divinely appointed engines of moral progress; therefore,
discriminatory duties on East Indian sugar manipulated the market and supported slave labor. In a letter to William Wilberforce in May 1821, Cropper
claimed West Indian planters asked for increased duties on East Indian sugar
because they feared free competition with East Indian sugar. "Is not this a
most decided admission that their system of cultivation cannot exist, unless
the country is taxed to support?" Cropper asked. British consumers paid
more than £1 million annually in duties and bounties to support West Indian
slavery.[43] Cropper and other members of the Anti-Slavery Society believed
West Indians' monopoly of trade had rendered the British colonies a liabil-
ity rather than an asset to the empire.[44] An article in the *Anti-Slavery Monthly
Reporter*, published in February 1830, calculated the cost of slavery. Break-
ing the cost into categories—army, ordnance, commissariat, miscellaneous,
and navy—the author concluded that these expenses were "but a part of
what it costs to maintain this cruel and criminal system." Adding the bounties and drawbacks, which favored West Indian sugar, annual expenditures to
support slavery were more than £3 million. Such "mischievous policy," the
author argued, "cramps the commerce of Great Britain, and paralyses the
industry . . . of our Asiatic fellow-subjects."[45] Leading abolitionist Zachary
Macaulay described the West Indian colonies as a "dead weight" on the country and "a source of enormous expense, without any adequate return." In
contrast, India "pours capital into this country," Macaulay wrote. Macaulay
claimed he avoided comparing the morality of the West Indies and India,
suggesting instead that because West Indian planters emphasized their contribution to British economic well-being, he would base his rebuttal on
similar grounds.[46] Other leading male abolitionists were not so circumspect,
linking financial support of slavery to a moral drain on the empire and claiming that continued support of slavery would "greatly aggravate the distress

of our countrymen at home" and impede the progress of "the general happiness and civilization of mankind" throughout the world.[47]

As head of Cropper, Benson, and Company, Liverpool's largest importer of East Indian sugar, Cropper had substantial economic ties to sugar production in East India. He was also an important member of the British abolitionist establishment; Cropper was a founding member of the Liverpool Society for the Amelioration and Gradual Abolition of Slavery as well as a member of the London committee of the national Antislavery Society.[48] For historians, Cropper's fusion of economic and humanitarian interests has served as an example of the link between capitalism and abolitionism. Historian Eric Williams presents Cropper as an example of an abolitionist motivated more by economic self-interest than humanitarian values.[49] In contrast, historian David Brion Davis describes him as a man in whom "the intensity of Quaker Quietism had fused with the economic optimism of Adam Smith." Cropper became an abolitionist because he believed in the "unity of moral and material progress."[50] Davis emphasizes the conflict between Cropper's commercial success and his Quaker beliefs, a conflict that ultimately found resolution in Smith's *The Wealth of Nations*. For Cropper, Smith resolved the tension between Christianity and profit; the invisible hand of the market was in reality the hand of God aiding the flow of goods toward their natural market in an "unfettered interplay of capital, labor, and resources."[51] Cropper's vested interest in East India sugar made suspect his support of economic tactics against West Indian sugar. In 1824, when the London committee of the Antislavery Society established a committee on East India sugar to promote its sale, West Indian planters responded, emphasizing the presence of slavery in British India. "Consult the respectable authorities [like Wilberforce]," one pamphlet urged in 1825, "and you will soon be convinced that the labourers who produce Sugar in the East Indies are generally wretched Slaves, whose situation, respecting essential comfort and protection, is far inferior, indeed, to that of the Negroes in our West India colonies."[52]

While Heyrick rejected abolitionists' plans to revise duties on East Indian sugar, she did not reject economic principles or the invisible hand of the market. Rather she rejected political change as too narrow in scope. Heyrick described the revision of duties as a form of "commercial speculation" that reduced the question of emancipation to matters of political comprise and financial profitability. "Speculations on the comparative profitableness of free and slave labour, may *ultimately* effect the destruction of slavery,—but christian charity will not wait the tardy uncertain result," Heyrick wrote. While she too believed that free labor was more efficient and more profitable than slave labor, she worried that reducing the question of abolition to economic principles would push aside moral commitments. Guiding consumers to buy correctly, Heyrick believed, was the "shortest, safest, most effectual" strategy for the abolition of slavery. Abstention was "more decisive, more efficient than words"; "more wise and rational, more politic and safe, as well as just and humane,—than gradual emancipation"; and "more lucrative . . . in the cultivation of . . . plantations." As Lasser argues, "For Heyrick, the invisible hand, driven by sympathetic consumer choices, would speedily bring about emancipation without the cumbersome mechanism of the state."[53]

Heyrick and Cropper each emphasized the substitution of sugar from the East Indies; yet, East Indian sugar proved problematic for supporters of the boycott. From a practical, economic standpoint, the artificially high cost of sugar from East India thwarted consumers' attempts to boycott slave-grown sugar. For the poor and the working class, East Indian sugar was often cost prohibitive. As one critic noted, the discriminatory bounties charged to East Indian sugar were "another rivet [that] has been added to the chain of the slave." While the duties imposed on East Indian sugar were charged to save West Indian planters from financial ruin, the duties further impoverished the poor because they paid a premium to maintain slavery through higher prices for sugar.[54]

In addition to being more expensive, East Indian sugar was produced under conditions that allowed it to be appropriated by West Indian plantation owners and their supporters to undermine the boycott of slave-grown sugar. As historian Andrea Major argues, "India occupied an anomalous place in the British Empire." British India was governed by the royal-chartered East India Company (EIC) and was characterized by a "large indigenous population and sophisticated social, political, and economic institutions," which resulted in a substantial difference between East India and the British colonies in the West Indies. The absence of a plantation economy, the lack of African slaves, and the integration of Indian slaves into affective networks all supported portrayals of East Indian slavery as indigenous and benign. Nonetheless, Indian slavery was "far from the innocuous social institution that some EIC officials claimed." After the EIC monopoly ended in 1813, East India was the focus of entrepreneurial efforts to increase commodity production in the region. Such efforts supported abolitionists' attempts to locate alternative sources for slave-labor goods such as sugar. Although Indian slavery was the subject of published reports in the 1820s, such as the voluminous collection of parliamentary papers documenting EIC correspondence on slavery since 1772, those reports received little attention in the abolitionist or missionary press. Instead, it was West Indian plantation owners and their supporters who brought the matter to public attention as they appropriated the issue of Indian labor to undermine abolitionists' moral arguments against West Indian slave-grown sugar.[55] As a result, for supporters and opponents of the boycott of West Indian sugar, East Indian sugar assumed a symbolic importance out of proportion to its actual ability to displace slave-grown sugar.

Opponents of East Indian sugar claimed the slaves of West India were better off than the slaves of the East whereas supporters of East Indian sugar sought to distance sugar production from Indian slavery. In arguments that bore a striking resemblance to the comparisons between the working class and the slave, supporters of slavery claimed slaves were the privileged group while abolitionists claimed East Indians were the better lot. As one critic of Cropper claimed, "It is only, I conceive because the labourers are obliged to work for next to nothing that sugar can be made in the East Indies so cheap as is asserted. However, then, the matter may be debated on political and commercial grounds, let us hear no more of the superior *humanity* of employing labourers at 3*d* per day in the East, rather than slaves in the West, to whom every comfort consistent with their humble position is undoubtedly afforded." In a series of comparisons between East and West Indian slavery, the anonymous author of *To the Consumers of Sugar* (1825) concluded that the situation of East Indians was much worse. To further emphasize his support for West Indian sugar, he noted that it "*goes farthest,* and is *cheapest* and *best.*"[56] Abolitionists countered these arguments, claiming that descriptions of Indian hardship were exaggerated and that freedom itself outweighed relief from poverty. Indian poverty, they claimed, did not cause misery or distress but represented instead a "voluntary acceptance of limited material wants." However, as Cobbett and other critics of abolitionists continued to emphasize the horrors of slavery, abolitionists found themselves unable to refute the existence of Indian slavery entirely. Instead, as Major argues, abolitionists "dismissed the importance of Indian slavery for their campaign on the grounds that it was not connected to sugar production and was a milder, more benign institution than West Indian slavery." Abolitionist arguments for East Indian sugar reveal the highly contextual nature of humanitarian reform. "[H]umanitarian agendas," Major concludes, functioned "within a complex matrix of moral, economic, political, and pragmatic imperatives that produced fissured and contested ideological formations that were applied unevenly across the sites of empire."[57]

Supporters and opponents of the second major boycott of slave-grown sugar, like their predecessors, linked the consumption of slave-grown sugar to other social and political issues, including women's activism and imperial reform. Heyrick made slavery and slave-labor goods a matter for woman's heart and for her pocketbook. As a result, she invested women with the ability to manipulate the market, viewing abstention as a morally directed economic strategy that had a direct impact on slavery. Cobbett and Cropper brought attention to the boycott through their respective arguments for working-class reform and for a revision of sugar tariffs. While their interests and their objectives were very different, Cobbett and Cropper nonetheless brought public attention to the issue of slave-grown sugar. There is no evidence that the second boycott was any more effective than the first in its impact on the market for sugar.[58] Still, the boycott did keep the issue of British slavery before the public, encouraging Britons to engage in practical action to pressure Parliament into abolishing slavery. The British boycott also reinvigorated the American abstention movement and sparked the reform work of the young Quaker poet Elizabeth Margaret Chandler.

CHAPTER 5

Woman's Heart: Free Produce and Domesticity

Elizabeth Heyrick's *Immediate, Not Gradual Ab-olition* was reprinted in the United States by Quaker printers in Philadelphia and New York shortly after its British publication. It was also serialized in Benjamin Lundy's *Genius of Universal Emancipation*.[1] Lundy's publication was an important source of information about women's activism and free produce in the 1820s. He printed reports, addresses, and publications from British female antislavery societies as well as accounts from American organizations. Two months after the last installment of *Immediate, Not Gradual Abolition* appeared in the *Genius*, Lundy published "The Slave Ship," an antislavery poem written by a young Quaker woman, Elizabeth Margaret Chandler.[2] That publication marked the beginning of a nearly decade-long partnership between Lundy and Chandler. In the 1820s, through their written work and their activism, Heyrick and Chandler defined the terms of feminine engagement with the antislavery movement and the boycott of slave labor. The two women were responsible for influencing hundreds of British and American women to join the free-produce and antislavery movements in the antebellum period.[3] Although both women died in the early 1830s—Heyrick in 1831 and Chandler in 1834—their written work and their activism continued to influence women until the American Civil War.

Chandler, unlike Heyrick, understood abstention from slave-labor goods as a matter of morality. Rather than a collective action that combined political

economy and moral appeals, Chandler instead urged women to purify themselves, their homes, and their nation of the stain of slavery. Consider, for
example, one of Chandler's most iconic poems, "Think of Our Country's
Glory," which illustrated how women's sympathy might be mobilized to
end slavery. The poem opens with the image of the American flag "stain'd
and gory" with the blood of Africa's children. Shifting attention to the personal, in the second stanza the poem describes the "frantic mother" who
cries out for her child all the while "falling lashes smother" her "anguish
wild!" This horrific scene is followed in the next stanza by the question
whether "woman's voice be hush'd." In the final stanza that question is answered with an emphatic, "Oh, no!"[4] Chandler's poem was widely reprinted
in the antebellum period. The poem and, in particular, the phrase, "Shall
woman's voice be hush'd," was used by many abolitionists to justify women's
activism.[5] The poem was set to music and sung in family circles and abolitionist gatherings, rallying women to the cause. On one notable occasion,
the women of the Boston Female Anti-Slavery Society sang "Think of Our
Country's Glory" after their meeting had been threatened by an antiabolitionist mob in 1835, suggesting the poem reassured women of the moral
power of their cause and the importance of female solidarity. The song was
later included in *Freedom's Lyre*, the hymnal compiled by Presbyterian minister Edwin F. Hatfield for the American Anti-Slavery Society (AASS).[6] The
phrase even appeared on a banner, appearing alongside of an image of slaveholders forcefully separating a slave mother and her children. Miss Smith of
Andover, Massachusetts, presented the banner to the West Parish Anti-Slavery
Society as part of the community's Fourth of July festivities.[7] Despite the
presence of patriotic imagery—particularly, the stained American flag—the
poem is an emotional appeal, calling on women as mothers, daughters, and
sisters to reject the violence of slavery. As one historian concludes, "Women
would read, and weep, and appeal to men who would do the political work
of emancipation."[8]

Although influenced by Heyrick, Chandler conceptualized abstention
from slave-labor goods as a moral response to slavery, appealing to women
in highly gendered religious terms.[9] Although the boycott of slave-labor
goods was a matter for all men and women, it was up to women to purify
the home and the family of the sin of slave-labor goods. In fashioning this
reinterpretation of Heyrick's arguments, Chandler drew on her Quaker up-
bringing, particularly the moral arguments of John Woolman. For Chandler, abstention and free produce was a testimony, a commitment to reject
the "gain of oppression," rather than an economic strategy. In her antislav-

ery writings, Chandler shifted the focus of the boycott from the marketplace to the home. Thus, abstention became a matter of individual choice and a statement of belief rather than a collective action and an economic tool.[10] The sentimentalization of abstention and free produce that began with Chandler remained a consistent characteristic of the movement throughout the remainder of its history.

Domesticity and Free Produce

Elizabeth Margaret Chandler was one of the most prolific antislavery authors in the United States in the antebellum period. Born in 1807 in Centreville, Delaware, Chandler's father moved her and her two brothers to Philadelphia in 1809, after the death of their mother. After her father died in 1815, she and her brothers were raised by their maternal grandmother and various aunts in the area. Chandler attended Quaker schools until she was twelve or thirteen and grew to adulthood in the divided Quaker community of Philadelphia. In 1827, at the time of the Quaker schism, Elizabeth and her brother Thomas were members of Philadelphia Northern District Monthly Meeting. That fall, after the split, they transferred to Green Street Monthly Meeting, the center of Hicksite influence in Philadelphia. They were subsequently disowned by Northern District Meeting.[11] Chandler played an important role in the development of American antislavery literary culture.[12] She became editor of the "Ladies' Repository," a new feature in Lundy's *Genius of Universal Emancipation*. The "Ladies' Repository" set conscience as the term on which women would engage in free-produce and antislavery activism. Chandler distinguished between male and female motivations for joining the abolitionist cause: men joined the cause for moral, political, or philanthropic motives whereas women were called to the cause "by *all* the holy charities of life." Describing her work in religious terms, Chandler professed her desire to be "useful" in "the advancement of . . . [the] holy cause" of abolition and pledged to "place the tribute of her services on the altar of Emancipation." She also urged women to abstain from slave-labor goods, to form antislavery societies, and to influence family and friends to do the same.[13]

Abstention, according to Chandler, was primarily a moral action that affected the individual consumer rather than an economic action that impacted the profitability of slavery. Although the economic consequences of abstention mattered, the moral foundation of abstention mattered more.

Abstention was a particularly feminine means of affirming antislavery sentiment. "Letters to Isabel," a series of eight free-produce essays written by
Chandler in 1829 and 1830, urged women to become active supporters of
abolitionism by abstaining from slave-labor goods. "Slavery, my friend, must
be either positively right, or positively wrong. There is no *middle* point on
which it may rest. It is not a thing to be merely *disapproved* of—coldly warred
with as a venial offence. It violates *all* the most essential principles of Christian religion," Chandler wrote. Anyone "who bears the name of a woman
and a Christian" should "fling from them the luxuries" produced by slave
labor "as if they were a deadly poison." Women were naturally suited to
antislavery work: "Woman was not formed to look upon scenes of suffering
with a careless eye" and should not "for an instant tolerate" the "wickedness" of slavery or the "luxuries that are purchased by such means." Chandler made an empathic appeal for women's abstention, describing a pound
cake as "the sepulcher of the broken heart" and a jam as filled with "briny
tears." Indifference to the blood-stained goods of slavery was a failure of
female sensibility: "If those who unscrupulously partake of these delicacies,
had beheld the horrors by which they are too often purchased . . . I believe
there are few females who would retain any desire to taste of the blood-
polluted banquet . . . why should the sight of blood be needed, when they
know it has been shed, to awaken their sleeping sensibilities?" She tolerated
no excuses for the consumption of slave-labor goods. Citing the parable of
the widow's mite, she dismissed the objection that free-labor goods were
too costly and too inconvenient.[14] While Chandler encouraged women to
join in associations, forming their individual decision to abstain into a
powerful, collective antislavery group, she reframed women's economic
power in moral terms, emphasizing instead the individual purification produced by moral female consumption.[15]

As an editor and a writer for the *Genius of Universal Emancipation*, Chandler was part of a broader pattern of change among American publications
in the 1820s that provided more opportunities for female authors and editors. Women benefited from the significant increase in publications for
women and by women; still, women often disagreed about the ways in which
women should use those opportunities, particularly when it came to political matters such as slavery. Sarah J. Hale, who was the most prominent female editor in this period, used her position as editor of the *Ladies Magazine*
to advocate for a separate feminine public sphere. While Hale accepted many
of the cultural ideals of womanhood, she did not accept the gendered distinction between the public and the private sphere. Instead, she urged women
to use the public sphere to engage and simultaneously challenge notions of

true womanhood. According to Hale, women should speak out publicly on domestic and moral matters. That view did not extend to political matters, however. For Hale, women could address the morality of slavery but not the politics; Chandler's pleas that women speak out and take action against slavery were too political.[16]

"An Appeal to the Ladies of the United States," written by Chandler in 1829, is a powerful call to action against slavery. Women had been educated by custom to believe slavery a "natural" and "necessary evil." The ideal of republican motherhood described women as the first educators of children who had the ability to influence national matters through the power of their influence. Women could "break the fetters of the oppressed." Chandler wrote: "Will you not stand boldly and nobly forth, in the face of the world, and declare that American women will never be tamely made the instruments of oppression?" Moreover, by giving "on every occasion the preference to the products of slave labor," those goods would become cheaper and more readily available. In a passage that echoed Heyrick, Chandler claimed: "As soon as sufficient inducement is held out, free labor will be liberally employed; the experiment of its comparative advantages with that of the slave, may then be fairly tried. . . . The demand for free labor products will become greater than for those of the other class; they may then be afforded cheaper, and Emancipation must necessarily follow."[17] "Appeal" appeared in *Genius of Universal Emancipation* in September 1829. It was reprinted two months later in Hale's *Ladies Magazine*. Hale explained that the article had appeared in the *Genius* and that it was being reprinted "by request." She attributed the essay to a "southern lady." Significantly, she abridged the essay, omitting the final paragraphs that explicitly outlined women's organizational activity and support for free produce. While Hale and Chandler shared similar views on female education and republican motherhood, their motivations for doing so were quite different. Hale believed female education would allow women to better fulfill their traditional feminine role; Chandler, in contrast, advocated female education as an important corrective to slavery. "In addressing her own sex, particularly on so momentous and really appalling subject as that of *slavery*," Hale said of Chandler's essay, "we presume the writer had no idea of advocating female interference or usurpation of authority, in directing the affairs of state." Hale cautioned her readers, "Let us beware of exerting our power *politically*." Woman's influence should "depend mainly on the respect inspired by her *moral* excellence, not on the political address or energy she may display."[18]

The following month, Chandler published her response to Hale's criticism, producing the short piece, "Opinions," as a review of a letter written by Hale to Chandler objecting "to the propriety of *females* becoming public advocates of Emancipation."[19] "Opinions" emphasized women's domestic role, urging women to use that role to aid the cause of the oppressed slave. Free produce was particularly suited to women's activism because it relied on women's domestic responsibilities. While Chandler admitted that emancipation was a political question, she claimed it rested on "the broader basis of humanity and justice." As a result, slavery was a moral question. And, Chandler asserted, "it is on *this* ground only, that we advocated the interference of women." She further denied any desire to transform women into a "race of politicians." Rather than emulating male political behavior, Chandler instead encouraged women to take female values into the world.[20]

The Hale-Chandler debate about the appropriate use of the feminine public sphere reflects the pliable nature of domesticity. Although both women used domestic ideology and both believed women should address moral issues, they differed when it came to political matters such as slavery. Hale believed women should not engage in political debate or create discord; therefore, she urged women to avoid the controversy of slavery and emancipation.[21] Chandler, in contrast, was troubled by women's indifferent acceptance of slavery. Continued feminine consumption of slave-labor goods reflected a callous disregard for the oppressed slave that rendered meaningless the ideals of feminine morality. Slave-labor goods transformed the home into a blood-soaked scene. Rather than food to nourish the family, the family banquet contained sweets that were "mix'd" with the "red-life drops" and the "scalding tears" of the slaves who had produced the goods.[22] Even families were rendered into shocking parodies by the commerce in slave-labor goods:

> The weary slave had left his toil;—it was an eve like this,
> But to his heart its loveliness would bring no throb of bliss . . .
>
> A cry of anguish caught his ear—in shrieks she breathed his name,
> And forward to his cot he sprung with heart and pulse of flame;
> Amid her weeping babes she knelt, and o'er her crouching head
> The white man's lash in mockery swung, all newly stain'd with red.[23]

Such scenes happened, Chandler claimed, because women were unwilling to forgo "the luxuries which have been wrung with heart-sickening inhumanity from the hands of the helpless and oppressed." American colonial women had "refused the use of *tea* during the revolutionary contest"; yet her contemporaries allowed themselves "to be ministered to by the hand of slavery." Chandler lamented, "It really is surprising how the gentle and the good can be so little offended by [slavery's] vileness."[24] It was woman's duty "to relax not [her] endeavours until it is *no longer* impossible" to purchase free-labor goods. "Besides promoting the consumption of free produce, the influence of woman may be widely felt in awaking a more general interest in the cause of Emancipation."[25] She called on women to "transform themselves mentally" into the slave, to "enter into the desolateness of that moment; stand alone and forsaken in the world; without religion, without a friend in earth or heaven, to whom they may turn for consolation in their hour of trial."[26] The immoral consumption of slave-labor goods made a mockery of domesticity. Thus, true womanhood must include moral commerce.

Early Organizations

Chandler encouraged women to take collective action by organizing free-produce and antislavery associations. Women's associational activity, she remarked, was part of the "conscientious discharge of an imperative duty." British women had demonstrated the effectiveness of publishing and distributing antislavery literature. "The same measure would, no doubt, here be productive of equally beneficial results," Chandler reasoned. Such associations would rouse the public from "their torpid insensibility." Moreover, associations were "evidence that the opinions expressed are not merely the effervescence of excited feeling in scattered individuals."[27] In the late 1820s, as Chandler began to speak out more frequently for free produce, her contemporaries in Philadelphia and elsewhere began to organize associations to promote antislavery and free produce.

The men and women of Philadelphia established gender-segregated free-produce societies in 1827 and 1829, respectively. Philadelphia men organized the Free Produce Society of Pennsylvania in January 1827 to locate and to promote free-labor goods. Of the sixty-four men of the Free Produce Society, most were Quakers including James Mott, Thomas McClintock, Abraham L. Pennock, and Isaac T. Hopper. The Female Association for Promoting the Manufacture and Use of Free Cotton organized two years later, in January 1829, the city's first female free-produce society and one of the earliest female antislavery associations in the United States. The group's initial meeting attracted thirteen women; the group's membership increased to more than one hundred in subsequent months. Although there are no membership lists for the association, it is likely that Lucretia Mott and Elizabeth Margaret Chandler were among the members. It is unclear why the women waited two years to establish a female association in Philadelphia; it is possible, however, that their organization was delayed by the Hicksite schism. Moreover, the Hicksite schism may have contributed to a decline in male free-produce activity in Philadelphia in this same period. A letter, published in the *African Repository and Colonial Journal* in October 1829, suggested the men's association had languished in the months after its establishment. The Free Produce Society of Pennsylvania, the letter writer remarked, had been recently "resuscitated from a state of torpidity . . . and now manifests strong symptoms of health and activity." The author also noted the presence of the female society, estimating the membership at seventy women, "most of them being house-keepers."[28]

In the 1820s and early 1830s, free-produce and antislavery associations were also organized outside the immediate Philadelphia area. Quakers Enoch Lewis, William Gibbons, and Benjamin Webb organized the Wilmington (Delaware) Society for the Encouragement of Free Labor in 1826. Like the Philadelphia groups, the Wilmington organization resolved to encourage the cultivation of free-labor goods and to disseminate information about the cause. Free-produce groups were organized in Ohio, including the Salem Abolition and Colonization Society (1827), the Free Produce Association of Green Plain (1832), the Free Produce and Anti-Slavery Society of Monroe County (1833), the New Garden Anti-Slavery Society (1834), and the Ohio Anti-Slavery Society (1835). In 1826 the Aiding Abolition Society of Monroe County, Ohio, sent a memorial to the merchants of Ohio and elsewhere urging them to give "the preference to the product of free labour, so as to discourage African Slavery, and to promote the amelioration of this degraded race of fellow beings." The memorial recited the lineage of the eighteenth-century abolitionist movement including Thomas Clarkson, William Wilberforce, and many other "individuals [who] conscientiously refused to use the produce of slavery." The members of the association "assure[d] the merchants, who will avoid procuring the produce of slavery, piracy, smuggling, &c. and will purchase such articles as are the produce of free labour, that they shall have their united and liberal support." Members cheered recent successful attempts by local merchants to secure free-labor goods.[29]

Quaker free-produce associations supported the development of similar groups in the African American community in Philadelphia. In October 1830, members of the Free Produce Society of Pennsylvania met with members of Richard Allen's Bethel Church to discuss the establishment of an African American free-produce association. Two months later, at a gathering that drew several hundred men, the Colored Free Produce Society of

Pennsylvania was organized, electing James Cornish as the secretary. Within months the officers of the association reported that demand for free-labor goods had exceeded expectations. It was reported that some members were buying up to fifty pounds of free-labor sugar at one time. In this same period, the women of Bethel Church formed the Colored Female Free Produce Society with Judith James as president and Laetitia Rowley as secretary. Like the Quaker-dominated associations, members linked consumers who purchased slave-labor goods to the support of slavery. The black free-produce societies also recognized the African American community's personal stake in slavery and the community's particular responsibility to break the chains of oppression. Throughout the 1830s and 1840s, black abolitionists organized local free-produce and antislavery societies in Philadelphia and elsewhere. For example, in 1838, a group of African American women in New York promoted a display of free-labor products at the Broadway Tabernacle with the proceeds going to the antislavery cause. In March 1834, black abolitionist William Whipper established a free-labor store next door to Richard Allen's Bethel Church in Philadelphia.[30]

While each of these organizations urged abstention from the products of slave labor, they also encouraged free produce, or the substitution of free-labor goods. In a tactic that was clearly borrowed from the British example, the men and women who formed these groups disseminated information about the availability of free-labor goods. They used the collective power of their associations and their stores to locate and to procure for interested consumers free-labor cotton, sugar, and other goods. These organizations marked a significant break from eighteenth-century Quaker abstention, which was both antislavery and anticommerce. In the nineteenth century, the men and women who opposed the consumption of slave-labor goods formed free-produce societies, disseminated information about free produce, and patronized free-produce stores. This emphasis on free produce reflected the expansion of ideas about the superiority of free labor and the rise of consumerism. The impact of consumerism on abstention is particularly evident in the children's poetry composed by Chandler.

Juvenile Abolitionists

The domestic ideology of the late eighteenth-century that aided distinctions between the domestic and the public spheres also supported new ideas about childhood that sharpened the distinction between adults and children. As it did with women, consumer culture had a profound influence on cultural ideas about childhood. Among the middle class, in particular, the idea of a separate children's physical and cultural space became entwined with consumer culture, leading to an expanded market for children's toys and books. These toys and books changed significantly in the late eighteenth and nineteenth centuries as parents adopted a more active model of child rearing that developed both mind and body. Increasingly, children's toys and books were used "to draw out children's talents and to teach the skills the middle classes believed to be most important for a respectable, happy and prosperous life."[31] These toys and books taught children cultural values, thus it is not unusual that Chandler and other abolitionists would use the consumer culture of childhood to teach children the importance of abstention and abolitionism.

As one of the earliest and most widely distributed American authors of children's abolitionist literature, Chandler was influential in encouraging children to abstain from the products of slave labor. Some of her most popular free-produce poems—"The Sugar Plums," "Oh Press Me Not to Taste Again," "Slave Produce," and "Christmas"—targeted a younger audience. Her antislavery texts written especially for children highlighted the importance of children to the abolitionist community. Abolitionists recognized that children were an important and receptive audience for antislavery literature.[32] Noting that "every body writes now for children," an editorial in the *Liberator* linked the growth in children's literature in general to the specific need to provide children with "correct information" about slavery.[33] Consuming abolitionist literature socialized young boys and girls into the abolitionist community and initiated them into the broader antebellum consumer culture. Abolitionist Henry C. Wright compared abolitionist instruction to religious instruction, calling for children to be "thoroughly imbued with the spirit and principles of Christian abolition."[34] Writing abolitionist literature for children provided women writers such as Chandler another literary venue to enter into the public debate about slavery.[35]

Children's stories about abstention dated to the late eighteenth century. Writers such as English Quakers Priscilla Wakefield and Amelia Opie used the expanding market for juvenile literature to craft antislavery tales.[36] Wakefield authored children's books on natural history as well as travelogues and moral tales often blending popular science writing with juvenile and didactic literature. Many of her works were published by the Quaker publishing firm Harvey and Darton, a leading publisher of children's books. Wakefield's *Mental Improvement* appeared in three volumes between 1794 and 1797. In a series of conversations among Mr. and Mrs. Harcourt and their four children, the father selected the subjects while the mother provided moral and spiritual commentary on a variety of subjects. The tenth conversation focused on sugar, transforming a lesson in the cultivation of sugar into a discussion of slavery. The conversation concluded with a pledge by the Harcourt children to abstain from the products of slave labor. *Mental Improvement* was reprinted by American publishers. Abraham Shearman, of New Bedford, Massachusetts, published the first American edition in 1799.[37] Opie, like Wakefield, published many of her works with Harvey and Darton in England. Her work was also widely reprinted in the United States. Her poem, "The Negro Boy's Tale: A Poem Addressed to Children," originally published during the slave-trade abolition campaign, was reprinted in 1824 by Harvey and Darton during the emancipation campaign.[38] Reprints of the poem appeared in a number of American antislavery publications including Enoch Lewis's *The African Observer*.[39] *The Black Man's Lament; or, How to Make Sugar*, published by Harvey and Darton in 1826, is an alternative history of sugar making. Like Wakefield's *Mental Improvement*, the cultivation and production of sugar cane is intimately linked to the abuses of slavery. Opie connected "the Black man's woes" to the "White man's crime." The "tall gold stems" of the sugar cane contained:

A sweet rich juice, which White men prize;
And that they may this *sugar* gain,
The Negro toils, and bleeds, and *dies*.[40]

In giving voice to the victimized slave, Opie rejected earlier children's abolitionist literature, which suggested slavery was acceptable if enforced by a benevolent master or mistress.[41] Instead Opie privileged the slave's right to equality and claimed European anxieties about emancipation were outweighed by the moral wrong of slavery.[42] In her poem, Opie made clear the link between sugar consumption and slavery; yet, she did not specifically call on children to abstain from sugar, relying instead on the moral weight of her tale to convince children to forgo the sweet substance.

Chandler, in contrast, appealed directly to children to reject slavery and the products of slave labor. In her study of abolitionist children's literature, literary scholar Deborah De Rosa argues that Chandler created a new fictional protagonist, the "abolitionist mother-historian." Female authors such as Chandler used the ambiguity of ideologies of motherhood to create "revisionist histories [that] employ everything from sentimental rhetoric to an increasingly radical, legalistic, and quasi-seditious rhetoric." Rather than the "sentimental, patriotic, or morally correct information" women traditionally used to educate their children, women may have instead opted for "seditious political works." Central to this revision of motherhood was the abolitionist mother-historian who reinterpreted American history for her children.[43] Two of Chandler's most widely reprinted children's poems— "What Is a Slave, Mother?" and "Looking at the Soldiers"—use the abolitionist mother-historian to create alternative historical narratives and encourage juvenile abolitionism. Both poems use a mother-child dialogue to heighten the child's political awareness of slavery.

The child protagonist of "What Is a Slave, Mother?" looks to the abolitionist mother-historian to refute the existence of slavery, particularly the slavery of children. In the first stanza the child asks the mother about slavery:

> Methinks I have heard a story told,
> Of some poor men, who are bought and sold,
> And driven abroad with stripes to toil,
> The live-long day on a stranger's soil;
>   Is this true mother?

In the second stanza, the child shifts focus from the "poor men" to "children as young as I" asking the mother to disprove that under slavery children were forcefully separated from their parents. However, the mother answers simply, "Alas, yes, my child." Clinging to hope, the child asks the mother whether "the master loves the slave child." When the mother responds in the negative, the child concludes, "The tales I have heard [must] be true." Stanza by stanza, Chandler uses the guise of the abolitionist mother-historian to emphasize the violent life of the slave child, a life so violent that the mother in the poem can only make the briefest replies to her child's disbelief. In the final stanza, the mother confirms her child's conclusions and completes the child's socialization into American political culture.[44]

The second poem, "Looking at the Soldiers," is a counterhistory of the founding of the United States. In the opening stanzas, the child describes the pageantry of the Fourth of July parade. The drums, the trumpets, the soldiers, and the horses are, for the child, a lesson in the history of events that "saw our country set free." But the mother reminds the child that liberty and revolution were "made in man's blood." More than bloodshed, however, the mother is distressed at the hypocrisy of the American Revolution. Through the persona of the abolitionist mother-historian, Chandler exposed the contradiction of celebrating American independence while holding millions of slaves in chains. Moreover, the abolitionist mother-historian urged her child to consider the different interpretations of revolution. The American colonists revolted against Great Britain, and their success was celebrated by subsequent generations. If American slaves revolted, however, it would be considered rebellion and lead to a much bloodier conclusion:

> We joy that our country's light bonds have been broke,
> But her sons wear, by thousands, a life-crushing yoke;
> And yon bayonets, dear, would be sheathed in their breast,
> Should they fling off the shackles that round them are prest.

In the final stanza, the mother asks the child to join her in protest by turning her back on the patriotic scene, thus transforming a moment of patriotism into a moment of abolitionist protest. Turning away in support of the slave, the mother introduced her child to a new form of civic virtue that challenged the child's traditional perceptions of American history.[45]

Still, Chandler sought more than abolitionist gestures; as in her adult works, Chandler encouraged readers to take pragmatic action against slavery, demonstrating individual commitment to the cause of the slave. Chandler used children's abstention from slave-grown sugar to model ideal abolitionist behavior. In the poems, "Christmas" and "The Sugar-Plums," the child protagonist rejects the gifts of sweets from the mother (or grandmother) and reminds the older women that the while such foods are pleasant to the taste, they were produced by the violence of slavery. "Oh Press Me Not to Taste Again" alludes to the trope of blood-stained sugar noting that "blood is 'neath the fair disguise" of "those luxurious banquet sweets." All three poems were published in the *Genius of Universal Emancipation*, the *Liberator*, and Lundy's collected works. "Oh Press Me Not to Taste Again" and "The Sugar-Plums" were also published in Garrison's collection, *Juvenile Poems for the Use of Free American Children of Every Complexion*.[46]

Chandler's antisugar poetry for children coincided with nonabolitionist debates about the increasing availability of confectionery. The *Moral Reformer*, the *Christian Watchman*, the *Friend*, and the *Boston Recorder* all published jeremiads against the consumption of sugar. The *Colored American* warned parents of the danger of confectionery shops and, through its advertisements, promoted the purchase of free-labor sugar, which suggests the two issues were mutually reinforcing. In an article published in 1837, the anonymous author despaired of parents withholding money from their children to spend in confectionery shops. "Most parents excuse themselves by saying that they don't spend a 'great amount' in confectionery, and don't go to a confectionery shop very often," the author noted. Still, "some men do not go to brothels very often; but then they go; and they go for the same purposes that those do, who go to them every night." Consumption of confectionery, the author concluded, supported "the whole iniquity" regardless of the number of purchases.[47] Some warnings linked the consumption of sugar to drinking. The *Temperance Advocate and Cold Water Magazine*, for example, published the story of Henry Haycroft, who began drinking as a youth. In one scene, Henry is offered a glass of peppermint cordial, which he finds so sweet that he takes "a large quantity." To further emphasize the connection between the peppermint of the alcohol and the peppermint of candy, the author follows Henry and his friend as they stumble to a candy stand to purchase sweets.[48]

Antisugar literature emphasized the dangers of intemperate consumption of sugar. Such tales urged parents, especially mothers, to instill discipline and virtue in their children. Regardless of the motivation—free produce and abolitionism or temperance—abstention from sugar heightened parents and children's awareness of the source of sugar and the consequences of excessive sugar consumption. Antisugar literature written for children trained boys and girls to an ascetic ideal that supported both abolitionism and temperance.

Another means of training children into virtuous behavior combined the discipline of alphabetization and the literacy of abolitionism. Inspired perhaps by Chandler, Hannah Townsend wrote *The Anti-Slavery Alphabet*, which was sold at the Philadelphia Anti-Slavery Fair in 1846 and 1847. *The Anti-Slavery Alphabet* drew on the tradition of alphabet books as a primary method of literacy training. Because women were the primary instructors of the alphabet, nineteenth-century alphabetization was influenced by accepted ideas about domesticity.[49] In *The Anti-Slavery Alphabet*, alphabetization was also shaped by the politics of abolitionism.[50] The letters of the alphabet were printed 1.5 inches high in standard alphabetic order, from the abolitionist to the zealous man, with each letter followed by its quatrain. The text alphabetizes the cultural terrain of slavery including the products of slave labor. For example, "M" represents the northern merchant "Who buys what slaves produce," emphasizing northern complicity in slavery, while "R" and "S" represent the rice and sugar, which the slave "is toiling hard to make." Reinforcing the role of children in abolitionism, the final two quatrains call for children to take an active role:

Y is for Youth—the time for all
    Bravely to war with sin;
And think not it can ever be
    Too early to begin.

Z is a zealous man, sincere,
    Faithful, and just, and true,
An earnest pleader for the slave—
    Will you not be so too?[51]

Townsend leaves her readers with this heroic image of the child abolitionist, the final question urging the reader's participation.[52]

Abolitionist literature was vital to socializing young abolitionists into the cause. In the 1830s, as youth organized antislavery societies and other associations to support abolitionism, many read or sang Chandler's poems at the meetings. For example, a group of Boston girls sang a musical rendition of Chandler's poem, "Peace of Berry," at their society's meeting. Likewise, Susan Paul's Boston Juvenile Choir sang a musical version of Chandler's "The Sugar-Plums."[53] Reading abolitionist literature to their children fit within the ideals of republican motherhood; yet, when poems such as Chandler's "Looking at the Soldiers" rejected traditional forms of patriotism and urged the consumption of only free produce, abolitionist juvenile literature suggested a radical overthrow of American political culture, one which made some women uncomfortable.

While her works appealed to women and children, Chandler's antislavery literature had a broad audience. As a result, she was the most widely read abolitionist author in the antebellum period, placing her in the vanguard of abolitionist and free-produce authors in the United States.[54] In addition to the *Genius of Universal Emancipation*, her poems and essays were published in the *Liberator*, the *Atlantic Souvenir*, the *Saturday Evening Post*, William Lloyd Garrison's *Juvenile Poems for the Use of Free American Children of Every Complexion*, and, in the 1840s, set to music by George W. Clark in his widely published abolitionist songbooks, *The Liberty Minstrel* and *The Harp of Freedom*.[55] Long after her death, abolitionists and boycotters used Chandler's literary works to promote the cause. These publications kept Chandler's works before antislavery supporters throughout the antebellum period regardless of their opinions about moral suasion or political abolitionism. Because her works were also widely anthologized outside the field of abolitionist works, her work reached far beyond the confines of the free-produce and abolitionist movements.[56]

Chandler asserted the morality of free produce and influenced men, women, and children to make the commitment to the cause of the slave by abstaining from the products of slave labor. The economic principles of Heyrick appeared occasionally in Chandler's works; still, Chandler focused on the simple morality of free produce rather than its economic principles. In particular, her emphasis on the morality of domestic consumption, rather than the coercion of market manipulation, deepened the connection between women and children and free produce. Quakers and non-Quakers alike formed free-produce societies in the 1820s and early 1830s in response to the appeals of Chandler and other supporters of abstention. In the 1830s, with the emergence of William Lloyd Garrison and the rise of radical abolitionism, supporters of free produce were confronted with a new challenge: how best to reconcile free produce and abolitionism.

CHAPTER 6

An Abstinence Baptism: American Abolitionism and Free Produce

Supporters of the boycott of slave labor, particularly after 1831, worked to reconcile free-produce principles with radical abolitionism. This effort is evident in the founding of three early antislavery societies. In January 1832, twelve men, including William Lloyd Garrison, gathered in the schoolroom of the African Baptist Church on Beacon Hill in Boston, Massachusetts, to approve and sign the constitutional document of the New England Anti-Slavery Society (NEASS), the first American association committed to the immediate abolition of slavery. The men did not include a free-produce statement in the constitution of the NEASS.[1] Eight months later, the women of Lenawee County, Michigan, met at the Friends meeting house near the Raisin River, where under the leadership of Elizabeth Margaret Chandler, they formed the Logan Female Anti-Slavery Society. Planning to meet monthly, the women pledged to abstain from "slave raised articles as much as possible."[2] In Boston, the following year, twelve women organized the Boston Female Anti-Slavery Society (BFASS), pledging their commitment to the immediate abolition of slavery. Their constitutional document did not mention free produce. In a subsequent annual report, however, the women affirmed their preference for "the product[s] of free labor."[3]

These three organizations reflect the variety of responses to free produce by the activists who joined the movement for the immediate abolition of slavery in the 1830s. Abolitionists who boycotted slave-labor goods asserted the importance of ideological consistency. Mary Grew, a member of the Philadelphia Female Anti-Slavery Society, described abstention as an "imperious" duty, which if neglected would "subject abolitionists to the charge of inconsistency, and disqualify them for efficiently promulgating their principles." Grew claimed free produce to be "among the most available and powerful means of promoting the great cause of emancipation."[4] Free produce encouraged consumers to identify with the enslaved, thereby supporting the Garrisonian emphasis on moral suasion and racial equality. Yet many abolitionists, including Garrison, agreed with the American abolitionist Theodore Weld who described free produce as a "collateral principle," one that would be acted on "*spontaneously*, if it be *first* anchored upon the main principle" of immediatism.[5] For American supporters of the boycott, the challenge in the 1830s was to broaden the appeal of free produce, particularly beyond the sectarian limits of the Society of Friends, to create a mass movement against the products of slave labor.

There were, however, significant obstacles to creating and sustaining such a broadly based movement. For many Quakers, who had just witnessed deep and bitter divisions among Friends, the abolitionist movement of the 1830s threatened similar disruptions in American society, particularly as opposition to abolitionism spread. As a result, many Quakers retreated from both organized free produce and antislavery. Moreover, convincing Garrison and like-minded abolitionists to continue their support of free produce, in the face of strident and often violent opposition to abolitionism, proved difficult. Garrison and his supporters could hardly be faulted for asking why abolitionists should urge abstinence when there was so much else to do. Garrison came to oppose free produce, in part, because free-labor goods were difficult to secure, leading abolitionist consumers to "fritter away great energies & respectable powers in controversies about yards of cotton-cloth & pounds of sugar," as the Garrisonian Samuel J. May noted.[6] Additionally, in this period, the free-produce movement, which had garnered support from both conservative and radical women, became entangled in debates about women's role in the abolitionist movement. Finally, free produce carried with it the taint of colonization. Quaker Benjamin Lundy, as we have seen, explored colonization opportunities in Texas and Haiti as possible sources for free-labor goods; however, Lundy did not support the American Colonization Society. The racist, anti-black attitudes of the ACS and its supporters tainted colonization schemes such as those promoted by Lundy. Still, free-produce activists worked hard to overcome these obstacles to create a dynamic, sustainable national free-produce community. Throughout the 1830s, a core group of activists, many of them Quakers, continued to assert free produce as a central tenet of abolitionism even as they struggled to reconcile free produce with Garrisonian immediatism.

Antislavery and Free Produce

The organization of the New England Anti-Slavery Society and especially the establishment of the American Anti-Slavery Society the following year signaled an important shift in the American abolitionist movement, one that had a profound effect on the free-produce movement in the 1830s. The AASS organized in December 1833 when an interracial group of abolitionists from nine states gathered in Philadelphia for the purpose of establishing a national organization. Among the delegates to the founding convention were several prominent black abolitionists, including Robert Purvis (founder of the Colored Free Produce Society) and James McCrummell. The official delegates and signatories were men, but there were at least eight women present, including Hicksite Quakers Lucretia Mott, Lydia White, and Esther Moore, and Orthodox Quaker Sidney Ann Lewis, sister-in-law of Enoch Lewis. Garrison and a committee of other delegates wrote the AASS's Declaration of Sentiments. Mott, however, suggested important revisions to the final document, which emphasized the importance of moral suasion, rejected compensated emancipation, and urged support for free produce.[7] The Declaration of Sentiments also reflected, in its support of free labor, the significant presence of Quaker delegates and an attempt to integrate free produce with abolitionism. Adoption of the Declaration of Sentiments affirmed supporters' break with earlier forms of antislavery and their commitment to the immediate abolition of slavery. This new form of immediatism originated in the anticolonization movement and was further refined by the arguments of Heyrick. While Heyrick defined immediatism as direct economic action, Garrison defined immediatism in terms of moral suasion. In the pages of the *Liberator*, which he started publishing in 1831, Garrison denounced slavery as a sin and all slaveholders as sinners, condemned the ACS, and demanded the immediate abolition of slavery. Reborn as an immediatist, Garrison attacked racial prejudice and fought for racial equality. By the time delegates met in 1832 to form the NEASS, Garrison had earned a reputation for his unequivocal attacks on colonization, his advocacy of immediatism, and his willingness to work with black abolitionists.[8]

Four days after delegates organized the AASS, the women who were present at that meeting gathered to organize the Philadelphia Female Anti-Slavery

Society. Lucretia Mott asked James McCrummell to assist. McCrummell, who had signed the Declaration of Sentiments, was a member of Philadelphia's black elite and the husband of Sarah McCrummell, who was appointed to the committee charged with drafting the constitution for the PFASS. The committee submitted a draft of the constitution on December 14. In January, the group revised the constitution, adding an additional article pledging to give preference to free-labor goods "at all times and on all occasions." The membership of the PFASS eventually exceeded two hundred; however, a core group ran the society and determined its direction.[9] Like British female antislavery societies, the PFASS gave structure to women's activism, sponsoring public addresses by abolitionists, purchasing and distributing antislavery literature, raising funds, and gathering signatures for petitions to Congress.[10] The women of the PFASS pledged to do all they could to eliminate prejudice and to promote racial uplift, a position that reflected the integrated membership of the organization. PFASS members worked together on a number of projects to aid the black community, including the improvement of education for blacks in Philadelphia.[11] Free produce also figured prominently in women's activities. The PFASS maintained an active correspondence with other antislavery societies about free-labor goods and served as an important source of information about the free produce movement.[12]

The PFASS, the Logan Female Anti-Slavery Society, and the Boston Female Anti-Slavery Society were among the more than 140 female antislavery societies established in the 1830s. Some of these societies, such as the Providence (Rhode Island) Female Anti-Slavery Society outlined their commitment to free produce in their organizing documents whereas others, such as the Salem Female Anti-Slavery Society (1832) and the Ladies' New-York City Anti-Slavery Society (1835), did not.[13] Female antislavery societies, particularly those that gave explicit support to free produce, encouraged women who boycotted slave-labor goods. While free produce was an extension of women's domestic role, boycotting slave-labor goods could lead to awkward social encounters, as Massachusetts abolitionist Deborah Weston discovered in 1836. Weston complained that free-produce principles had prevented her from eating "almost everything good" while visiting in New Bedford. Still, she consoled herself with the hope that she had embarrassed her hostess into switching to free-labor goods. In another incident, the confrontation was much more painful. Mary Ann, a young woman who visited Weston's sister Ann in Groton, was humiliated when she refused slave-labor goods while visiting at "Dr. Cutter's." As Anne Weston explained, "on declining slave labour, some how or other the mine exploded." Too upset to describe the incident in detail, Mary Ann pleaded with Anne not to press for details: " 'for if I talk I shall get to crying.' " Anne comforted the young woman and offered her free-labor cake and assured her "the storm would blow over."[14] Meeting regularly with those who shared their free-produce principles comforted and strengthened women like Deborah, Anne, and Mary Ann.

In mid-1836, this idea of shared values and community led antislavery women in Boston, Philadelphia, and New York to consider a national association of women's antislavery societies, similar to the American Anti-Slavery Society. The Boston Female Anti-Slavery Society proposed establishing an executive committee of female abolitionists to better coordinate the work of female antislavery activists throughout the United States.[15] New York women also supported the idea of an executive committee, preferring an organization that united women, rather than an integrated association to unite women and men. Such a female association, they believed, would better coordinate the arduous work of gathering signatures on petitions without violating accepted gender norms. The women of the PFASS, however, preferred to seek recognition of female delegates to the national and state meetings of the male associations. In a compromise measure, in January 1837, the Boston women called for a general meeting of all female abolitionists, rather than form an executive committee, believing "the united wisdoms of *all* the societies" might better serve the development of a plan of cooperation among women's antislavery societies.[16] American abolitionist women held three annual national meetings in New York (1837) and Philadelphia (1838 and 1839). Although many of the women involved in these associations had corresponded for years, these national meetings provided them an opportunity to meet face to face.

At each of the three conventions, the female delegates endorsed free produce. In 1837, delegates approved Lucretia Mott's free-produce resolution. Purchasing slave-labor products continued southern slavery, Mott noted; therefore, it was the duty of abolitionists to avoid "this unrighteous participation" in the consumption of slave produce.[17] Again, in 1838 and 1839, delegates passed free-produce resolutions. In 1838, Thankful Southwick, a member of the BFASS, claimed it was the duty of female abolitionists "to make the *most vigorous efforts* to procure for the use of their families the products of *free labor*." Southwick's resolution emphasized women's leadership in advancing the cause of free produce. Abby Kelley of the Female Anti-Slavery Society of Lynn, Massachusetts, introduced a resolution that noted the support northern "social and commercial intercourse" gave to "slaveholding communities."[18] In 1839, delegates endorsed a resolution introduced by

BFASS founder Martha Ball who urged women to refuse "participation in the sin" and to maintain "a pure example." During the subsequent discussion, radical members of the convention, including Lucretia Mott, encouraged women to "regard slave labor produce as the fruits of the labor of our own children, brothers, and sisters, and from such a view decide on the propriety of using it." In doing so, Mott and others promoted free produce as an act of radical identification with the slave, embracing identification with African Americans even as many abolitionists retreated from racial equality in the face of violent protests by antiabolitionist mobs.[19]

Of the resolutions passed by the women at these conventions, the most controversial revolved around issues of gender and race. At the first convention, in May 1837, Angelina Grimké of the Philadelphia Female Anti-Slavery Society challenged women to move beyond traditional religious and cultural ideas about gender. Grimké urged women to recognize that "certain rights and duties are common to all moral beings." She described women's reform work as a "duty" that was within the "province" of woman's sphere. Woman, Grimké argued, must "do all that she can by her voice, and her pen, and her purse, and the influence of her example" to abolish slavery. After much discussion, the resolution was adopted; however, twelve women, most of them from New York, dissented and requested their names be listed in the proceedings as doing so. Abolitionist and author Lydia Maria Child proposed a resolution rebuking evangelical associations that accepted contributions from slaveholders. Three of the twelve women who had refused to approve Grimké's resolution also dissented from Child's resolution.[20]

Angelina and Sarah Grimké were early advocates of free produce as well women's equality. Natives of South Carolina, the sisters had migrated north to escape the influence of slavery. The Grimkés joined the Society of Friends and the PFASS. Both women were outspoken supporters of free produce, maintaining their personal boycott until the Civil War.[21] When Angelina wed abolitionist Theodore Weld in 1838, the couple transformed the event into a testimonial to their antislavery views. In addition to an interracial guest list, the couple hired a black confectioner to make a wedding cake of free-labor sugar.[22] In 1837, the Grimkés, at the invitation of the American Anti-Slavery Society, traveled the abolitionist lecture circuit. Their popularity soon drew mixed-gender audiences. In June 1837, the General Association of Massachusetts Congregational Churches met to discuss the sisters' flagrant violation of gender norms. Three years earlier, in 1834, Congregationalist ministers in Boston had voted by a large majority to refuse to read abolitionist meeting notices from the pulpit. In 1836, the ministers passed a resolution against "itinerant agents" speaking in churches without the consent of the pastors and the ecclesiastical bodies. The sisters' antislavery lectures to mixed-gender audiences provided another opportunity for the Congregationalists to issue a harsh rebuke against antislavery lecturers, particularly women. Though the pastoral letter does not specifically identify the Grimkés, they were clearly the focus of the ministers' concerns that women had assumed "the place and tone of man as a public reformer."[23]

In contrast to the lively debates about gender at the 1837 convention and in the wake of the Congregational rebuke of the Grimkés, discussions of women's role at the 1838 and 1839 conventions were much more restrained. The resolutions introduced in 1838 tapped into gender-specific ideas about women's appropriate role and, as a result, generated little discussion. The delegates resolved that "one of the most appropriate fields of exertion of the influence of woman" was abolitionism. Additional resolutions by abolitionists Abigail Ordway (Massachusetts) and Mary Grew (Pennsylvania) affirmed that woman's responsibility to act against slavery was rooted in her role as a mother and a Christian.[24] In 1839, the delegates consciously avoided the issue of women's rights, a strategy made easier by the Grimkés' absence from the convention that year.[25]

Race also figured prominently at the women's conventions. In 1837, Angelina Grimké presented a resolution against racial prejudice, calling on women to "mingle with our oppressed brethren" and "to act out the principles of Christian equality by associating with them as though the color of the skin was of no . . . consequence." At the 1838 convention, Angelina's sister Sarah Grimké's resolution against race prejudice sparked strong opinions on either side of the debate. Grimké claimed that abolitionists had a duty to "identify themselves with these oppressed Americans by sitting with them in places of worship, by appearing with them in our streets, by giving them our countenance in steam-boats and stages, by visiting them at their homes and encouraging them to visit us, receiving them as we do our white fellow citizens." Several delegates voted against the resolution claiming it would hinder rather than help the abolitionist cause. After the convention, several delegates attempted to remove the resolution from the convention transcription. Although the convention proceedings do not provide an explanation for these actions, the women may have acted out of racial prejudice, or fear of antiabolitionist mobs like those that burned Pennsylvania Hall, in 1838, during the second convention.[26]

Thankful Southwick and Martha Ball each introduced free-produce resolutions at the women's antislavery conventions; yet the two women held different views about women's abolitionist activity. Southwick was proud of the Boston Female Anti-Slavery Society's success in petitioning Congress and running an annual antislavery fair. Southwick, as well as other women, including Lucretia Mott and the Grimké sisters, believed women and men shared the same rights and duties when it came to political questions such as slavery. In contrast, Ball and like-minded women affirmed the tenets of domesticity. For Ball, a well-ordered society, like a well-ordered household, was arranged around the natural distinction between the sexes. While conservative women, such as Ball, used these ideas to argue for women's participation in reform movements, that activism did not translate into arguments for women's equality. Increasingly, in the late 1830s, women who supported free produce and abolitionism linked the movements to more radical ideas about gender and race. As a result, Martha Ball and other conservative women retreated into reform work that affirmed the maternal and domestic roles of women, consciously avoiding political issues such as women's rights.[27] Although Ball agreed with Angelina Grimké that it was "the province of woman, to plead the cause of the oppressed," she disagreed with the implications of Grimké's argument that woman should "no longer remain satisfied in the circumscribed limits with which corrupt custom and a perverted application of Scripture have encircled her."[28] When the Congregational ministers reprimanded the Grimké sisters in 1837, several female antislavery societies, including the Buckingham Female Anti-Slavery Society of Pennsylvania, expressed their support of the sisters. In a letter that echoed the moral resolve of Elizabeth Heyrick, the Buckingham women reminded the Grimkés that moral right mattered more than masculine custom: "Whatever is right must be expedient. . . . Let then, the right be done tho' all the associations of men be dissolved, and their glory laid low in the dust."[29] Regardless of the consequences, the Buckingham women noted, women must act on their beliefs.

The women of the Buckingham group linked radical ideas about gender and political action to the boycott of slave labor. In a letter to the Philadelphia Female Anti-Slavery Society in August 1837, the women of the Buckingham Female Anti-Slavery Society asserted the duty of abolitionists to abstain from slave-labor products and lamented the lack of free-labor goods. Anti-slavery societies, they argued, had to become in practice free-produce societies: "There are now about 1100 Anti-Slavery Societies in the United States, embracing at least 100,000 members; now if these societies would individually, as well as collectively, use their influence to encourage the labor of free men, to the exclusion of that of slaves, can any one doubt that such influence would have a most salutary effect in promoting a market for free products." The Buckingham women urged opponents of free produce to imagine those "dear to them . . . writhing beneath the gory lash of a cruel task-master or loaded and bowed down with the galling chains of slavery." In addition to applying "moral bearing" to "political action," women should merge the moral and the political in daily activities: "Take [your principles] also to the grocers, and dry-goods store, to the tables of our friends, and into every social circle and thus make them have a moral bearing on the social and commercial interests of the whole community." Abstention "should not breathe . . . forth in words only, but interweave [in] every action of our lives."[30] In their vision of free produce, the Buckingham women suggested a radical reordering of American society, one that affected not only the domestic world of women but the public realm of politics and economics as well. For the Buckingham women, free produce formed the core of equal rights for all.

Black abolitionists' support of free produce made similar connections between the boycott of slave labor and equal rights. In 1827, in his famous anticolonization letter, Richard Allen, founder of the African Methodist Episcopal Church, criticized the American Colonization Society and claimed African colonization denied black claims to American citizenship. In language reminiscent of the first slave-sugar boycott, Allen reasserted blacks' right to citizenship: "This land which we have watered with our tears and our blood is now our mother country." Rather than contamination of domestic goods, African blood, sweat, and tears became the means by which blacks would claim civil and political rights.[31] David Walker, in his 1829 *Appeal to the Coloured Citizens of the World*, reprinted Allen's letter verbatim before elaborating on Allen's metaphor of blood-stained soil. "America is more our country, than it is the whites," Walker wrote. "We have enriched it with our blood and tears. The greatest riches in all America have arisen from our blood and tears:—and will they drive us from our property and homes, which we have earned with our blood?"[32] In a July 4, 1830, speech, black minister Peter Williams connected black service during the Revolutionary War to black toil on the land as markers of citizenship: "We are natives of this country . . . not a few of our fathers suffered and bled to purchase its independence . . . we have toiled to cultivate it, and to raise it to its present prosperous condition; we ask only to share equal privileges with those who come from distant lands to enjoy the fruits of our labour."[33] Boycotting slave-labor goods would end the theft of African labor and restore to the enslaved the fruits of their labor.

For black abolitionists, free produce and racial uplift were inextricably joined; as a result, black abolitionists often integrated support for the boycott of slave labor with other reform activities. In the early 1830s, in a series of conventions, black abolitionists passed resolutions in support of free produce and encouraged moral reform and economic independence. In 1833, delegates approved a resolution supporting the establishment of free-labor stores by black entrepreneurs. The following year, black businessman William Whipper established a free-labor and temperance grocery store next door to Bethel Church in Philadelphia. In this same period, in an attempt to improve the supply of free-labor goods, the Colored Free Produce Society of Pennsylvania offered premiums above the market price for rice produced by free labor. At the fifth convention in 1835, delegates described free produce as "the duty of every *lover of freedom*." Delegates also considered a report from France that sugar had been successfully manufactured from the beet root. Members were asked to explore the potential for producing beet sugar in the United States and "to report to the next convention, the result of their efforts."[34] In 1836, black abolitionists in Philadelphia organized the American Moral Reform Society, adopting the principles of education, temperance, economy, and universal liberty. In an "Address to the Colored Churches in the Free States," the society criticized free blacks who condemned slavery yet continued to purchase slave-labor goods.[35] Connecting the economic activities of free blacks to slave labor, black abolitionists asserted the importance of racial solidarity and ideological consistency. In 1838, black abolitionists in New York celebrated the end of slavery in the British Empire in an event supplied with free-labor goods.[36] For black abolitionists, abolishing the market for slave-labor goods was critical to the fight for emancipation and racial equality.

In the 1830s, the male-only or integrated (by gender or race) antislavery societies established by men at the local and regional level also debated the relationship between free produce and abolitionism. The Clarkson Anti-Slavery Society, organized in 1832 by residents of Lancaster and Chester Counties, Pennsylvania, asked its members, "Is it consistent with the principles of Abolitionists, to use the products of slave labor?"[37] In 1837, at the second annual meeting of the East Fallowfield Anti-Slavery Society, supporters passed a free-produce resolution. The Schuylkill Township Anti-Slavery Society adopted a similar measure the following year.[38] Also, in 1838, members of the East Fallowfield, Clarkson, and Schuylkill Anti-Slavery Societies, as well as other groups such as the Kennett and West Chester Anti-Slavery Societies, met in Philadelphia to discuss free produce at the Requited Labor Convention.[39] Despite this apparent agreement on the issue of free produce, many of these same societies struggled with the relationship between free produce and abolitionism. For example, in 1837, the Clarkson Anti-Slavery Society failed to pass a resolution calling for "total abstinence" from slave-labor products.[40] Such discussions were not limited to the local level.

Although free produce had been included in the American Anti-Slavery Society's Declaration of Sentiments, supporters and opponents continued to debate the role of free produce in the abolitionist movement, particularly at the national level. In 1836, William Jay, son of the famous jurist John Jay, protested the passage of New York abolitionist Gerrit Smith's free-produce resolution at the society's annual meeting. Jay believed free produce was an individual principle, which should be promoted through free-produce societies and not through the national antislavery society: "Abolitionists who embrace this doctrine have an unquestionable right to maintain and defend it *on their own responsibility*, and to form Societies avowing it in their constitutions; but they have no right to use the meetings, the periodicals, or the funds of the American Society for the purpose of propagating it." In a letter to the *Liberator*, Smith defended his action, claiming he had substituted a "far milder Resolution" than the one introduced by abolitionist Charles Stuart, who was described by Smith as "a man, who never consents to sacrifice a hair's breadth of principle." Smith justified his support of free produce: "I have long thought, that there is no single thing, which abolitionists could do, that would contribute so far to the abolition of slavery, as their abstinence from the products of slave labor." Smith believed the self-denying example of 100,000 boycotters "would carry more conviction to the minds of slaveholders of the truth and power of antislavery doctrines and of the sincerity with which they are held, than all the testimony of types and *pens*." The following year, at the fourth annual meeting of the AASS in May 1837, Stuart tried once again to introduce the issue of free produce, but the resolution "was laid upon the table, and subsequently, indefinitely postponed." Likewise, in 1838, a free-produce resolution was considered but not acted on.[41] Likely, Garrison's intervention prevented action in support of free produce at the annual AASS meetings.[42]

Garrison's dismissal of free produce frustrated abolitionist consumers like Smith. It is unclear exactly when Garrison rejected free produce as an antislavery tactic; however, articles in the *Liberator* suggest his disaffection developed in the mid to late 1830s. In 1835, for example, Garrison published a letter he received from Rowland T. Robinson, a Vermont Quaker and supporter of free produce, encouraging Garrison to give "more than a mere recommendation" to abstain from slave-labor products.[43] Gerrit Smith, in his defense of free produce, called on Garrison "to increase the power and efficacy of your writings and of your uncompromising integrity and fearless vindication of the truth, by your thorough espousal of the doctrine of abstinence from the products of slave labor."[44] In a letter to British abolitionist Elizabeth Pease in August 1839, Angelina Grimké lamented Garrison's rejection of free produce "because the weight of his example & his influence are very extensive."[45] Still, the presence of free-produce supporters, such as Lucretia Mott, at the annual AASS meetings meant free produce would come up for discussion even if Garrison did not support the boycott. For example, at the twentieth anniversary of the AASS in 1853, Mott "urged attention" to the Declaration of Sentiments, "which relates to our giving preference to the products of *free labor* over those of *slave labor*."[46]

In the 1830s, as abolitionists formed antislavery societies to promote the immediate abolition of slavery, men and women such as Jay, Smith, Garrison, and Mott worked to reconcile free produce with radical abolitionism. Traditionally, free produce was associated with the Quakers. In the 1820s, free produce became closely associated with colonization schemes through the activism of Benjamin Lundy who sought opportunities for free blacks in Texas and in Haiti. As a result, for many abolitionists in the 1830s, free produce was associated with the strategies and tactics of an outmoded form of antislavery activism. Still, among the more radical, often women and black abolitionists, free produce represented an absolute moral position, one that supported individual identification with enslaved blacks. Even after Garrison distanced himself from free produce, many Garrisonian abolitionists continued to assert the importance of the boycott of slave-labor goods. This ongoing connection to radical abolitionism worried many Quakers who struggled to define the relationship between free produce and the Society of Friends.

Quakers

Although free produce figured prominently in Elias Hicks's conflict with Quaker elders, Quakers on either side of the schism continued to abstain from slave-labor goods. In the 1830s, Friends' participation in free produce was influenced by internal conflicts among Hicksite and Orthodox Quakers and by external events, particularly the rise of radical abolitionism. Friends' views of free produce and abolitionism were shaped by the schism of 1827–28, which opened to reinterpretation every fundamental belief and practice of Friends. Friends' participation in abolitionism was influenced by the development of immediatism. Immediatist abolitionists sought support from Quakers. Yet most Quakers were wary of the radical abolitionist movement. Garrison denounced slaveholders and advocated disunion, activities which violated Friends' testimonies about the inward light and peace. Indeed, for most Quakers, Garrison sounded more like Benjamin Lay than John Woolman. Moreover, the outspoken and often violent antiabolitionist response to Garrisonian radicalism, as well as opposition from Quaker meetings, discouraged most Friends from participating in abolitionism. In many ways, Friends' participation in free produce followed a similar trajectory. Free produce retained its Quaker core while responding to the developments in the abolitionist movement. Increasingly, supporters of the boycott asserted the economic argument of free produce, namely that support for free produce would force slaveholders to emancipate their slaves and to use free labor. Such arguments reflected criticism from abolitionists who questioned the efficacy of boycotting slave-labor goods. Similarly, supporters used Quakers' moral argument for free produce to demand consumers identify with the enslaved and to seek racial equality, core tenets of the abolitionist movement. For Quakers in the 1830s, the free-produce movement was marked by conflicting demands to retain traditional free-produce activism and to align free produce with radical abolitionism.[47]

Quakers who participated in the abolitionist movement risked being denounced as a radical abolitionist. Consider, for example, the petition of Caln Quarterly Meeting (Hicksite). In November 1835, members of Caln Quarterly Meeting (Hicksite) in Chester County, Pennsylvania, drew up a petition to the U.S. Senate praying for the abolition of slavery in the District of Columbia. The Caln petition arrived in January 1836 as the Senate was debating two antislavery petitions from Ohio. Senator James Buchanan of Pennsylvania presented the Caln petition, asking the Senate accept the petition but reject the attached prayer. South Carolina Senator John C. Calhoun reacted strongly against the Ohio and Pennsylvania petitions. Though the Quaker petition was more respectfully worded, Calhoun claimed "the same principles were embodied in [both petitions], and the innuendoes conveyed [in the Quaker petition] were as far from being acceptable as the barefaced insolence" of the Ohio petitions.[48] Defenders of the Quaker petition made a clear distinction between Quakers and abolitionists. New Jersey Senator Garrett Wall demanded the Caln petition be heard. The Caln petition, Wall claimed, did not "come from the great laboratory of abolition *incendiarism*. It [did] not spring from the *heated* atmosphere produced by the contention of men struggling for political power; nor [did] it come from men, who under pretence of conscience, cloak worldly, selfish, or unholy designs." Friends were not seeking "to destroy the constitution or endanger the peace and permanency of the Union." Using "the calm, mild, and dispassionate voice of *reason*," Wall said the Caln petitioners had exercised their political rights in a manner consistent with the principles of the Constitution and the discipline of their society.[49] Opponents of the Quaker petition, however, condemned the Society of Friends for agitating the slavery question. On March 9, the Senate voted to receive the Quaker petition and to reject the petitioners' prayer. Afterward the Senate adopted the rule to lay all antislavery petitions on the table, a practice that had the same practical effect as the gag rule passed in the House of Representatives.[50]

Reaction to the Caln petition convinced some Quakers that while they might use their voices as members of the Society of Friends to speak out against slavery, they risked receiving the same treatment as radical abolitionists. In a comparison of the abolitionist and the colonizationist, the *Friend* noted that Quakers must remain in a state of "forbearance"; otherwise, they were likely to "[sow] the seeds of disagreement and discord." After the Caln controversy, the *Friend* warned against petitions to Congress and suggested that Friends' actions "in behalf of oppressed humanity, ought ever to be characterized by mildness, by prudence, by a proper regard to fitness as to the time and the occasion."[51] In the 1830s, Orthodox and Hicksite meetings warned Friends against joining antislavery societies. Philadelphia Yearly Meeting (Hicksite) refused to take any action as a corporate body other than to encourage its members "to embrace every right opening, to maintain & exalt our righteous testimony against slavery."[52] Farmington Quarterly Meeting (Orthodox) proposed New York Yearly Meeting (Orthodox) prepare a petition to Congress for members of subordinate meetings to sign, but this suggestion was not adopted by the Yearly Meeting.[53] In September 1839, members of the Meeting for Sufferings, Philadelphia Yearly Meeting (Orthodox), noted their desire to "stand open, individually and collectively, to the tendering influences of that Spirit which breathes peace on earth and good will to men . . . [and] be prepared to take such measures as Divine Wisdom may point out to clear our own hands and to espouse [the slaves'] cause whenever the way may clearly present."[54] Similarly, Quaker meetings were cautious in their admonitions about free produce, urging support for free produce but not making it a point of discipline. For example, the Hicksite meetings in New York (1837) and Philadelphia (1839) advised against the use of slave produce. Also, in 1839, Philadelphia Yearly Meeting (Hicksite), in response to the sixth query asking Friends to remain clear of prize goods among other things, noted that some members "consider the use of slave goods . . . a departure." Other Quakers were less circumspect in their support of free produce. In the early 1840s, several Quaker meetings, including Farmington Quarterly Meeting (Orthodox) and New York Yearly Meeting (Orthodox), issued statements on free produce while other meetings, such as Genesee Yearly Meeting and Indiana Yearly Meeting of Anti-Slavery Friends, made abstention from slave-labor goods a point of discipline.[55]

As a traditional Quaker practice, free produce provided a seemingly apolitical solution for Quakers who wished to pursue what one *Friend* editorialist described as a "noiseless path" while promoting the "general good." Friends could provide an effective example by remaining aloof from the passions of American social and political life. As the writer explained, Friends' "examples of uprightness and religious stability give a useful tone wherever they exist, and when commotions arise, they are peculiarly valuable, in drawing those who are in danger of being swept away by the various currents, which rush hither and thither, to enquire what it is, which makes such unmoved, in the midst of storm and distress."[56] Some Quakers urged Friends against associating with non-Friends in reform associations. Friends, as one writer noted, "are more likely to advance the cause by acting very much alone." Citing Anthony Benezet and John Woolman (but not Elias Hicks) as useful examples, the author suggested Friends could maintain their traditional antislavery principles in the midst of the chaos created by Garrisonian abolitionism only by remaining apart from the secular movement.[57]

Quakers' reluctance to take collective measures against slavery led Philadelphia Hicksites to organize the Association of Friends for Advocating the Cause of the Slave, and Improving the Condition of the Free People of Colour in May 1837. The group had more than one hundred charter members. Organized as a Quaker antislavery society, the association was an attempt by Friends to provide their co-religionists an opportunity to work within the abolitionist movement without joining secular societies. However, the presence of Quaker abolitionists James and Lucretia Mott, Caleb Clothier, Daniell Neal, Daniel Miller Jr., and Emmor Kimber gave the organization a decidedly abolitionist slant. Though not strictly a free-produce association, the group made abstention a central tenet of their activism. The association created the Committee on Requited Labor, which met for the first time on September 12, 1837. Caleb Clothier, Lydia White, Priscilla Hensey, and William C. Betts formed the core of the committee. The Committee on Requited Labor compiled a list of free-labor grocers, supported the American Free Produce Association after its establishment in 1838, and wrote addresses for the association.[58] Most likely the committee was responsible for the pamphlet, *An Address to the Members of the Religious Society of Friends, on the Propriety of Abstaining from the Use of the Produce of Slave Labour,* issued by the association in its first year. In the *Address,* the association urged Friends to consider the issue of abstinence and adopt it as part of their abolitionist testimony. According to the *Address,* Quaker discipline prohibited the use of or trade in prize goods, including the products of slave labor. The *Address* also referred to the antislavery testimony of John Woolman and Elias Hicks, reminding Friends of their collective tradition of antislavery testimony. Abstention from the products of slave labor purified the individual and the community from the stain of slavery and delivered slaves from oppression by choking off demand for the products of forced labor.[59] The association published two other pamphlets in 1838: one appealing to women and the other a general statement on the evils of slavery.[60] In 1840, the association changed its name to the Association for Promoting the Abolition of Slavery. The association provided an outlet for Quakers' abolitionist energy. Still, the organization was controversial. Many in the Philadelphia Yearly Meeting (Hicksite) objected to it while others argued the association did not go far enough in its abolitionist work.[61]

In 1839, Charles Marriott of New York Yearly Meeting (Hicksite) helped organize the New York Association of Friends for the Relief of those Held in Slavery and the Improvement of Free People of Color, an association most likely modeled after the Philadelphia association. In the 1830s and early 1840s, Marriott stood at the epicenter of debates about Friends' relationship with the antislavery movement. Born in England in 1782, Marriott came to America in 1801 with his parents and sisters. A member of Hudson Monthly Meeting, Marriott served on the Meeting for Sufferings, New York Yearly Meeting. After the schism, Marriott joined with the Hicksites. In the 1830s, Marriott published articles in the *Genius of Universal Emancipation* and the *Liberator*.[62] In 1835, he published an address on the duty of abstinence from slave-labor goods. Marriott challenged the traditional Quaker argument that antislavery activism was an attempt *"to do good in our own wills"* and, therefore, contrary to the Quaker view that Friends should wait on the prompting of the inward light. Instead, Marriott asked, "Would it not be as charitable, and more useful to inquire what our reward will be, for persisting *to do evil in our own wills.* And, whether, when our understandings are *convinced*, if it be not presumptuous to ask a further extension of Divine revelation, ere we consent to cease to oppress our fellow-creatures." Marriott claimed nothing but Quaker unfaithfulness had prevented incorporation into the discipline an article requiring abstention from the products of slave labor. Friends, he warned, must actively pursue their antislavery testimony or forgo any further witness against slavery. "What is morally wrong can never be religiously right," Marriott concluded. He submitted the tract to the Meeting for Sufferings, New York Yearly Meeting, for publication, but the group rejected it, leaving Marriott to proceed on his own responsibility.[63] Despite this setback, Marriott continued to work within the structure of the Society of Friends, refusing to join any organized antislavery societies, for example, because of Friends' admonitions against such participation. Finally, in 1840,

Marriott joined the American Anti-Slavery Society.[64] That same year, Marriott signed the *Address*, published by the New York Association of Friends, which challenged conservative Friends' objections to participation in the wider antislavery movement. Consistent with his earlier statements, Marriott insisted Friends had a moral responsibility to oppose slavery by every available means.[65] Conservative Quakers disagreed. In 1842, Marriott was disowned.[66]

By the late 1830s, slavery was for many Friends *the* defining issue. Increasingly, Friends judged one another not by their adherence to Quaker tenets, such as plainness but instead by how consistently they advocated the cause of the slave. Collectively, Quaker meetings sought what one historian calls "a moderate tone of moral suasion."[67] Many meetings such as New York Yearly Meeting (Orthodox) made public statements against slavery, but cautioned members against getting caught up in the excitement of the radical abolitionist movement.[68] Abstention from slave-labor products urged Friends to high levels of personal morality and responsibility rather than active involvement in non-Quaker reform societies. Moreover, abstention might succeed in rendering slavery uneconomical, ultimately leading to its abolition. And if free produce did not succeed in abolishing slavery, Friends had at least purified themselves and their community from the taint of slavery.[69] As long as free produce remained an individual, moderate antislavery statement, it was unobtrusive enough for most Quakers to adopt the practice. When Quakers began to organize with non-Quakers in free-produce and antislavery associations, however, abstention increasingly took on the radical tone of Garrisonian abolitionism.

Juvenile Antislavery Societies

In addition to the various free-produce and antislavery societies formed by men and women, Quaker and non-Quaker, the 1830s also witnessed the development of juvenile antislavery. Although the editor of the *Slave's Friend* credited the publication with inspiring the creation of juvenile abolitionist groups, juvenile antislavery societies actually predated publication of the newspaper, as evidenced by a report in the *Liberator*, in December 1835, from the newly formed Providence Juvenile Anti-Slavery Society. The young women reported reading antislavery literature and raising funds for the cause through the solicitation of donations and the sale of handmade items. The Providence group soon opened their membership to include young black women eventually calling themselves a "sugar-plum society," which most likely referenced their pledge to abstain from slave-grown sugar.[70] In 1836, young abolitionists in New York organized the Chatham Street Chapel Juvenile Anti-Slavery Society, which served as an auxiliary society to the New York City Anti-Slavery Society. The juvenile abolitionists invited New York abolitionist Lewis Tappan to address their first meeting.[71] That same year, young men in Philadelphia formed the Junior Anti-Slavery Society of Pennsylvania.[72] By the late 1830s, there were groups in Richmond, Ohio; Pawtucket, Rhode Island; Portland, Maine; and Newark, Patterson, and Whippany, New Jersey, as well as least three juvenile societies in New York City.[73] In 1838, African American juvenile societies were established in Troy, Carlisle, Pittsburgh, and Providence. The Pittsburgh society, for example, was established in July 1838 as a "cent a week" society. By 1839, the group had grown to forty members and had raised money to support the *Colored American*, the weekly published by black minister and abolitionist Samuel Cornish.[74]

Like adult antislavery societies, juvenile associations promoted the free-produce movement. In January 1837, for example, the Junior Anti-Slavery Society invited abolitionist printer Lewis C. Gunn to address the group on the preselected discussion question: "Is it consistent with the principles of abolition to partake of the produce of slave labor?" After Gunn's address, the group resolved to give preference to free-labor produce and abstain "as far as practicable" from slave-labor produce. The following January, the group renewed their commitment to free produce. Despite repeated resolutions against slave-labor produce, however, the group lamented that more members had not made the commitment.[75] In Boston, a female juvenile antislavery society boycotted the products of slavery and raised funds for the cause. In August 1837, the young women "had quite a discussion on self-denial and on the use of sugar and butter and at last came to the conclusion that we would deny ourselves of something so as to contribute one cent weekly to the society."[76] In New York, R. G. Williams addressed the initial gathering of the Juvenile Anti-Slavery Society. He encouraged the children to sacrifice on behalf of the slave. "When you feel a desire to spend your money for confectionery, or any unnecessary thing to eat or drink," Williams said, "think of the thousands of poor slave children who are naked, hungry, ignorant, whipped and destitute of the good things you enjoy." The society adopted a free-produce resolution: "We do not like to eat sugar, or rice, or any thing else, made by the poor slaves, seeing they are forced to work every day with out pay, under the lash, and are fed no better than brutes."[77]

Juvenile antislavery societies, perhaps more so than any other group, struggled with identifying appropriate activities. Organizers encouraged activities similar to those of adult abolitionist societies, including learning about the slave's experience, boycotting slave-labor goods, and encouraging others to join the organization. Free produce, in particular, was an important, pragmatic tactic for juvenile abolitionists. Publications for young abolitionists urged children to adopt free produce as one of several means for aiding the abolitionist cause. The *Slave's Friend*, published as a monthly periodical from 1836 to 1838, included articles, stories, and poems written for an eight- to twelve-year old audience. Garrison included a juvenile column in the *Liberator* and published a collection of poems for children. *Juvenile Poems for the Use of Free American Children, of Every Complexion*, published in 1835, included several of Elizabeth Margaret Chandler's free-produce poems. Children were also urged to refrain from calling slaves vulgar names, to imitate the moral courage of their parents, and even to sign Petitions for Minors. Young girls were also encouraged to sew and to knit for antislavery fairs.[78]

In the 1830s, whether the association was organized by men or women, adults or children, Quakers or non-Quakers, white or black abolitionists, free-produce as an antislavery tactic was discussed and often included particularly as a resolution. Seemingly, free produce was widely discussed and, by implication, widely adopted. And, initially, free produce seemed a promising strategy for abolitionist Quakers and non-Quakers. However, as resistance to radical abolitionism and women's activism deepened and spread in the 1830s, some prominent abolitionists including William Lloyd Garrison and Theodore Weld began to question the efficacy of free produce. By the late 1830s, Garrison had given up on free produce while Weld dismissed abstinence as a "*collateral* principle" although he had abstained from slave-labor goods "for years" as a duty.[79] Still, supporters of the boycott of slave-labor remained optimistic that abstention could indeed apply economic and moral pressure on slaveholders. In an effort to spread the word about slave-labor goods and to increase the supply of free-labor goods, abolitionist consumers in the 1830s began to consider the benefits of a national free-produce association. In 1837, abolitionists decided to organize a national convention to consider the question.

Requited Labor Convention

Planning for the Requited Labor Convention began with a call sent out by the Clarkson Anti-Slavery Society in 1837 to other abolitionists—individuals and societies—to join in a general convention of men and women committed to abstinence from the products of slave labor. In September, the society named a committee of three men and three women to correspond with other individuals and groups to discuss the organization of a free-labor convention "to devise the best means for the procurement and manufacturing of articles obtained by free labor." The committee contacted the PFASS for help in organizing the convention. By the following spring, the society had generated enough support to publish a circular inviting groups and individuals to attend a free-produce convention scheduled for mid-May.[80]

The Requited Labor Convention met May 17, 1838, at Pennsylvania Hall, along with the second annual Anti-Slavery Convention of American Women. Although the Requited Labor Convention drew representatives primarily from Pennsylvania-based antislavery societies, representatives William Bassett and James P. Boyce of the Lynn Anti-Slavery Society, Massachusetts, were also present. James and Lucretia Mott as well as Lydia White served as delegates from the Quaker Association of Friends for Advocating the Cause of the Slave, and Sarah Pugh, Grace Douglass, and Sarah Grimké were among the representatives from the PFASS. Individual attendees included Mary Grew, Abraham Pennock, Mary L. Cox, and Susan H. Luther.[81] The conservative Pennsylvania Society for Promoting the Abolition of Slavery (PAS), however, declined the invitation to attend. Established in 1775, the PAS preferred political lobbying and opposed all forms of grassroots activism, including the "holding of 'promiscuous meetings' of men and women, blacks and whites," believing such meetings "threatened the Union's well-being by arousing the people's passions."[82] Although organizers hoped to draw a broad cross-section of the abolitionist community, most of the attendees were Quakers, Hicksite and Orthodox.

The convention resolved to form the National Requited Labor Association and appointed a committee to draft a constitution for the new association. Committees were also formed to prepare and publish an address on the duty of abstinence and to identify sources of free-labor goods. At the end of the first afternoon, Alanson St. Clair, a Unitarian minister from Massachusetts, offered a strong free-produce resolution that members should "in all cases give a preference to the products of free labor over those of slaves; and never, if we can have a choice between the two give countenance to slaveholding, by purchasing, trafficking in, or using the latter." The resolution was tabled after "an animated discussion," and the convention adjourned to meet the next morning. Pennsylvania Hall, however, was destroyed that evening by antiabolitionist mobs. When the Requited Labor Convention met the next morning "at the *ruins* of the *Pennsylvania Hall*," the group adjourned to meet instead at the home of James and Lucretia Mott.

After appointing a Committee of Correspondence authorized to call a convention together at an appropriate time, the Requited Labor Convention adjourned.[83]

In September 1838, convention delegates met again, this time with a much smaller group in attendance. Lewis C. Gunn reported on a draft of the association's constitution, which was accepted. The members agreed to call the new association the American Free Produce Association. Gunn was appointed to prepare and publish an address on the duty of abstinence. The members of the association also appointed a committee to consider the propriety of establishing free-labor stores as well as a committee to prepare a memorial to Congress requesting a repeal of duties on free-labor goods to allow such goods to compete equally with slave-labor goods. Though absent, the group elected Gerrit Smith as president. Abraham L. Pennock, William Bassett, William H. Johnson, and Lewis Tappan were elected as vice presidents. Other officers included Lewis C. Gunn, Lucretia Mott, Lydia White, Henry Grew, Abby Kelly, and Sarah Pugh.[84] The organizers of the convention and the AFPA attempted to appeal to a broad cross-section of abolitionists as evidenced by the election of the non-Quakers Smith as president and Lewis Tappan as one of the vice presidents. Smith, an outspoken supporter of free produce and a friend of Quaker Abraham L. Pennock, had been invited by Gunn to participate in the convention, but other commitments prevented Smith's attendance. A letter from Smith was read to the convention and included in the published minutes.[85]

Radical reformer William Goodell had also been invited to attend the convention. Goodell, like Elizabeth Heyrick, believed the abolition of slavery and the reform of labor conditions were inextricably linked. In the 1820s, Goodell edited the *Investigator and General Intelligencer*, the *Genius of Temperance*, the *Emancipator*, and the *Friend of Man*, all reform journals. His articles addressed both colonization and immediatism. However, after Nat Turner's rebellion in 1831, and the harassment of Prudence Crandall after she admitted black students to her school in 1833, Goodell was influenced by Garrison to focus his editorial and journalistic skills on abolitionism. Goodell was among the first to link abolitionism to the broader issue of black civil rights and racial equality. He was one of the few abolitionists to connect these issues to women's rights and working-class reform. Goodell advocated for suffrage reform in Rhode Island and challenged the exploitation of women and children who were paid starvation wages. He believed just and equitable laws as important as personal reform. In his publications, Goodell reprinted material from the workingman's press and provided space for the discussion of women's issues. Goodell also used his publications to challenge the decline in morals and the rise in aristocracy that were, he believed, the result of the market revolution.[86]

The problem with free produce, according to Goodell, was that it did not go far enough in targeting oppressive labor conditions. In declining the invitation sent by Gunn, Goodell observed that at the founding of the American Anti-Slavery Society delegates had adopted a free-produce resolution despite concerns that "its incorporation into our enterprise would cripple our efforts, and shut us out of the manufacturing districts of the North." Yet little had been done "to make any decisive advances in relation to it." For many, introducing the discussion of the boycott of slave-labor "appears to be a wandering from the specific object of association, if not an impertinent attempt to press the organization into a service for which it was never intended," a reference to William Jay's criticism of Gerrit Smith in 1836. Moreover, the oppression of "kitchen domestics and cotton factory operatives," Goodell observed, "has been known to give serious offence to some who are sufficiently zealous for *Southern* emancipation." Goodell asked whether the AFPA, through "its periodicals and official publications," would consider publishing "kindred discussion[s] of the propriety of abstinence from the products of *other* forms of oppression besides that of our American slaveholding." Citing his experiences on the island of Java, Goodell noted that his awareness of other forms of oppressive labor had strengthened his "repugnance to the use of slave labor products." If the AFPA were successful in "*procuring supplies of free labor goods*, for all parts of the country," Goodell concluded, the association would accomplish much in removing objections to the free-produce movement. The increased supply of free-labor goods would lead many consumers to "examine the subject, and not only examine, but *act*, by giving the *preference*, to say the least, for free goods."[87] For Goodell, it was critical that the AFPA retain both its moral and its market focus.

The Requited Labor Convention marked a significant shift in the American free-produce movement. The convention represented American activists' first attempt to organize a national movement against slave-labor goods. The delegates hoped the association would impress on abolitionists the importance of moral consistency. Integrated by race and gender, the AFPA reflected "the fusion of moral passion and political demands" identified as unique to women's antislavery associations in the 1830s. Influenced in large part by Quaker women such as Lucretia Mott, Sarah Pugh, and Lydia White, the Requited Labor Convention and the American Free Produce Association likewise brought together the moral and the political.[88] Despite the conflagration at Pennsylvania Hall that forced convention delegates to re-convene in September, supporters of the AFPA were optimistic about the future.

In addition to ideological support, the organization of the American Free Produce Association promised a solution for the problems of supply that continued to plague the movement. The various free-produce societies that organized in the 1820s and 1830s sought alternatives for slave-labor goods. Often these limited efforts yielded few goods that were not more costly than the slave-labor alternative. For example, in 1828, Charles Collins of New York purchased a few bales of cotton from Francis Williamson in North Carolina. The manufactured cotton sold for nineteen to twenty-one cents per yard, well above the price for similar goods made from slave-labor cotton.[89] In 1831, a committee of the Pennsylvania Free Produce Society published an extensive summary of available sources for free-labor goods, out-lining the challenges of acquiring such goods. Maple sugar was the only source of free-labor sugar in the United States; additionally, cotton supplies were in-adequate and rice was so scarce premiums were offered.[90] Supply, as well as quality, challenged supporters of the movement. And the two problems worked in dynamic relationship. Limited supplies meant limited choices for consumers. Limited consumer demand, in turn, became a disincentive for producers of free-labor goods. Still, abolitionist merchants opened free-labor stores: at least six in the 1820s and more than twenty in the 1830s. Free-labor stores were concentrated in major cities such as New York and Philadelphia.[91] For example, in 1837, E. Robinson of New York City claimed to regularly supply nearly two hundred abolitionists with free-labor goods. Robinson even offered to deliver those goods free of charge. Samuel Cornish, editor of the *Colored American*, drew his readers' attention to the store of Perkins and Town, also located in New York, who supplied free-labor molasses, sugar, rice, and coffee, "which can be relied upon as really free, of an excellent quality and very cheap." Cornish urged "the friends of the slave" to make it a matter of conscience not "to partake of the slaveholders' deeds by eating of the fruits of slave labor."[92] In addition to clothing and dry goods, free-labor stores offered goods such as shoes, paper, ice cream, and candy "free from the taint of slavery."[93] Abolitionist consumers also bought and sold free-labor goods at the annual antislavery fairs organized by women's antislavery asso-ciations. The Boston Female Anti-Slavery Society's early antislavery fairs in-cluded treats made with free-labor sugar and sugar bowls inscribed "Sugar not made by slaves" while the Western Anti-Slavery Fair featured "*free labor* cotton shirts, collars, and bosoms."[94] Services, using free-labor goods, were also available to consumers. Boarders at the Graham House in Boston, for example, were fed only "the products of free labor."[95] In Philadelphia, Quaker Nathan Thorne offered tailoring services that used only free-labor goods.[96] For supporters of the boycott, a national organization held the potential to better coordinate these myriad efforts to supply free-labor goods to the market.

In the 1830s, men and women, Quaker and non-Quaker alike, worked to integrate Quaker views about slave labor and free produce into the anti-slavery societies they organized. For American supporters of the boycott, free produce offered a pragmatic way to fight slavery, citing the British example as evidence. In the 1790s, the boycott of slave-grown sugar preceded the abolition of the slave trade in 1807; in the 1820s, a second major boycott of slave-labor goods had culminated in parliamentary passage of the Emancipation Act in 1833 and in full emancipation in 1838. Events in Britain encouraged American abolitionist consumers to persist in spite of the internecine disputes that divided American abolitionists in the late 1830s. Moreover, the protean meanings of free-produce activism encouraged participation by conservative and radical abolitionists. Even as free produce united disparate groups of abolitionist consumers, free produce divided abolitionists over the use of the boycott in the fight against slavery. For many reformers, free produce remained an individual question. Still, the establishment of the American Free Produce Association, as well as the founding of a similar organization in Britain, the British India Society, encouraged many supporters of the boycott, who looked forward to more abolitionists joining the cause of free produce.

CHAPTER 7

Yards of Cotton Cloth and Pounds of Sugar: The Transatlantic Free-Produce Movement

British and American supporters of the boycott of slave labor were encouraged by Parliament's abolition of the apprenticeship system and the full emancipation of the British Empire's slaves in August 1838. Political success led British abolitionists to establish three national organizations in 1839. In March, Quakers Joseph Pease and William Howitt and British abolitionist George Thompson organized the British India Society (BIS). All three men were known for their activism. Pease had helped found the Peace Society in 1817 while Thompson had toured the United States in the 1830s on behalf of the abolitionist cause. Howitt, a popular writer, had recently published *Colonization and Christianity*, describing conditions in British India. The following month, in April, Quaker Joseph Sturge and other British abolitionists organized the British and Foreign Anti-Slavery Society (BFASS), and, in July, parliamentary abolitionist Thomas Fowell Buxton organized the African Civilization Society (ACS). The BIS and the ACS focused on reform and free-labor crop alternatives in British India and Africa, respectively. All three organizations clarified British abolitionists' decision, after 1838, to focus their reform energies on the abolition of slavery in the United States and elsewhere. Within weeks of its organization, the BFASS proposed an international antislavery meeting for the following year in London, sending out a broadly worded invitation to "the friends of the slave of every nation and every clime."[1]

These national developments held the promise of an international movement against the products of slave labor. National groups such as the American Free Produce Association and the British India Society, as well as regional groups such as the Philadelphia Female Anti-Slavery Society, worked hard to sway public sentiment toward a free-labor stance in the marketplace; however, their efforts were often hampered by supply problems. Thus, an international movement, with expanded sources for free-labor crops, suggested that problems of supply and quality might be resolved. Yet, these associations and their members were also caught up in debates about race, gender, and sectarian support of radical reform that caused tension among the larger community of reformers in Britain and the United States. While questions of race, gender, and religion limited the impact of national organizations, the boycott continued to attract new supporters.

American Free Produce Association

In September 1838, Requited Labor Convention delegates appointed Lewis C. Gunn to prepare an address on the duty of abstinence. A New York Quaker, Gunn was active in the American Anti-Slavery Society. In the winter of 1837–1838, he and Connecticut abolitionist Charles C. Burleigh spent six months in Haiti on a fact-finding trip, establishing connections with abolitionists in Port-au-Prince.[2] In *An Address to Abolitionists*, Gunn laid out the moral foundation of the American Free Produce Association. By purchasing slave produce, consumers sanctioned "the plunder of slaves." Moreover, through his purchase of slave-labor goods, the consumer "tempt[ed] the commission" of the crime of slaveholding; thus, the consumer became "virtually the plunderer of the slaves." By using slave produce, abolitionists were withholding a "very important testimony against slavery as a sin" and "diminish[ing] the influence of [their] antislavery efforts."[3] Gunn's *Address* invoked the free-produce rhetoric of Elias Hicks and Elizabeth Heyrick, as well as early Quaker reformers such as John Woolman, consciously placing the AFPA within the broader, transatlantic history of the abstention movement. Recounting the ideological origins of the abstention movement, Gunn and the members of the AFPA reminded supporters and opponents alike of the importance of moral consistency.

The members of the AFPA also recognized the importance of increasing the supply of free-labor goods. At the Requited Labor Convention, Lydia White, a member of the PFASS and a Hicksite Quaker, was appointed to a committee to identify sources for free-labor goods.[4] As the owner of a

free-labor store in Philadelphia, White was a logical choice for the committee. She understood, probably better than any other member of the committee, the difficulty of obtaining regular supplies of free-labor goods. When
White opened her dry goods store in Philadelphia in 1830, Elizabeth Margaret Chandler promoted the store and its owner in the "Ladies' Repository" of the *Genius of Universal Emancipation*: "We are proud to know that the
projector of so laudable a design is one of our own sex."[5] By 1831, White
was receiving orders from Vermont, Michigan, Rhode Island, New York,
Ohio, Indiana, New Jersey, and Delaware as well as Pennsylvania. White also
purchased small quantities of cotton for manufacture and sale in her shop.[6]
White advertised her store in the *Liberator* and the *Genius of Universal Emancipation* as well as the *National Reformer*, an African American weekly.[7] White
and other owners of free-labor stores had difficulty obtaining a steady supply of free-labor goods. Writing in 1831 to Garrison, White apologized that
she did not "have a full supply and a better assortment of domestic cotton
goods." In a letter later that year, White again lamented the lack of free-labor
goods, "It is truly mortifying to have [to] say that we have not enough of
either of the articles [you requested] on hand at present worth sending."
White suggested a free-labor cotton factory might address supply problems
and convince southern cotton growers to switch to free labor.[8] Samuel Philbrick, who was one of the first and most active abolitionists in Brookline,
Massachusetts, complained free-labor cotton "cannot be had in Boston." He
suggested that abstention might gain favor among Boston consumers if a
steady supply of free-labor goods were made available at a price competitive
with slave-labor goods.[9]

The AFPA committee appointed to identify supplies of free-labor goods
proposed two plans to address the problem. The first plan was based on voluntary contributions from individuals; the other plan proposed forming a
joint stock association. After the September meeting, the AFPA distributed
a circular presenting both plans and requesting supporters indicate their preference and pledge their support.[10] Massachusetts abolitionist William Bassett was among the first to respond sending a ten dollar contribution. Bassett
also suggested Miller send circulars to other abolitionists, including Abby Kelley, Maria Weston Chapman, Samuel Philbrick, and Aaron L. Benedict.[11] In
their responses, Philbrick and Benedict raised doubts about the efficacy of
the venture. Both worried that the joint stock association would render stock-
holders liable for the financial obligations of the society. Philbrick also worried about "subscribing for any certain am[oun]t of goods, without knowing
whether the quality & kind of goods wanted, can be obtained."[12] When the
AFPA met in October 1839 for their first annual meeting, the Executive

FIGURE 6.   Label used by the American Free Produce Association. Courtesy of Middletown Historical Society, Middletown, Connecticut.

Committee lamented the lack of progress, noting the response to the circular was "not sufficiently encouraging to justify us in taking the proposed step." While the AFPA had failed to collect funds to establish free-labor stores, the committee believed the proposal "a measure of the highest importance." Attributing the failure of the store venture to a lack of steady supply, the committee suggested instead "the creation of a fund for the encouragement of the production of cotton by free labour." Funds raised could be used to purchase free-labor cotton and to hire agents who could ensure that free-labor cotton was not "intermixed with that produced by slaves."[13] The delegates adopted the measure and appointed a committee to raise the necessary funds.

Raising nearly four hundred dollars, the AFPA recruited Esther and Phineas Nixon from Randolph County, North Carolina, to procure free-labor cotton from local farmers. In early 1840, the AFPA purchased more than thirteen hundred pounds of cotton, which was subsequently manufactured and sold.[14] Procuring free-labor cotton from the slave-labor South was problematic, as the Nixons reported to the AFPA. The couple had trouble convincing local farmers to adopt free-labor practices and often had to price their cotton above market value. Producing free-labor cotton was also dangerous. "All it needs is a match to create an explosion," Esther Nixon noted.[15]

With more than one hundred people in attendance at its first annual meeting, the AFPA seemed a vibrant but struggling community of dedicated reformers. Although they worried about their lack of progress, members looked forward to the World Anti-Slavery Convention scheduled to meet in London in June 1840. The AFPA selected nine delegates—seven men and two women, including James and Lucretia Mott, Sarah Pugh, William Bassett, and Abraham Pennock—to represent the association's interests at the international meeting. Delegates also passed a resolution calling on recalcitrant abolitionists "to reflect upon the glaring inconsistency of protesting against slavery as an immorality, and yet paying for its support." More than anything, members of the AFPA hoped to end abolitionists' "lamentable apathy" toward free-produce. AFPA members also celebrated the end of apprenticeship and full emancipation in the West Indies and the subsequent formation of the BIS. These events, members claimed, were "calculated to have an important bearing on the cause of freedom generally and on our enterprise in particular." The delegates resolved to begin correspondence with the BIS.[16] American supporters of the boycott believed reform in India would open new sources for the production of free-labor goods, which in turn would aid the abolitionist cause in the United States.

British India Society

The organization of the British India Society was a watershed moment. As we have seen, in the 1820s, abolitionist consumers distanced free produce from East Indian slavery. In the 1790s and the 1820s, East Indian sugar held symbolic importance for supporters of the boycott of slave-grown sugar. Abolitionists insisted that East Indian labor, however cheap, was fundamentally free; they distinguished between East Indian and West Indian slavery, claiming the former was indigenous and less severe than African slavery in the West Indies. In 1833, Parliament excluded British India from the Emancipation Act, leaving it to the East India Company to eradicate slavery in India. By the late 1830s, however, EIC inaction led abolitionists to focus more closely on labor conditions in India. Conditions in British India became increasingly significant to abolitionists and other reformers who "sought to reposition the subcontinent within newly emerging relationships of trade and labor in a post-emancipation empire," as one scholar notes. Supporters of the boycott of slave-labor goods were anxious to exploit India's economic potential as a supplier of free-labor goods while others saw in India an important market for British goods. Moreover, reform in India took on added urgency as free labor increasingly became the only legitimate mode of capitalist production.[17] British abolitionists' emphasis on India reflected and reinforced their new, expansive vision of antislavery activism.

Organizing for the BIS began in 1838, following the formation of the Aborigines' Protection Society a year earlier in London. Though events in India, in particular, were important in leading to the founding of the Aborigines' Protection Society, the association focused on the conditions of indigenous populations throughout the British Empire.[18] In the summer of 1838, George Thompson and Joseph Pease helped with the publication of a circular to outline conditions in India. The circular was then distributed to members of Parliament and the Aborigines' Protection Society. At the August meeting of the society, a resolution was passed to engage Thompson's aid in presenting a series of lectures to inform the public of the need for reform in India.[19] In a letter to William Lloyd Garrison in January 1839, Thompson noted his affiliation with the Aborigines' Protection Society. He also emphasized his particular interest in Indian reform, noting that most of his addresses in late 1838 and early 1839 had focused on conditions in British India.[20] In another letter, Thompson wrote of his growing interest in a British India association: "I incline more and more to the plan of a separate, independent, thorough-going society for prosecuting, as its exclusive work, the cause of the Hindoo." Still, Thompson waited for the "way to open" in order to establish such an organization.[21]

In late January, Thompson found the opening he sought in a fortuitous meeting with the Orientalist William Adam.[22] Born in Scotland in 1796, Adam studied classical and vernacular Indian languages before traveling to India, in 1818, as a Baptist missionary. While in India, Adam worked with Indian reformer Rammohun Roy, who converted Adam to Unitarianism in 1821.[23] Cut off from Baptist financial support, Adam worked as a clerk and newspaper editor in India throughout the 1820s. In 1829, Adam became editor of the radical *India Gazette*, which he used as a platform to challenge traditional British depictions of Indians as illiterate and uncivilized. From 1834 through 1838, Adam surveyed the state of education in India. He supported education in the vernacular languages, a plan the British government in India rejected as "impracticable," "complicated," and "expensive." In 1838, Adam left India to join his wife and children in Boston, Massachusetts.[24] Adam convinced Thompson and Pease and his daughter Elizabeth Pease to establish an association to specifically seek reform on behalf of the people of India. Adam declined to take a leadership role in the organization, however, since he had already accepted a teaching appointment at Harvard University.[25]

After the meeting with Adam, Thompson and the Peases worked to generate support for a British India reform association. Elizabeth Pease accompanied Thompson to the towns where he was scheduled to lecture, helping him organize local societies in a fashion similar to the antislavery societies organized in Britain in the 1820s. In March 1839, a provisional committee was appointed to organize the British India Society. Excluded from formal membership in the BIS because of her gender, Elizabeth Pease used other means to generate interest and support for the organization. In April, Pease's friend Mary Wigham wrote Boston abolitionist Maria Weston Chapman that Thompson's lectures and British affairs in India had "claimed [the] serious attention . . . of the Emancipation Society." The Peases, along with Thompson, also attended London Yearly Meeting where Thompson outlined the goals of the BIS. A reprint of Quaker William Howitt's prospectus for the organization was distributed at the meeting. The prospectus assured supporters of the Quaker foundations of the BIS, noting that the organization would be "found[ed] upon the strictest principles of justice and humanity— upon a basis which will permanently exclude the adoption of party, of sectarian, or mercenary views. They contemplate the use of those means only which are moral, peaceful, and constitutional."[26]

British and American abolitionists celebrated the first formal meeting of the BIS in June 1839. In a series of speeches, British reformers urged the reformation of conditions in India for the benefit of the indigenous population, the prosperity of British business, and the emancipation of the slave. Improving labor conditions would provide opportunities for expanded agricultural development in India, which would increase Indian supplies of cotton for British mills and in turn would increase Indian demand for British manufactures. As one lecturer noted, "If every man in India could afford to purchase a dress a year, Britain would send $50 million worth of goods to India."[27] Reform in India would also affirm Britain's moral standing, particularly in relationship to the United States. Lecturers noted the hypocrisy of slavery in the midst of American democracy. Cotton for British mills, one lecturer noted, came almost "wholly from the United States of America, which still allowed their land of freed, (O, mockery of the name of freedom!) to pander to the cause of Slavery: dimming the luster of their flag of stars, and making it too often the harbinger of darkness instead of light."[28] The BIS is "doing your work for you & aim at the very object you are seeking to accomplish," Elizabeth Pease told Maria Weston Chapman.[29] In response, Chapman congratulated Pease, praising the establishment of the BIS: "I see at a glance what its effect must be on American slavery, & cast my whole spirit across the Atlantic, towards you in England."[30] Angelina Grimké wrote Pease that the BIS had "claimed a large share of our sympathy" and wrote of her pleasure to see free produce being agitated in Britain once again.[31] Boston abolitionist Maria Weston Chapman praised the British India Society for "bringing the free labor of British India in direct competition with slave labor." The BIS also promised prosperity to England by removing British dependence on American cotton. American statesmen, Chapman noted, will "see both the patriotism and the cupidity of Britain ready to aid her philanthropists . . . to secure to British India the undivided demand of the British cotton-market."[32] Though not all supporters of the BIS were interested in its humanitarian efforts, British and American reformers looked to the organization as yet another important development in the international abolitionist movement.

Unlike the American Free Produce Association, the British India Society functioned solely as a pressure group. The AFPA had two goals: to convince other abolitionists to adopt free produce and to increase the availability of free-labor goods by direct participation in the manufacture of those goods. In contrast, the BIS identified as its primary duty the widest possible dissemination of information about India, believing that political reform would then create the conditions for businessmen to produce free-labor goods.[33] In his extensive lecture series, Thompson linked the success of the abolition of slavery in the West Indies to the planned objective for British India: "The spirit that never tired, that never quailed, while pursuing the great object of negro emancipation, has been invoked, has been awakened, is now stirring; and what we did for the slave of the West shall, with the help of God, be done for the Hindoo of the East."[34] Political and economic reform in India would address the shortcomings of the Emancipation Act of 1833 and, at last, emancipate all of the empire's slaves. In the United States, Garrison edited a volume of Thompson's India speeches while William Adam lectured on his experiences in British India.[35] Through her extensive correspondence with American abolitionists, Elizabeth Pease also aided the flow of information about the BIS and its efforts. Pamphlets, reports, and letters sent by Pease to American abolitionists were, as Lucretia Mott's son-in-law Edward M. Davis noted, kept in "constant motion."[36] American supporters of the boycott believed reform in India would increase the supply of free-labor goods and further the cause of abolition in the United States.

Not all abolitionists were convinced that cotton cultivation in India would have the desired effect on slavery in the southern United States. William Adam claimed he did not share George Thompson's "sanguine expectations."

While Adam was convinced increased cotton cultivation, "in combination with other causes" might improve the situation of "the starving & degraded population of India," its effect on American slavery might only be "*collateral*." Still, Adam resolved "to stand before the American public as its advocate to the full extent of the object."[37]

Abolitionists' desire to increase cotton cultivation in British India received unexpected reinforcement in this period from the East India Company and the cotton manufacturers in Liverpool, Manchester, and Glasgow. American cotton prices rose and supplies declined in the late 1830s, prompting British businessmen to explore the potential for cotton cultivation in East India. India had been a major supplier of cotton until it was superseded by American cotton in the nineteenth century. In 1839, the EIC recruited Captain Thomas Bayles, an officer of the Indian army on furlough in England, to introduce American-style cotton production to India using indigenous labor. In an allegedly covert operation, the EIC sent Bayles to America "to engage parties qualified for the purpose of instructing and superintending the natives in the cultivation of cotton, and the proper method of cleaning it by machinery."[38] Given the amount of publicity Bayles's mission received in the British and American press, Bayles's objectives were far from secret. The editors of the New Orleans *Daily Picayune*, for example, claimed the Mississippi press had exposed Bayles's purpose after he recruited individuals to go to India.[39] Bayles spent time in South Carolina, Georgia, and Louisiana as well as Mississippi. In 1840, Bayles returned to England with ten recruits. The Washington, D.C., *Daily National Intelligencer* mocked the American planters who traveled with Bayles as "pure philanthropists" and claimed the misguided American "anti-Slavery and Abolition societies" wished to deprive American cotton "of a foreign market, as the produce of *slave labor*" because they believed "the Hindoos" enjoyed "an admirable freedom."[40] The EIC operation worried some supporters of American cotton, who feared increased cotton production in British India, Texas, South America, and elsewhere would damage the market for American-grown cotton.[41] In the end, the EIC operation failed despite a total investment of £100,000.[42] While rumor attributed its failure to sabotage by American planters, Isaac Watts, secretary of the Cotton Supply Association in Manchester, blamed the poor infrastructure of British India, which hindered efforts to bring cotton to the British market. Nonetheless, businessmen and abolitionists persisted in their efforts to produce cotton in East India for British textile mills.[43] Supporters of free-labor goods from India looked forward to the World Anti-Slavery Convention, believing international cooperation would aid the boycott and the abolitionist cause.

World Anti-Slavery Convention

Responsibility for organizing the World Anti-Slavery Convention fell to British Quaker Joseph Sturge and members of the London Committee, the executive committee of the British and Foreign Anti-Slavery Society. Considered among the more radical of the British abolitionists, Sturge embraced immediatism earlier than many of his male abolitionist counterparts. Sturge had also opposed compensating slaveholders. Like Cropper and Heyrick, Sturge recognized the connection between the abolition of slavery and relief for the poor, believing the abolition of slavery would improve conditions for the working class. He, like Cropper, also worried that a widespread boycott of slave-grown cotton, for example, would close mills and displace British workers. In planning for the convention, Sturge recruited support from British antislavery societies and supervised efforts to gather information about slavery for presentation at the convention. The London Committee also issued an invitation to "the friends of the slave of every nation and every clime."[44] When the London Committee learned that some American antislavery societies had appointed female delegates to the World Anti-Slavery Convention, they issued a second call, specifically asking for male delegates. Female delegates, Sturge claimed, would hinder rather than aid the cause. If female delegates did attend the convention, he warned, "they will have to encounter the strong feeling against it, which exists here, standing alone."[45] Still, American associations, such as the American Free Produce Association persisted, sending as delegates Lucretia Mott and Sarah Pugh. As the female delegates arrived in London, in the days before the convention began, the London Committee made repeated efforts to convince them to accept their exclusion from the convention. At one meeting, a black delegate from Jamaica told Mott, "It would lower the dignity of the Convention and bring ridicule on the whole thing if ladies were admitted." Mott replied, noting that "similar reasons were urged in Pennsylvania for the exclusion of colored people from our meetings—but had we yielded on such flimsy arguments, we might as well have abandoned our enterprise." Mott's response is an important reminder of the different social and political contexts in which British and American abolitionists worked. In the United States, female and African American support and leadership were vital to the cause.[46]

American abolitionist Wendell Phillips brought the woman question before all of the delegates on the first day of the convention. William Lloyd Garrison, delayed by the annual meeting of the American Anti-Slavery Society, was not present. Although the London Committee had already decided to exclude female delegates, Phillips insisted that the convention as a whole should decide whether the women should be recognized, an argument first made by Sarah Pugh in a written protest the previous day. British abolitionist George Thompson, who had been instrumental in bringing American women into the movement, urged Phillips to withdraw the motion. Phillips, however, persisted. William Adam also spoke in favor of the women delegates. In the end, an overwhelming majority of convention delegates voted against admission of the women, and they were forced to sit in the gallery, witnesses to but not participants in the proceedings.[47]

Delegates debated two topics—British India and free produce—that were of particular importance to supporters of the boycott. On the second day of the convention, William Adam delivered a lecture to the delegates, highlighting the continued existence of slavery in the territories of the East India Company. Abridged from a series of open letters Adam had written to parliamentary abolitionist Thomas Fowell Buxton and published in Boston and in London earlier that year, Adam's lecture challenged traditional arguments about the character and the source of slavery in British India. The EIC had failed to abolish slavery and had given tacit sanction to its continued presence. "Slavery in India does not rest on law but custom," Adam remarked, "and this illegal custom has been invested by the British government in India, with the desecrated forms and sanctions of law and justice." Moreover, slavery in India was not as benign as previously claimed. Using a rhetorical strategy from the abolitionist movement, Adam emphasized specific instances of physical cruelty, alluding to "the unnatural and atrocious barbarity" practiced on slave eunuchs, for example. Female slaves, he added, were kept "for licentious purposes" and often subject to "mutilation and murder." While Adam admitted that slavery was not the worst social evil from which India suffered, he maintained that Indian bondage was far from harmless. Highlighting the horrors of slavery, Adam contradicted earlier assumptions that Indian slavery was "divested of all the cruel features which characterized the African trade." He called for renewed abolitionist effort to end slavery in British India, thus completing the abolition of slavery in the British Empire. "Nothing has been done to mitigate the condition of the slaves, or to lead to the extinction of slavery," Adam told the delegates. "You have, therefore, strong, clear, defined ground upon which to proceed; and I earnestly hope that you will proceed."[48]

The delegates received Adam's speech with approbation, noting that the political compromises of the Emancipation Act of 1833 had limited action against slavery in India. "We have long talked of the evil [of slavery in British India], but what have we done to remove it," Joseph Pease asked. The delegates appointed a committee, including Adam, Pease, Charles Stuart, and George Thompson to consider Adam's paper and to deliver to the convention a resolution or resolutions based on it. Joseph Sams, a Quaker bookseller from Darlington, urged the committee to do more than consider Adam's report. Instead, he urged the committee to also consider the subject of free labor. If "we as a nation were to use only free labour produce," Sams said, "it would be one of the severest blows which could possibly be given to slavery." R. R. R. Moore, a political economist from Dublin, objected. "We shall gain nothing by mixing up the subjects," Moore claimed. George Thompson agreed. The delegates unanimously approved the resolution, limiting the committee's review to the information contained in Adam's report.[49]

On the eighth day of the convention, Charles Stuart introduced a free-produce resolution, recommending "the disuse of slave-labour produce, and instead of it the use of free-labour produce, as far as practicable." Stuart, a native of Jamaica and a retired army officer, had been active in antislavery in the United States and the West Indies. In the 1830s, as we have seen, Stuart was unsuccessful in his attempts to introduce a free-produce resolution at the annual meetings of the American Anti-Slavery Society. At the World Anti-Slavery Convention, Stuart's resolution triggered an intense debate. Those critical of the resolution noted the challenge of abstaining from slave-labor goods, particularly in the United States. "Slave-labour, in some form or other, enters into nearly all the substantial articles of commerce, that are in ordinary use, and ranked as necessaries," American abolitionist James G. Birney remarked. Other delegates debated the meaning of the phrase, "as far as practicable," asking whether the resolution should be reworded or the phrase omitted altogether. American abolitionist and Unitarian minister George Bradburn claimed the phrase "as far as practicable" amounted to "nothing." "Great diversity of opinion will be entertained as to what *is* practicable," he said. Several delegates were concerned that the consequences of the boycott had not been fully considered. Noting the importance of cotton to British industry, one delegate believed any free-produce resolution would impede the abolitionist cause. "I think we ought to pause, and to deeply consider the consequences of this motion," he warned. Delegates who supported a free-produce resolution noted the thousands of Americans who abstained from slave-labor goods. "Americans . . . eschew every article of slave produce, and would pay fifty cents instead of five, if it were required, to put down American slavery," bragged one American delegate while another claimed hundreds more abstained in the United States than in Britain. George Thompson believed passage of the resolution, or a modified version of it, "would strengthen the hands of abolitionists very materially." In the end, the delegates refused to endorse Stuart's resolution. Instead, delegates agreed to form a committee to examine possible sources for free-labor goods.[50] Immediately after the free-produce debate, William Adam introduced the resolutions drafted by the committee charged with examination of his report on East India slavery. The committee presented a series of eight resolutions, highlighting the nature and extent of slavery in India. The resolutions, which restated the key points of Adam's lecture, passed unanimously. The resolutions did not reference free labor or identify India as a potential source of free-labor goods.[51]

In her diary, Lucretia Mott wrote approvingly of William Adam's lecture earlier in the week though she lamented that "the convention [was] not disposed to entertain the question, altho' many had something to say on it." It was Nathaniel Colver, the stout Baptist minister from Tremont Temple in Boston, who received the harshest criticism from Mott. Colver, she wrote, "told how tender he was *once* on the subject [of free produce], how he gathered his little ones about him, and explained to them the cruelty & wickedness of such participancy," but he discovered that "self-denial was not easy & gave it up & [gave] his children full latitude in robbery & spoil & the gain of oppression." After giving his speech against free produce, Colver "sallied forth to our bar," challenging Mott to speak out, "if the spirit moves you . . . say on—you'll be *allowed* to say what you wish." Instead, Mott sat in silent protest. Later she noted, "Our Free Produce society will have to double their diligence & do their own work—and so will American Abolitionists generally—& especially women."[52] Colver's taunt marginalized both the free-produce movement and the women who supported the movement. Subsequent reports of the free-produce debate focused on the silencing of Mott. According to Sarah Pugh, Mott's report to the AFPA, in October 1840, revealed "how her heart burned within her to speak for the wronged & the outraged," and how she had not been granted the opportunity to counter the "false reasoning" of the delegates. Had Mott been able to do so, Pugh claimed, "they would have mourned for the wrong they had done to the slave in this gagging one of his best and most able advocates." The *National Anti-Slavery Standard* noted that "the rules of the Convention had placed a padlock upon [Mott's] lips, and [she was] obliged to listen to flimsy sophistry in defence of wrong, in silence."[53]

The free-produce debate at the World Anti-Slavery Convention reveals the limits of moral commerce. During the convention, delegates spent considerable time debating the "general axiom, that free-labour is more profitable to the employer, and consequently cheaper, than slave-labour." On the seventh day of the convention, delegates considered a series of resolutions emphasizing the profitability of free labor and encouraging abolitionists to seek alternate sources for slave-labor goods. Such measures relied on economic coercion to force slave-labor goods from the market. "The unrestricted competition of free-labour in the cultivation of sugar, would necessarily introduce a new system, by which the cost of production would be further diminished, and the fall of prices that must ensue, would leave no profits upon slave-grown sugar."[54] Many of the delegates agreed with Stuart, who believed the market for slave-labor goods must be destroyed before abolitionists could begin to convert the hearts of slaveholders.[55] For Lucretia Mott, such appeals to "avarice" displayed a "want of confidence in moral power." As historian Carol Faulkner argues, "abstinence was an aspect of the practical Christianity that [Mott] advocated in her sermons: an everyday action that shook the religious, political, and economic foundations of slavery." Consuming free produce, "the individual freed herself from custom and the market even as she contributed to the liberation of slaves."[56] While Mott and other members of the American Free Produce Association worked to replace slave-labor goods with free-labor alternatives, their efforts emphasized the moral purity of free-labor goods rather than their economic superiority. The free-produce debate reflected abolitionist consumers' struggle to reconcile the fundamental elements of free produce: economics and morals. Mott's son-in-law Edward M. Davis looked forward to a future when cotton from British India would drive slave-grown cotton from the market. "American slavery will have recd. its death blow," he remarked.[57] Yet, Davis also questioned the objectives of the British India Society. "*You* force Slavery from its present location by appealing to the avaricious feelings of the slaveholder," he wrote British abolitionist Elizabeth Pease in March 1840. "*We* exterminate it by appealing to his conscience and understanding." Even if British reformers were successful in supplying their country with free-labor cotton from India, Davis suggested that would still not reform American slaveholders. "Would this prove to our planters that slavery is sinful?" Davis asked. "No! only that his business is unprofitable. The result might & I doubt not would be, to do away with our slave holding Laws but not our slave holding spirit."[58] Davis, Mott, and others made a sharp distinction between the morals and the economics of free produce. The morality of free produce reformed the heart while economics reformed the market. Delegates to the World Anti-Slavery Convention were unable to come to an agreement about the relationship between economic principles and moral commitments. While delegates chose to focus on questions of supply rather than matters of conversion, the conflict between economic principles and moral commitments continued to stress the free-produce movement even as free produce attracted new supporters and lost old ones on either side of the Atlantic.

Doing Their Own Work: American Free Produce in the 1840s

In October 1840, the American Free Produce Association held its second annual meeting at Clarkson Hall in Philadelphia. As it had with other anti-slavery and free-produce meetings that fall, the events of the World Anti-Slavery Convention dominated the meeting's discussions. Henry Grew provided the only dissenting vote when AFPA delegates passed a resolution stating the association was "deeply aggrieved" by events in London. At the convention, Grew had voted against recognition of the female delegates, in-cluding his daughter Mary. Lucretia Mott and Sarah Pugh presented their report to the membership, noting that while many delegates to the conven-tion expressed support of the theory of free produce, delegates did little "to aid us in our plans." James Mott and Henry Grew also presented a report to the association, noting with regret "that the consistent practice we advocate, of abstaining from the use of the fruits of cruel and unrequited toil, has ob-tained to a very limited extent among the professed friends of the injured slave." Delegates to the convention, though expressing support of abstention, claimed that "impracticability" and "inexpediency" made it impossible for them to remain consistent. The slaveholder, Mott and Grew remarked, used the same excuses "to fortify his trembling conscience." The establishment of the British India Society, however, gave the two men reason to hope that free produce was gaining in appreciation by the larger abolitionist commu-nity.[59]

Despite the hopes of Mott and Grew, the AFPA had limited support in the 1840s. After peaking in 1839, participation steadily declined. The meeting minutes for 1839 contain a complete list of delegates whereas most minutes for subsequent years contain no such listing. In 1845, the annual meeting had to be rescheduled because delegates were lacking; in 1846 and 1847, delegates appointed the same set of officers who had served the association the previous year. In the 1840s, as the organization lost members, the membership narrowed to a small core group of supporters, mostly Quak-ers, including Sarah Pugh, James and Lucretia Mott, Abraham Pennock, Ca-leb Clothier, and Daniel Miller Jr. Still, members of the AFPA continued to seek support from abolitionist societies. In 1841, the Executive Committee of the AFPA sent a letter to each state antislavery society urging their members to embrace "the principle of abstinence." The group also issued an "Address to Abolitionists."[60] The following year, members issued the *American Free Produce Journal*, a two-page circular, issued in October 1842, to present the free-produce idea "to the serious attention of their antislavery brethren."[61]

The AFPA also struggled to supply boycotters with free-labor goods. In 1840, the group purchased nearly 1,400 pounds of North Carolina cotton to be manufactured into free-labor yard goods. The following year, the AFPA received a large quantity of "free Texas cotton," which the group had made into ginghams, canton flannel, bed-ticking, calicoes, knitting cotton, and other articles. Cotton prices declined sharply in 1842, forcing the group to take a loss on some of its goods. At the annual meeting that year, members passed a resolution to create a fund "for the purchase & manufacture of Free Cotton." Each member, by annual subscription, would pay one dollar into a manufacturing fund. In 1843, the AFPA's Committee on Finance outlined a four-step plan to raise funds to continue manufacturing free-labor goods. The annual report for 1843 noted that the market and the quality of goods had improved, which is evidenced by the AFPA's purchase of more than 30,000 pounds of free-labor cotton that was subsequently manufactured into 40,000 yards of cloth. In 1844 and 1845, the group manufactured 41,000 and 62,000 yards of cloth, respectively. Increasingly, in the 1840s, manufacturing seemed to be the only business of the association although manufacturing reports are unavailable after 1845. In 1846, James Mott noted that since "the business of the association is conducted chiefly by our manufacturing committee, the details of its operation will be found in their report." Success was short-lived, however; sales declined in 1847 as the AFPA faced competition from the newly formed Free Produce Association of Friends of Philadelphia Yearly Meeting. "Storekeepers and others" had divided their purchases between the two groups. Moreover, the Free Produce Association of Friends "had a larger stock and better variety of articles" and received "the best attention" of the two groups. The Free Produce Association of Friends was not the AFPA's most significant problem, however. "The chief reason" for declining sales, the committee reported, could be attributed to inability of the association's agents "to give the business the time and attention requisite to its proper management." As a result, the Executive Committee recommended liquidating the business.[62]

Even as the Executive Committee of the AFPA struggled with problems, such as membership and supplies, the group continued to frame those discussions in moral terms and to assert the moral imperative of free produce. At the third annual meeting of the AFPA, in October 1841, the Executive Committee lamented the apathy many abolitionists demonstrated toward free produce. "The great mass of abolitionists . . . need an abstinence baptism," president pro tem Sarah Pugh asserted in the annual report. In a pointed reference to Garrison's dismissal of free produce, she noted that many abolitionists had "sacrificed political party and religious sect for the cause of freedom, yet the taint of slavery still clings to them, and they need to be pointed to the stain that dims their otherwise consistent testimony." Pugh described the AFPA as an association under siege. Editors of antislavery papers did not reprint an address published by the association in the *Pennsylvania Freeman*; thus, the report reached only "a comparatively small portion of abolitionists" rather than "the great mass of . . . antislavery brethren." Likewise, England continued to purchase American slave-grown cotton rather than improve labor conditions and increase production of free-labor cotton in India. The AFPA's efforts were further hampered by high duties on free-labor cotton. At the annual meeting, members reviewed and approved a memorial to Congress requesting that duties on foreign and raw cotton be removed, claiming that current duties paid by the association constituted "a tax upon conscientious scruples."[63]

In 1842, at the fourth annual meeting, Sarah Pugh presented a motion to dissolve the association. After an "animated discussion," the motion was voted down "by an apparently unanimous vote."[64] During the "animated discussion" of Pugh's motion, the membership read a letter from Aaron L. Benedict of Delaware County, Ohio, reporting the successful organization of the Western Free Produce Association (WFPA). Benedict's letter was reprinted in full in the AFPA's annual report, suggesting its importance to the membership. "No house in the vicinity being half large enough to convene the people, the [free-produce] meeting was held in a grove," Benedict wrote. According to Benedict, a plan had been established to form free-produce societies in every county in Ohio where "friends of abstinence reside." Benedict described an energetic free-produce movement under development in the West, one which the newly formed society hoped the AFPA would support through the supply of free-labor goods.[65] Developments in Ohio and Indiana were promising enough to postpone any plans of dissolving the AFPA.

Even as free produce declined in the East, western free produce gained momentum, which in turn helped revitalize the movement in Philadelphia. Of an estimated sixteen free-produce societies that formed in the 1840s, seven were located in Ohio, Indiana, Iowa, and Michigan, including the Marion County Free Produce Association, Whetstone, Ohio; the Wayne County

Free Produce Association, Wayne County, Indiana; the Iowa Free Produce Association (formerly the Salem Anti-Slavery Society, established in 1841), Salem, Iowa; and the Young's Prairie Free Labor Association, Young's Prairie, Michigan.[66] Many of the antislavery societies that organized in the West in the 1840s also adopted free produce. In the spring of 1841, nearly one hundred women gathered in Spiceland, Indiana, to organize the Henry County Female Anti-Slavery Society. Initially, the women focused on influencing their "fathers, husbands and brothers" to vote for Liberty Party candidates. By fall, however, the women had adopted their first free-produce resolution. Four other women's associations quickly adopted similar free-produce resolutions.[67] When the Western Free Produce Association organized in 1842, as an auxiliary to the American Free Produce Association, supporters asked antislavery societies throughout Ohio, Indiana, Illinois, Michigan, and Iowa to hold meetings to discuss free produce and to select delegates to the WFPA's inaugural meeting, which was held on August 8, 1842, in Green Plain, Ohio.[68] All of this activity supported the establishment of free-produce stores. Of the estimated twenty-one free produce stores established in the 1840s, nine were located in Ohio, Iowa, and Indiana.[69]

When the Western Free Produce Association organized in 1842, the group laid out ambitious plans for promoting the free-produce cause. By leaving the manufacturing to the American Free Produce Association, the WFPA could focus solely on supplying goods through wholesale and retail free-labor stores. In his letter to the AFPA, Benedict suggested the Pennsylvania Anti-Slavery Society hire an agent "to go through the country and form free-labor societies, and rouse the minds of abolitionists to a sense of the importance of abstinence from the productions of slave-labor; and of establishing a monthly periodical, devoted to this subject."[70] In 1843, when the WFPA met in Greensboro, Indiana, members reported little progress. The group had struggled to acquire free-labor goods, to raise funds, and to recruit experienced leaders to promote the cause. In 1844 the officers of the WFPA did not attend the meeting, and in 1845 the organization did not hold a meeting. The following year, the group reorganized and resolved to raise funds to establish a wholesale free-produce store in Cincinnati that would be operated by Levi Coffin, a Quaker merchant from Newport, Indiana. Initially, Coffin declined for personal and professional reasons; however, when the group failed to find someone else to run the operation, Coffin relented. Chronically underfunded, Coffin managed to keep the business afloat until 1857 when he sold out and returned to Newport.[71]

Levi Coffin's influence on free produce in the West was not limited to his work with the WFPA, however. In the early 1840s, Coffin was instrumental in organizing the Indiana Yearly Meeting of Anti-Slavery Friends, which formed after Quakers in Indiana split over the issue of abolitionism. In the 1830s, Quakers in Indiana led opposition to slavery in the state, including vigorous protests against the state's infamous Black Laws, which limited black immigration to Indiana and denied citizenship to blacks already living in the state. Levi Coffin and his distant cousin, Elijah Coffin, were among those Quakers who petitioned the state legislature for repeal of the laws. Radical Quakers such as Levi Coffin advocated for immediate emancipation and full racial equality. In contrast, Elijah Coffin and other conservative Quakers favored gradual emancipation through colonization. As clerk of the Meeting for Sufferings, Elijah Coffin was also among the powerful elite of Indiana Quakers. Until 1839, these two groups, conservative and radical, maintained an uneasy truce. In 1839, Arnold Buffum arrived in Indiana. An agent of the American Anti-Slavery Society, Buffum had been disowned by the Society of Friends in the East. His arrival in Indiana was followed by letters and traveling ministers who denounced Buffum as an infidel and a deceiver. Buffum established antislavery societies, edited the abolitionist journal, the *Protectionist*, and organized antislavery lectures throughout the state. Not surprisingly, radical Quakers such as Levi Coffin, as well as Walter Edgerton and Charles Osborn, welcomed Buffum's efforts. In 1840, Edgerton unsuccessfully attempted to modify the Quaker discipline, making the purchase of slave-labor goods an offense subject to disownment. Two years later, tensions among Quakers reached a boiling point when presidential candidate Henry Clay appeared in Richmond, Indiana, during the yearly meeting. His warm reception by conservative Friends stood in sharp contrast to the "stinging rebuke" of abolitionist Quakers, who publicly demanded Clay free his slaves. As a result, the Meeting for Sufferings removed eight of its members for their abolitionist sympathies, including Levi Coffin and Charles Osborn. Indiana Yearly Meeting also warned its subordinate meetings not to appoint abolitionists to positions of power, and continued to caution against the "excitement and zeal" of the antislavery movement. In the end, nearly two thousand Friends, or about one-tenth of the Yearly Meeting's membership, left to form the Anti-Slavery Friends.[72] Having "come out" of the Indiana Yearly Meeting, Anti-Slavery Friends were freed of the hostile Quaker authority that had limited their abolitionist agitation.

The Indiana Yearly Meeting of Anti-Slavery Friends sought to transform abolitionist practice into enforceable doctrine, the only corporate body of Quakers to do so. Anti-Slavery Friends required their members, primarily Orthodox Quakers, to support the Liberty Party and to adopt free produce. In 1849, the Anti-Slavery Friends revised their discipline, making the boycott of slave-labor goods a requirement. Deficiencies reported by subordinate meetings prompted the group to issue epistles in 1853 and 1855, reminding the quarterly and monthly meetings, as well as individual Quakers, of the importance of "a faithful testimony against Slavery." Anti-Slavery Friends never received widespread support from American Quakers. In 1857, the group dissolved for lack of members.[73]

The American Free Produce Association, the Western Free Produce Association, and the Indiana Yearly Meeting of Anti-Slavery Friends framed their support of free produce in moral terms. The members of the AFPA and the WFPA, in particular, gave priority to the morality of free produce above all else. Free produce, they argued, was a sacrifice, a duty, and an act of consistency required of all true abolitionists. Urging abolitionists' identification with the slave, Quaker Benjamin S. Jones claimed, "if we have faith in the principles we advocate, we should be willing to sacrifice luxury, comfort, and convenience in the cause of universal liberty; preferring rather to suffer with the captive, than share the spoils with the oppressor." In the mid-1840s, members of the AFPA celebrated their ability to "maintain [their] principles amidst opposing influences within, as well as without, the anti-slavery ranks." Their critics, however, were quick to point out their inconsistency, citing the unavoidable infiltration of slave-labor products into northern society. Other critics of free produce were frustrated by what they saw as a proliferation of tests for abolitionist membership. "We should have not only the political and ecclesiastical tests, but 'free produce tests,' the 'kitchen table or cast' test, the test of paying taxes to the government that supports slavery, the test of neglecting to do *all* in our power . . . and so on, indefinitely," Samuel Lightbody complained. Instead, Lightbody called on reformers to simply "abolitionize the people and then leave them to act individually."[74] In their quest to bring abolitionists into the free-produce movement, abolitionist consumers instead seemed to push them away with their narrow focus on individual purity and moral consumption.

William Lloyd Garrison was a particularly visible target for supporters of free produce. An early supporter of free produce, by the late 1830s, Garrison had rejected the tactic as impractical. While in London for the World Anti-Slavery Convention, Lucretia Mott tried unsuccessfully to change Garrison's mind. "Rather inconsistent," she noted in her diary.[75] Lea Gause was not so charitable, publicly accusing Garrison of adopting the motto, "No Union with Slaveholders" in theory but not in practice.[76] Time and again, abolitionist consumers pointed out the hypocrisy of abolitionists who purchased slave-labor products, strengthening the very shackles abolitionists were attempting to break.[77] Garrison later defended his stance, arguing that free produce would not convince slaveholders who were motivated "not [by] the love of gain, but the possession of absolute power, unlimited sovereignty."[78] When Garrison claimed abolitionists were particularly entitled to use slave-labor goods because they were fighting for the slave, the AFPA responded, "It is even said, by men of well-known zeal for the cause of freedom, that the friends of the slave have a peculiar, and, indeed, the only right to use the blood-stained fruit of his extorted toil, as if we, whose eyes have been opened to the enormous injustice of the system which extorts that toil, and whose souls burn with indignation at its very name, may appropriate its fruits to our use more guiltlessly than they who are comparatively blind to its inherent sinfulness!"[79] In the 1840s, Garrison continued to assert the impossibility of avoiding all slave-labor products. Garrison criticized those who would use free produce as "a test of moral character." While he expressed respect for those who abstained and who could be described as "the most intellectual, the most courageous, the most self denying, and the most sincerely conscientious antislavery men and women in the land," Garrison chastised Quakers, such as those in Indiana, who abstained from slave-labor goods all the while "upholding the pro-slavery position of the Society with which they are connected." Such free-produce supporters, Garrison remarked using a biblical figure, "strain at a gnat, and swallow a camel."[80]

In the 1840s, American supporters of the free-produce movement were unable to reconcile the economic principles and the moral commitments of abstention. The Quakers who dominated the free-produce movement continued to assert the moral imperative of abstention, driving away potential supporters of the boycott. Although the boycott suffered from chronic problems of supply, the boycott suffered more from the inflexibility of the movement's supporters.

As American supporters of free produce attempted to maintain associations to coordinate the work of the movement, British reformers struggled to continue the British India Society. In August 1840, Manchester replaced London as the center of the Indian reform movement. Five months later, the association established the newspaper, the *British Indian Advocate*, edited by William Adam, who had relocated to Britain from Massachusetts after the World Anti-Slavery Convention. The *Advocate* was short-lived, however. In 1841, the British India Society entered into a formal alliance with the Anti-Corn Law League (ACLL). In an effort to increase free trade, the ACLL sought repeal of British laws restricting the importation of foreign grain. While many British and American abolitionists supported free trade and the Anti-Corn Law League, many others worried that the movement would distract attention from abolitionism, particularly after George Thompson agreed to set aside agitation for the BIS temporarily in order to work for the league. As Elizabeth Pease noted, "they [the League] will not let us have GT to ourselves, *peaceably*." Thompson, Joseph Pease, and the leadership of the BIS agreed to the alliance. In return, the leaders of the Anti-Corn Law League promised to throw the weight of their influence behind Indian reform once the Corn Laws had been repealed. The leaders of the BIS thought they had negotiated a good bargain; however, the alliance proved disastrous for the BIS. The British India Society lost all public momentum for the cause and gained the enemies of the Anti-Corn Law League. By the time the Corn Laws were repealed in 1846, Indian reform and the British India Society were nearly forgotten.[81]

The demise of the American Free Produce Association and the British India Society did not mean the end of free produce in the United States or Britain, however. Supporters of both the AFPA and the BIS regrouped to form new associations. In 1845 and 1846, American Quakers established the Free Produce Association of Friends of Philadelphia Yearly Meeting and the Free Produce Association of Friends of New York Yearly Meeting, respectively.[82] British Quaker Anna Richardson organized the Newcastle Ladies' Free Produce Association in 1846, one of a growing network of British free-produce societies in this period. Three years later, Joseph Sturge chaired a meeting to establish the British Free Produce Association.[83] These associations sustained the free-produce movement in the 1840s and initiated a new wave of free-produce activity in the 1850s.

CHAPTER 8

Bailing the Atlantic with a Spoon: Free Produce in the 1840s and 1850s

Debates over antislavery ideology and strategy prompted a decline in the membership of the Philadelphia Female Anti-Slavery Society in the 1840s. In this period, the society initiated new standards for membership, requiring adherence to nonresistance. The members of the PFASS also shifted their attention away from organizing public lectures and collecting signatures on petitions, focusing instead on the annual antislavery fair. Increasingly, the society narrowed its definition of "proper antislavery work."[1] In 1844, Lucretia Mott acknowledged the "diversity of operations" in the abolitionist movement, but warned abolitionists to exercise caution lest they become too "engrossed with [their] favorite department" in the cause. Supporters of free produce should view abstinence from the products of slave labor "as the beginning, rather than the fulfillment of their duty."[2] In 1846, Esther Moore, the society's first president, resigned to devote more time to the Philadelphia Vigilance Committee. Moore's resignation prompted "a discussion as to how far these mere branches of the Anti-Slavery cause had claims on Abolitionists for their support. The general expression seemed to be 'These things ought ye to do, and not to leave the other undone.'"[3] In the 1840s, the society adopted what one scholar describes as a "more restrictive ideological position." As a result, as historian Carol Faulkner argues, "members . . . chose not only between antislavery societies and vigilance committees, but also between free produce and the inexpensive fruits of slavery, and between moral power and political action."[4] For Mott, abolitionists were to focus on the overthrow of slavery. "Our efforts must still be to destroy the system, root and branch, to lay the axe at the root of the corrupt tree" of slavery, Mott reminded the membership of the PFASS in 1856.[5]

In the 1840s in the free-produce movement, as in the abolitionist movement, supporters debated what constituted "proper antislavery work." Many supporters of free produce continued to assert the importance of free produce as a statement of ideological consistency and, for some, economic power. Others disagreed. Abolitionist and Unitarian minister Samuel J. May compared the use of free produce "as a principal weapon of offence" in abolitionism to "bailing out the Atlantic with a spoon."[6] May's assessment of free produce captured the attitude of many American abolitionists, including Garrison, in the 1840s and 1850s. Still, support for free produce remained strong among the movement's most ardent supporters. Nonetheless, the boycott of slave labor experienced a noticeable shift in its base of support and in its focus. Beginning in the mid-1840s, black abolitionists joined with Quakers in the free-produce movement. Although the movement remained active in the United States, attention shifted back to Britain because of the efforts of black abolitionists like Henry Highland Garnet and because of the increasing emphasis on finding free-labor alternatives for slave-grown cotton. In the 1840s and 1850s, moral commitments and economic principles competed for primacy in the movement as supporters initiated free-labor projects in Massachusetts, Texas, Africa, and beyond. Supporters simultaneously emphasized the moral and the economic benefits of these projects. These efforts reveal the ways in which race, gender, and sectarian support influenced activists' efforts to dislodge slavery from the Atlantic economy.

Quakers and Free Produce

The divisions of the 1830s continued to influence Quakers' response to antislavery and free produce in the 1840s and 1850s. While Quaker meetings on either side of the Hicksite schism continued to issue statements on slavery, abolitionism, and free produce, earlier debates intensified, resulting in additional schisms among Friends. Among Orthodox Quakers, schism came after the visit of British evangelical Quaker minister Joseph John Gurney, who traveled among American Friends from 1837 through 1840. His views were similar to those found in mainstream evangelical culture. Gurney supported Quaker efforts to work with non-Quakers in a variety of reforms, including antislavery, temperance, Bible reading, and prison reform. Rhode Island Quaker John Wilbur, described by one scholar as "a model of the quietist Friend," attacked Gurney's teachings, claiming the British minister's views were unsound. The Gurney-Wilbur conflict led to formal separations in New England and Ohio Yearly Meetings and increased divisions in Philadelphia Yearly Meeting.[7] In the 1840s and 1850s, Hicksites experienced similar divisions as disaffected Friends left their established meetings to form independent associations of Congregational, or Progressive Friends. As it did in the Orthodox split, social reform played a role in the Hicksite division.[8] By the 1850s, there were four distinct groups of Quakers. Among the Orthodox and Hicksite Quakers were others who attempted to tread a middle ground of compromise. Despite these conflicts, Quakers continued to support abstention from the products of slave labor, either individually or collectively in the various free-produce societies.

Among Orthodox Quakers, debates about slavery focused on Friends' participation in abolitionist societies. Of the eleven Quarterly Meetings that composed New York Yearly Meeting (Orthodox), Farmington was most active in promoting antislavery measures. In 1836, for example, in an *Address to Its Members*, the meeting suggested that Friends had failed to make a thorough exertion of "moral influence" in the "cause of emancipation" and, as a result, manifested "a degree of apathy." Farmington Quarterly Meeting urged its members to reject indifference and to exercise "active virtue" on behalf of the slave. Farmington urged New York Yearly Meeting to prepare petitions to the national government and to establish a standing committee on slavery. New York Yearly Meeting, however, continued to limit Friends' antislavery activism to public statements—such as those issued by the Yearly Meeting in 1837, 1844, and 1852—and to abstinence from the products of slave labor. In 1842, Farmington Quarterly Meeting's Committee on Slavery issued its own statement on free produce. Reiterating Quakers' traditional stand against the products of slave labor, Farmington Quarterly urged abstinence as a moral duty. In 1845, New York Yearly Meeting issued a similar address on free produce.[9] In the 1840s, Philadelphia Yearly Meeting (Orthodox) issued its own statements on slavery, including a tract on free produce written by Samuel Rhoads in 1844. Rhoads challenged Friends to examine their testimony on slave-labor produce. Citing the example of John Woolman, Rhoads argued that Friends had for more than a century practiced individual abstinence from slave-labor products. Still, Quakers as a sect had failed to adopt abstinence despite the society's stance against slave trading and slave owning. "We are told that we shall have no reward for attempting *to do good in our own wills*," Rhoads wrote quoting New York Quaker Charles

Marriott. "Would it not be as well to inquire what our reward will be for persisting *to do evil in our own wills*," he asked, countering conservative Friends' claims that joining secular antislavery societies was an attempt to correct that which was better left to divine guidance.[10] The debates among Orthodox Quakers in New York and Philadelphia reveal Friends' efforts to discern the limits of Quaker antislavery. Despite admonitions to avoid "mingling with the world," many Orthodox Quakers continued to actively promote free produce and antislavery, joining in both sectarian and secular societies.[11]

Of the Orthodox Quakers active in these free-produce associations, the majority were Gurneyites. In the 1840s, Orthodox Friends in the Philadelphia, New York, Ohio, and New England Yearly Meetings organized free-produce associations. Rhoads, Abraham Pennock, and George W. Taylor organized the association for the Philadelphia Yearly Meeting. Following a meeting in April 1845, the three were part of the committee charged with drafting a constitution and issuing a call for a general meeting in June.[12] In his history of the Underground Railroad, William Still described Rhoads as having "a keen sense of justice and humanity . . . he never wavered, but as long as slavery existed by law in our country his influence, both publicly and privately, was exerted against it." Rhoads adopted early the traditional Quaker testimony against the products of slave labor, later joining the American Free Produce Association in 1841. He traveled to England twice, in 1834 and again in 1847. It was on his second trip that Rhoads "enlarged his connection and his correspondence with antislavery friends there," including British Quaker Anna Richardson. Rhoads assisted the Vigilance Committee with material assistance and often supplemented his own financial assistance with funds from Richardson and other English supporters. In the 1850s he supported financially Myrtilla Miner's efforts to educate free black girls in Washington, D.C. Working with Pennock and Enoch Lewis, Rhoads edited the *Non-Slaveholder*. He served as editor of the *Friends' Review* from 1856 to 1867, taking over after Lewis's death in 1856.[13] Pennock helped establish the Free Produce Society of Pennsylvania in 1827 and was active in the AFPA, recruiting Gerrit Smith to the organization. He was also active in the Bible Association of Friends, which organized in 1829. Pennock was one of the few Orthodox Friends to play a prominent role in the secular abolitionist movement, hosting British abolitionist George Thompson when he lectured in Philadelphia, for example. Pennock's abolitionist activities were not without controversy among his co-religionists. In 1845, British Quaker Alex Derkin cautioned Pennock against taking "too active a part in the Abolition societies." While Derkin did not want to discourage Pennock from doing all he could for the slave, he cautioned him to work within the bounds of the society in order to preserve his "use & influence" in it.[14] Taylor had studied with Enoch Lewis, later graduating to teach at Quaker schools in Philadelphia, Wilmington, and Long Island where he had come under the influence of Lindley Murray Moore. As a result of his friendship with Moore, Taylor had joined with the Orthodox Quakers when Friends divided in 1827–28. Taylor had been active in the Bible Association of Friends and served as a publishing agent for the *Friend*, an Orthodox Quaker publication. Taylor was also active in the temperance movement.[15] The three men, who exemplified the reformist activity of Gurneyite Quakers, formed the core leadership of the new organization and also assumed editorial responsibilities of the *Non-Slaveholder*, the free-produce newspaper that was established in January 1846.

The Free Produce Association of Friends of Philadelphia Yearly Meeting pledged to increase the manufacture and production of free-labor goods.[16] The economic basis of the organization was quickly established as the board of managers announced, at the first annual meeting, the manufacture of ten thousand yards of cloth. In 1847, sixty thousand yards of cloth were manufactured with similar increases in quantity and quality reported in 1848. In addition to increasing supplies of free-labor goods, members of the association corresponded with British Quakers to promote the use of free-labor products and to share information including an address to the aging Thomas Clarkson, requesting from him any information about the effect of the 1791–1792 boycott on the abolition of the slave trade. Similar groups were formed in New York (1845), Ohio (1846), and New England (1848). All four organizations focused on the supply of free-labor goods. The Philadelphia group maintained close ties to Taylor's free-labor store in Philadelphia and Levi Coffin's store in Cincinnati while the New York society's store was operated by George Wood, Lindley M. Hoag, and Robert Lindley Murray.[17] Although the focus of these free-produce associations remained on increased supplies of free-labor goods, the organizations also urged Friends to remember their moral duty to the slave. For example, the board of managers of the Ohio group issued *The Plea of Necessity* in 1851, examining Friends' plea that necessity led them to use the products of slave labor. "It is . . . to be regretted that many, even of those who believe abstinence from the use of slave products is called for at the hands of sincere opponents of slavery, have, to too great an extent, admitted the weight of this plan," the managers noted. The tract examined the question of abstinence and denied the legitimacy of "the plea of necessity." "The Plea of Necessity" was the second of two free-produce tracts produced that year by the Ohio group. The previous year the group had reissued Farmington Quarterly Meeting's 1836 *Address to Its Members*.[18]

Despite *The Plea of Necessity* and the other antislavery tracts, the various Free Produce Associations of Yearly Meetings focused more on economic principles, leaving explicit statements of moral commitments to the various yearly meetings.

Free-produce activism deepened the divisions that already existed between Wilburite and Gurneyite Orthodox Quakers. The supporters of Wilbur and Gurney held distinct theological views that shaped their response to social reform. Wilburites emphasized the writings of early Friends, investing them with a sort of infallibility in the belief that "early Friends had been given a greater measure of understanding than others in grasping the truths of Christianity." Those Wilburites who were committed to the complete guidance of the Holy Spirit refused to read the Bible unless they felt a special leading. Although the Gurneyites read the early Friends, they based their religious views on the Bible. In matters of social reform, the two groups adopted distinct stands. Wilburites emphasized disengagement with the world, participating in exclusively Quaker organizations. Gurneyites, in contrast, were active in reform and often joined with non-Quakers in social reforms such as free produce and antislavery. For Wilburites, reform work drew Friends into the spirit of the world. Reform work originated in self-will rather than waiting to learn the divine will. Ohio Quaker Joseph Edgerton warned Friends that "joining with those who do not believe in the immediate direction of Christ in such matters, and therefore do not wait for it, you will very likely become like them." Edgerton was one of the most influential ministers in Ohio Yearly Meeting and one of the foremost opponents of abolitionism, describing it as an "overactive, restless spirit" that "like the locust, the cankerworm, and the caterpillar" was "ready to eat up every green thing." Participation in reform, Wilburites believed, would result in an inability to discern the moving of the Holy Spirit. "What a pity! What a pity!" a voice in a dream warned Indiana Quaker Charles Osborn in 1833, "that for the abolition of slavery, and the spreading of the Bible, people should be turned against Christ." In 1842, Osborn was one of the radical Quaker abolitionists removed from Indiana Yearly Meeting's Meeting for Sufferings, later helping to organize the Indiana Yearly Meeting of Anti-Slavery Friends. For Friends like Osborn and Gurney, good works were an essential part of Christianity.[19] The divisions among Orthodox Quakers influenced individual participation in reform movements, such as free produce, and limited the effectiveness of such movements as supporters were forced to defend their activism.

Orthodox Quaker merchant William Bassett of Lynn, Massachusetts, was a member of New England Yearly Meeting's Meeting for Sufferings. In the late 1830s, Bassett came to believe that Quakers had "lost the spirit of Him who was no respecter of persons and who came to 'preach deliverance to the captive.' "[20] During this period, he came out in support of the American Anti-Slavery Society, presided at the Requited Labor Convention in 1838, and was active in the American Free Produce Association. Bassett also helped found the New England Non-Resistance Society. When he was criticized by Quakers for his antislavery activism, Bassett responded by publishing a number of pamphlets and articles condemning New England Quaker leaders for closing the meetinghouse to antislavery lecturers and for their objections to reform societies. He also attacked Quaker meetings that segregated seating for white and black members. Bassett published a *Letter to a Member of the Society of Friends*, defending his participation in antislavery societies. In 1840, after several years of tension between Bassett and the New England Quaker leadership, Bassett was disowned. In 1844, Bassett decided to move with his family to the Northampton Association of Education and Industry (NAEI), a cooperative community founded in 1842 to produce free-labor silk as an alternative to slave-grown cotton.[21]

The NAEI occupied 470 acres about two and a half miles from the center of Northampton, Massachusetts, on a site that included "farm- and woodland, a four story, brick silk factory, a boardinghouse, various outbuildings, and several private houses." The factory building included manufacturing space as well as a dormitory, a common kitchen and dining room, and schoolrooms. Members worked a variety of trades in addition to the community's primary activity, raising silkworms and manufacturing thread. Membership was based on the purchase of stock as well as on shared principles. As Bassett explained to British abolitionist Elizabeth Pease, "Our association is based on the principle of a community of interests—not on that of a community of property. Each person is credited with the amount he invests, and on withdrawal he is entitled to receive the amount to his credit." From its incorporation in 1842 until its dissolution in 1846, the community attracted 240 men, women, and children, including black abolitionists David Ruggles and Sojourner Truth. William Lloyd Garrison and Frederick Douglass were also active in the association's activities.[22]

Bassett joined the NAEI in 1844 after experiencing several years of financial difficulties as well as problems with Quaker leaders. Unemployed and disowned by the Quakers, Bassett saw in the NAEI an opportunity to address the injustices of an economic system that oppressed wage workers as much as it did slaves. As he recounted in a letter to Elizabeth Pease in 1844, "When I was engaged in manufacturing business, with 150 persons in my employ, I became deeply impressed with the ways of the system in which I was involved. I could not reconcile with my ideas of justice the inequality that exists between the employer & the employed. I could not see why those who were laboring for me 15 or 16 hours a day should receive only just enough to sustain life, while I, with leisure for intellectual improvement, was accumulating of the products of their industry." Bassett's description of the injustices of wage labor sounds very much like John Woolman's pleas for an equitable economy in *A Plea for the Poor*. Bassett connected his own behavior as a manufacturer to that of the slaveholder: "If the Southern Slaveholder is guilty of *robbery* in appropriating to himself the earnings of others, how much better am I?" The solution, Bassett decided, was a radical reordering of the relationship between employer and employee:

> It seemed to me as clear as the sun at noon-day, that if an equal amount of labor were bestowed by me and my journeymen, the proceeds of our joint industry should be *equally* distributed amongst us. On investigating the subject I soon became convinced that the evils which I saw and deplored were inherent in the system and that no remedy could be provided but in its subversion. I was satisfied that the system of *hired labor* was false & necessarily unequal in its operation. In short, it seemed that the existing institutions of civilization were based on a most mischievous falsehood, *ie.* that the interests of men are *diverse*— and, hence, that no change in those institutions could satisfy the demands of humanity—The defect was radical and fatal; and a *Reorganization of Society* alone could provide a remedy. Instead of *individual competition*, humanity demands *mutual cooperation*.

The pursuit of wealth had corrupted American society, according to Bassett. Slaveholding was but one symptom of that problem. "If the God of *Love* were worshipped with half the devotedness that is bestowed upon Mammon, what a Paradise this earth would be!" Bassett concluded.[23] However, as historian Christopher Clark argues, Bassett's time in Northampton marked "the high point of his radicalism." After he withdrew from the community and returned to his home in Lynn, Massachusetts, Bassett drifted away from Garrisonian radicalism and toward political abolitionism. Bassett later became a Unitarian.[24]

Hicksite Quakers were as divided as the Orthodox on the issue of Friends' participation in popular reform movements, particularly abolitionism. One area of conflict centered on the use of Quaker meetinghouses for antislavery lectures. This prohibition, which was generally a matter of local option, applied equally to all advocates of reform, including antislavery and temperance. Even gatherings of free-produce supporters were subject to censure because some Friends believed such meetings "dese-crated" the meetinghouse.[25] As New England Yearly Meeting explained, "to open our meetinghouses to lecturers whose opinions and principles on many subjects that *we* consider of primary importance are widely different from ours . . . will have a tendency to draw off the minds of our members from an establishment in the Truth of those principles which have ever been maintained by us."[26] In Indiana, the Yearly Meeting closed meeting-houses to antislavery lecturers in response to criticism from British Friends, such as Joseph Sturge, who believed American Friends were too conserva-tive on the question of slavery.[27] One of the more dramatic closures came in East Fallowfield, Pennsylvania, where a riot broke out during a meeting of the Chester County Anti-Slavery Society in January 1845. The meeting included three antislavery lecturers, including the well-known Abby Kelley from Massachusetts. On the second day, a large crowd gathered for the eve-ning lecture. Quaker Joseph Pennock, who was present, noted the presence of "half a dozen or dozen mobocrats, and a few loose fellows of the baser sort." Just as Quaker physician Edwin Fussell commenced speaking, a riot broke out. Pennock described what ensued: "A mobocrat, in the back part of the house, cried out, 'There, you have talked enough, you talk as if you were going to talk all night.' Then came the din of war. Whistling, shrieks, cries of 'drag him out, clear the house,' resounded on all sides. The stove-pipe was knocked down: brimstone was flung on the stove; panes of glass were knocked out; the women rushed from the house. . . . Some others leapt out the windows; and all was delightful confusion . . . Benjamin Jones stood up on a bench in the midst of the disturbers, and asserted to good purpose the right of every human being to utter his free thoughts upon any question."[28] In the wake of the riot, Fallowfield Preparative Meeting debated whether the meetinghouse should be closed to any meetings other than those of worship and discipline of the Society of Friends. After exten-sive discussion, Friends decided to close the meetinghouse even though the majority of the membership supported keeping the meetinghouse open for antislavery lecturers. That summer the more radical among the local Quak-ers opened the People's Hall. Located next to Fallowfield Meetinghouse in Ercildoun, the People's Hall would serve as a "Free Hall wherein to discuss any and every subject of Interest in Religion, Morals, Physics, Politics, or any subject of interest to the family of man irrespective of clime, class, cast, sex, sects, or party."[29] The closure of meetinghouses to antislavery and free-produce activists exacerbated theological conflicts among Hicksite Quakers. Similar to the divisions among the Orthodox, divisions among the Hicksites centered on theological questions as well as concerns about Quakers involvement in secular reform movements. This division is particularly evident in the ministry of New York Hicksite George Fox White.

White's crusade against secular reform movements reflects the ways in which Quaker involvement could simultaneously advance and limit the boycott of the products of slave labor. Quaker historian Thomas Hamm describes White as "the most controversial, most polarizing figure in Hicksite Quakerism." In the 1840s, White's crusade against popular reform movements "help[ed] fracture every Hicksite yearly meeting except Baltimore and change the course of Hicksite Quakerism."[30] White's theological views were consistent with the positions espoused by leading Hicksites in the 1820s. White's "antireform argument was a logical and consistent outgrowth of the Hicksite Reformation," Hamm argues. "Its roots lay in a quietism that eschewed undertaking any action without a clear divine leading, in worries about the impact that joining with non-Friends even in good causes would have on Quakers, and in fear of the ambitions and influence of evangelical Protestant reformers, especially the clergy, in American society." White was an opponent of slavery who, when he felt led, could denounce slavery in terms consistent with the most fervent of abolitionists. White also abstained from the products of slave labor. Yet White vehemently opposed nonsectarian reform societies, believing they were a threat to Quakerism. Non-Quaker abolitionists, notably Oliver Johnson, who was editor of the American Anti-Slavery Society's newspaper the *National Anti-Slavery Standard*, criticized White. In 1840, Johnson and White exchanged a series of letters in which Johnson took White to task for a range of failures. In February 1841, Johnson published the exchange. The following month Johnson published "A Rare Specimen of a Quaker Preacher," an even more scathing attack on White. Johnson's conflict with White led to charges being brought against Quakers Isaac T. Hopper, Charles Marriott, and James S. Gibbons, who as members of the board of directors of the AASS were held responsible for promoting discord and disunity among Friends. When Hopper, Marriott, and Gibbons denied any wrongdoing, they were disowned. White also attacked Lucretia Mott for her participation in antislavery and nonresistance organizations. Joining with like-minded Hicksite leaders, White posed a threat to Mott's membership in the Society of Friends. In the end, Mott was able to resist her enemies and retain her membership.[31]

White's crusade against nonsectarian reform divided Hicksite Quakers, contributing to the polarization among Hicksites over the issue of antislavery. In the late 1840s and early 1850s, Hicksite Quakers in New York, Michigan, Ohio, and Pennsylvania withdrew from their respective yearly meetings. In New York, the separation came in 1848 when about two hundred members of the Genesee Yearly Meeting withdrew and established the Congregational Friends. The Yearly Meeting of Congregational Friends rejected the structure of the Society of Friends; they also embraced reform causes such as antislavery and temperance. That same year witnessed similar divisions among Hicksites in Michigan and Ohio. In Pennsylvania, the split came later, in 1851, in Kennett Monthly Meeting. That split culminated in 1853 with the formal establishment of the Pennsylvania Yearly Meeting of Progressive Friends.[32]

In the 1840s and 1850s, Quaker debates about Friends' involvement in nonsectarian reform movements, such as free produce and antislavery, influenced both the participation in and the development of those movements. The schisms of the 1840s resulted in four distinct groups of Quakers: Gurneyite Orthodox, Wilburite Orthodox, Hicksite, and Progressive. The presence of supporters of abstention in each of these groups suggests the enduring importance of free produce as a form of Quaker antislavery. While the practice of abstaining from the products of slave labor could transcend theological differences, it also deepened the divisions among Quakers, for example, when individuals such as George Fox White used the practice of free produce as a weapon to attack the reform work of their coreligionists. Significantly, for the boycott of slave labor, the Quaker schisms of the 1840s limited the effectiveness of abstention. Of the four groups formed out of the separations of the 1840s, only the Gurneyite Quakers actively promoted the economic objectives of abstinence. While Hicksites such as Lucretia Mott continued to assert the moral commitment of abstinence as a form of ideological consistency, it was Gurneyites such as George W. Taylor who worked to accomplish the economic principles of abstinence. As the most radical of Quakers, Progressive Friends seemed most likely to carry the mantle of free produce. Yet, many Progressives such as Chester County Quaker J. Williams Thorne, an ardent opponent of slavery, did not practice free produce.[33] For those Progressives who did support free produce, abstention was an element of a broader practice of social reform, including antislavery, women's rights, and temperance.

Britain, Black Abolitionists, and Free Produce

British Quakers provided critical support to the Free Produce Association of Friends of Philadelphia Yearly Meeting and, by extension, to the American free-produce movement in the 1840s and 1850s. Joseph Sturge, founder of the British and Foreign Anti-Slavery Society, provided financial support to aid the free-produce association as well as making funds available to Samuel Rhoads for the use of the Vigilance Committee.[34] In 1846, the American pacifist Elihu Burritt joined the free-produce cause, providing a vital link between Sturge in Britain and Rhoads and Taylor in the United States. In the fall of that year, Burritt traveled to England at Sturge's expense to promote his newly formed peace organization, the League of Universal Brotherhood. While in England, Burritt made the decision to include free produce in his plan for the league. He intended "to adopt the little plan of the [Free Produce Association of Friends of Philadelphia Yearly Meeting], and expand it to a great system which should finally bring every mother's son of the non-slaveholders of the South into antagonism to their feudal barons of the lash," Burritt wrote Garrison, "thus arraying against slavery the powerful interest of free labor right on its bloodstained territory." Burritt explained his ambitious plan to establish free-labor cotton factories in America, England, and France.[35] Three weeks later, Burritt wrote Taylor, outlining his plan and requesting information about free produce. "I am desirous of presenting this movement to the British public in a way that it has never been done," Burritt wrote. "I believe the people here are ready for it." He believed "the exclusive consumption of Free Labor products" should be an integral aspect of the league's program. "I want you to keep me supplied with the facts necessary for a full exposition of the subject [of free produce]." For Burritt, reinvigorating the American free-produce movement would move British abolitionists to action. "The Abolitionists here have nothing large to do," Burritt told Taylor in November 1846. "This measure would be the greatest one that ever was originated." In England, women organized female auxiliaries known as Olive Leaf Circles to raise funds for the league by selling sewn articles, most of which were, at Burritt's encouragement, made from free-labor goods. There were about 150 of these circles in England by 1850, creating a ready-made market for free-labor goods. Despite this optimistic start, Burritt's peace crusade eclipsed his interest in free produce and antislavery until 1852 when the publication of *Uncle Tom's Cabin* rekindled his interest.[36]

In 1852, Burritt once again promoted the free-produce cause in Britain and the United States, suggesting a number of ideas to increase the supply of free-labor goods. Burritt proposed the creation of a company to support free produce. Supporters of free produce would purchase shares in the company, which would then pay dividends to farmers who raised free-labor cotton. Another plan proposed sending European immigrants to the American South to establish free-labor cotton farms. This plan would provide large amounts of free cotton for the market and would demonstrate to southern slaveholders the superiority of free labor. Burritt also established a free-produce depot in London in 1853. When Calvin and Harriet Beecher Stowe toured England in 1854, Burritt explained the project to them. The Stowes pledged their support. Harriet encouraged Burritt to tour the southern states and offered to cover the expenses of such a trip. In this same period, Burritt began to edit a new monthly, *Citizen of the World*, to be published by Taylor in Philadelphia. *Citizen of the World* promoted free produce. Burritt also took over editorial duties of *The Slave*, a weekly started by British Quaker and free-produce supporter Anna Richardson. Burritt also published *The Bond of Brotherhood*, which complemented and promoted his League of Universal Brotherhood. By the mid-1850s, however, Burritt's efforts were severely limited by the failure of the league and the stagnation of Taylor's cotton manufacturing. With the depression of 1857, the free-produce movement was in near collapse.[37]

Burritt's free-produce work was supported by British Quakers Henry and Anna Richardson who were leaders in the British free-produce movement. From 1851 through 1855, Anna edited the free-produce periodical *The Slave*. Henry and Anna had been involved in the abolitionist movement since the 1830s. In 1846, Anna founded the Ladies Free Produce Association. In addition to antislavery, the Richardsons were also involved in the peace movement. In 1850, Reverend Henry Highland Garnet accepted an invitation from the Richardsons to tour Britain to promote free produce. Historian R. J. M. Blackett describes American black abolitionists who visited England in this period as a "third force," providing an alternative to political abolitionists and Garrisonians who vied for British attention. As a "third force"—independent, active contributors to the transatlantic abolitionist movement—black abolitionists provided British supporters an opportunity to remain involved in the movement without necessarily having to take sides. Garrisonians opposed free produce and Garnet's tour because they worried it would erode support for other, more efficient abolitionist tactics. Frederick Douglass also opposed Garnet's tour, claiming Garnet had never supported free produce in America. Despite the criticism, Garnet's tour was a success, leading to the establishment of twenty-six free-produce societies by the end of January 1851.[38]

Garnet spent three years abroad. He toured Scotland, England, and Ireland. Additionally, he and Henry Richardson attended a peace conference in Germany. Little is known of Garnet's German tour, which is credited with the establishment of the German Anti-Slavery Society. Garnet also influenced an effort to establish free-labor stores in Germany. After leaving England, Garnet and J. W. C. Pennington traveled to Jamaica.[39] Garnet promoted free produce as a powerful weapon against slavery though it mattered little to him whether supporters were drawn to the movement by economic or moral motives. Garnet along with the Richardsons sustained the free-produce movement and drew other abolitionist consumers into their circle of influence. In the black abolitionist community, Samuel Ringgold Ward and Alexander Crummell promoted free produce as a practical tactic and a moral responsibility. Garnet, like Elihu Burritt, provided a vital link between American and British supporters of free produce.

Cheap Cotton

By the 1850s, through the work of the American Free Produce Association, the British India Society, and other free-produce and antislavery associations, the focus of the boycott of slave labor had expanded to include more explicitly the need to find free-labor alternatives for slave-grown cotton. Consumer demand for cotton textiles in Europe and the United States fueled an expansion of cotton production in Britain, making Britain the largest global producer of cotton in the 1840s. Centered in Manchester, which was dubbed "Cottonopolis" by *The Times*, and Lancashire, the British textile industry was the principal consumer of the global raw-cotton crop and, as a result, heavily dependent on American slave-grown cotton. "American slavery is principally supported by the demand of Great Britain for the cotton of the United States," British abolitionists observed in 1846. British consumption of cotton helped revitalize the free-produce movement in Britain and stimulated interest among British and American abolitionists in the 1840s and 1850s.[40] Africa and Texas were of particular focus in the 1850s as sites for free-labor cotton colonies.

In *Cotton Cultivation in Africa*, published in 1858, American Orthodox Quaker Benjamin Coates laid out his argument for an international reform movement connected to the cultivation of free-labor cotton in Africa. Coates argued that African cotton would be less expensive than American cotton and would, as a result, garner the support of both English and American consumers. African cotton would thrive and as a result so would African society while American slavery, once rendered unprofitable, would wither away. Philadelphia Yearly Meeting (Orthodox) endorsed the cotton-growing plan in a statement against slavery. Influenced by Coates's pamphlet, Garnet devoted much of his time for the next three years to the African cotton project, establishing the African Civilization Society in 1859 to civilize and evangelize Africa and to promote cotton cultivation.[41] Support in the African American community was divided. Reverend J. Sella Martin "believed the Civilization Society would tend to break the link which held England to this country, and makes her dependent on the Southern States for cotton."[42] Unfortunately, the involvement of colonizationists such as Coates limited the organization's appeal among American supporters of free produce.[43]

The desire for free-labor cotton led supporters of the boycott to once again consider Texas, now part of the United States, as a site for the production of free-labor sugar and cotton. Texas land merchant Jacob de Cordova gave a series of lectures in the United States and England, promoting the state and its suitability for cotton production. Born in 1808 in Jamaica, de Cordova was raised in England by an aunt. In the 1820s, he migrated to Philadelphia where he joined his father who had become president of the Congregation Mikveh Israel in 1820. De Cordova settled in Texas in 1839, living in Galveston and Houston where he served as one of the founders of Beth Israel. In the 1840s and 1850s, de Cordova traveled throughout the state of Texas. He laid out the central Texas town of Waco in 1848 and 1849 before settling in Guadalupe County near Seguin in 1852. By 1859 de Cordova had acquired nearly one million acres of Texas land and was widely recognized as an expert on Texas.[44] In 1858, de Cordova lectured in Pennsylvania, New Jersey, and New York before traveling to England at the invitation of the Cotton Supply Association of Manchester. De Cordova's lectures, which were drawn from his book *The Texas Immigrant and Traveller's Guide Book* (1856), lauded the state as a new home for emigrants. De Cordova described a land abundant in natural resources and rich in opportunity.[45] As one reviewer noted of de Cordova's book *Texas: Her Resources and Her Public Men* (1858), "Everything grows in Texas, or would grow if it were planted. There is room for slave-labour among the canes, and free-labour among the corn and the wine—and for slave or free labour, according to the taste or circumstances of the planter, among the cotton, which will remunerate either method of production." Cotton cultivation, in particular, allowed an antislavery man "to sink his principles in his personal practice." For the emigrant, who was able to purchase land and "work for his own hand, . . . Texas [would] become not only an 'earthly paradise' . . . but 'a little heaven below' to the contemplation of the Northern abolitionist, whose real prospect of ever trampling out the 'guaranteed institution' is through competition alone."[46] In England, de Cordova glossed over his proslavery leanings, emphasizing instead the potential for free-labor cotton in Texas. "Whilst you are directing your attention to [the cultivation of cotton] in India, and receiving reports of cotton prospects from Africa, I come before you to tell you of a State . . . [which] if encouraged by emigration and nourished by capital, is capable of producing every year, by European labor—from three to five million bales of cotton," de Cordova told his listeners. He cited the example of German immigrants who grew nearly one-fifth of the cotton produced in Texas and asserted his view that "white labor" was "the most economical." Only in Texas could cotton be successfully produced by free labor, de Cordova remarked, and "those who visit the State of Texas must soon be convinced of its importance as a cotton-growing country."[47] De Cordova's speeches were published and read widely on both sides of the Atlantic. As a result of de Cordova's efforts, his land company, which he co-owned with his brother Phineas, became one of the largest ever operated in the southwestern United States.[48]

Jacob de Cordova was not alone in promoting Texas as a productive site for free-labor cotton. From 1852 through 1857, journalist and landscape architect Frederick Law Olmsted embarked on an extensive research journey through the South and Texas, writing a series of articles for the *New York Daily Times*, which were collected into three volumes, including *A Journey through Texas* (1857). Like de Cordova, Olmsted celebrated the cotton production of the antislavery German immigrants in Texas. Olmsted had for several years been involved in efforts to bring free-soil settlers to Texas. In 1857, Olmsted turned his attention to immigration, hoping to use the positive reception his book had received in the North to generate interest in free-labor immigration to Texas. Olmsted distributed copies of *A Journey through Texas* to abolitionists, including Samuel Gridley Howe, Theodore Parker, and John Greenleaf Whittier. The *Texas* book was translated into German in an attempt to encourage further German immigration to Texas. Olmsted also sent copies of his book to the Cotton Supply Associations of Manchester and Liverpool. In his correspondence with British cotton interests, he pointed out that the supply of cotton was limited only by the labor supply, and a tenfold increase in the production of cotton was possible if there were a significant increase in the number of free immigrants into the Southwest. Moreover, the cotton crop of the United States, Olmsted wrote, "might be doubled on the land as yet unoccupied" in Texas. "There is nothing in the laws, nor, under discreet direction, need there be anything in the prejudices of the people, to prevent free settlers occupying this land," Olmsted concluded. By 1858, however, personal difficulties forced Olmsted to drop his active promotion of Texas.[49]

The efforts of de Cordova and Olmsted generated considerable interest in the Northeast in the idea of a free-labor cotton colony in Texas. In 1861, New England businessman Edward Atkinson published the pamphlet *Cheap Cotton by Free Labor*. Like Olmsted, Atkinson sought the transformation of cotton production by bringing free labor to Texas by convincing northern textile manufacturers that slavery was not the most effective way to grow cotton. Displacing slave-labor from cotton production would break the "slave oligarchy" that had deprived working men of "participation in a branch of agriculture capable of being made the most profitable and self-sustaining of any which can be followed in this country," Atkinson argued. The system of slave-labor had proved inefficient. The high cost of slaves had kept planters from increasing production of cotton. If Texas lands were instead "occupied by an intelligent yeomanry" rather than "the whiskey-drinking, pork-eating race which now occupies them," cotton production would increase. Echoing the arguments of de Cordova and Olmsted, Atkinson claimed Texas had enough cotton and sugar land "to supply three times the entire crop now raised in this country." Using free labor to produce these staples more cheaply than they could be produced by slave labor would bring an end to slavery—"the law of competition is inexorable." Atkinson declared the slave-labor system a failure. "Have not the cotton spinners of the world the right to say to the slaveholder:—You have proved by the experience of the last few years that with your slave labor you cannot give us cotton enough." While Atkinson believed free blacks could grow cotton more efficiently than enslaved blacks, the bulk of his argument focused on free white labor.[50] Atkinson's pamphlet was well received by northern and British businessmen. Olmsted told Atkinson he had read his pamphlet "with more satisfaction than anything hitherto published on the slavery question."[51]

Atkinson promoted a plan to send the federal army to Texas to emancipate the slaves, compensating their owners so they might have capital enough to transition to free labor. Occupying Texas would isolate the "old slave states," leaving slavery "to die a certain and a peaceful death." In a letter to Gustavus Fox, assistant secretary of the navy, Massachusetts Governor John Andrew outlined the military and economic benefits of Atkinson's Texas plan. In addition to flanking the southern rebellion, the plan would restore the cotton supply for northern manufacturers and encourage loyal men to remain in Texas. "These points are urged, not in the interest of Abolitionists," Andrew emphasized, "but by leading commercial men and capitalists, as fairly coming under the necessities and rules of war."[52] Andrew sent copies of his letter to other government officials as well as friends in New York. The plan had the support of many in the federal government, including Secretary of the Treasury Salmon P. Chase and Secretary of War Edwin M. Stanton. Despite such support, President Abraham Lincoln refused to support the plan, citing other military priorities. Lincoln later relented, as a result of pressure from his own cabinet and from Texas Unionists, and authorized Nathaniel P. Banks to lead an expedition to the Gulf Coast of Texas. By the time Banks launched a Texas expedition up the Red River in 1864, Atkinson had turned his attention elsewhere. In late 1863, Atkinson, with support from Boston businessmen, organized the Free Labor Cotton Company, which leased southern cotton plantations "on humane business principles." The group hired A. H. Kelsey as their agent. Kelsey and his son traveled to the lower Mississippi Valley where they leased a large cotton plantation, hired workers, and proceeded to plant a cotton crop. Unstable economic conditions as well as Confederate raids limited the outcome of the project.[53]

Free-produce stalwarts Taylor and Burritt had also explored the possibility of free-labor cotton from Texas. Nathan Thomas, an agent for the Free Produce Association of Friends of Philadelphia Yearly Meeting, traveled through Louisiana, Mississippi, Texas, and Arkansas to determine the prospects for free-labor production in the region. In his letters to Taylor and Rhoads, Thomas provided an extensive description of the region. Thomas believed Texas might become a viable source of free-labor goods, but in the late 1840s the region was too sparsely settled and too far from reliable transportation to be considered.[54] Elihu Burritt suggested that the success of German immigrants in Texas in producing free-labor cotton might be reproduced in Georgia, Alabama, or Mississippi.[55] In 1850, the Free Produce Association of Friends of New York Yearly Meeting considered a proposal to raise $100,000—half of which would be raised in England—to award prizes to planters in Texas who produced the largest amount of free-labor cotton. Benjamin Tatham, the New York Quaker who proposed the scheme, pledged $500 a year to help "crowd slavery out of Texas." His co-religionist Richard Carpenter described Tatham's pledge as "very liberal," but noted also that "he is very safe in making it." While Carpenter claimed "an increasing interest in the success" of free produce, he did not feel a similar "increase of hope that it will succeed."[56] Philadelphia Friends, like many non-Quakers, lauded the success of the German immigrants in Texas in the 1850s. "The production of a thousand bales, untouched by servile hands, within a small district of that fertile region," Samuel Rhoads and Enoch Lewis remarked, "certainly gives encouragement to the belief, that with proper exertions a supply might be obtained more than equal to existing demands."[57] Nonetheless, the Quaker efforts did not lead to an increase in the production of free-labor cotton.

The efforts of free-produce activists to increase the production of free-labor cotton faced formidable challenges in the 1840s and 1850s. As slaveholders migrated west toward new cotton regions such as Texas, they also created, as historian Edward Baptist argues, "practices, attitudes, and material goods—whips, slates, pens, paper, and the cotton plant itself—that made" their "cotton-picking method as efficient as possible." New practices were reinforced by the use of torture, extorting "new efficiencies" from the "most skillful hands and contriving minds ever harder." As a result, cotton production by slave labor continued to expand, doubling in the 1850s from two million to four million bales. World consumption of cotton experienced similar increases, from one and one-half billion pounds at the beginning of the decade to two and one-half billion pounds by the end of the decade, with nearly two-thirds of that amount coming from American fields. By 1860, seven of the eight wealthiest states had been created by cotton's march south and west.[58]

By the end of the 1850s, despite nearly one hundred years of arguments against the products of slave labor, the so-called "gains of oppression" had deepened their hold on the transatlantic economy. Among Garrisonian abolitionists, support for free produce declined rapidly in this period. Even among Quakers, those first supporters of the boycott of slave labor, the boycott lost its relevance for many, particularly as they worried about the continued divisions among Orthodox and Hicksite Quakers. While some Quakers asserted the moral imperative of free produce, others—notably Gurneyite Quakers—focused their efforts on increasing the production of free-labor goods. Free-labor cotton from Texas or Africa would provide sufficient economic leverage to permanently dislodge slave-labor cotton from the Atlantic market. These efforts were unsuccessful, however, revealing how dependent consumers were on slave-labor goods. Yet, free produce as a statement of moral commitment and economic principle persisted and even, to an extent, flourished as the movement attracted new supporters, particularly black abolitionists like Henry Highland Garnet. The presence of new supporters such as Garnet and Atkinson reveals the resilience of the idea of moral commerce.

Conclusion
There Is Death in the Pot!

> She little thinks that to enable her to sweeten her daily
> meal, the African village may have been fired—the
> horrors of the middle-passage inflicted—human beings
> brought to the auction-block and sold into intermi-
> nable Slavery, the wife from the husband, and the child
> from the parent—the gang, male and female, driven to
> the cane-field with a cart-whip—herded together at
> night like cattle—systematically kept in heathen
> darkness and degradation!
>
> —Anna Richardson, *There Is Death in the Pot!*, c. 1850

Henry and Anna Richardson produced three pamphlets in support of Garnet's free-produce tour of England: *A Revolution of the Spindles for the Overthrow of American Slavery, Conscience versus Cotton*, and *There Is Death in the Pot!* The first two tracts reflect the boycott's shift in focus to slave-grown cotton in the nineteenth century while the third, with its graphic title, captured both the past and the present of the boycott of slave labor. The phrase, "there is death in the pot," is a reference to the prophet Elisha who commanded his servant to gather herbs to make a stew for the sons of the prophets. The servant mistakenly gathers poisonous gourds, prompting one man to cry out, "O, man of God, there is death in the pot." Elisha added flour to the pot, miraculously transforming the con-taminated stew into a wholesome, nourishing meal.[1] *There Is Death in the Pot!* invoked in its title the specter of James Gillray's "Barbarities in the West Indias," the eighteenth-century political caricature of a slave boiled to death in a pot of sugar cane juice, and the specter of blood-stained sugar (see Figure 3). It also referenced Frederick Accum's scandalous work, *A Treatise on the Adulteration of Food and Culinary Poisons*, which was first published in 1820 and reprinted widely in England, the United States, and Germany. Using the phrase, "there is death in the pot," Accum urged consumers to take action against contaminated foodstuffs. A "lurid production," according to one historian, *Treatise* went through multiple editions, even after the author left England in disgrace and fear.[2]

There Is Death in the Pot! traced the contamination of consumer goods by slave labor and the role of consumers in transforming the marketplace. Linking slave-labor goods to domestic consumption, Richardson wrote, "The grocer takes your [money for sugar], and retaining a fraction as his profit, hands all the remainder to the wholesale dealer, the dealer hands it to the importer, the importer to the Cuban merchant; the merchant to the Slaveholder, to whom it becomes a premium for the maintenance of slavery." Although total abstinence from slave-labor goods was impossible, that was not sufficient justification for "consuming some hundred-weights of Slave-grown sugar, or some scores of pounds of Slave-grown coffee, while the same articles, in Free produce, are within our reach." The tract concluded with a table headlined, "The Free-Man or the Slave; Which Shall Supply Your Table?" Three columns labeled "Produce of Free Labour," "Produce of Slave Labour," and "Partly Free, Partly Slave, or Uncertain" mapped for consumers the progress of emancipation in the Atlantic world, emphasizing the availability of free-labor sugar, coffee, and tobacco from the British West Indies and the continued oppressive labor conditions in Cuba, Brazil, and the American South. *There Is Death in the Pot!* documented the accomplishments of the boycott as well as the work that remained. In mapping the availability of free-labor goods, the tract emphasized consumers' ability to act as moral agents in the market. Like the flour used to transform the poisonous stew of the Old Testament, consumers could transform the market through their individual purchases of free-labor goods.[3]

There Is Death in the Pot! also makes clear the limits of the boycott as evidenced by the continued presence of slave-labor goods. The boycott was most effective in Britain in the 1790s and the 1820s when activists garnered widespread support for a boycott of slave-grown sugar by linking the boycott to other political and social issues such as women's activism, parliamentary reform, and colonial expansion. Estimates for the 1791–1792 boycott vary widely ranging from three hundred thousand to as many as one-half million participants. The door-to-door canvas of the 1820s likely yielded an even higher figure.[4] Compare those figures to estimates for the American movement. At the height of its popularity, an estimated five to six thousand individuals attempted to buy only free-labor goods; free-produce societies attracted about fifteen hundred members. In 1847, the *Non-Slaveholder* placed the number far higher, estimating that ten thousand Friends or 10 percent of all Quakers abstained from slave-labor goods.[5] The stark difference between the British and American movements is instructive. British supporters, especially in the 1790s and the 1820s, targeted slave-grown sugar, thus effectively limiting the scope of the boycott. Although such a political strategy limited the general economic impact on slaveholders, it did focus considerable attention on the violent production of slave-grown sugar, giving rise to graphic images of Britons consuming the flesh and blood of African slaves. Such a focus may well have contributed to the popularity of the boycott because consumers, repulsed by the thought of eating contaminated sugar, rejected the commodity. In contrast, American supporters targeted a broad range of slave-labor goods, including sugar, cotton, indigo, rice, and coffee. For Quakers, such as George W. Taylor, the morality of free produce called on consumers to forgo *all* products of slave labor. While Taylor and others invoked the violence of slave labor, suggesting, for example, that cotton had been stained by the blood of slaves, such rhetoric lacked the intense lurid focus that distinguished antisugar rhetoric. Moreover, this comprehensive boycott of slave labor forced supporters, including Taylor, to spend considerable time and effort locating free-labor alternatives. American supporters of the boycott often framed abstention and free produce as an absolute choice—demanding complete abstinence as proof of ideological consistency. This moral absolutism led many abolitionists, including Garrison, to reject boycotting as an antislavery tactic.

Taylor's free-produce activism reveals how much Quaker abstention had changed since the ministry of John Woolman. For Woolman, the rise of consumer society imperiled the individual's soul. Consumer goods, whether made by slaves or free men, hindered an individual's relationship with God. Thus Woolman's abstention was both antislavery and anticommerce. Where Woolman saw danger, Taylor saw redemption. Taylor believed the market held the potential to act as an agent of moral reform, purifying the market of slave-labor goods and bringing the individual closer to God by aligning faith and action. That many Quakers, individually and collectively, continued to practice abstention and free produce despite the many schisms of the nineteenth century suggests the protean meanings of the boycott. While many Quakers believed activism in the free produce and antislavery movements would lead Friends away from their religious tenets, others believed such activism was an important means of putting faith into action. In 1884, reflecting back on the movement, Taylor noted that the predictions of Friends had not materialized: "Some [Friends] looked upon [free produce] with suspicion, as likely to lead Friends away from communion with our religious Society. . . . [This] prediction was not verified in a single instance to my knowledge."[6] The flexibility of free produce provided for the presence of both groups of Quakers—conservative Quakers who abstained as an individual statement of renunciation of the sin of slavery, and evangelical Quakers (such as Taylor) who abstained as part of a broader statement of reform. Additionally, the presence in the movement of radical Quaker abolitionists such as Lucretia Mott serve as further evidence of the multiplicity of meanings activists gave to abstention and free produce. For Mott and like-minded activists, free produce affirmed their unequivocal commitment to racial equality.

The women who supported abstention and free produce were as diverse as the Quakers. The boycott of slave-labor goods transformed women from the unreliable abolitionists of the eighteenth century to the movement's moral core in the nineteenth century. The movement accommodated a multitude of female voices, including the economic analysis of Heyrick, the sentimental arguments of Chandler, and the racial radicalism of Mott. Even as moral suasion lost ground in the 1840s, many women continued to assert the imperative of free produce, citing ideological consistency as an important signifier of antislavery commitment and as an important statement of radical identification with the slave. Free produce assured both conservative and radical women of a place in the antislavery movement. Moreover, the multivocal networks of the free-produce movement connected radical women such as the pacifist Mott—"who proclaimed she was a belligerent in the face of slavery"—to the militant black abolitionist Henry Highland Garnet who simultaneously advocated slave insurrection and free produce.[7]

Garnet and other black abolitionists in the 1840s and 1850s embraced the economic principles of free produce, which they saw as a practical response to the failure of moral suasion. For Garnet, free produce had the potential to provide the economic foundation necessary for racial equality. In the 1840s and 1850s, many British abolitionists aided the efforts of black abolitionists to establish free labor. In 1848, Douglass's *North Star* reprinted Henry Richardson's *Revolution of the Spindles*, in which he connected British consumption of American cotton to slavery, claiming a revolution of the spindles would overthrow American slavery. Echoing the words of Garrison, Richardson demanded "No Commercial Union with Slaveholders!"[8] Richardson urged consumers to "come out" of the marketplace and to create instead an alternate economy based on justice and equality. Seeking alternate sources for southern, slave-grown cotton, British abolitionists supported the efforts of Garnet and other black abolitionists who planned to establish free-labor colonies in Africa and the Caribbean. These projects would restore to black laborers the fruits of their labor. More significantly, these projects were a critical step in achieving racial equality. Black abolitionists asserted both the moral commitment and the economic principle of the boycott. "Tell the planters that you will no longer, by buying the produce of their slaves, suffer them to get rich by the sweat, and agony, and blood of your fellow creatures—that you will reduce them from affluence to poverty and bankruptcy, and immediately the system will come to an end," Alexander Crummell told the British and Foreign Anti-Slavery Society in 1849.[9]

Still, supporters of free produce never came close to displacing slave-labor goods from the Atlantic marketplace. In her history of the free-produce movement, Ruth Nuermberger claims the boycott of slave labor failed because it placed too heavy a demand on the individual consumer: "Voluntary self-denial can be expected only of the conscientious few, never of the mass."[10] While Nuermberger is correct, the failure of the boycott reveals more than a lack of economic and moral commitment by the mass of abolitionists. Instead, we need to understand the sheer audacity of the boycott. Garrison correctly recognized just how indispensable slave-labor goods had become in the nineteenth century.[11] While northerners abolished slavery, manufacturers and consumers in New England remained connected to slavery through their commercial transactions, perhaps most visibly in the links between the ever-expanding cotton frontier and the textile manufacturers in places such as Pawtucket, Rhode Island, and Lowell, Massachusetts. More than cotton connected the industrial North and the plantation South, however, as northern manufacturers produced critical goods such as hoes, shoes, and clothing for slaves.[12] Among consumers, early crops from the South allowed northerners to enjoy an extended growing season. "Early in the spring from the South . . . many rare vegetables and other edibles are brought to market by the facilities afforded by rail cars and steamboats, thus inducing, as it were, in these latitudes, artificial seasons," observed Thomas De Voe, a butcher and New York City's future superintendent of markets.[13] In the nineteenth century, as slave-labor goods expanded the breadth and depth of their economic reach, antislavery consumers found it increasingly difficult to remain free of slave-labor goods. According to historian Seth Rockman, as historians have turned more attention to the relationship between slavery and capitalism, their works "hold a great deal of promise for recognizing slavery's centrality to the *capital* at the heart of capitalism. . . . Following the money has allowed scholars to see slavery less as a regional system and more as the wellspring of national economic development."[14] The men and women who supported the boycott of slave labor as well those who gave up on the boycott recognized that challenge. "I have myself, for many years, endeavored to carry out this principle [free produce] . . . as far as I could do so," Samuel J. May wrote in 1848, before comparing the boycott to "bailing out the Atlantic with a spoon."[15] That May felt compelled to defend his habits of consumption, even as he criticized the boycott, suggests the success of the boycott of slave labor cannot be measured by purely economic means. Supporters of the boycott made the connection between slavery and capitalism an inescapable reality. In the process, they pioneered a new conception of consumer activism that has, as one scholar notes, "become the lingua franca of consumer activists ever since."[16]

For more than one hundred years, support for abstention and free produce waxed and waned; yet, support for the movement never completely disappeared, which is a testament to activists' resilience and persistence. The rhetoric of abstention and free produce emphasized consumers' complicity in slavery and called on men and women to reject the immoral commerce in slaves and slave-labor goods. Invoking the ideals of humanity and justice, supporters of the boycott envisioned a deep-rooted transformation of the Atlantic economy. For supporters of moral commerce, each individual decision in the marketplace was freighted with moral significance. Therein rests the success of the movement. As supporters and opponents debated the meaning and the role of moral commerce in the fight for the abolition of slavery, they made it impossible to remain fully neutral in the slavery debate.

NOTES

Introduction. A Principle Both Moral and Commercial

1. Free Produce Society of Pennsylvania, *Constitution of the Free Produce Society of Pennsylvania* (Philadelphia: D. & S. Neall, 1827); Judith Wellman, *The Road to Seneca Falls: Elizabeth Cady Stanton and the First Woman's Rights Convention* (Urbana: University of Illinois Press, 2004), 74, 93, 109. "Boycott" is a late nineteenth-century term, referring to the anticolonial protest of Irish peasants against British landlords. The word "boycott" is derived from the name of British land agent, Captain Charles Boycott, and was popularized in the nineteenth century by Scottish-born American journalist, James Redpath. In 1880, when Boycott attempted to evict tenants from his employer's land, local residents protested Boycott's action by refusing to work his fields or to trade with him. Ostracized and isolated, Boycott and his family were forced to work the fields themselves. In the United States, reporting on the protest, Redpath coined the word "boycott," claiming the word more effectively described the tactic of ostracism. As historian Lawrence Glickman argues, Redpath "invented the word 'boycott' because it was short and catchy, more likely to be adopted by both the press and the protestors." See Lawrence Glickman, *Buying Power: A History of Consumer Activism in America* (Chicago: University of Chicago Press, 2009), 121–127; Monroe Friedman, *Consumer Boycotts: Effecting Change through the Marketplace and the Media* (New York: Routledge, 1999). Since 1880, the word "boycott" has been applied to an array of consumer protests at the local, national, and international levels. For the modern reader and consumer, "boycott" is more descriptive than the less familiar phrase "free produce," which was used most regularly by antislavery activists, though both "boycott" and "free produce," as well as "abstention," refer to forms of consumer activism.

2. William Lloyd Garrison to Richard P. Hunt, May 1, 1840, in *The Letters of William Lloyd Garrison*, ed. Walter M. Merrill and Louis Ruchames (Cambridge, Mass.: Harvard University Press, 1971–1981), 2:594–596; William Lloyd Garrison to Thomas McClintock, May 1, 1840, McClintock-Neeley Collection, Women's Rights National Park Historic Park, Seneca Falls, New York.

3. *Genius of Universal Emancipation*, October 30, 1829; Wendell Phillips Garrison and Francis Jackson Garrison, *William Lloyd Garrison, 1805–1879: The Story of His Life Told by His Children*, 4 vols. (Boston: Houghton, Mifflin, 1894), 1:152, 264. Ruth Ketring Nuermberger claims Garrison was responsible for the inclusion of a free-produce resolution in the American Anti-Slavery Society's "Declaration of Sentiments" in 1833, a view Carol Faulkner challenges noting the presence at the

convention of free-produce supporters Lucretia Mott, Sidney Ann Lewis, and Lydia White. See Ruth Ketring Nuermberger, *The Free Produce Movement: A Quaker Protest against Slavery* (New York: AMS Press, 1942), 21; Carol Faulkner, "The Root of the Evil: Free Produce and Radical Antislavery, 1820–1860," *Journal of the Early Republic* 27 (2007): 390–391.

4. *Liberator*, June 18, 1836; March 5, 1847; March 1, 1850; Glickman, *Buying Power*, 83–84, 332n33.

5. Florence Kelley, "My Philadelphia," *Survey* 57 (October 1, 1926): 54; *A Memorial to Sarah Pugh: A Tribute of Respect from Her Cousins* (Philadelphia: J. B. Lippincott, 1888), 14, 23, 33–34; Minutes of the American Free Produce Association, October 15, 1839, reel 31, Pennsylvania Abolition Society, Historical Society of Pennsylvania, Philadelphia (hereafter cited as AFPA, HSP).

6. *Liberator*, July 18, 1835; Angelina Grimké Weld to Elizabeth Pease, August 14, 1839, in *British and American Abolitionists: An Episode in Transatlantic Understanding*, ed. Clare Taylor (Edinburgh: Edinburgh University Press, 1974), 79; *Liberator*, March 1, 1850.

7. *Liberator*, March 5, 1847; June 18, 1847; *Non-Slaveholder*, April 1847.

8. *Liberator*, March 1, 1850.

9. Wendell Phillips Garrison, "Free Produce among the Quakers," *Atlantic Monthly*, October 1868, 493.

10. Nuermberger, *Free Produce Movement*, 59, 113.

11. For American abstention and free produce, see Faulkner, "The Root of the Evil"; Glickman, *Buying Power*, 61–89; Stacey Robertson, *Hearts Beating for Liberty: Women Abolitionists in the Old Northwest* (Chapel Hill: University of North Carolina Press, 2010), 67–90; Julie Roy Jeffrey, *The Great Silent Army of Abolitionism: Ordinary Women in the Abolitionist Movement* (Chapel Hill: University of North Carolina Press, 1998), 20–22; Beth Salerno, *Sister Societies: Women's Antislavery Organizations in Antebellum America* (DeKalb: Northern Illinois University Press, 2005), 17–19. For the British movement, see Charlotte Sussman, *Consuming Anxieties: Consumer Protest, Gender, and British Slavery, 1713–1833* (Stanford, Calif.: Stanford University Press, 2000), 110–29; Clare Midgley, *Women against Slavery: The British Campaigns, 1780–1870* (London: Routledge, 1992); Clare Midgley, *Feminism and Empire: Women Activists in Imperial Britain* (London: Routledge, 2007); Elizabeth Kowaleski-Wallace, *Consuming Subjects: Women, Shopping, and Business in the Eighteenth Century* (New York: Columbia University Press, 1997), 37–51; Anna Vaughan Kett, "Quaker Women, the Free Produce Movement and British Anti-Slavery Campaigns: The Free Labour Cotton Depot in Street, 1852–1858" (doctoral thesis, University of Brighton, 2012). To date, no full history of the British free-produce movement has been written.

12. Glickman, *Buying Power*, 35–36, 322n9. See also E. P. Thompson, "The Moral Economy of the English Crowd in the Eighteenth Century," *Past and Present* 50 (February 1971): 79; Barbara Clark Smith, "Food Rioters and the American Revolution," *William and Mary Quarterly* 51 (January 1994): 11; Phyllis Whitman Hunter, *Purchasing Identity in the Atlantic World: Massachusetts Merchants, 1670–1780* (Ithaca, N.Y.: Cornell University Press, 2001), 104. The food riots described by Thompson, Smith, and Hunter were attempts by the working poor to restore what they perceived as their right to a supply of food at a reasonable price.

13. Mimi Sheller, "Bleeding Humanity and Gendered Embodiments: From Antislavery Sugar Boycotts to Ethical Consumers," *Humanity: An International Journal of Human Rights, Humanitarianism, and Development* 2 (Summer 2011): 188.

14. The fair-trade movement is just one example of modern consumer activism. See Keith R. Brown, *Buying into Fair Trade: Culture, Morality, and Consumption* (New York: New York University Press, 2013).

15. British and American abolitionists who supported the immediate and unconditional abolition of slavery used the word "immediatism" to define their style of activism. See John Stauffer, "Immediatism," in *The Historical Encyclopedia of World Slavery*, ed. Junius P. Rodriguez (Santa Barbara, Calif.: ABC-CLIO, 1997), 1:364.

16. Faulkner, "The Root of the Evil," 392; *Proceedings of the Anti-Slavery Convention of American Women*, Philadelphia, May 15, 16, 17, and 18, 1838 (Philadelphia, 1838), 7.

17. Roger Bruns, "Benjamin Lay: The Exploits of an Ardent Abolitionist," *American History Illustrated* 14 (May 1979): 14–22; David Waldstreicher, "Benjamin Franklin, Religion, and Early Antislavery," in *The Problem of Evil: Slavery, Freedom, and the Ambiguities of American Reform*, ed. Steven Mintz and John Stauffer (Amherst: University of Massachusetts Press, 2007), 168–169. "Guerilla theater" is from Waldstreicher.

18. John Woolman, *A Plea for the Poor; or, A Word of Remembrance and Caution to the Rich*, repr., John Woolman, *The Journal and Major Essays of John Woolman*, ed. Phillips P. Moulton (New York: Oxford University Press, 1971), 238.

19. Kirsten Sword, "Remembering Dinah Nevil: Strategic Deceptions in Eighteenth-Century Antislavery," *Journal of American History* 97 (2010): 324–325; Christopher Leslie Brown, *Moral Capital: Foundations of British Abolitionism* (Chapel Hill: University of North Carolina Press, 2006), 406–424.

20. Barbara Welter, "The Cult of True Womanhood: 1820–1860," *American Quarterly* 18 (1966): 151–174. An extensive literature examines the concept of "separate spheres." For two of the most helpful, see Linda Kerber, "Separate Worlds, Female Worlds, Woman's Place: The Rhetoric of Women's History," *Journal of American History* 75 (1988): 9–39; Amanda Vickery, "Golden Age to Separate Spheres? A Review of the Categories and Chronology of English Women's History," *Historical Journal* 36 (1993): 383–414.

21. The historiography of the consumer revolution is quite extensive. For the most useful works, see Neil McKendrick, John Brewer, and J. H. Plumb, *The Birth of a Consumer Society: The Commercialization of Eighteenth Century England* (Bloomington: Indiana University Press, 1982); John Brewer and Roy Porter, eds., *Consumption and the World of Goods* (New York: Routledge, 1993); Grant McCracken, *Culture and Consumption: New Approaches to the Symbolic Character of Consumer Goods and Activities* (Bloomington: Indiana University Press, 1988); T. H. Breen, *The Marketplace of Revolution: How Consumer Politics Shaped American Independence* (New York: Oxford University Press, 2004); Ann Smart Martin, *Buying into the World of Goods: Consumers in Backcountry Virginia* (Baltimore, Md.: Johns Hopkins University Press, 2008); Ann Smart Martin, "Makers, Buyers, and Users: Consumerism as a Material Culture Framework," *Winterthur Portfolio* 28 (1993): 141–157; Cary Carson, "The Consumer Revolution in Colonial British America: Why Demand?" in

Of Consuming Interests: The Style of Life in the Eighteenth Century, ed. Cary Carson, Ronald Hoffman, and Peter J. Albert (Charlottesville: University Press of Virginia, 1994), 483–697.

22. Kowaleski-Wallace, *Consuming Subjects*, 5.

23. See S. Bradley Shaw, "The Pliable Rhetoric of Domesticity," in *The Stowe Debate: Rhetorical Strategies in Uncle Tom's Cabin*, ed. Mason I. Lowance, Ellen E. Westbrook, and R. D. DeProspo (Amherst: University of Massachusetts Press, 1994), 73–98.

24. Richard S. Newman, "'A Chosen Generation': Black Founders and Early America," in *Prophets of Protest: Reconsidering the History of American Abolitionism*, ed. Timothy Patrick McCarthy and John Stauffer (New York: New Press, 2006), 63, 67.

25. *Freedom's Journal*, November 2, 1827.

26. See Gary B. Nash, *Forging Freedom: The Formation of Philadelphia's Black Community, 1720–1840* (Cambridge, Mass.: Harvard University Press, 1988), 5. Nash argues that free blacks in Philadelphia "pursued their goal of a dignified and secure existence. . . . Recognizing the obstacles they faced, and maneuvering within boundaries that most of them had only limited resources to redefine, they tested, contested, sometimes transcended, and sometimes succumbed to the power of white Philadelphians above, among, and around them" (5).

27. Seymour Drescher, Capitalism and Antislavery: British Mobilization in Comparative Perspective (New York: Oxford University Press, 1987), x.

28. Elihu Burritt, *Twenty Reasons for Total Abstinence from Slave-Labour Produce* (Bucklersbury, UK: J. Unwin, n.d.).

29. Geoffrey Plank, *John Woolman's Path to the Peaceable Kingdom: A Quaker in the British Empire* (Philadelphia: University of Pennsylvania Press, 2012), 83.

30. See, e.g., Nuermberger, *Free Produce Movement*, 83–99.

31. Samuel J. May to John Estlin, May 2, 1848, Samuel J. May Papers, Boston Public Library, Boston (hereafter cited as May Papers, BPL).

32. Nuermberger, *Free Produce Movement*, 89–91; Carol Lasser, "Immediatism, Dissent, and Gender: Women, and the Sentimentalization of Transatlantic Anti-Slavery Appeals," in *Women, Dissent, and Anti-Slavery in Britain and America, 1790–1865*, ed. Elizabeth J. Clapp and Julie Roy Jeffrey (New York: Oxford University Press, 2011), 111–112.

33. See Ellen Hartigan-O'Connor, "'She Said She Did Not Know Money': Urban Women and Atlantic Markets in the Revolutionary Era," *Early American Studies* 4 (2006): 323.

34. *Liberator*, March 5, 1847.

35. Elizur Wright Jr., "On Abstinence from the Products of Slave Labor," *Quarterly Anti-Slavery Magazine* 1 (1836): 395.

36. William Goodell to Lewis C. Gunn, August 29, 1838, repr., *Minutes of the Required Labor Convention*, Philadelphia, May 17 and 18, 1838; September 5 and 6, 1838 (Philadelphia: Merrihew and Gunn, 1838), 16.

37. Edward E. Baptist, *The Half Has Never Been Told: Slavery and the Making of American Capitalism* (New York: Basic Books, 2014), 321–322. For the connection between slavery and economic growth, see also Sven Beckert, *Empire of Cotton: A Global History* (New York: Alfred A. Knopf, 2014); Walter Johnson, *River of Dark*

Dreams: Slavery and Empire in the Cotton Kingdom (Cambridge, Mass.: Harvard University Press, 2013); Joshua Rothman, *Flush Times and Fever Dreams: A Story of Capitalism and Slavery in the Age of Jackson* (Athens: University of Georgia Press, 2012); Craig Steven Wilder, *Ebony and Ivy: Race, Slavery, and the Troubled History of America's Universities* (New York: Bloomsbury Press, 2013). For a broader geographic and temporal perspective, see Joseph Inikori, *Africans and the Industrial Revolution in England: A Study in International Trade and Economic Development* (New York: Cambridge University Press, 2002).

38. Seth Rockman, "Slavery and Capitalism," *Journal of the Civil War Era*, http://journalofthecivilwarera.org/forum-the-future-of-civil-war-era-studies/the-future-of-civil-war-era-studies-slavery-and-capitalism.

39. Elihu Burritt to George W. Taylor, September 29, 1846, Taylor Family Papers, Coll. No. 1179, Quaker Collection, Haverford College, Haverford, Penn. (hereafter cited as QC, HC).

40. Sarah Pugh, Diary Entry, January 1846, in *A Memorial to Sarah Pugh*, 35–36.

41. Ibid., August 1844, 33–34.

1. Prize Goods

1. Ruth Ketring Nuermberger, *The Free Produce Movement: A Quaker Protest against Slavery* (New York: AMS Press, 1942), 4–5. See also Ryan P. Jordan, *Slavery and the Meetinghouse: The Quakers and the Abolitionist Dilemma* (Bloomington: Indiana University Press, 2007), 36; Geoffrey Plank, *John Woolman's Path to the Peaceable Kingdom: A Quaker in the British Empire* (Philadelphia: University of Pennsylvania Press, 2012), 152; Thomas P. Slaughter, *The Beautiful Soul of John Woolman: Apostle of Abolition* (New York: Hill and Wang, 2008); David Waldstreicher, "Benjamin Franklin, Religion, and Early Antislavery," in *The Problem of Evil: Slavery, Freedom, and the Ambiguities of American Reform*, ed. Steven Mintz and John Stauffer (Amherst: University of Massachusetts Press, 2007), 168–169.

2. There is some debate about the length of Lay's residency in Barbados with estimates ranging from one to thirteen years. See Roberts Vaux, *Memoirs of the Lives of Benjamin Lay and Ralph Sandiford: Two of the Earliest Public Advocates for the Emancipation of the Enslaved Africans* (Philadelphia: Solomon W. Conrad, 1815), 17–20; C. Brightwen Rowntree, "Benjamin Lay," *Journal of the Friends' Historical Society* 33 (1936): 3–13. For the debate, see David Brion Davis, *The Problem of Slavery in Western Culture* (New York: Oxford University Press, 1966), 322n59.

3. Nuermberger, *Free Produce Movement*, 4; Waldstreicher, "Benjamin Franklin," 168; Plank, *John Woolman's Path*, 100–101; Brycchan Carey, *From Peace to Freedom: Quaker Rhetoric and the Birth of American Antislavery, 1657–1761* (New Haven, Conn.: Yale University Press, 2012), 164–172. See also Vaux, *Memoirs*.

4. Plank, *John Woolman's Path*, 101, 102–104, 105–106; Geoffrey Plank, "The First Person in Antislavery Literature: John Woolman, His Clothes, and His Journal," *Slavery and Abolition* (March 2009): 70–71; John Woolman, *The Journal and Major Essays of John Woolman*, ed. Phillips P. Moulton (New York: Oxford University Press, 1971), 36–38, 119; Jean R. Soderlund, *Quakers and Slavery: A Divided Spirit* (Princeton, N.J.: Princeton University Press, 1985), 15–17.

5. Ross Martinie Eiler, "Luxury, Capitalism, and the Quaker Reformation, 1737–1798," *Quaker History* 97 (Spring 2008): 14–18.

6. James Walvin, "Slavery, the Slave Trade and the Churches," *Quaker Studies* 12 (March 2008): 190, 191. Walvin cites the examples of George Whitefield and John Newton: "George Whitefield, an evangelist in America, did not approve of slavery—but he nonetheless owned slaves. The young slave captain, John Newton, saw nothing odd as he put rebellious Africans in the thumbscrews before settling down to pray for a safe and profitable passage to the Americas. . . . Throughout [this period], whatever unease or discomfort, there was no sense that slave ownership was irreligious; it was a matter of rendering unto Caesar" (190). Until recently, scholars have dismissed early Quaker antislavery as being of little consequence. Historians, according to Brycchan Carey, recognize the intimate connection between the early history of Quakerism and the early history of abolitionism; yet, those same historians generally dismiss these early efforts, dated between 1650 and 1750, as having "little impact" on the eventual development of abolitionism. As Carey argues, historians "have paid more attention to results and outcomes than to process." Carey, *From Peace to Freedom*, 2–3. Geoffrey Plank makes a similar argument in his biography of John Woolman, noting the presence of an older strand of abolitionist historiography that dismisses early abolitionism as of little consequence. More recent work has adopted what Plank describes as a "deeper chronological perspective, which allows us to assess the full contribution of the Quakers." Plank, *John Woolman's Path*, 239n18. In addition to Carey's and Plank's work, see also Christopher Leslie Brown, *Moral Capital: Foundations of British Abolitionism* (Chapel Hill: University of North Carolina Press, 2006); Maurice Jackson, *Let This Voice Be Heard: Anthony Benezet, Father of Atlantic Abolitionism* (Philadelphia: University of Pennsylvania Press, 2009).

7. Pink Dandelion, *The Quakers: A Very Short Introduction* (New York: Oxford University Press, 2008), 2–8. In his longer examination of Quaker theology, Dandelion claims, "this intimacy with Christ, this relationship of direct revelation, is alone foundational and definitional of the movement. It does not describe any period or branch of Quaker theology sufficiently . . . [rather] Quakerism has had its identity constructed around this experience and insight." Pink Dandelion, *An Introduction to Quakerism* (New York: Cambridge University Press, 2007), 22. See also Hugh Barbour, *The Quakers in Puritan England* (New Haven, Conn.: Yale University Press, 1964); H. Larry Ingle, *First among Friends: George Fox and the Creation of Quakerism* (New York: Oxford University Press, 1994).

8. Dandelion, *Introduction to Quakerism*, 13–24.

9. Thomas D. Hamm, *The Transformation of American Quakerism: Orthodox Friends, 1800–1907* (Bloomington: Indiana University Press, 1988), 7–8; Carey, *From Peace to Freedom*, 30–31; A. Glenn Crothers, *Quakers Living in the Lion's Mouth: The Society of Friends in Northern Virginia, 1730–1865* (Gainesville: University Press of Florida, 2012), 20–21.

10. Crothers, *Quakers Living in the Lion's Mouth*; Dandelion, *Quakers*, 22, 37–43; Carey, *From Peace to Freedom*, 28–30. See also Barry Levy, *Quakers and the American Family: British Settlement in the Delaware Valley* (New York: Oxford University Press, 1988). In the 1660s, as Friends were formalizing their meeting structure, separate men's and women's business meetings were recommended at all levels, each with their own areas of responsibility. George Fox believed this was necessary for women to

have their own voice. The first women's yearly meeting was not established until 1784, more than one hundred years after Fox's call for such meetings. See Dandelion, *Quakers*, 22.

11. Dandelion, *Quakers*, 23; Crothers, *Quakers Living in the Lion's Mouth*, 20–21.

12. See, e.g., Deuteronomy 24:7: "If a man be found stealing any of his brethren of the children of Israel, and maketh merchandise of him, or selleth him; then that thief shall die; and thou shalt put evil away from among you."

13. "Germantown Friends' Protest against Slavery," in *The Quaker Origins of Antislavery*, ed. J. William Frost (Norwood, Penn.: Norwood Editions, 1980), 69. Frost's version is based on a nineteenth-century transcription. See also Carey, *From Peace to Freedom*, 71–86. Carey reproduces the original manuscript, recovering the original orthography.

14. Thomas E. Drake, *Quakers and Slavery in America* (New Haven, Conn.: Yale University Press, 1950), 11–14; Soderlund, *Quakers and Slavery*, 18; Carey, *From Peace to Freedom*, 83–85.

15. Travis Glasson, *Mastering Christianity: Missionary Anglicanism and Slavery in the Atlantic World* (New York: Oxford University Press, 2012), 52–53; Drake, *Quakers and Slavery in America*, 14–15; Carla Gardina Pestana, *Protestant Empire: Religion and the Making of the British Atlantic World* (Philadelphia: University of Pennsylvania Press, 2009), 111. See also Ethyn Williams Kirby, *George Keith, 1693–1716* (New York: American Historical Association, 1942); J. William Frost, *The Keithian Controversy in Early Pennsylvania* (Norwood, Penn.: Norwood Editions, 1980); Jon Butler, " 'Gospel Order Improved': The Keithian Schism and the Exercise of Quaker Ministerial Authority in Pennsylvania," *William and Mary Quarterly*, 3rd ser., 31 (July 1974): 431–452.

16. William Bradford and George H. Moore, "The First Printed Protest against Slavery in America," *Pennsylvania Magazine of History and Biography* 13 (October 1889): 265–270; Carey, *From Peace to Freedom*, 91–92. For the fruits of the Spirit, see Galatians 5:22–23.

17. "Robert Piles," in Frost, *Quaker Origins of Antislavery*, 71–72; Carey, *From Peace to Freedom*, 101.

18. See Maxine Berg, "Luxury, the Luxury Trades, and the Roots of Industrial Growth: A Global Perspective," in *The History of Consumption*, ed. Frank Trentmann (New York: Oxford University Press, 2012), 173–191; Sidney W. Mintz, *Sweetness and Power: The Place of Sugar in Modern History* (New York: Viking, 1985).

19. John Hepburn, *The American Defence of the Christian Golden Rule; or, An Essay to Prove the Unlawfulness of Making Slaves of Men. By Him who Loves the Freedom of the Souls and the Bodies of All Men* (New York, 1715), 82–122; Drake, *Quakers and Slavery in America*, 34–35; Carey, *From Peace to Freedom*, 123–142; Davis, *Problem of Slavery in Western Culture*, 317.

20. Hepburn, *American Defence of the Golden Rule*, 82–122, esp. 90–91, 118. See also Drake, *Quakers and Slavery in America*, 34–35; Carey, *From Peace to Freedom*, 123–142; Davis, *Problem of Slavery in Western Culture*, 317.

21. Robert Bruns, ed., *Am I Not a Man and a Brother: The Antislavery Crusade of Revolutionary America, 1688–1788* (New York: Chelsea House, 1977), 16; Carey, *From Peace to Freedom*, 127.

22. As quoted in Oliver Pickering, " 'The Quakers Tea Table Overturned': An Eighteenth-Century Moral Satire," *Quaker Studies* 17 (March 2013): 252.

23. Society of Friends, *London Yearly Meeting: Extracts from the Minutes and Advices of the Yearly Meeting of Friends Held in London, from its First Institution* (London: James Phillips, 1783), 186.

24. As quoted in Pickering, "'Quakers Tea Table,'" 252.

25. Ralph Sandiford, *The Mystery of the Iniquity: In a Brief Examination of the Practice of the Times, by the Foregoing and Present Dispensation* (Philadelphia, 1730), 5; Ralph Sandiford, *A Brief Examination of the Practice of the Times, by the Foregoing and the Present Dispensation* (Philadelphia, 1729).

26. J. William Frost, "Quaker Antislavery: From Dissidence to Sense of the Meeting," *Quaker History* 101 (Spring 2012): 18. As Frost argues, "Unlike Hepburn . . . the Quaker belief in authoritative personal revelation and his knowledge that there were many who agreed with him gave Sandiford the confidence to disagree with the weighty Friends who dominated the meeting." See also Davis, *Problem of Slavery in Western Culture*, 320. Davis claims Sandiford had more in common with his successor Benjamin Lay than with his predecessor Hepburn. Unlike Hepburn, Sandiford and Lay "were ready to be ostracized or even to die for the cause; and their works drip with blood and smell of the smoke and ash of hell." Brycchan Carey describes Sandiford's book as "an amalgam of the previous half-century's writing on slavery, embedded within a particularly dense piece of religious rhetoric." It was, as Carey notes, "a strategic intervention in the political debate" about the slave trade. "Its rhetoric, while certainly thundering forth from the pulpit . . . also betrays moments of conciliation and even of political shrewdness." Carey, *From Peace to Freedom*, 131, 147.

27. Sandiford, "Dedication," in *Brief Examination*, n.p. See also Carey, *From Peace to Freedom*, 150.

28. Sandiford, "Dedication," in *Brief Examination*; Sandiford, *Mystery of the Iniquity*, 107.

29. Sandiford, *Mystery of the Iniquity*, 7. See also Carey, *From Peace to Freedom*, 159.

30. Vaux, *Memoirs*, 39–43.

31. Alexander X. Byrd, *Captives and Voyagers: Black Migrants across the Eighteenth-Century British Atlantic World* (Baton Rouge: Louisiana State University Press, 2008), 6; Michelle Craig McDonald, "Transatlantic Consumption," in *The Oxford Handbook of the History of Consumption*, ed. Frank Trentmann (New York: Oxford University Press, 2012), 115–119. See also Eric Williams, *Capitalism and Slavery* (Chapel Hill: University of North Carolina Press, 1994); Richard S. Dunn, *Sugar and Slaves: The Rise of the Planter Class in the English West Indies, 1624–1713* (Chapel Hill: University of North Carolina Press, 1972); Richard B. Sheridan, *Sugar and Slavery: An Economic History of the British West Indies, 1623–1775* (Barbados: Caribbean Universities Press, 1973); Daniel Littlefield, *Rice and Slaves: Ethnicity and the Slave Trade in Colonial South Carolina* (Baton Rouge: Louisiana State University Press, 1981); Judith A. Carney, *Black Rice: The African Origins of Rice Cultivation in the Americas* (Cambridge, Mass.: Harvard University Press, 2001); Allan Kulikoff, *Tobacco and Slaves: The Development of Southern Cultures in the Chesapeake, 1680–1800* (Chapel Hill: University of North Carolina Press, 1986). In his discussion of the Anglican Church's involvement in slavery and the slave trade, James Walvin notes that the church was not alone: "Slavery ensnared each and every institution in Britain, from Parliament itself, to the

humblest of manufacturers and workers laboring in slave-related industries." Walvin, "Slavery, the Slave Trade and the Churches," 195.

32. Grant McCracken, *Culture and Consumption: New Approaches to the Symbolic Character of Consumer Goods and Activities* (Bloomington: Indiana University Press, 1988), 22, 19.

33. T. H. Breen, *The Marketplace of Revolution: How Consumer Politics Shaped American Independence* (New York: Oxford University Press, 2004), 304.

34. K. N. Chaudhuri, *The Trading World of Asia and the English East India Company, 1660–1760* (Cambridge: Cambridge University Press, 1978), 385.

35. Elizabeth Kowaleski-Wallace, *Consuming Subjects: Women, Shopping, and Business in the Eighteenth Century* (New York: Columbia University Press, 1997), 22; Francis S. Drake, ed., *Tea Leaves: Being a Collection of Letters and Documents Relating to the Shipment of Tea to the American Colonies in the Year 1773, by the East India Company* (Boston: A. O. Crane, 1884), 200; Breen, *Marketplace of Revolution*, 304.

36. Beth Carver Wees, *English, Irish, and Scottish Silver at the Sterling and Francine Clark Art Institute* (New York: Hudson Hills Press, 1997), 267–269; Andrew White, "A 'Consuming' Oppression: Sugar, Cannibalism and John Woolman's 1770 Slave Dream," *Quaker History* 96 (Fall 2007): 14–15; Jennifer Anderson, *Mahogany: The Costs of Luxury in Early America* (Cambridge, Mass.: Harvard University Press, 2012); Clare Midgley, *Feminism and Empire: Women Activists in Imperial Britain* (London: Routledge, 2007), 46; Breen, *Marketplace of Revolution*, 304.

37. Chaudhuri, *Trading World of Asia*, 385; Wendy Woloson, *Refined Tastes: Sugar, Confectionery, and Consumers in Nineteenth-Century America* (Baltimore: Johns Hopkins University Press, 2002), 22–23. See also Mintz, *Sweetness and Power.*

38. Charlotte Sussman, *Consuming Anxieties: Consumer Protest, Gender, and British Slavery, 1713–1833* (Stanford, Calif.: Stanford University Press, 2000), 29–30.

39. Mintz, *Sweetness and Power*, 21–22, 46–47, 53; White, "A 'Consuming' Oppression," 8–9.

40. Russell R. Menard, *Sweet Negotiations: Sugar, Slavery, and Plantation Agriculture in Early Barbados* (Charlottesville: University of Virginia Press, 2006), 83–84.

41. John G. Stedman, *Narrative, of a Five Years' Expedition: Against the Revolted Negroes of Surinam, in Guiana, on the Wild Coast of South America, from the Year 1772 to 1777* (London: J. Johnson and J. Edwards, 1796), 1:315–316.

42. B. W. Higman, *Slave Population and Economy in Jamaica, 1807–1834* (Kingston, Jamaica: University of West Indies Press, 1995), 121–123. Sugar plantations experienced the highest rates of mortality among the enslaved. Mortality rates declined slightly in the coffee, livestock, and pimento (allspice) industries. Mortality rates declined significantly on plantations where the cultivation of minor staples, such as pimento, was combined with coffee growing or livestock raising. See Vincent Brown, *The Reaper's Garden: Death and Power in the World of Atlantic Slavery* (Cambridge, Mass.: Harvard University Press, 2008), 51–52.

43. As quoted in Robert L. Paquette, *Sugar Is Made with Blood: The Conspiracy of La Escalera and the Conflict between Empires over Slavery in Cuba* (Middletown, Conn.: Wesleyan University Press, 1988), 56.

44. Peter Motteux, *A Poem upon Tea*, repr., *Literary Representations of Tea and the Tea-Table*, vol. 1 of *Tea and the Tea-Table in Eighteenth-Century England*, ed. Markman Ellis (London: Pickering and Chatto, 2010), 38–48.

45. *The Tea-Drinking Wife, and Drunken Husband*, repr. *Literary Representations of Tea and the Tea-Table*, 163–171.

46. Jonas Hanway, *A Journal of Eight Days Journey from Portsmouth to Kingston upon Thames . . . To Which Is Added, An Essay on Tea . . .* (London: H. Woodfall, 1756); Sussman, *Consuming Anxieties*, 25–28; Kowaleski-Wallace, *Consuming Subjects*, 21–23.

47. John Wesley, *A Letter to a Friend, Concerning Tea* (London, 1825); Sussman, *Consuming Anxieties*, 35–36.

48. As quoted in Pickering, " 'Quakers Tea Table,' " 254.

49. "Joshua Evans's Journal," in *Friends' Miscellany* 10 (1837): 25–26. See also Plank, *John Woolman's Path*, 83.

50. Jackson, *Let This Voice Be Heard*, 55.

51. Soderlund, *Quakers and Slavery*, 32–53; Carey, *From Peace to Freedom*, 177–182.

52. Frost, "Quaker Antislavery," 27; Plank, *John Woolman's Path*, 105–106; Phillips P. Moulton, "Woolman Chronology," in Woolman, *Journal*, 17–20. For a discussion of the circumstances surrounding the publication of Woolman's journal, including the differences between the British and the American editions, see Plank, "The First Person in Antislavery Literature," 76–79.

53. John Woolman, *Considerations on Pure Wisdom, and Human Policy; on Labour; on Schools; and on the Right Use of the Lord's Outward Gifts* (Philadelphia: D. Hall and W. Sellers, 1768), 4.

54. John Woolman, *Considerations on Keeping Negroes: Recommended to the Professors of Christianity, of Every Denomination, Part Second* (Philadelphia: B. Franklin and D. Hall, 1762), 26–27; Woolman, *Considerations on Pure Wisdom*, 12–17.

55. John Woolman, *Considerations on the True Harmony of Mankind; and How It Is to Be Maintained* (Philadelphia: Joseph Crukshank, 1770), 13–14.

56. Woolman, *Considerations on Pure Wisdom*, 12–17, 23; John Woolman, *A Plea for the Poor; or, A Word of Remembrance and Caution to the Rich*, repr., Woolman, *Journal*, 240.

57. Woolman, *Some Considerations on the Keeping of Negroes*, repr., Woolman, *Journal*, 208.

58. Woolman, *Considerations on Pure Wisdom*, 12–17, 23; Plank, *John Woolman's Path*, 85–86.

59. Woolman, *Considerations on Pure Wisdom*, 13, 15; Woolman, *A Plea for the Poor*, 247.

60. Woolman, *Considerations on Keeping Negroes, Part Second*, , 43–44.

61. Woolman, *Journal*, 36–38; Plank, *John Woolman's Path*, 67–68, 114–115.

62. Woolman, *Journal*, 59; Plank, *John Woolman's Path*, 111.

63. Woolman, *Journal*, 28; Woolman, *Considerations on the True Harmony of Mankind*, 13.

64. Woolman, *Journal*, 59. See also Plank, "The First Person in Antislavery Literature," 69–70; Plank, *John Woolman's Path*, 111–115.

65. Woolman, *Journal*, 60.

66. See Isaiah 33:15: "He that walketh righteously, and speaketh uprightly; he that despiseth the gain of oppressions, that shaketh his hands from holding of bribes, that stoppeth his ears from hearing of blood, and shutteth his eyes from seeing evil."

67. Plank, *John Woolman's Path*, 120; Andrew White, "'Keeping Clear from the Gain of Oppression': 'Public Friends' and the De-Mastering of Quaker Race Relations in Late Colonial America" (PhD diss., University of Washington, 2003), 148–153.

68. Plank, "The First Person in Antislavery Literature," 69.

69. Woolman, *Journal*, 65.

70. Woolman, *Considerations on Keeping Negroes, Part Second*, 24, 31–32; Woolman, *A Plea for the Poor*, 250, 259, 266; Woolman, *Journal*, 65, 66.

71. Woolman, *Journal*, 161.

72. Plank, "The First Person in Antislavery Literature," 70.

73. As quoted in Henry J. Cadbury, *John Woolman in England: A Documentary Supplement* (Philadelphia: Friends' Historical Society, 1971), 95, 97.

74. Woolman, *Journal*, 190.

75. Woolman, *A Plea for the Poor*, 250, 259. For a full discussion of Woolman's clothes, see Plank, "The First Person in Antislavery Literature," 67–91.

76. Plank, "The First Person in Antislavery Literature," 79.

77. Vaux, *Memoirs*, 23–24, 67.

78. Kenneth Carroll, *Joseph Nichols and the Nicholites: A Look at the "New Quakers" of Maryland, Delaware, North and South Carolina* (Easton, Md.: Easton Publishing, 1962), 42–43.

79. Plank, "The First Person in Antislavery Literature," 80.

80. "Joshua Evans Journal," 21–24, 32.

81. Plank, "The First Person in Antislavery Literature," 79–80; "Some Account of the Religious People Called 'Nicholites,'" in *Friends Miscellany* 4 (1833): 245; Carroll, *Joseph Nichols*, 18, 20, 26.

82. DeFoe as quoted in Brown, *Reaper's Garden*, 24. For more about Woolman and DeFoe, see Thomas L. Haskell, "Capitalism and the Origins of the Humanitarian Sensibility, pt. 2," in *The Antislavery Debate: Capitalism and Abolitionism as a Problem in Historical Interpretation*, ed. Thomas Bender (Berkeley: University of California Press, 1992), 158–160; John Ashworth, "The Relationship between Capitalism and Humanitarianism," in Bender, *Antislavery Debate*, 186.

83. Woolman, *Journal*, 161.

84. White, "A 'Consuming' Oppression," 1–27.

85. Plank, "The First Person in Antislavery Literature," 79.

86. Joseph Woods, *Thoughts on the Slavery of Negroes* (London: James Phillips, 1784), 7, 18–19.

2. Blood-Stained Sugar

1. Sidney W. Mintz, *Sweetness and Power: The Place of Sugar in Modern History* (New York: Viking, 1985), 67; Beth Carver Wees, *English, Irish, and Scottish Silver at the Sterling and Francine Clark Art Institute* (New York: Hudson Hills Press, 1997), 267, 269; Clare Midgley, *Feminism and Empire: Women Activists in Imperial Britain* (London: Routledge, 2007), 46; Rodris Roth, *Tea-Drinking in Eighteenth-Century America*, repr., *Material Life in America, 1600–1860*, ed. Robert Blair St. George (Boston: Northeastern University Press, 1988); Mary Douglas and Baron Isherwood,

The World of Goods: Towards an Anthropology of Consumption (New York: Routledge, 2002). See also Martin, *Buying into the World of Goods*, 8, 173–193. In her analysis of retail trade in eighteenth-century Virginia, Ann Smart Martin notes that slaves made up a significant portion of merchant John Hook's business: "The number of slaves who made purchases had grown so large and their activity so regular that by the turn of the century, Hook's storekeeper at Hale's Ford began keeping a separate account book for their purchases."

2. Ellen Hartigan-O'Connor, *The Ties That Buy: Women and Commerce in Revolutionary America* (Philadelphia: University of Pennsylvania Press, 2009), 192.

3. Ferdinand M. Bayard, *Travels of a Frenchman in Maryland and Virginia with a Description of Philadelphia and Baltimore in 1791 . . .*, trans. Ben C. McCary (Williamsburg, Va.: Edwards Brothers, 1950), 35, 47. Bayard noted his frustration with his lack of familiarity with the coded placement of the spoon: "When the cup is sent back, care is taken to place the spoon in such a manner that it indicates whether you wish another cup, or whether you have had enough. A Frenchman who did not speak any English, and not being acquainted with this sign language, and very distressed to see the sixteenth cup arrive, hit upon the idea after having emptied it, of keeping it in his pocket until they had finished serving."

4. Ibid., 130, 73. For more about Bayard's American tour, see Warren R. Hofstra, *The Planting of New Virginia: Settlement and Landscape in the Shenandoah Valley* (Baltimore: Johns Hopkins University Press, 2004), 336–337. See also Breen, *The Marketplace of Revolution*, 282, 284.

5. Elizabeth Kowaleski-Wallace, *Consuming Subjects: Women, Shopping, and Business in the Eighteenth Century* (New York: Columbia University Press, 1997), 5; Nancy Armstrong, *Desire and Domestic Fiction* (New York: Oxford University Press, 1987), 95.

6. See Thomas L. Haskell, "Capitalism and the Origins of the Humanitarian Sensibility, Part 1," and "Capitalism and the Origins of the Humanitarian Sensibility, Part 2," in *The Antislavery Debate: Capitalism and Abolitionism as a Problem in Historical Interpretation*, ed. Thomas Bender (Berkeley: University of California Press, 1992), 107–135, 136–160; John Ashworth, "The Relationship between Capitalism and Humanitarianism," in Bender, *Antislavery Debate*, 180–199; Clare Midgley, "Slave Sugar Boycotts, Female Activism and the Domestic Base of British Antislavery Culture," *Slavery and Abolition* 17 (1996): 150–152. Midgley, building on the arguments of Haskell and Ashworth, suggests that the rise of consumer society with its concomitant emphasis on individual choice was necessary for the development of the abstention campaign.

7. Judith Jennings, "Joseph Woods, 'Merchant and Philosopher': The Making of the British Anti-Slave Trade Ethic," *Slavery and Abolition* 14 (December 1993): 163–164; Christopher Leslie Brown, *Moral Capital: Foundations of British Abolitionism* (Chapel Hill: University of North Carolina Press, 2006), 412–433; Betty Fladeland, *Men and Brothers: Anglo-American Antislavery Cooperation* (Urbana: University of Illinois Press, 1972), 32, 39–40; Kirsten Sword, "Remembering Dinah Nevil: Strategic Deceptions in Eighteenth-Century Antislavery," *Journal of American History* 97 (2010): 336–337; Judith Jennings, *The Business of Abolishing the Slave Trade, 1783–1807* (London: Frank Cass, 1997), 5–16, 22–23; Judith Jennings, *Gender, Religion, and*

Radicalism in the Long Eighteenth Century: The "Ingenious Quaker" and Her Connec-tions (Burlington, Vt.: Ashgate, 2006), 41.

8. Jennings, "Joseph Woods," 163–164; Jennings, *Business of Abolishing the Slave Trade*, 23–25; Brown, *Moral Capital*, 424–433; Sword, "Remembering Dinah Nevil," 336–337.

9. Joseph Woods, *Thoughts on the Slavery of Negroes* (London: James Phillips, 1784), 7, 15, 18–19, 29; Jennings, "Joseph Woods," 165–167.

10. Jennings, "Joseph Woods," 163–164; Brown, *Moral Capital*, 412–433; Flade-land, *Men and Brothers*, 32, 39–40; Sword, "Remembering Dinah Nevil," 336–337; J. R. Oldfield, *Popular Politics and British Anti-Slavery: The Mobilization of Public Opinion against the Slave Trade, 1787–1807* (Portland, Ore.: Frank Cass, 1998), 42–46.

11. Brown, *Moral Capital*, 430–431. See also Sword, "Remembering Dinah Nevil," 316–318, 336–337.

12. Brown, *Moral Capital*, 433–450, 457; Sword, "Remembering Dinah Nevil," 318.

13. Fladeland, *Men and Brothers*, 44–60; Jennings, *Business of Abolishing the British Slave Trade*, 34–62; Sword, "Remembering Dinah Nevil," 335. See also C. L. R. James, *The Black Jacobins: Toussaint L'Ouverture and the San Domingo Revolution* (New York: Vintage Books, 1989).

14. Jennings, "Joseph Woods," 171–172.

15. For an analysis of Fox's identity, see Timothy Whelan, "William Fox, Martha Gurney, and Radical Discourse of the 1790s," *Eighteenth-Century Studies* 42, no. 3 (2009): 404–408. See also Thomas Clarkson, *The History of the Rise, Progress and Ac-complishment of the Abolition of the African Slave-Trade by the British Parliament* (London: Longman, Hurst, Rees and Orme, 1808), 2:348.

16. See, e.g., Richard Hillier, *A Vindication of the Address to the People of Great Britain on the Use of West India Produce, with Some Observations and Facts Relative to the Situation of the Slaves* (London: M. Gurney, 1791); Andrew Burn, *A Second Address to the People of Great Britain Containing a New, and Most Powerful Argument to Abstain from the Use of West India Sugar* (London: M. Gurney, 1792); William Allen, *The Duty of Abstaining from the Use of West India Produce: A Speech Delivered at Coach-maker's Hall*, January 12, 1792 (London: M. Gurney, 1792).

17. Whelan, "William Fox, Martha Gurney, and Radical Discourse," 398–401, 403. See also Ian Maxted, *The London Book Trades, 1775–1800: A Preliminary Check-list of Members* (Kent, U.K.: Dawson, 1977), 84, 97.

18. Clarkson, *History*, 2:349–350. Methodist Samuel Bradburn estimated that more than 400,000 people participated in the boycott. Samuel Bradburn, *An Ad-dress to the People Called Methodists Concerning the Evil of Encouraging the Slave Trade* (Manchester: T. Harper, Smithy-Door, 1792).

19. As quoted in Earl Leslie Griggs, *Thomas Clarkson: The Friend of Slaves* (Ann Arbor: University of Michigan, 1938), 69; Oldfield, *Popular Politics*, 58. In this same letter, Clarkson noted that sugar revenue was down £200,000. In reply, Wedgwood proposed printing 2,000 copies and adding a woodcut of the seal of the kneeling slave. Wedgwood also offered to pay the cost of preparing the print.

20. *Strictures on an Address to the People of Great Britain, on the Propriety of Abstaining from West-India Sugar and Rum* (London: T. Boosey, 1792), 3.

21. Whelan, "William Fox, Martha Gurney, and Radical Discourse," 397, 402. See also Charlotte Sussman, "Women and the Politics of Sugar, 1792," *Representations* 48 (Autumn 1994): 51; Clarkson, *History*, 1:571.

22. E.g., see Peter C. Hogg, *The African Slave Trade and Its Suppression: A Classified and Annotated Bibliography of Books, Pamphlets, and Periodical Articles* (London: Frank Cass, 1973), 169–175. Hogg includes four editions of Fox's *Address*, but fails to note the change in title that occurred with the seventh edition. See also Whelan, "William Fox, Martha Gurney, and Radical Discourse," 403; John H. Y. Briggs, "Baptists and the Campaign to Abolish the Slave Trade," *Baptist Quarterly* 42, no. 3 (2007): 279. According to Briggs, Fox's tract "spawned more than twenty responses, both in support and opposition, from Dissenters and Anglicans, male and female, between the summer of 1791 and the spring of 1792." Given the transient character of these pamphlets, many more may have been printed.

23. William Fox, *An Address to the People of Great Britain on the Propriety of Abstaining from West India Sugar and Rum*, 24th ed. (London: M. Gurney, 1792), 10, 2–3.

24. Ibid., 12. Antisugar literature often used statistics such as these to support their claims. E.g., see *New York Journal and Patriotic Register*, April 25, 1792. The newspaper reporter noted claims that if 37,000 British families would abstain from sugar, slavery would be abolished!

25. Fox, *An Address to the People of Great Britain*, 2–3.

26. See Seymour Drescher, *Capitalism and Antislavery: British Mobilization in Comparative Perspective* (New York: Oxford University Press, 1987), 78–79; Clare Midgley, *Women against Slavery: The British Campaigns, 1780–1870* (London: Routledge, 1992), 35. As Drescher argues, abstention "brought women and children directly into the orbit of the campaign." Although abstention did bring women into the eighteenth-century abstention movement, activists such as William Fox did not specifically seek women's support, at least in the early weeks of the campaign.

27. Kowaleski-Wallace, *Consuming Subjects*, 22.

28. Motteux, *Poem in Praise of Tea*, 7.

29. William Cowper, "The Task, Book IV," in *Cowper: Verse and Letters*, ed. Brian Spiller (Cambridge, Mass.: Harvard University Press, 1968), 464, 466.

30. Eliza Haywood, *The Female Spectator* (London: A. Millar, W. Law, and R. Cater, 1775), 2:80.

31. Joseph Addison, "The Lover," in *The Miscellaneous Works, in Verse and Prose, of the Right Honourable Joseph Addison* (London: J. and R. Tonson, 1765), 2:348.

32. Charles Jenner, *Town Eclogues*, 2nd ed. (London: T. Caddell, 1773), 11.

33. *The Tea Drinking Wife, and Drunken Husband* (NewCastle upon Tyne: n.p., 1749), in *Literary Representations of Tea and the Tea-Table*, ed. Markman Ellis, vol. 1 of *Tea and the Tea-Table in Eighteenth-Century England*, ed. Markman Ellis (London: Pickering & Chatto, 2010), 165.

34. Karen Harvey, "Barbarity in a Teacup? Punch, Domesticity, and Gender in the Eighteenth Century," *Journal of Design History* 22, no. 3 (2008): 211; Jenner, *Town Eclogues*, 11.

35. Amanda Vickery, *The Gentleman's Daughter: Women's Lives in Georgian England* (New Haven, Conn.: Yale University Press, 1998), 206–208.

36. John Galt, *The Annals of the Parish and the Ayrshire Legatees, with a Memoir of the Author* (Edinburgh: William Blackwood, 1841), 11; Alexander Warrack, comp., *A*

Scot's Dialect Dictionary, Comprising the Words in Use From the Latter Part of the Seventeenth Century to the Present Day (London: W. R. Chambers, 1911), 341. See also Kowaleski-Wallace, *Consuming Subjects*, 34–36. Kowaleski-Wallace argues that the tea table conversation of working class women is a form of resistance of "patriarchal hierarchy as well as male economic and sexual control. Even though her rebellion operates only within her circle, it nonetheless suggests the subversive power of women's speech across class lines: women's voice retains the power to subvert discipline, to speak audibly of needs and desires."

37. Hanway, *A Journal of Eight Days Journey*, 244–245, 263; Charlotte Sussman, *Consuming Anxieties: Consumer Protest, Gender, and British Slavery, 1713–1833* (Stanford, Calif.: Stanford University Press, 2000), 25–31; Kowaleski-Wallace, *Consuming Subjects*, 19–37.

38. As quoted in Elizabeth Kowaleski-Wallace, "Tea, Gender, and Domesticity in Eighteenth-Century England," *Studies in Eighteenth-Century Culture* 23 (1994): 132; Eliza Haywood, *The Tea-Table; or, A Conversation Between Some Polite Persons of Both Sexes, at a Lady's Visiting Day . . .* (London: J. Roberts, 1725), 1.

39. Haywood, *Tea-Table*, 1; *The Tea Drinking Wife, and Drunken Husband*, 165; Edward Young and Eliza Haywood, quoted in Kowaleski-Wallace, *Consuming Subjects*, 30.

40. Mary Wollstonecraft, *A Vindication of the Rights of Woman*, in *The Vindications: The Rights of Men, The Rights of Woman*, ed. D. L. Macdonald and Kathleen Scherf (Orchard Park, N.Y.: Broadview Literary Texts, 1997), 282.

41. Wollstonecraft, *Vindication of the Rights of Woman*, 282, 286, 287, 335. See also Sussman, *Consuming Anxieties*, 125–126; Moira Ferguson, *Subject to Others: British Women Writers and Colonial Slavery, 1670–1834* (New York: Routledge, 1992), 186–189.

42. For a discussion of economy in this period, see Karen Harvey, "Men Making Home: Masculinity and Domesticity in Eighteenth-Century Britain," *Gender and History* 21 (November 2009): 532–536.

43. Cruikshank referenced a contemporary case involving Captain John Kimber, who was tried for his part in the murder of an African woman who refused to dance naked for him on the deck of his ship. A week before Cruikshank published "The Gradual Abolition of the Slave Trade," he published a caricature of the Kimber case, "The Abolition of the Slave Trade." For a discussion of Kimber and of the Cruikshank satire, see Brycchan Carey, *British Abolitionism and the Rhetoric of Sensibility: Writing, Sentiment, and Slavery, 1760–1807* (New York: Palgrave, 2005), 179–185; Oldfield, *Popular Politics*, 175.

44. Allen, *Duty of Abstaining*, 23; *An Address to Her Royal Highness the Dutchess of York, against the Use of Sugar* (London, 1792), 10. In the fall of 1791, Princess Frederica of Prussia wed Prince Frederick, Duke of York. See H. M. Stephens, "Frederick, Prince, duke of York and Albany (1763–1827)," rev. John Van der Kiste, in *Oxford Dictionary of National Biography*, ed. H. C. G. Matthew and Brian Harrison (Oxford: Oxford University Press, 2004).

45. Mary Birkett, *A Poem on the African Slave Trade, Addressed to Her Own Sex, Part I* (Dublin: J. Jones, 1792), 13–15.

46. Carey, *British Abolitionism and the Rhetoric of Sensibility*, 7–8; G. J. Barker-Benfield, *The Culture of Sensibility: Sex and Society in Eighteenth-Century Britain* (Chicago: University of Chicago Press, 1992), 37.

47. Kate Davies, "A Moral Purchase: Femininity, Commerce, and Abolition," in *Women and the Public Sphere: Writing and Representation, 1700–1830*, ed. Elizabeth Eger, Charlotte Grant, Cliona O'Gallchoir, and Penny Warburton (Cambridge: Cambridge University Press, 2001), 133–159.

48. *Manchester Mercury*, December 7, 1787.

49. *Gentleman's Magazine*, July 1788.

50. Hester Thrale, *Thraliana: The Diary of Mrs. Hester Lynch Thrale (Later Mrs. Piozzi), 1776–1809*, ed. Katherine C. Balderston (Oxford: Oxford University Press, 1951), 2:714.

51. *Gentleman's Magazine*, July 1788.

52. Hannah More, *Slavery, a Poem* (London: T. Cadell, 1788); Carey, *British Abolitionism and the Rhetoric of Sensibility*, 38–39.

53. Samuel Taylor Coleridge, "Lecture on the Slave Trade," in *Lectures 1795: On Politics and Religion*, ed. Lewis Patton and Peter Mann (Princeton, N.J.: Princeton University Press, 1971), 249.

54. Wollstonecraft, *Vindication of the Rights of Woman*, 282. See also Sussman, *Consuming Anxieties*, 125–126; Ferguson, *Subject to Others*, 186–189.

55. *Gentleman's Magazine*, April 1789; Carey, *British Abolitionism and the Rhetoric of Sensibility*, 90.

56. *Strictures on an Address*, 4.

57. *European Magazine and London Review*, March 1792.

58. *Monthly Review*, October 1791.

59. Carey, *British Abolitionism and the Rhetoric of Sensibility*, 88.

60. House of Commons, Select Committee Appointed to Take the Examination of Witnesses Respecting the African Slave Trade, *An Abstract of the Evidence Delivered before a Select Committee of the House of Commons in the Years 1790 and 1791; On the Part of the Petitioners for the Abolition of the Slave Trade* (Edinburgh, 1791), 70–72. See also Deidre Coleman, "Conspicuous Consumption: White Abolitionism and English Women's Protest Writing in the 1790s," *ELH* [*English Literary History*] 61 (Summer 1994): 356. Coleman argues that "women's cruelty was not random and indiscriminate"; rather, women's punishment of their slaves was "for sexual reasons." She continues, "The slave-master husband who has right of sexual access to his wife also has right of access to his slaves; thus it comes about that oppressed white women victimize their even more oppressed women slaves."

61. Mary Wollstonecraft, *Vindication of the Rights of Men*, in *The Vindications*, 79.

62. Benjamin Flower, *The French Constitution . . .* , 2nd ed. (London: G. G. J. and J. Robinson, 1792), 452–453.

63. Coleman, "Conspicuous Consumption," 355–356.

64. Anna Letitia Barbauld, *Epistle to William Wilberforce, Esq.: On the Rejection of the Bill for Abolishing the Slave Trade* (London: T. Johnson, 1791).

65. Wollstonecraft, *Vindication of the Rights of Woman*, 282. See also Sussman, *Consuming Anxieties*, 125–126; Ferguson, *Subject to Others*, 186–189.

66. Clarkson, *History*, 2:190–191.

67. See, e.g., Rachel Hope Cleves, *The Reign of Terror in America: Visions of Violence from Anti-Jacobinism to Antislavery* (New York: Cambridge University Press, 2009).

68. "The Slaves: An Elegy," *Scot's Magazine*, April 1788.

69. Ian Haywood, "Bloody Vignettes," in *Bloody Romanticism: Spectacular Violence and the Politics of Representation, 1773–1832* (New York: Palgrave, 2006), 11.

70. Thomas Tryon, *Friendly Advice to the Gentleman Planters of the East and West Indies: In Three Parts* (London: Andrew Sowle, 1684), 96.

71. Ralph Sandiford, dedication, to *A Brief Examination of the Practice of the Times, by the Foregoing and the Present Dispensation* (Philadelphia, 1729); Fox, *Address to the People of Great Britain*, 4.

72. Thomas Cooper, *Letters on the Slave Trade: First Published in Wheeler's Manchester Chronicle; and Since Re-Printed with Additions and Alterations* (Manchester: C. Wheeler, 1787), 25.

73. Coleridge, "Lecture on the Slave Trade," 248.

74. Burn, *Second Address*, 1–12.

75. Clarkson, *History*, 2:269; Oldfield, *Popular Politics*, 174–175. Oldfield suggests that by embellishing Francis's testimony before the House of Commons, Gillray "cast doubt on the authenticity of the story and the reliability of the source." Francis's testimony was reported in the United States. See "Observations upon Negro Slavery," *Universal Asylum and Columbian Magazine*, November 1790.

76. *European Magazine and London Review*, March 1792.

77. Although Hillier's pamphlet is included in Hogg's substantial bibliography of the slave trade debate, the female apologist's tract is not. See Hogg, *African Slave Trade*, 169–175.

78. *An Answer to a Pamphlet Intituled [sic] An Address to the People of England against the Use of West India Produce* (Whitechapel: W. Moon, 1791), 4–7.

79. Carey, *British Abolitionism and the Rhetoric of Sensibility*, 124, 127, 130.

80. Hillier, *Vindication of an Address to the People of Great Britain*, 18.

81. Ibid., 3; Midgley, *Women against Slavery*, 26.

82. *Answer to a Pamphlet*, 3: "The Writer of this little piece, considering that God made of one blood all the nations which dwell on the face of the earth, has no more partiality to the colour of the skin than the Author of the Pamphlet can have; nor is she so devoid of the feelings of humanity or of Christian principles, as to wish slavery and oppression to any individual of the human race." This is the only reference to the author's gender.

83. Susan Staves, "'The Abuse of Title Pages': Men Writing as Women," in *A Concise Companion to the Restoration and the Eighteenth Century*, ed. Cynthia Wall (Malden, Mass.: Blackwell, 2005), 162–182; John Mullan, *Anonymity: A Secret History of the English Language* (London: Faber and Faber, 2007), 128–129.

84. Richard Hillier, *A Vindication of the Address to the People of Great-Britain on the Use of West India Produce with Some Observations and Facts Relative to the Situation of the Slaves. In Answer to a Female Apologist for Slavery. The Second Edition, with Strictures on Her Reply to a Reply* (London: M. Gurney, 1791), 24.

85. Srividhya Swaminathan, *Debating the Slave Trade: Rhetoric of British National Identity, 1759–1815* (Burlington, Vt.: Ashgate, 2009).

86. Adam Hochschild, *Bury the Chains: Prophets and Rebels in the Fight to Free an Empire's Slaves* (New York: Houghton Mifflin, 2005), 226–234.

87. Ibid., 235–236. *The Times* as quoted in Hochschild.

88. William Fox, *Thoughts on the Death of the King of France* (London: J. Ridgway, W. Richardson, T. Whieldon and Butterworth, M. Gurney, 1793), 16. See John Barrell, *Imagining the King's Death: Figurative Treason, Fantasies of Regicide, 1793–1796* (New York: Oxford University Press, 2000), 1, 81.

89. Barrell, *Imagining the King's Death*, 82, 86.

90. Hochschild, *Bury the Chains*, 193; Midgley, *Women against Slavery*, 38–40; Drescher, *Capitalism and Slavery*, 79, 216–217n47; Seymour Drescher, *Econocide: British Slavery in the Era of Abolition*, 2nd ed. (Chapel Hill: University of North Carolina Press, 2010), 116–117; Coleman, "Conspicuous Consumption," 342; Oldfield, *Popular Politics*, 185–187.

3. Striking at the Root of Corruption

1. Dunlap's *Daily American Advertiser*, May 11, 1792; May 14, 1792; *New-York Journal and Patriotic Register*, May 19, 1792; *New York Magazine, or Literary Repository*, March 1793. *Daily American Advertiser* May 11, 1792; May 14, 1792, quoted in David N. Gellman, *Emancipating New York: The Politics of Slavery and Freedom, 1777–1827* (Baton Rouge: Louisiana State University Press, 2006), 92.

2. *New-York Journal and Patriotic Register*, March 14, 1792; *New Jersey Journal*, March 14, 1792.

3. Kirsten Sword, "Remembering Dinah Nevil: Strategic Deceptions in Eighteenth-Century Antislavery," *Journal of American History* 97 (2010): 317.

4. Geoffrey Plank, "The First Person in Antislavery Literature: John Woolman, His Clothes, and His Journal," *Slavery and Abolition* (March 2009): 79.

5. See Plank's discussion of the important differences between the British and American editions of Woolman's journal; Plank, "The First Person in Antislavery Literature," 76–79.

6. Geoffrey Plank, *John Woolman's Path to the Peaceable Kingdom: A Quaker in the British Empire* (Philadelphia: University of Pennsylvania Press, 2012), 208–210.

7. John Woolman, *Considerations on Keeping Negroes: Recommended to the Professors of Christianity, of Every Denomination, Part Second* (Philadelphia: B. Franklin and D. Hall, 1762), 232–233; Maurice Jackson, *Let This Voice Be Heard: Anthony Benezet, Father of Atlantic Abolitionism* (Philadelphia: University of Pennsylvania Press, 2009), 72–80.

8. Joshua Evans, Journal Transcription, 1731–1798, Joshua Evans Papers, RG 5/190, Friends Historical Library, Swarthmore College, 190–191, 194, 216.

9. Benjamin Franklin, *Observations Concerning the Increase of Mankind, Peopling of Countries, &c.* (Boston: S. Kneeland, 1755), 5–6, 8; Benjamin Rush, *An Address to the Inhabitants of the British Settlements, on the Slavery of Negroes* (Philadelphia: John Dunlap, 1773), 6–7; Eva Sheppard Wolf, "Early Free-Labor Thought and the Contest over Slavery in the Early Republic," in *Contesting Slavery: The Politics of Bondage and Freedom in the New American Nation*, ed. John Craig Hammond and Matthew Mason (Charlottesville: University of Virginia Press, 2011), 32–37.

10. Wolf, "Early Free-Labor Thought," 32–34, 37–38; "Rusticus," quoted by Wolf, 38.

11. Alan Taylor, *William Cooper's Town: Power and Persuasion on the Frontier of the Early American Republic* (New York: Alfred A. Knopf, 1995), 30–34; Gellman, *Emancipating New York*, 92.

12. David W. Maxey, "The Union Farm: Henry Drinker's Experiment in Deriving Profit from Virtue," *Pennsylvania Magazine of History and Biography* 107 (October 1983): 614; Taylor, *William Cooper's Town*, 115–117, 119–126. See also David W. Maxey, "Of Castles in Stockport and Other Strictures: Samuel Preston's Contentious Agency for Henry Drinker," *Pennsylvania Magazine of History and Biography* 110 (July 1986): 413–446.

13. Maxey, "The Union Farm," 612–613, 618; Taylor, *William Cooper's Town*, 115–126; Henry Drinker, quoted in Maxey, 612.

14. *Remarks on the Manufacturing of Maple Sugar: With Directions for Its Further Improvement; Collected by a Society of Gentlemen, in Philadelphia, and Published for the General Information and Benefit of the Citizens of the United States* (Philadelphia: James and Johnson, 1790).

15. *Remarks on the Manufacturing of Maple Sugar: With Directions for Its Further Improvement; Collected by a Society of Gentlemen, in Philadelphia, and Published for the General Information and Benefit of the Citizens of the United States* (London: James Phillips, 1791); *New-York Literary Magazine, or Literary Repository*, January 1791, 34–37; February 1791, 69–72.

16. Benjamin Rush, *An Account of the Sugar-Maple Tree of the United States, and of the Methods of Obtaining Sugar from It, Together with Observations upon the Advantages Both Public and Private of This Sugar: In a Letter to Thomas Jefferson, Esq. Secretary of State of the United States, and One of the Vice-Presidents of the American Philosophical Society* (London: James Phillips, 1792). See also David N. Gellman, "Pirates, Sugar, Debtors, and Slaves: Political Economy and the Case for Gradual Emancipation in New York," *Slavery and Abolition* 22 (August 2001): 56.

17. Jacques Brissot de Warville, *New Travels in the United States of America: Including the Commerce of America with Europe; Particularly France and Great Britain*, 2 vols. (London: J. S. Jordan, 1794), 1: 255–260; *New York Magazine, or Literary Repository*, August 1792; David Brion Davis, *The Problem of Slavery in the Age of Revolution, 1770–1823* (Ithaca, N.Y.: Cornell University Press, 1975), 94–95.

18. *Albany Journal*, November 3, 1788.

19. Supporters of maple sugar production, quoted in Gellman, *Emancipating New York*, 93.

20. Editors of the *Daily Advertiser*, quoted in Wolf, "Early Free-Labor," 38.

21. *New Jersey Journal*, May 19, 1792; March 14, 1792.

22. *New York Journal and Patriotic Register*, March 14, 1792; May 19, 1792.

23. Gellman, *Emancipating New York*, 93.

24. Wendy Woloson, *Refined Tastes: Sugar, Confectionery, and Consumers in Nineteenth-Century America* (Baltimore: Johns Hopkins University Press, 2002), 29.

25. Anna Davis Hallowell, *James and Lucretia Mott: Life and Letters* (Boston: Houghton Mifflin, 1884), 88.

26. Gary B. Nash, *Forging Freedom: The Formation of Philadelphia's Black Community, 1720–1840* (Cambridge, Mass.: Harvard University Press, 1988), 43–44, 92–94, 103–109. See also Beverly C. Tomek, *Colonization and Its Discontents: Emancipation, Emigration, and Antislavery in Antebellum Pennsylvania* (New York: New York University Press, 2011), 1–8, 27–34.

27. Edward E. Baptist, *The Half Has Never Been Told: Slavery and the Making of American Capitalism* (New York: Basic Books, 2014), 8–11.

28. "Supply of Sugar," *Federal Republican* (Elizabethtown, NJ), November 28, 1803; Wolf,; Alan Magruder, quoted in Wolf, "Early Free-Labor Thought," 40.

29. Gellman, *Emancipating New York*, 93.

30. Ellen Ross, "'Liberation Is Coming Soon': The Radical Reformation of Joshua Evans (1731–1798)," in *Quakers and Abolition*, ed. Brycchan Carey and Geoffrey Plank (Urbana: University of Illinois Press, 2014), 25–26.

31. John Woolman, *The Journal and Major Essays of John Woolman*, ed. Phillips P. Moulton (New York: Oxford University Press, 1971), 190; Geoffrey Plank, "'The Flame of Life Was Kindled in All Animal and Sensitive Creatures': One Quaker Colonist's Views of Animal Life," *Church History* 76 (September 2007), 569–590; Plank, "The First Person in Antislavery Literature," 67–91.

32. Evans, Journal Transcription, 26–27; Ross, "'Liberation Is Coming Soon,'" 20–23; Jack D. Marietta, *The Reformation of American Quakerism, 1748–1783* (Philadelphia: University of Pennsylvania Press, 1984), 110.

33. Evans, Journal Transcription, 238; Ross, "'Liberation Is Coming Soon,'" 24–25.

34. David Cooper, Diary, Journals, Diaries, Etc., 1683–ongoing, Ms. Coll. 975-C, p. 50, QC, HC.

35. Warner Mifflin, *The Defence of Warner Mifflin Cast against Him on Account of His Endeavors to Promote Righteousness, Mercy and Peace among Mankind* (Philadelphia, 1796); Thomas E. Drake, *Quakers and Slavery in America* (New Haven, Conn.: Yale University Press, 1950), 75–76, 93, 95, 107–108; Davis, *Problem of Slavery in the Age of Revolution*, 100–101, Smith quote on 101.

36. Bliss Forbush, *Elias Hicks: Quaker Liberal* (New York: Columbia University Press, 1996), 31, 52, 54, 90.

37. Forbush, *Elias Hicks*, 90, 144–145.

38. Elias Hicks, *Observations on the Slavery of the Africans and Their Descendants, and on the Use of the Produce of Their Labour* (New York: Samuel Wood, 1811), 7, 13–14, 15; Forbush, *Elias Hicks*, 144–149; Drake, *Quakers and Slavery*, 116; Ross, "'Liberation Is Coming Soon,'" 25.

39. Ross, "Liberation Is Coming Soon," 25; Carol Faulkner, "The Root of the Evil: Free Produce and Radical Antislavery, 1820–1860," *Journal of the Early Republic* 27 (2007): 389.

40. Elijah E. Hoss, *Elihu Embree, Abolitionist* (Nashville, Tenn.: University Press Company, 1897), 6–7; Matilda Wildman Evans, "Elihu Embree, Quaker Abolitionist, and Some of His Co-Workers," *Bulletin of Friends' Historical Association* 21 (Spring 1932): 5–17; Ruth Ketring Nuermberger, *The Free Produce Movement: A Quaker Protest against Slavery* (New York: AMS Press, 1942), 100–101; Merton Dillon, *Benjamin Lundy and the Struggle for Negro Freedom* (Urbana: University of Illinois Press, 1966), 5, 34–42; Joseph J. Lewis, *Memoir of Enoch Lewis* (West Chester, Penn.: F. S. Hickman, 1882).

41. *Emancipator*, July 31, 1820; August 31, 1820; repr., *Emancipator (Complete), 1820* (Nashville, Tenn.: B. H. Murphy, 1932); Lawrence B. Goodheart, "Tennessee's Antislavery Movement Reconsidered: The Example of Elihu Embree," *Tennessee Historical Quarterly* 41 (Fall 1982): 224–238; Drake, *Quakers and Slavery*, 127–128.

42. Dillon, *Benjamin Lundy*, 5, 34–42; *Genius of Universal Emancipation*, July 4, 1823.

43. *Genius of Universal Emancipation*, June 19, 1823.

44. *Genius of Universal Emancipation*, October 1824; June1825; September 1825; October 8, 1825; January 21, 1826; August 5, 1826; November 25, 1826; March 31, 1827; September 29, 1827; October 14, 1827; April 26, 1827; May 3, 1828; Crothers, *Quakers Living in the Lion's Mouth*, 125, 128; Dillon, *Benjamin Lundy*, 88–102; Nuermberger, *Free Produce Movement*, 119; James Oliver Horton and Lois E. Horton, *In Hope of Liberty: Culture, Community, and Protest Among Northern Free Blacks, 1700–1860* (New York: Oxford University Press, 1997), 194.

45. H. G. Ward, *Mexico in 1827*, 2 vols. (London: Henry Colburn, 1828), 1:21–22, 40–90.

46. Dillon, *Benjamin Lundy*, 179–220. See also Benjamin Lundy, *The Life, Travels, and Opinions of Benjamin Lundy, including His Journeys to Texas and Mexico* (Philadelphia: W. D. Parrish, 1847).

47. *Friends' Review*, February 9, 1856; October 26, 1850; Lewis, *Memoir of Enoch Lewis*, 83; Paul W. Grasek, "Quaker, Teacher, Abolitionist: The Life of Educator-Reformer Enoch Lewis, 1776–1856," (PhD diss., University of Connecticut, 1996), 143–144.

48. Enoch Lewis, "Redemption of Slaves by Purchase," *Non-Slaveholder*, November 1853; Lewis, *Memoir of Enoch Lewis*, 52; Grasek, "Quaker, Teacher, Abolitionist," 143–144.

49. *Friends' Review*, March 5, 1853.

50. *African Observer*, July 1827; August 1827; repr., *The African Observer, 1827–1828* (Westport, Conn.: Negro Universities Press, 1970), 108–111, 141–145.

51. American Convention for Promoting the Abolition of Slavery and Improving the Condition of the African Race, *Minutes of the Proceedings of the Third Convention of Delegates from the Abolition Societies Established in Different Parts of the United States, Assembled at Philadelphia . . .* (1796), 28; American Convention, *Minutes* (1816), 4; American Convention, *Minutes* (1823), 24; American Convention, *Minutes* (1825), 22; repr., *The American Convention for Promoting the Abolition of Slavery and Improving the Condition of the African Race: Minutes Constitution, Addresses, Memorials, Resolutions, Reports, Committees and Anti-Slavery Tracts*, 3 vols. (New York: Bergman, 1969); Nuermberger, *Free Produce Movement*, 11–12.

52. Herbert Aptheker, ed., *A Documentary History of the Negro People in the United States* (New York: Citadel Press, 1951), 5–12, 14–16.

53. Joanna Brooks, "The Early American Public Sphere and the Emergence of a Black Print Counterpublic," *William and Mary Quarterly*, 3rd ser., 62 (June 2005): 68.

54. Richard S. Newman, "Prince Hall, Richard Allen, and Daniel Coker: Revolutionary Black Founders, Revolutionary Black Communities," in *Revolutionary Founders: Rebels, Radicals, and Reformers in the Making of the Nation*, ed. Alfred F. Young, Gary B. Nash, and Ray Raphael (New York: Alfred A. Knopf, 2011), 306.

55. Richard S. Newman, "'A Chosen Generation': Black Founders and Early America," in *Prophets of Protest: Reconsidering the History of American Abolitionism*, ed. Timothy Patrick McCarthy and John Stauffer (New York: New Press, 2006), 61–62.

56. Aptheker, *Documentary History*, 17.

57. Newman, "Prince Hall," 312–316.

58. Tomek, *Colonization and Its Discontents*, 43–62; Dillon, *Benjamin Lundy*, 23–28. See also Eric Burin, *Slavery and the Peculiar Solution: A History of the American Colonization Society* (Gainesville: University of Florida Press, 2008).

59. Aptheker, *Documentary History*, 71.

60. Adam Carman, *An Oration Delivered on the Fourth Anniversary of the Abolition of the Slave Trade* (New York: John C. Totten, 1811), 11, 13.

61. J. William Frost, "Years of Crisis and Separation: Philadelphia Yearly Meeting, 1790–1860," in *Friends in the Delaware Valley: Philadelphia Yearly Meeting, 1681–1981*, ed. John M. Moore (Haverford, Penn.: Friends Historical Association, 1981), 65.

62. H. Larry Ingle, *Quakers in Conflict: The Hicksite Reformation* (Wallingford, Penn.: Pendle Hill, 1998), 13.

63. Thomas D. Hamm, *The Transformation of American Quakerism: Orthodox Friends, 1800–1907* (Bloomington: Indiana University Press, 1988), 11.

64. Ingle, *Quakers in Conflict*, 68, 77–78; Elbert Russell, *The History of Quakerism* (New York: Macmillan, 1942), 296–297.

65. Philadelphia and Baltimore Yearly Meetings Discipline (1806), quoted in Bliss Forbush, *Elias Hicks: Quaker Liberal* (New York: Columbia University Press, 1956), 195.

66. Ingle, *Quakers in Conflict*, 68.

67. New York Yearly Meeting Discipline (1783), quoted in Forbush, *Elias Hicks*, 120.

68. New York Yearly Meeting Discipline, in *The Old Discipline: Nineteenth-Century Friends' Disciplines in America* (Farmington, Maine: Quaker Heritage Press, 1999), 400.

69. Carol Faulkner, *Lucretia Mott's Heresy: Abolition and Women's Rights in Nineteenth-Century America* (Philadelphia: University of Pennsylvania Press, 2011), 48–49; Hugh Barbour Thomas Bassett, Christopher Densmore, H. Larry Ingle, Alson D. Van Wagner, "The Orthodox-Hicksite Separation," in Hugh Barbour, Christopher Densmore, Elizabeth H. Moger, Nancy C. Sorel, Alson D. Van Wagner, and Arthur J. Worrall, eds., *Quaker Crosscurrents: Three Hundred Years of Friends in the New York Yearly Meetings* (Syracuse, N.Y.: Syracuse University Press, 1995), 121.

70. Elias Hicks, *Letters of Elias Hicks, Including Also a Few Short Essays Written on Several Occasions, Mostly Illustrative of His Doctrinal Views* (New York: Isaac Hopper, 1834), 181.

71. Stephen Grellet, quoted in Edwin Bronner, *"The Other Branch": London Yearly Meeting and the Hicksites, 1827–1912* (London: Friends Historical Society, 1975), 4.

72. Elias Hicks, *The Letters of Elias Hicks* (Philadelphia, 1861), 44, 45, 40, 63; Faulkner, *Lucretia Mott's Heresy*, 44–45; Forbush, *Elias Hicks*, 182–184; Ingle, *Quakers in Conflict*, 81–83.

73. Robert H. Abzug, *Cosmos Crumbling: American Reform and the Religious Imagination* (New York: Oxford University Press, 1994), 5–6; Bruce Allen Dorsey, "Friends Becoming Enemies: Philadelphia Benevolence and the Neglected Era of American Quaker History," *Journal of the Early American Republic* 18 (Autumn 1998): 395–428.

74. William Bacon Evans, *Jonathan Evans and His Time, 1759–1839* (Boston: Christopher Publishing House, 1959), 42.

75. Ingle, *Quakers in Conflict*, 17–21; Faulkner, *Lucretia Mott's Heresy*, 45.

76. Evans, *Jonathan Evans*, 42.

77. Jeremiah H. Foster, *An Authentic Report of the Testimony in a Cause at Issue in the Court of Chancery of the State of New Jersey, between Thomas L. Shotwell, Complainant, and Joseph Hendrickson and Stacy Decow, Defendants* (Philadelphia: J. Harding, 1831), 2:39.

78. Foster, *Authentic Report*, 1:354, 2:39–40; Elias Hicks to Valentine Hicks, October 28, 1819, Elias Hicks Papers, Friends Historical Library, Swarthmore College, Swarthmore, Penn.; Forbush, *Elias Hicks*, 190. See also Ingle, *Quakers in Conflict*, 84–85.

79. Ingle, *Quakers in Conflict*, 85; Forbush, *Elias Hicks*, 189.

80. Evans, *Jonathan Evans*, 42.

81. Lydia Maria Child, *Isaac T. Hopper: A True Life* (Boston: J. P. Jewett, 1853), 276.

82. *Philanthropist*, August 21, 1819; Drake, *Quakers and Slavery*, 117.

83. *Miscellaneous Repository* 1 (1828): 346.

84. George W. Taylor, *Autobiography and Writings of George W. Taylor* (Philadelphia, 1891), 22; George W. Taylor to Jacob Taylor, January 10, 1828, Taylor Family Papers, Coll. No. 1233, QC, HC.

85. *Journal of the Life and Religious Labours of John Comly, Late of Byberry, Pennsylvania: Published by His Children* (Philadelphia: T. Ellwood Chapman, 1853), 38–39. See also Samuel M. Janney, *History of the Religious Society of Friends: From Its Rise to the Year 1828*, 4 vols. (Philadelphia: T. Ellwood Zell, 1867), 4:213.

86. Betty Fladeland, *Men and Brothers: Anglo-American Antislavery Cooperation* (Urbana: University of Illinois Press, 1972), 74, 80–124.

4. I Am a Man, Your Brother

1. Betty Fladeland, *Men and Brothers: Anglo-American Antislavery Cooperation* (Urbana: University of Illinois Press, 1972), 168–177; Adam Hochschild, *Bury the Chains: Prophets and Rebels in the Fight to Free an Empire's Slaves* (New York: Houghton Mifflin, 2005), 309–311; 322–324; David Brion Davis, *Inhuman Bondage: The Rise and Fall of Slavery in the New World* (New York: Oxford University Press, 2006), 237; Emilia Viotti da Costa, *Crowns of Glory, Tears of Blood: The Demerara Slave Rebellion of 1823* (New York: Oxford University Press, 1994), 177–178. For Buxton's speech as well as the full debate of May 15, 1823, see *Hansard's Parliamentary Debates*, new ser., 9 (May 15, 1823): 257–360.

2. Da Costa, *Crowns of Glory*, 197–202, 219–220, 222–227, 242–244; Davis, *Inhuman Bondage*, 217–218.

3. Elizabeth Heyrick, *Immediate, Not Gradual Abolition; or, An Inquiry into the Shortest, Safest, and Most Effectual Means of Getting Rid of West Indian Slavery* (London: Hatchard and Son, 1824), 3, 4, 7; Carol Lasser, "Immediatism, Dissent, and Gender: Women, and the Sentimentalization of Transatlantic Anti-Slavery Appeals," in *Women, Dissent, and Anti-Slavery in Britain and America, 1790–1865*, ed. Elizabeth J. Clapp and Julie Roy Jeffrey (New York: Oxford University Press, 2011), 112.

4. Carol Faulkner, "The Root of the Evil: Free Produce and Radical Antislavery, 1820–1860," *Journal of the Early Republic* 27 (2007): 380–381. The "provocative image" featured on the cover of the first British edition was not reprinted on subsequent American editions.

5. Clare Midgley, *Women against Slavery: The British Campaigns, 1780–1870* (London: Routledge, 1992), 62.

6. Clare Midgley, "The Dissenting Voice of Elizabeth Heyrick: An Exploration of the Links between Gender, Religious Dissent, and Anti-Slavery Radicalism," in Clapp and Jeffrey, *Women, Dissent, and Anti-Slavery in Britain and America*, 94–95, 100; Shirley Aucott, *Elizabeth Heyrick, 1769 to 1831: The Leicester Quaker Who Demanded the Immediate Emancipation of the Slaves in the British Colonies* (Leicester, U.K.: Gartree Press, 2007), 5–15; J. R. Oldfield, *Popular Politics and British Anti-Slavery: The Mobilization of Public Opinion against the Slave Trade, 1787–1807* (Portland, Ore.: Frank Cass, 1998), 140.

7. Midgley, "Dissenting Voice of Elizabeth Heyrick," 100; Kenneth Corfield, "Elizabeth Heyrick: Radical Quaker," in *Religion in the Lives of English Women, 1760–1930*, ed. Gail Malmgreen (Bloomington: Indiana University Press, 1986), 52–59; Hochschild, *Bury the Chains*, 325.

8. Midgley, "Dissenting Voice of Elizabeth Heyrick," 91–101; Lasser, "Immediatism, Dissent, and Gender," 112–114. See also Jennifer Rycenga, "A Greater Awakening: Women's Intellect as a Factor in Early Abolitionist Movements, 1824–1834," *Journal of Feminist Studies in Religion* 21 (Fall 2005): 31–59.

9. William Felkin, *A History of the Machine-Wrought Hosiery and Lace Manufactures* (London: Longmans, Green, 1867), 441–442; Corfield, "Elizabeth Heyrick," 56.

10. Hochschild, *Bury the Chains*, 320; Robert Poole, "'By Law or By Sword': Peterloo Revisited," *History* 91 (April 2006): 254–276; Donald Read, *Peterloo: The "Massacre" and its Background* (Manchester, U.K.: Manchester University Press, 1958).

11. Elizabeth Heyrick, *Exposition of One Principal Cause of the National Distress: Particularly in Manufacturing Districts; with Some Suggestions for Its Removal* (London, 1817), 3.

12. Heyrick, *Exposition*, 21, 22, 29, 34–36; Clare Midgley, *Feminism and Empire: Women Activists in Imperial Britain* (London: Routledge, 2007), 59.

13. Brycchan Carey, *British Abolitionism and the Rhetoric of Sensibility: Writing, Sentiment, and Slavery, 1760–1807* (New York: Palgrave, 2005), 124–130; Seymour Drescher, "Cart Whip and Billy Roller: Antislavery and Reform Symbolism in Industrializing Britain," *Journal of Social History* 15 (1981): 12.

14. The spinners of Stockport, quoted in Drescher, "Cart Whip and Billy Roller," 8, 16.

15. *Christian Observer* 8 (August 1824): 479–487.

16. Heyrick, *Exposition*, 20.

17. Midgley, *Feminism and Empire*, 59–60.

18. Hochschild, *Bury the Chains*, 318–320; da Costa, *Crowns of Glory*, 197–202, 219–220, 222–227, 242–244; Davis, *Inhuman Bondage*, 217–218.

19. Edward Rugemer, *The Problem of Emancipation: The Caribbean Roots of the American Civil War* (Baton Rouge: Louisiana State University Press, 2008), 53–65.

20. Da Costa, *Crowns of Glory*, 252–292; Davis, *Inhuman Bondage*, 215–218; Rugemer, *Problem of Emancipation*, 65, 86–91. See also David Brion Davis, "Review: The Role of Ideology in the Anglo-American Connection," *Reviews in American History* 1 (September 1973): 386.

21. Heyrick, *Immediate, Not Gradual Abolition*, 12, 22; Heyrick, *An Enquiry Which of the Two Parties Is Best Entitled to Freedom? The Slave or the Slave-Holder? An Impartial Examination of the Conduct of Each Party, at the Bar of Public Justice* (London: Baldwin,

Cradock and Joy, 1824), 5, 10, 16–190; Gelien Matthews, *Caribbean Slave Revolts and the British Abolitionist Movement* (Baton Rouge: Louisiana State University Press, 2006), 82; Midgley, *Feminism and Empire*, 58.

22. Heyrick, *Immediate, Not Gradual Abolition*, 5, 6, 11–12, 23; Elizabeth Heyrick, *Apology for Ladies' Anti-Slavery Associations* (London: J. Hatchard and Sons, 1828), 12; Lasser, "Immediatism, Dissent, and Gender," 112–115.

23. Elizabeth Heyrick, "Address to the Ladies of Great Britain," in *The Hummingbird; or, Morsels of Information on the Subject of Slaver; with Various Miscellaneous Articles* (Leicester, U.K.: A. Cockshaw, 1825), 198.

24. *The First Report of the Female Society for Birmingham, West Bromwich, Wednesbury, Walsall and Their Respective Neighbourhoods for the Relief of British Negro Slaves* (Birmingham, U.K.: Benjamin Hudson, 1826), 14–17.

25. For example, Benjamin Lundy reprinted numerous articles about the Birmingham group in the pages of the *Genius of Universal Emancipation*. The society's first report was reprinted in its entirety in the September 8 and 15, 1827, issues of the *Genius*.

26. Midgley, *Women against Slavery*, 47, 218n24; *The Third Report of the Female Society for Birmingham, West Bromwich, Wednesbury, Walsall and Their Respective Neighbourhoods for the Relief of British Negro Slaves* (Birmingham, U.K.: Benjamin Hudson, 1828), 18.

27. *The Second Report of the Female Society for Birmingham West Bromwich, Wednesbury, Walsall and Their Respective Neighbourhoods for the Relief of British Negro Slaves* (Birmingham, U.K.: Benjamin Hudson, 1827), 17; *Third Report of the Female Society for Birmingham*, 17; Minutes, November 26, 1829, Birmingham Ladies' Society for the Relief of Negro Slaves, Minute Book, *Records Relating to the Birmingham Ladies' Society for the Relief of Negro Slaves, 1825–1919*, reel 2, Birmingham Reference Library, Birmingham, U.K. (hereafter cited as BLS, BRL); Catherine Hutton Beale, *Catherine Hutton and Her Friends* (Birmingham, U.K.: Cornish Brothers, 1895), 206; *Report of the Sheffield Female Antislavery Society* (Sheffield: J. Blackwell, 1827), 3; Midgley, *Women against Slavery*, 58–59; Hochschild, *Bury the Chains*, 326.

28. *What Does Your Sugar Cost? A Cottage Conversation on the Subject of British Negro Slavery* (Birmingham, 1828); Midgley, *Women against Slavery*, 61.

29. *Reasons for Substituting East India Sugar for West India Sugar, Chiefly Selected from a Recent Publication, on the Subject of Emancipation* (Birmingham, U.K.: Benjamin Hudson, 1826).

30. *East India Sugar* (Sheffield, U.K.: J. Blackwell, n.d.); Midgley, *Women against Slavery*, 61; Louis Billington and Rosamund Billington, "'A Burning Zeal for Righteousness': Women in the British Anti-Slavery Movement, 1820–1860," in *Equal or Different: Women's Politics, 1800–1914*, ed. Jane Rendall (Oxford: Blackwell, 1987), 87–88; Hochschild, *Bury the Chains*, 326.

31. As quoted in Midgley, *Women against Slavery*, 57.

32. *Genius of Universal Emancipation*, October 20, 1827.

33. *First Report of the Female Society for Birmingham*, 7; *Second Report of the Female Society for Birmingham*, 10; Minutes, April 8, 1828, April 12, 1831, BLS, BRL; Midgley, *Women against Slavery*, 57; *The Second Report of the Ladies' Association for Calne, Melksham, Devizes and Their Respective Neighbourhoods in Aid of the Cause of Negro Emancipation* (1827), 14.

34. Midgley, *Women against Slavery*, 61–62.

35. Lasser, "Immediatism, Dissent, and Gender," 112–115.

36. David Brion Davis, *Slavery and Human Progress* (New York: Oxford University Press, 1984), 183–184.

37. Hochschild, *Bury the Chains*, 327; Midgley, *Feminism and Empire*, 61.

38. *Report of the Sheffield Female Anti-Slavery Society* (Sheffield, U.K.: J. Blackwell, 1827), 10–11.

39. Minutes, April 8, 1830, Birmingham Ladies' Society for the Relief of Negro Slaves, Minute Book, BLS, BRL; *Account of the Receipts and Disbursements of the Anti-Slavery Society, for the Years 1829 and 1830; with a List of Subscribers* (London: S. Bagster, Jr., 1830); Midgley, *Women against Slavery*, 115.

40. Heyrick, *Immediate, Not Gradual Abolition*, 24.

41. *First Report of the Ladies' Association of Liverpool*, 7–8.

42. Davis, *Slavery and Human Progress*, 181, 183; Fladeland, *Men and Brothers*, 162–164.

43. James Cropper, *Letters Addressed to William Wilberforce, M.P.: Recommending the Encouragement of the Cultivation of Sugar in Our Dominions in the East Indies as the Natural and Certain Measures of Effecting the Total and General Abolition of the Slave-Trade* (London: Longman, Hurst, 1822); Davis, *Slavery and Human Progress*, 181; David Brion Davis, "James Cropper and the British Antislavery Movement, 1821–1823," *Journal of Negro History* 45 (October 1960): 246.

44. Zachary Macaulay, *East and West India Sugar; or, A Refutation of the Claims of the West India Colonists to a Protecting Duty on East India Sugar* (London: Lupton Relfe and Hatchard and Son, 1823), 63–65; *Anti-Slavery Monthly Reporter*, October 1826, 247–248; Matthews, *Caribbean Slave Revolts*, 152.

45. *Anti-Slavery Monthly Reporter*, February 1830, 175–181.

46. Macaulay, *East and West Indian Sugar*, 63.

47. *Anti-Slavery Monthly Reporter*, October 1826, 248.

48. Davis, *Slavery and Human Progress*, 179–191.

49. Eric Williams, *Capitalism and Slavery* (Chapel Hill: University of North Carolina Press, 1994), 186–187.

50. David Brion Davis, "James Cropper and the British Antislavery Movement, 1823–1833," *Journal of Negro History* 46 (April 1961): 173. See also Davis, "James Cropper and the British Antislavery Movement, 1821–1823," 241–258.

51. Davis, *Slavery and Human Progress*, 180.

52. *To the Consumers of Sugar [A Reply to the Arguments Recommending the Purchase of East Indian Sugar . . .]* (1825), 2.

53. Heyrick, *Immediate, Not Gradual Abolition*, 23, 11, 39; Lasser, "Immediatism, Dissent, and Gender," 114.

54. Anthropos, *The Rights of Man (Not Paines), but the Rights of Man, in the West Indies* (London: Knight and Lacey, 1824), 35, 36.

55. Andrea Major, "'The Slavery of East and West': Abolitionists and 'Unfree' Labour in India, 1820–1830," *Slavery and Abolition* 31 (December 2010): 503–506; Andrea Major, *Slavery, Abolitionism, and Empire in India, 1772–1843* (Liverpool, U.K.: Liverpool University Press, 2012), 293–320.

56. *Liverpool Mercury*, August 17, 1821, in Major, *Slavery, Abolitionism, and Empire*, 309; *To the Consumers of Sugar*, 3–8.

57. Major, "'The Slavery of East and West,'" 515–519.

58. Midgley, *Women against Slavery*, 62.

5. Woman's Heart

1. Elizabeth Heyrick, *Immediate, Not Gradual Abolition; or, An Inquiry into the Shortest, Safest, and Most Effectual Means of Getting Rid of West Indian Slavery* (repr., Philadelphia: Joseph Rakestraw, 1824); Elizabeth Heyrick, *Immediate, Not Gradual Abolition; or, An Inquiry into the Shortest, Safest, and Most Effectual Means of Getting Rid of West Indian Slavery* (repr., New York: James V. Seaman, 1825); *Genius of Universal Emancipation*, November 26, 1825; December 10, 17, 24, and 31, 1825.

2. See *Genius of Universal Emancipation*, February 4, 1826; *The Casket*, February 1826. "The Slave Ship" was later reprinted in the *Liberator*, March 31, 1832. See also Benjamin Lundy, ed. *The Poetical Works of Elizabeth Margaret Chandler: With a Memoir of Her Life and Character* (Philadelphia: Lemuel Howell, 1836), 12.

3. Beth A. Salerno, *Sister Societies: Women's Antislavery Organizations in Antebellum America* (DeKalb: Northern Illinois University Press, 2005), 21; Merton Dillon, *Benjamin Lundy and the Struggle for Negro Freedom* (Urbana: University of Illinois Press, 1966), 143.

4. "Think of Our Country's Glory," *Genius of Universal Emancipation*, May 1830; *Liberator*, January 8, 1831.

5. See, e.g., Angelina Grimké, *Appeal to the Christian Women of the South* (New York: s.n., 1836); Frederick Douglass, "American Prejudice against Color: An Address Delivered in Cork, Ireland, October 23, 1845," *Cork Examiner*, October 27, 1845, in *The Frederick Douglass Papers*, ser. 1, *Speeches, Debates, and Interviews* (New Haven, Conn.: Yale University Press, 1979), 1:59; William Lloyd Garrison, "To the Abolitionists of Massachusetts," *Liberator*, July 19, 1839 in *The Letters of William Lloyd Garrison*, ed. Walter M. Merrill and Louis Ruchames (Cambridge, Mass.: Harvard University Press, 1971–1981), 2:497–517.

6. Edwin F. Hatfield, comp., *Freedom's Lyre: or, Psalms, Hymns, and Sacred Songs for the Slave and His Friends* (New York: American Anti-Slavery Society, 1840), 101. Chandler's poetry was included in other hymnals, including two compiled by the minister George W. Clark. Clark's *The Liberty Minstrel* was first published in 1844 and reprinted seven times. Clark also published *The Free Soil Minstrel*, which was *The Liberty Minstrel* adapted for the Free Soil Party. *A Selection of Anti-Slavery Hymns, for the Use of Friends of Emancipation*, compiled by William Lloyd Garrison, and *Songs of the Free and Hymns of Christian Freedom*, compiled by Maria Weston Chapman, also included Chandler's poems.

7. *True Wesleyan*, August 10, 1844.

8. Carol Lasser, "Immediatism, Dissent, and Gender: Women, and the Sentimentalization of Transatlantic Anti-Slavery Appeals," in *Women, Dissent, and Anti-Slavery in Britain and America, 1790–1865*, ed. Elizabeth J. Clapp and Julie Roy Jeffrey (New York: Oxford University Press, 2011), 121.

9. For the connection between women and religion and abolitionism, see Stacey Robertson, "'On the Side of Righteousness': Women, the Church and Abolition," in Clapp and Jeffrey, *Women, Dissent, and Anti-Slavery in Britain and America*, 155–174.

10. Lasser, "Immediatism, Dissent, and Gender," 122.

11. Wade Hinshaw Index to Quaker Meeting Records, Friends Historical Library, Swarthmore College, Swarthmore, Penn. See also Jane Howell to Elizabeth Margaret Chandler, June 3, 1832, in *Remember the Distance That Divides Us: The Family Letters of Philadelphia Quaker Abolitionist and Michigan Pioneer Elizabeth Margaret Chandler, 1830–1842*, ed. Marcia J. Heringa (East Lansing: Michigan State University Press, 2004), 119.

12. Holly M. Kent, "All Reform Depends upon You: Femininity, Authority, and the Politics of Authorship in Women's Antislavery Fiction, 1821–1861" (PhD diss., Lehigh University, 2010), 36, 39.

13. "Address," *Genius of Universal Emancipation*, September 2, 1829.

14. The parable of the widow's mite may be found in Mark 12:41–44 and Luke 21:1–4. In the parable, the widow donates two mites (the least valuable coins at the time), which is all she owns. Although the wealthy men of the parable donate much more, it is only a small proportion of their wealth. The widow's simple offering provides a striking contrast to the pride and pretentiousness of the wealthy men. Jesus explains to the disciples that the widow's humble and heartfelt offering means more to God than the offering made by the wealth men.

15. "If and But," *Genius of Universal Emancipation*, May 1831; "Letters to Isabel," *Genius of Universal Emancipation*, October 30, 1829; November 6, 13, 27, 1829; December 4, 18, 1829; January 15, 1830; March 5, 1830; "The New Year," *Genius of Universal Emancipation*, January 1, 1830; "Slave Luxuries," Elizabeth Margaret Chandler, *Essays, Philanthropic and Moral, by Elizabeth Margaret Chandler: Principally Relating to the Abolition of Slavery*, ed. Benjamin Lundy (Philadelphia: Lemuel Howell, 1836), 87–88; "Appeal to the Ladies of the United States," *Genius of Universal Emancipation*, September 16, 1829; "Opposition to Slavery," *Genius of Universal Emancipation*, January 1, 1830; "Associations," *Genius of Universal Emancipation*, January 22, 1830. The last installment of "Letters to Isabel" was incorrectly listed as "No. 7" in the *Genius*. It was correctly listed as "No. 8" in Lundy's later compilation. See Chandler, *Essays*, 53–64.

16. Frank Luther Mott, *A History of American Magazines* (Cambridge, Mass.: Harvard University Press, 1938–1968), 1:340–343; Patricia Okker, *Our Sister Editors: Sarah J. Hale and the Tradition of Nineteenth-Century American Women Editors* (Athens: University of Georgia Press, 1995), 9; Janet Gray, *Race and Time: Women's Poetics from Antislavery to Racial Modernity* (Iowa City: University of Iowa Press, 2004), 64–65; Alma Lutz, *Crusade for Freedom: Women of the Antislavery Movement* (Boston: Beacon Press, 1968), 8–9; Jacqueline Bacon, "The *Liberator*'s 'Ladies' Department,' 1832–1837: Freedom or Fetters?" in *Sexual Rhetoric: Media Perspectives on Sexuality, Gender, and Identity*, ed. Meta G. Carstarphen and Susan C. Zavoina (Westport, Conn.: Greenwood Press, 1999), 5.

17. *Genius of Universal Emancipation*, September 16, 1829. For a discussion of republican motherhood, see Linda K. Kerber, *Women of the Republic: Intellect and Ideology in Revolutionary America* (New York: W. W. Norton, 1986).

18. [Sarah J. Hale], "Introduction to 'An Appeal to the Ladies of the United States,'" *Ladies Magazine*, November 11, 1829; [Sarah J. Hale], "Review of Letters on Female Character," *Ladies Magazine*, June 1829; "Female Education," *Genius of Universal Emancipation*, September 2, 1829; "Indifference," *Genius of Universal Emancipation*, October 30, 1829. According to Hale, "The domestic station is woman's

appropriate sphere, and it will be honorable if she but adorn it with the graces, dignify it by intelligence, and hallow it by sentiment, tenderness, and piety. An ignorant woman cannot do this." See also Benjamin Lundy, "Memoir," in Lundy, ed., *Poetical Works*, 21. Lundy claimed that shortly after the publication of "Appeal," Chandler "found herself engaged in a great controversy with a lady of great celebrity, an author, residing in New England." Though neither Lundy nor Chandler identified Hale as Chandler's critic, the timing of Hale's reprint and its introduction suggest that the "lady of great celebrity" was most likely Hale.

19. Lundy, "Memoir," 21.

20. "Opinions," *Genius of Universal Emancipation*, December 11, 1829. For a discussion of "female politicians," see Rosemarie Zaggari, *Revolutionary Backlash: Women and Politics in the Early American Republic* (Philadelphia: University of Pennsylvania Press, 2007), 75–81.

21. S. Bradley Shaw, "The Pliable Rhetoric of Domesticity," in *The Stowe Debate: Rhetorical Strategies in Uncle Tom's Cabin*, ed. Mason Lowance Jr. (Amherst: University of Massachusetts Press, 1994), 91; Gray, *Race and Time*, 64.

22. "Slave Produce," *Genius of Universal Emancipation*, July 1, 1831.

23. "The Grave of the Unfortunate," *Genius of Universal Emancipation*, August 1, 1830.

24. "Slavery," *Genius of Universal Emancipation*, November 1, 1830.

25. "Opposition to Slavery," *Genius of Universal Emancipation*, January 1, 1830.

26. "Mental Metempsychosis," in Chandler, *Essays*, 117–118.

27. "Opposition to Slavery," *Genius of Universal Emancipation*, January 1, 1830; "Associations," *Genius of Universal Emancipation*, January 22, 1830.

28. American Convention for Promoting the Abolition of Slavery and Improving the Condition of the African Race, *Minutes of the Proceedings of the Twenty-First Biennial American Convention for Promoting the Abolition of Slavery, and Improving the Condition of the African Race Convened at the City of Washington . . .* (Philadelphia, 1829), 57–60; *African Repository and Colonial Journal*, October 1829. For Chandler's involvement, see Elizabeth Margaret Chandler, "To the Ladies Free Produce Society," in Lundy, *Poetical Works*, 175. The poem was not published in the *Genius*. Most likely the poem was composed between 1830 and 1833. Chandler moved to Michigan in 1830, and the women's free-produce group dissolved in 1833. For more about the Female Association, see Ruth Ketring Nuermberger, *The Free Produce Movement: A Quaker Protest against Slavery*, 16–18. See also Carol Faulkner, *Lucretia Mott's Heresy: Abolition and Women's Rights in Nineteenth-Century America* (Philadelphia: University of Pennsylvania Press, 2011), 55.

29. *Genius of Universal Emancipation*, July 1, 1826; Nuermberger, *Free Produce Movement*, 19.

30. *Genius of Universal Emancipation*, February, May, August 1831; *Liberator*, April 5, 1834. See also Nuermberger, *Free Produce Movement*, 18–19; Benjamin Quarles, *Black Abolitionists* (New York: Oxford University Press, 1969), 74–75; Faulkner, *Lucretia Mott's Heresy*, 55; Carol Faulkner, "The Root of the Evil: Free Produce and Radical Antislavery, 1820–1860," *Journal of the Early Republic* 27 (2007): 390.

31. Teresa Michals, "Experiments before Breakfast: Toys, Education and Middle-Class Childhood," in *The Nineteenth-Century Child and Consumer Culture*, ed. Dennis Denisoff (Burlington, Vt.: Ashgate, 2008), 29–42.

32. See, e.g., "Juvenile Anti-Slavery Agent," *Slave's Friend* 2, no. 8 (1837): 2. Note this article is published on the second page of the cover. The editor of the *Slave's Friend* lauded the appointment of Henry C. Wright as the American Anti-Slavery Society's agent appointed to work with children: "Woe to slavery . . . when the present race of juveniles are grown up." See also Henry C. Wright, "Juvenile Anti-Slavery Societies," *Liberator*, January 14, 1837. Wright noted that at that time there were four juvenile antislavery societies in New York averaging about one hundred members each and that two or three societies were in the process of organizing.

33. *Liberator*, January 22, 1831. See also Mary Lystad, *From Dr. Mather to Dr. Seuss: 200 Years of American Books for Children* (Boston: G. K. Halle, 1980), 50. Lystad notes that in this period 60 percent of books written for children "focused on moral instruction," and 38 percent provided "instruction in social behavior."

34. *Pennsylvania Freeman*, August 24, 1837. Children, according to Wright, were essential to the future of abolitionism: "I hope you, and all engaged in this holy struggle in behalf of our afflicted fellow citizens in chains, will never forget that our duty is but half done by struggling ourselves; we must also raise up and discipline a generation to carry this work to complete triumph after we are laid aside from our labors."

35. Deborah De Rosa, *Domestic Abolitionism and Juvenile Literature, 1830–1865* (Albany, N.Y.: State University of New York Press, 2003), 1. According to De Rosa, women took advantage of the developing market for children's literature and the cult of domesticity to discuss political issues such as slavery. In turn, women and children were politicized: "Through their publications, these authors politicize women and children, transcend the ideology of separate spheres, and enter into the public discourse about slavery to which they had limited access."

36. Moira Ferguson, *Subject to Others: British Women Writers and Colonial Slavery, 1670–1834* (New York: Routledge, 1992), 133–134; J. R. Oldfield, *Popular Politics and British Anti-Slavery: The Mobilization of Public Opinion against the Slave Trade, 1787–1807* (Portland, Ore.: Frank Cass, 1998), 142–148.

37. Priscilla Wakefield, *Mental Improvement*, ed. Ann B. Shteir (East Lansing, Mich.: Colleagues Press, 1995), 73–82; Margaret Hope Bacon, *Valiant Friend: The Life of Lucretia Mott* (New York: Walker, 1980), 13. As a child, Lucretia Mott memorized passages from *Mental Improvement*. See also Priscilla Wakefield, *Mental Improvement; or, The Beauties and Wonders of Nature and Art* (New Bedford, Mass.: Abraham Shearman, 1799).

38. Moira Ferguson dates the original publication of "The Negro Boy's Tale" to 1795. *The Oxford Dictionary of National Biography*, ed. H. C. G. Matthew and Brian Harrison (Oxford: Oxford University Press, 2004), dates the poem to 1802, when it was included in Opie's book. See Amelia Opie, *Poems* (London: Longman and Rees, 1802). See Ferguson, *Subject to Others*, 361n17; Gary Kelly, "Opie, Amelia (1769–1853)," in Matthew and Harrison, *Oxford Dictionary of National Biography*, doi:10.1093/ref:odnb/20799/. Deborah De Rosa notes only the 1824 reprint. De Rosa, *Domestic Abolitionism and Juvenile Literature*, 14.

39. See, e.g., *African Observer*, July 1827, 126–128.

40. Amelia Opie, *The Warrior's Return / The Black Man's Lament*, ed. Donald H. Reiman (New York: Garland, 1978), 3–4.

41. See, e.g., Maria Edgeworth, *The Grateful Negro* (1804). As Karen Sands-O'Connor argues, Edgeworth argued only for the humane treatment of slaves

rather than treating slaves as humans. Karen Sands-O'Connor, *Soon Come Home to This Island: West Indians in British Children's Literature* (New York: Routledge, 2008), 30–32.

42. Sands-O'Connor, *Soon Come Home to This Island*, 36.

43. De Rosa, *Domestic Abolitionism and Juvenile Literature*, 79–81, 96–97.

44. "What Is a Slave, Mother?" in *Juvenile Poems for the Use of Free American Children of Every Complexion*, ed. William Lloyd Garrison (Boston: Garrison and Knapp, 1835), 13–14. "What Is a Slave, Mother?" was also printed in Lundy, *Poetical Works*, 70–71. See also De Rosa, *Domestic Abolitionism and Juvenile Literature*, 96.

45. "Looking at the Soldiers," in Garrison, *Juvenile Poems*, 47–48. See Nina Baym, *American Women Writers and the Work of History, 1790–1860* (New Brunswick, N.J.: Rutgers University Press, 1995), 76; De Rosa, *Domestic Abolitionism and Juvenile Literature*, 97.

46. "Oh Press Me Not to Taste Again" and "The Sugar-Plums," in Garrison, *Juvenile Poems*, 68–69, 19.

47. *Colored American*, April 8, 1837. An earlier article in the *Episcopal Recorder* made similar links between confectionary shops and brothels. See "Where Are Your Children?" *Episcopal Recorder*, December 20, 1834.

48. Thomas Teetotal, "Henry Haycroft: A Story for Youth," *Temperance Advocate and Cold Water Magazine* 1 (1843): 38–40.

49. Patricia Crain, *The Story of A: The Alphabetization of America from* The New England Primer *to* The Scarlet Letter (Stanford, Calif.: Stanford University Press, 2000), 218, 4, 103–140.

50. See Martha Sledge, "'A is an Abolitionist': *The Anti-Slavery Alphabet* and the Politics of Literacy," in *Enterprising Youth: Social Values and Acculturation in Nineteenth-Century American Children's Literature*, ed. Monika Elbert (New York: Routledge, 2008), 69–82. Shirley Samuels connects *The Anti-Slavery Alphabet* to the pedagogical concerns of the *Slave's Friend*. Shirley Samuels, "The Identity of Slavery," in *The Culture of Sentiment: Race, Gender, and Sentimentality in Nineteenth-Century America*, ed. Shirley Samuels (New York: Oxford University Press, 1992), 157–171. Elizabeth Margaret Chandler's poem, "The Sugar-Plums" was reprinted in the *Slave's Friend* in 1836.

51. Hannah Townsend, *The Anti-Slavery Alphabet* (Philadelphia: Anti-Slavery Fair/Merrihew & Thompson, 1847). See also Deborah C. De Rosa, *Into the Mouths of Babes: An Anthology of Children's Abolitionist Literature* (Westport, Conn.: Praeger, 2005), 73–76.

52. De Rosa, *Domestic Abolitionism and Juvenile Literature*, 117.

53. Ibid., 113; Lois Brown, "Out of the Mouths of Babes: The Abolitionist Campaign of Susan Paul and the Juvenile Choir of Boston," *New England Quarterly* 75 (March 2002): 72.

54. For a list of publications in which Chandler's work appeared, see Mary Patricia Jones, "Elizabeth Margaret Chandler: Poet, Essayist, Abolitionist" (PhD diss., University of Toledo, 1981), 266–268. Significantly, in her history of the American free-produce movement, Nuermberger fails to note the wide distribution of Chandler's work. Rather she dismisses Chandler as the movement's lone poet and as an author of "highly moralistic" prose. See Nuermberger, *Free Produce Movement*, 112.

55. George W. Clark was a preacher and a teacher as well as a political abolitionist. *The Liberty Minstrel* was first published in 1844 and reprinted seven times. Clark

also published *The Free Soil Minstrel,* which was *The Liberty Minstrel* adapted for the Free Soil Party. Chandler's works were included in other antislavery hymnals and songbooks including *A Selection of Anti-Slavery Hymns, for the Use of Friends of Emancipation,* comp. William Lloyd Garrison; *Songs of the Free and Hymns of Christian Freedom,* comp. Maria Weston Chapman; and *Freedom's Lyre: or, Psalms, Hymns, and Sacred Songs for the Slave and His Friends,* comp. Edwin F. Hatfield for the American Anti-Slavery Society.

56. See Rufus Wilmot Griswold, ed., *Poets and Poetry of America* (Philadelphia: Carey and Hart, 1842); Rufus Wilmot Griswold, ed., *Gems from American Female Poets, with Brief Biographical Notes* (Philadelphia: H. Hooker, 1842); Rufus Wilmot Griswold, ed., *The Female Poets of America* (Philadelphia: Moss, 1849); Evert A. and George L. Duyckinck, eds., *Cyclopaedia of American Literature: Embracing Personal and Critical Notices of Authors, and Selections from Their Writings; from the Earliest Period to the Present Day,* vol. 2 (New York: Charles Scribner, 1855); Sarah Josepha Hale, ed., *Woman's Record* (New York: Harper and Bros., 1842); Caroline May, ed., *The American Female Poets: With Biographical and Critical Notices* (Philadelphia: Lindsay and Blakiston, 1853); Thomas Buchanan Read, ed., *The Female Poets of America with Portraits, Biographical Notices, and Specimens of Their Writings,* 7th ed. rev. (Philadelphia: E. H. Butler, 1857).

6. An Abstinence Baptism

1. Roman J. Zorn, "The New England Anti-Slavery Society: Pioneer Abolition Organization" *Journal of Negro History* 42 (July 1957): 157–176; *Constitution of the New-England Anti-Slavery Society: Together with its By-Laws, and a List of its Officers* (Boston: Garrison and Knapp, 1832).

2. Ruth Evans to Jane Howell, October 22, 1832, in *Remember the Distance That Divides Us: The Family Letters of Philadelphia Quaker Abolitionist and Michigan Pioneer Elizabeth Margaret Chandler, 1830–1842,* ed. Marcia J. Heringa (East Lansing: Michigan State University Press, 2004), 147; Laura S. Haviland, *A Woman's Life Work: Labors and Experiences of Laura S. Haviland* (Chicago: C. V. Waite, 1887), 32; Merton Dillon, "Elizabeth Chandler and the Spread of Antislavery Sentiment in Michigan," *Michgan History* 39 (December 1955): 491; Maurice Ndukwu, "Antislavery in Michigan: A Study of Its Origin, Development, and Expression from Territorial Period to 1860" (PhD diss., University of Michigan, 1979), 16–17.

3. *Report of the Boston Female Anti-Slavery Society: With a Concise Statement of Events, Previous and Subsequent to the Annual Meeting of 1835* (Boston: Boston Female Anti-Slavery Society, 1836), 79, 102–103. See also Debra Gold Hansen, *Strained Sisterhood: Gender and Class in the Boston Female Anti-Slavery Society* (Amherst: University of Massachusetts Press, 1993).

4. *Genius of Universal Emancipation,* October 1837.

5. Theodore Weld to J. F. Robinson, May 1, 1836, in *Letters of Theodore Dwight Weld, Angelina Grimké Weld, and Sarah Grimké,* ed. Gilbert H. Barnes and Dwight L. Dumond, 2 vols. (New York: Da Capo Press, 1970), 2:296.

6. Samuel J. May to John Estlin, May 2, 1848, May Papers, BPL.

7. Carol Faulkner, *Lucretia Mott's Heresy: Abolition and Women's Rights in Nineteenth-Century America* (Philadelphia: University of Pennsylvania Press, 2011), 64–66;

Beth A. Salerno, *Sister Societies: Women's Antislavery Organizations in Antebellum America* (DeKalb: Northern Illinois University Press, 2005), 26–27.

8. James Brewer Stewart, *Holy Warriors: The Abolitionists and American Slavery* (New York: Hill and Wang, 1976), 35–59; W. Caleb McDaniel, *The Problem of Democracy in the Age of Slavery: Garrisonian Abolitionists and Transatlantic Reform* (Baton Rouge: Louisiana State University Press, 2013), 37–44; Faulkner, *Lucretia Mott's Heresy*, 64–66; Salerno, *Sister Societies*, 26–27.

9. Philadelphia Female Anti-Slavery Society, Minutes, December 14, 1833, Papers of the Pennsylvania Abolition Society, reel 30, Historical Society of Pennsylvania, Philadelphia (hereafter cited as PFASS, HSP); Faulkner, *Lucretia Mott's Heresy*, 66–67; Julie Winch, *Philadelphia's Black Elite: Activism, Accommodation, and the Struggle for Black Autonomy, 1787–1848* (Philadelphia: Temple University Press, 1988), 85–87.

10. See, e.g., Minutes, August 11, 1835, December 8, 1836, April 13, 1837, PFASS, HSP. See also Jean R. Soderlund, "Priorities and Power: The Philadelphia Female Anti-Slavery Society," in *The Abolitionist Sisterhood: Women's Political Culture in Antebellum America*, ed. Jean Fagan Yellin and John C. Van Horne (Ithaca, New York: Cornell University Press, 1994), 69–71; Sarah Pennock Sellers, *David Sellers, Mary Pennock Sellers* (n.p., 1926), 47.

11. Shirley Yee, *Black Women Abolitionists: A Study in Activism, 1828–1860* (Knoxville: University of Tennessee Press, 1992), 96–97.

12. See, e.g., Minutes, August 11, 1834; March 9, August 10, 1837, PFASS, HSP.

13. *Genius of Universal Emancipation*, November 1832; *Liberator*, July 14, 1832; Salerno, *Sister Societies*, 24–48. For the Boston Female Anti-Slavery Society, see Hansen, *Strained Sisterhood*; Amy Swerdlow, "Abolition's Conservative Sisters: The Ladies' New York City Anti-Slavery Societies, 1834–1840," in *The Abolitionist Sisterhood: Women's Political Culture in Antebellum America*, ed. Jean Fagan Yellin and John C. Van Horne (Ithaca, New York: Cornell University Press, 1994), 31–44.

14. Deborah Weston to Aunt Mary, November 6, 1836; June 15, 1837; Deborah Weston to Anne Weston, November 13–17, 1836; Anne Weston to Caroline Weston, August 7, 1837, all in Weston Papers, BPL. See also Julie Roy Jeffrey, *The Great Silent Army of Abolitionism: Ordinary Women in the Antislavery Movement* (Chapel Hill: University of North Carolina Press, 1998), 48–49.

15. Maria Weston Chapman to Philadelphia Female Anti-Slavery Society, August 4, 1836, PFASS Incoming Correspondence, PFASS, HSP.

16. Minutes, August 11, September 8, 1836; February 9, 1837; March 9, 1837, PFASS, HSP; Maria Weston Chapman to Philadelphia Female Anti-Slavery Society, January 12, 1837, PFASS, HSP; Salerno, *Sister Societies*, 52–54.

17. *Proceedings of the Anti-Slavery Convention of Women*, New York City, May 9–12, 1837 (New York: William S. Dorr, 1837), 9, 10, 13. In the fall of 1837, the Philadelphia Female Anti-Slavery Society passed similar resolutions. See *Pennsylvania Freeman*, September 21, 1837.

18. *Proceedings of the Anti-Slavery Convention of Women*, May 15–18, 1838 (Philadelphia: Merrihew and Gunn, 1838), 7, 8.

19. *Proceedings of the Anti-Slavery Convention of American Women*, Philadelphia, May 1–3, 1839 (Philadelphia: Merrihew and Gunn, 1839), 7; Salerno, *Sister Socie-*

ties, 97–99; Carol Faulkner, "The Root of the Evil: Free Produce and Radical Antislavery, 1820–1860," *Journal of the Early Republic* 27 (2007): 392–393.

20. *Proceedings* . . . (1837), 9, 10, 13.

21. Gerda Lerner, *The Grimké Sisters from South Carolina: Pioneers for Woman's Rights and Abolition* (New York: Schocken Books, 1967), 71–74, 88–91.

22. Angelina Grimké to Theodore Weld, May 6, 1838, in Barnes and Dumond, *Letters . . . Weld,* 2:665. See also Benjamin Quarles, *Black Abolitionists* (New York: Oxford University Press, 1969), 75; Lerner, *Grimké Sisters,* 239–242.

23. *Boston Recorder,* July 14, 1837; Lerner, *Grimké Sisters,* 171, 188–189. See also Salerno, *Sister Societies,* 68–71; Anna M. Speicher, *The Religious World of Antislavery Women: Spirituality in the Lives of Five Abolitionist Lecturers* (Syracuse, N.Y.: Syracuse University Press, 2000), 109–121.

24. *Proceedings* . . . (1838), 6, 8; Salerno, *Sister Societies,* 82–85.

25. Salerno, *Sister Societies,* 99.

26. *Proceedings* . . . (1838), 6, 8; Salerno, *Sister Societies,* 82–85.

27. Hansen, *Strained Sisterhood,* 144.

28. *Proceedings* . . . (1837), 9.

29. Buckingham Anti-Slavery Society to Sarah and Angelina Grimké, July 27, 1837, Sarah M. Grimké Papers, Center for American History, University of Texas at Austin.

30. Minutes, August 10, 1837, PFASS, HSP; Buckingham Female Anti-Slavery Society to Mary Grew, August 4, 1837, PFASS Incoming Correspondence, PFASS, HSP; *Genius of Universal Emancipation,* October 1837; *Pennsylvania Freeman,* August 30, 1838.

31. *Freedom's Journal,* November 2, 1827; Richard S. Newman, *Freedom's Prophet: Richard Allen, the AME Church, and the Black Founding Fathers* (New York: New York University, 2008), 258–259.

32. David Walker, *David Walker's Appeal to the Coloured Citizens of the World,* ed. Peter P. Hinks (University Park: Pennsylvania State University Press, 2000), 67.

33. William Lloyd Garrison, *Thoughts on African Colonization* (Boston: Garrison and Knapp, 1832), 66. See also Richard S. Newman and Roy E. Finkenbine, "Forum: Black Founders in the New Republic; Introduction," *William and Mary Quarterly,* 3rd ser., 64 (January 2007), 89.

34. *Minutes of the Third Annual Convention for the Improvement of the Free People of Colour in the United States* (New York: n.p., 1833), 30; *Minutes of the Fifth Annual Convention for the Improvement of the Free People of Colour in the United States* (Philadelphia: William P. Gibbons, 1835), 12; Quarles, *Black Abolitionists,* 74–76.

35. Faulkner, "Root of the Evil," 391; Winch, *Philadelphia's Black Elite,* 105–106, 111. See also Howard Holman Bell, "The American Moral Reform Society, 1836–1841," *Journal of Negro Education* 27 (Winter 1958): 34–40.

36. *Colored American,* July 28, 1838.

37. *Genius of Universal Emancipation,* July 1833; *Liberator,* September 13, 1834.

38. William C. Patten, "The Anti-Slavery Movement in Chester County, Pennsylvania" (M.A. thesis, University of Delaware, 1963), 69–70; William C. Kashatus, *Just Over the Line: Chester County and the Underground Railroad* (West Chester, Penn.: Chester County Historical Society, 2002), 41.

39. *Minutes of the Proceedings of the Requited Labor Convention*, Philadelphia, May 17–18, September 5–6, 1838 (Philadelphia: Merrihew and Gunn, 1838), 3–6.

40. Patten, "The Anti-Slavery Movement," 70.

41. *Liberator*, June 2, 1837; June 4, June 18, July 2, 1836; *Fourth Annual Report of the American Anti-Slavery Society with the Speeches Delivered at the Anniversary Meeting*, New York City, May 9, 1837 (New York: William S. Dorr, 1837), 23; *Fifth Annual Report of the Executive Committee of the American Anti-Slavery Society, with the Minutes of the Meetings of the Society for Business, and the Speeches Delivered at the Anniversary Meeting*, May 8, 1838 (New York: William S. Dorr, 1838), 14.

42. Anthony J. Barker, *Captain Charles Stuart: Anglo-American Abolitionist* (Baton Rouge: Louisiana State University Press, 1986), 126–127.

43. *Liberator*, July 18, 1835.

44. Ibid., July 2, 1836.

45. Angelina Grimké Weld to Elizabeth Pease, August 14, 1839, in *British and American Abolitionists: An Episode in Transatlantic Understanding*, ed. Clare Taylor (Edinburgh: Edinburgh University Press, 1974), 79.

46. *Proceedings of the American Anti-Slavery Society, at Its Second Decade*, Philadelphia, December 3–5, 1853 (New York: American Anti-Slavery Society, 1854), 162.

47. J. William Frost, "Why Quakers and Slavery? Why Not More Quakers?" 29–40; Carleton Mabee, *Black Freedom: The Nonviolent Abolitionists from 1830 through the Civil War* (New York: Macmillan, 1970), 189–191.

48. 12 Reg. Deb. 100 (1836), 100; Thomas E. Drake, *Quakers and Slavery in America* (New Haven, Conn.: Yale University Press, 1950), 146.

49. *Speech of Mr. Wall, of New Jersey, on the Memorial of the Caln Quarterly Meeting of the Society of Friends, of Lancaster County, Pennsylvania, Praying for the Abolition of Slavery and the Slave Trade in the District of Columbia*, U.S. Senate, February 29, 1836 (Washington, D.C.: Blair and Rives, 1836), 3–4.

50. Cong. Globe, 24th Cong., 1st Sess., 95–99, 100 (1836); *Liberator*, January 30, 1836; *Christian Reporter and Boston Observer*, January 30, 1836; Drake, *Quakers and Slavery*, 146–147. See also Daniel Wirls, " 'The Only Mode of Avoiding Everlasting Debate': The Overlooked Senate Gag Rule for Antislavery Petitions," *Journal of the Early Republic* 27 (2007): 115–138.

51. *Friend*, May 16, 1835; November 5, 1836. See also J. William Frost, "Years of Crisis and Separation: Philadelphia Yearly Meeting, 1790–1860," in *Friends in the Delaware Valley: Philadelphia Yearly Meeting, 1681–1981*, ed. John M. Moore (Haverford, Penn.: Friends Historical Association, 1981), 95:

"The spectacular growth of the new form of antislavery attracted and repelled Friends. Garrison's followers preached immediate emancipation but riots resulted and the hostility of the South mounted. Quaker sympathizers created new abolition groups modeled on Garrison's principles, but Quaker opponents saw the new movement as fostering hatred for the South rather than meaningful reform and did not wish to be associated with violence. Before 1840 Philadelphia Yearly Meeting Orthodox and Hicksite Yearly Meetings in New York, Baltimore, and Philadelphia issued strong warnings against Friends joining in activities for good purposes with those who had not the proper religious sensitivities."

52. Minutes of Philadelphia Yearly Meeting (Hicksite), April 14, 1837, Friends Historical Library, Swarthmore College, Swarthmore, Penn. (hereafter cited as FHL, SC).

53. Christopher Densmore, "The Dilemma of Quaker Anti-Slavery: The Case of Farmington Quarterly Meeting, 1836–1910," *Quaker History* (1993): 82.

54. Minutes of Philadelphia Yearly Meeting (Orthodox), Meeting for Sufferings, September 20, 1839, FHL, SC.

55. Minutes of Philadelphia Yearly Meeting (Hicksite), April 14, 1837, 24; Ryan P. Jordan, *Slavery and the Meetinghouse: The Quakers and the Abolitionist Dilemma* (Bloomington: Indiana University Press, 2007), 37; Densmore, "Dilemma of Quaker Anti-Slavery."

56. *Friend*, March 15, 1834.

57. Ibid., May 23, 1835.

58. Minutes of the Committee on Requited Labor, 1837–1839, Philadelphia Yearly Meeting of Friends, Papers of the Pennsylvania Abolition Society, reel 31 HSP. The microfilm guide and the catalog record associate the Committee on Requited Labor with the Philadelphia Yearly Meeting of Friends. The minutes, however, indicate this committee was affiliated with the Association of Friends for Advocating the Cause of the Slave, and Improving the Condition of the Free People of Colour. Priscilla Hensey is also listed in the minutes as Priscilla Henszey.

59. Association of Friends for Advocating the Cause of the Slave, and Improving the Condition of Free People of Colour, *An Address to the Members of the Religious Society of Friends, on the Propriety of Abstaining from the Use of the Produce of Slave Labour* (Philadelphia: Merrihew and Gunn, 1838).

60. Ruth Ketring Nuermberger, *The Free Produce Movement: A Quaker Protest against Slavery* (New York: AMS Press, 1942), 34–35; Drake, *Quakers and Slavery*, 154–155. The other pamphlets issued by the association were *An Address to the Citizens of the United States, on the Subject of Slavery* (Philadelphia: Neall and Shann, 1838); *An Appeal to the Females of the North, on the Subject of Slavery by a Female of Vermont* (Philadelphia: John Thompson, 1838).

61. Drake, *Quakers and Slavery*, 154–155.

62. Christopher Densmore and Thomas Bassett, "Quakers, Slavery, and the Civil War," in *Quaker Crosscurrents: Three Hundred Years of Friends in the New York Yearly Meetings*, ed. Hugh Barbour, Christopher Densmore, Elizabeth H. Moger, Nancy C. Sorel, Alson D. Van Wagner, and Arthur J. Worrall (Syracuse, N.Y.: Syracuse University Press, 1995), 188; Elizabeth H. Moger, "Quakers as Abolitionists: The Robinsons of Rokeby and Charles Marriott," *Quaker History* 92 (Fall 2003): 54.

63. Charles Marriott, *An Address to the Religious Society of Friends on the Duty of Declining the Use of the Products of Slave Labour* (New York: Isaac T. Hopper, 1835), 12; *Testimony of New-York Association of Friends for the Relief of Those Held in Slavery, &c. Concerning Charles Marriott, Deceased* (New York, 1844), 6–7; Nuermberger, *Free Produce Movement*, 23n33.

64. Moger, "Quakers as Abolitionists," 54–55; Densmore and Bassett, "Quakers, Slavery, and the Civil War," 185.

65. *Address from the New-York Association of Friends, for the Relief of Those Held in Slavery, and the Improvement of Free People of Color, to Its members and Friends Generally* (New York, 1842).

66. Drake, *Quakers and Slavery*, 161–162; Nuermberger, *Free Produce Movement*, 31; Densmore and Bassett, "Quakers, Slavery, and the Civil War," 188.

67. Densmore, "Dilemma of Quaker Anti-Slavery," 82.

68. As quoted in ibid.

69. Ibid., 83; Frost, "Years of Crisis and Separation," 91–93.

70. Deborah De Rosa, *Domestic Abolitionism and Juvenile Literature, 1830–1865* (Albany: State University of New York Press, 2003), 108; *Liberator*, December 25, 1835; Quarles, *Black Abolitionists*, 29.

71. *Slave's Friend* 2, no. 5 (1837): 2–3.

72. Minutes of the Junior Anti-Slavery Society, June 24, 1836, Papers of the Pennsylvania Abolition Society, reel 31 Historical Society of Pennsylvania (hereafter cited as JASS, HSP).

73. De Rosa, *Domestic Abolitionism and Juvenile Literature*, 109.

74. Quarles, *Black Abolitionists*, 30; *Colored American*, November 23, 1839.

75. Minutes, January 20, 1837, JASS, HSP; *National Enquirer*, January 14, 1837; Minutes, January 5, 1838, JASS, HSP; Minutes, June 15, 1838, JASS, HSP.

76. As quoted in De Rosa, *Domestic Abolitionism and Juvenile Literature*, 113.

77. *Slave's Friend* 2, no. 5 (1837): 11, 15.

78. De Rosa, *Domestic Abolitionism and Juvenile Literature*, 108–114.

79. Angelina Grimké to Elizabeth Pease, August 14, 1839; Theodore D. Weld to J. F. Robinson, May 1, 1836, both in Barnes and Dumond, *Letters . . . Weld*, 1:295–298, 2:781–787.

80. *Liberator*, October 20, 1837; *Pennsylvania Freeman*, October 5, 1837; Clarkson Anti-Slavery Society to Mary Grew, PFASS Incoming Correspondence, 1837, reel 31, PFASS, HSP; *Liberator*, March 9, April 13, 1838; *Pennsylvania Freeman*, March 15, 1838.

81. *Minutes of the Proceedings of the Requited Labor Convention* Philadelphia May 17–18, September 5–6, 1838, 6; Susan H. Luther to William Lloyd Garrison, May 21, 1838, William Lloyd Garrison Papers, Boston Public Library (hereafter cited as Garrison Papers, BPL). The PFASS appointed thirty delegates to the Requited Labor Convention. See Minutes for April 12, 1838, PFASS, HSP.

82. Nuermberger, *Free Produce Movement*, 23–24; Richard S. Newman, *The Transformation of American Abolitionism: Fighting Slavery in the Early Republic* (Chapel Hill: University of North Carolina, 2002), 173–174.

83. *Minutes of the Proceedings of the Requited Labor Convention*, Philadelphia May 17–18, September 5–6, 1838, 3–8. Italics in the original. See also *History of Pennsylvania Hall, Which Was Destroyed by a Mob, on the 17th of May 1838* (Philadelphia: Merrihew and Gunn, 1838); *Pennsylvania Freeman*, May 7, 24, 31, 1838. On antiabolitionist mobs, see Leonard L. Richards, *Gentlemen of Property and Standing: Anti-Abolition Mobs in Jacksonian America* (New York: Oxford University Press, 1970); David Grimsted, *American Mobbing, 1828–1861: Toward Civil War* (New York: Oxford University Press, 1998), 3–82. Ira V. Brown argues that the integrated meeting of the Anti-Slavery Convention of American Women provoked public hostility and led to the destruction of Pennsylvania Hall: "Not even Pennsylvania was ready for racial integration and women's liberation in 1838." Ira V. Brown, "Racism and Sexism: The Case of Pennsylvania Hall," *Phylon* 37 (1976): 128. Brown incorrectly identifies the Requited Labor Convention as the Recruited

Labor Convention. He also overlooks the integrated membership of the Requited Labor Convention.

84. *Minutes of the Proceedings of the Requited Labor Convention*, Philadelphia May 17–18, September 5–6, 1838, 9–14. For Gunn's address, see Lewis C. Gunn, *Address to Abolitionists* (Philadelphia: Merrihew and Gunn, 1838).

85. Gerrit Smith to Lewis C. Gunn, August 19, 1838, Committee on Requited Labor; *Minutes of the Proceedings of the Requited Labor Convention*, Philadelphia May 17–18, September 5–6, 1838, 15; Daniel L. Miller Jr. to Gerrit Smith, November 3, 1838, Gerrit Smith Papers, Special Collections Research Center, Syracuse University Library (hereafter cited as Smith Papers, SUL).

86. Paul Goodman, *Of One Blood: Abolitionism and the Origins of Racial Equality* (Berkeley: University of California Press, 1998), 69–80; Bruce Laurie, *Beyond Garrison: Antislavery and Social Reform* (New York: Cambridge University Press, 2005), 23.

87. William Goodell to Lewis C. Gunn, August 29, 1838, repr., *Minutes of the Proceedings of the Requited Labor Convention*, Philadelphia May 17–18, September 5–6, 1838, 16–18.

88. Salerno, *Sister Societies*, 158–159. Women's antislavery societies in this period "were quite up-front about their desire to change the ways in which power was used and citizenship distributed in the United States," according to Salerno. Women believed they had the right and the responsibility "to influence what their political representatives believed and how they voted. A small coalition of men agreed with them." When the antislavery movement divided over the woman question, the "fusion" of the moral and the political was lost and took decades to regain.

89. *Genius of Universal Emancipation*, January 26, 1828.

90. Ibid., June 11, 1831.

91. Nuermberger, *Free Produce Movement*, 62–63, 119.

92. *Colored American*, July 22, 1837; October 10, 1840.

93. *Genius of Universal Emancipation*, September 2, 1829; *National Enquirer and Constitutional Advocate of Universal Liberty*, February 5, 1836; Lawrence Glickman, *Buying Power: A History of Consumer Activism in America* (Chicago: University of Chicago Press, 2009), 69–72.

94. *Liberator*, December 20, 1834; Stacey Robertson, *Hearts Beating for Liberty: Women Abolitionists in the Old Northwest* (Chapel Hill: University of North Carolina Press, 2010), 125.

95. *Liberator*, March 4, 1837.

96. *Pennsylvania Freeman*, September 17, 1840.

7. Yards of Cotton Cloth and Pounds of Sugar

1. Betty Fladeland, *Men and Brothers: Anglo-American Antislavery Cooperation* (Urbana: University of Illinois Press, 1972), 195–256, 263–264; Clare Midgley, *Women against Slavery: The British Campaigns, 1780–1870* (London: Routledge, 1992), 121–122; J. Gallagher, "Fowell Buxton and the New African Policy, 1838–1842," *Cambridge Historical Journal* 10 (1950): 36–58; William Howitt and Mary Howitt, eds., *Howitt's Journal of Literature and Popular Progress* (London: William Lovett), 2:259; *Liberator*, October 11, 1839.

2. *Liberator*, February 9, 1838; *National Enquirer and Constitutional Advocate of Universal Liberty*, November 30, 1837; February 8, 15, 22, 1838; March 1, 1838; Ira V. Brown, "An Antislavery Agent: C. C. Burleigh in Pennsylvania, 1836–1837," *Pennsylvania Magazine of History and Biography* 105, no. 1 (1981): 84. See also Lucretia Mott to James Miller McKim, March 15, 1838 and Lucretia Mott to Edward M. Davis, June 18, 1838, both in *Selected Letters of Lucretia Coffin Mott*, ed. Beverly Wilson Palmer (Urbana: University of Illinois Press, 2002), 37–45; Anna Lee Marston, ed., *Records of a California Family: Journals and Letters of Lewis C. Gunn and Elizabeth Le Breton Gunn* (San Diego, Calif.: n.p., 1928), 4–6.

3. Lewis C. Gunn, *An Address to Abolitionists* (Philadelphia: Merrihew and Gunn, 1838), 5, 6, 10.

4. *Minutes of the Proceedings of the Requited Labor Convention*, Philadelphia May 17–18, September 5–6, 1838 (Philadelphia: Merrihew and Gunn, 1838), 7.

5. *Genius of Universal Emancipation*, May 1830. White operated her store until 1846, the second-longest running of the free-labor stores in this period.

6. Ruth Ketring Nuermberger, *The Free Produce Movement: A Quaker Protest against Slavery* (New York: AMS Press, 1942), 81. After their move to Michigan, Elizabeth Margaret Chandler and her aunt Ruth Evans ordered goods from White's store. See, e.g., Elizabeth Chandler to Jane Howell, December 13, 1832, *Remember the Distance That Divides Us: The Family Letters of Philadelphia Quaker Abolitionist and Michigan Pioneer Elizabeth Margaret Chandler, 1830–1842*, ed. Marcia J. Heringa (East Lansing: Michigan State University Press, 2004), 155.

7. See, e.g., *National Reformer*, October 1838.

8. Lydia White to William Lloyd Garrison, May 9, 1831; Lydia White to William Lloyd Garrison, October 19, 1831, both in Garrison Papers, BPL.

9. Samuel Philbrick to Daniel L. Miller, December 30, 1838, Incoming Correspondence, American Free Produce Association, AFPA, HSP.

10. *Pennsylvania Freeman*, November 8, 1838. See also Daniel L. Miller Jr. to Gerrit Smith, November 3, 1838, Smith Papers, SUL.

11. William Bassett to Daniel L. Miller, November 9, 1838, Incoming Correspondence, American Free Produce Association, AFPA, HSP.

12. Samuel Philbrick to Daniel L. Miller, December 30, 1838; Aaron L. Benedict to Daniel L. Miller, January 18, 1839, Incoming Correspondence, American Free Produce Association, AFPA, HSP.

13. Minutes, October 15, 1839, AFPA, HSP.

14. Minutes, October 20, 1840, AFPA, HSP.

15. Esther Nixon to the American Free Produce Association, February 7, March 6, May 1, 1840; Phineas Nixon to the American Free Produce Association, September 25, October 2, 1840, Incoming Correspondence, American Free Produce Association, AFPA, HSP.

16. Minutes, October 15, 1839, AFPA, HSP.

17. Andrea Major, *Slavery, Abolitionism, and Empire in India, 1772–1843* (Liverpool, U.K.: Liverpool University Press, 2012), 325–326.

18. S. R. Mehrota, "The British India Society and Its Bengal Branch, 1839–1846," *Indian Economic and Social History Review* 4 (Summer 1967); 131; Anne Stoddart, *Elizabeth Pease Nichol* (London: J. M. Dent, 1899), 72; Kenneth D. Nworah,

"The Aborigines' Protection Society, 1889–1909: A Pressure Group in Colonial Policy," *Canadian Journal of African Studies* 5, no. 1 (1971): 79–81.

19. Stoddart, *Elizabeth Pease Nichol*, 73–79.

20. George Thompson to William Lloyd Garrison, January 5, 1839, in *British and American Abolitionists: An Episode in Transatlantic Understanding*, ed. Clare Taylor (Edinburgh: Edinburgh University Press, 1974), 67–68. See also George Thompson to Richard D. Webb, February 15, 1839, in *British and American Abolitionists*, 69.

21. George Thompson to unknown, January 7, 1838, as quoted in Stoddart, *Elizabeth Pease Nichol*, 85.

22. Scholarship on William Adam is limited. For an early biographical study of Adam, see S. C. Sanial, "The Rev. William Adam," *Bengal Past and Present: The Journal of the Calcutta Historical Society* 8 (1914): 251–272. See also Julie L. Holcomb, "'The Second Fallen Adam': William Adam and Nineteenth-Century Transatlantic Reform," in *Currents in Transatlantic History: Encounters, Commodities, Identities*, ed. Steven Reinhardt (College Station, Texas: Texas A & M University Press, forthcoming 2016).

23. Born in 1772 in British-ruled Bengal, Rammohun Roy's family belonged to the Brahman caste, the highest ranking of the four varnas, or social classes, in Hindu India. Raised within the Hindu tradition, Rammohun was exposed to the Islamic tradition at an early age. In the 1810s, he became interested in Unitarianism. Rammohun wrote and spoke confidently within each of these three religious traditions. He was fluent in English, Greek, and Hebrew, as well as Sanskrit and Persian. Rammohun published widely in Bengali, English, and Hindustani. He fought for an end to sati, or widow burning, supported education, and criticized British censorship of the Indian press and the exclusion of Indians from British juries. See Dermot Killingley, *Rammohun Roy in Hindu and Christian Tradition: The Teape Lectures, 1990* (Newcastle-upon-Tyne: Grevatt and Grevatt, 1993); Lynn Zastoupil, "'Notorious and Convicted Mutilators': Rammohun Roy, Thomas Jefferson, and the Bible," *Journal of World History* 20 (September 2009): 399–434; Lynn Zastoupil, *Rammohun Roy and the Making of Victorian Britain* (New York: Palgrave Macmillan, 2010).

24. Joseph DiBona, ed., *One Teacher, One School: The Adam Reports on Indigenous Education in Nineteenth-Century India* (New Delhi: Biblioa Impex, 1983), 6–10.

25. Stoddart, *Elizabeth Pease Nichol*, 85; John Hyslop Bell, *British Folks and British India Fifty Years Ago: Joseph Pease and His Contemporaries* (London: John Heywood, 1891), 61; DiBona, *One Teacher, One School*, 11.

26. Stoddart, *Elizabeth Pease Nichol*, 85–86, 89–90; Bell, *British Folks and British India*, 58–60, 62–64; Mary Wigham to Maria Weston Chapman, April 1, 1839, in Taylor, *British and American Abolitionists*, 69–70; *Speeches, Delivered at a Public Meeting, for the Formation of a British India Society*, Freemasons' Hall, July 6, 1839 (London: British India Society, 1839), 67.

27. *Speeches, Delivered at a Public Meeting*, 14.

28. Ibid., 44.

29. Elizabeth Pease to Maria Weston Chapman, July 11, 1839, in Taylor, *British and American Abolitionists*, 72–73.

30. Maria Weston Chapmen to Elizabeth Pease, August 20, 1839, in Taylor, *British and American Abolitionists*, 81–82.

31. Angelina Grimké to Elizabeth Pease, August 14, 1839, Anti-Slavery Collection, Boston Public Library, Boston, Mass. (hereafter cited as ASC, BPL).

32. Maria Weston Chapman, "The British India Society," *Liberty Bell*, January 1, 1839.

33. *Speeches Delivered at a Public Meeting*, 68.

34. George Thompson, *Six Lectures on the Condition, Resources, and Prospects of British India, and the Duties and Responsibilities of Great Britain to Do Justice to That Vast Empire* (London: John W. Parker, 1842), 128.

35. George Thompson, *Six Lectures on British India, Delivered in the Friends' Meeting-House in Manchester, England, in October 1839* (Pawtucket, R.I.: William and Robert Adams, 1840); William Adam to Maria Weston Chapman, November 5, 1839, in Taylor, *British and American Abolitionists*, 86–87; William Adam to Maria Weston Chapman, December 5, 1839, ASC, BPL; *Liberator*, February 5, 15, 1840; *Christian Register and Boston Observer*, March 7, 1840.

36. Edward M. Davis to Elizabeth Pease, December 11, 1839, ASC, BPL.

37. Edward M. Davis to Elizabeth Pease, December 11, 1839, ASC, BPL.

38. Arthur W. Silver, *Manchester Men and Indian Cotton, 1847–1872* (Manchester: Manchester University Press, 1966), 38–39; Frenise A. Logan, "A British East India Company Agent in the United States, 1839–1840," *Agricultural History* 48 (April 1974): 267–276. See also Brian Schoen, *The Fragile Fabric of the Union: Cotton, Federal Politics, and the Global Origins of the Civil War* (Baltimore: Johns Hopkins University Press, 2009), 171.

39. *Daily Picayune*, August 4, 1840. See also *Southern Quarterly*, 1 (April 1842), 459; *Niles Register*, March 27, 1841.

40. *Daily National Intelligencer*, September 21, 1840.

41. Ibid., November 25, 1841.

42. Silver, *Manchester Men*, 38.

43. Isaac Watts, *Cotton Supply Association* (Manchester: Tubbs & Brook, 1871), 122.

44. Betty Fladeland, *Abolitionists and Working-Class Problems in the Age of Industrialization* (Baton Rouge: Louisiana State University Press, 1984), 49–73; Fladeland, *Men and Brothers*, 258–267; Douglas H. Maynard, "The World's Anti-Slavery Convention of 1840," *Mississippi Valley Historical Review* 47 (December 1960): 455; Donald R. Kennon, "'An Apple of Discord': The Woman Question at the World's Anti-Slavery Convention of 1840," *Slavery and Abolition* 5 (December 1984): 250.

45. *Liberator*, May 8, 1840; Lewis Tappan to Theodore Weld, May 4, 1840, in *Letters of Theodore Dwight Weld, Angelina Grimké Weld and Sarah Grimké, 1822–1844*, ed. Gilbert H. Barnes and Dwight L. Dumond (Gloucester, Mass.: Peter Smith, 1965), 2:834; Kennon, "'An Apple of Discord,'" 248–249.

46. Frederick B. Tolles, ed., *Slavery and the "Woman Question": Lucretia Mott's Diary of Her Visit to Great Britain to Attend the World's Anti-Slavery Convention of 1840* (Haverford, Penn.: Friends' Historical Association, 1952), 23, 27, 28–29; Kathryn Kish Sklar, "'Women Who Speak for an Entire Nation': American and British Women at the World Anti-Slavery Convention, London, 1840," in *The Abolitionist Sisterhood: Women's Political Culture in Antebellum America*, ed. Jean Fagan Yellin and John C. Van Horne (Ithaca, N.Y.: Cornell University Press, 1994), 308.

47. Tolles, *Slavery and the "Woman Question,"* 27–31; *Liberator*, December 11, 1840; Maynard, "World's Anti-Slavery Convention," 459–460; Kennon, "'An Apple of Discord,'" 250–251; William Lloyd Garrison to Helen Garrison, June 29, 1840, in Taylor, *British and American Abolitionists*, 91–93.

48. British and Foreign Anti-Slavery Society, *Proceedings of the General Anti-Slavery Convention Called by the Committee of the British and Foreign Anti-Slavery Society*, London, June 12–23, 1840 (London: British and Foreign Anti-Slavery Society, 1841), 77–86. See also Major, *Slavery, Abolitionism, and Empire*, 321–324.

49. BFASS, *Proceedings of the General Anti-Slavery Convention*, London June 12–23, 1840, 90.

50. Ibid., 437–447.

51. Ibid., 447–454.

52. Tolles, *Slavery and "The Woman Question,"* 39–40. Emphasis in the original. See also Carol Faulkner, "The Root of the Evil: Free Produce and Radical Antislavery, 1820–1860," *Journal of the Early Republic* 27 (2007): 393–394.

53. Sarah Pugh to Richard D. Webb, November 18, 1840, ASC, BPL; *National Anti-Slavery Standard*, November 12, 1840.

54. BFASS, *Proceedings of the General Anti-Slavery Convention*, London June 12–23, 1840, 430–432.

55. Carleton Mabee, *Black Freedom: The Nonviolent Abolitionists from 1830 through the Civil War* (New York: Macmillan, 1970), 190–191.

56. Tolles, *Slavery and "The Woman Question,"* 39–40. Emphasis in the original. See also Faulkner, "Root of the Evil," 393–394.

57. Edward M. Davis to Elizabeth Pease, December 28, 1839, in Taylor, *British and American Abolitionists*, 88.

58. Edward M. Davis to Elizabeth Pease, March 30, 1840, ASC, BPL.

59. Minutes, October 20, 1840, AFPA, HSP; Sarah Pugh to Elizabeth Pease, November 16, 1840, ASC, BPL; *Liberator*, December 11, 1840.

60. Minutes, October 15, 1839; October 18, 1841; October 21, 1842; October 21, 1845; October 26, 1846; October 4, 1847, AFPA, HSP. The *Philanthropist* reprinted the letter to the Ohio Anti-Slavery Society in the June 30, 1841, issue.

61. *American Free Produce Journal*, October 1, 1842.

62. Minutes, October 18, 1841; October 21, 1842; October 17, 1843; October 21, 1845; October 26, 1846; October 4, 1847, AFPA, HSP.

63. Minutes, October 18, 1841, AFPA, HSP; *New York Evangelist*, April 28, 1842.

64. Minutes, October 21, 1842, AFPA, HSP.

65. Ibid.; *National Anti-Slavery Standard*, November 17, 1842; Nuermberger, *Free Produce Movement*, 50–51.

66. Nuermberger, *Free Produce Movement*, 117–118; Stacey Robertson, *Hearts Beating for Liberty: Women Abolitionists in the Old Northwest* (Chapel Hill: University of North Carolina Press, 2010), 76, 230n39.

67. Robertson, *Hearts Beating for Liberty*, 73–76.

68. *National Anti-Slavery Standard*, April 7, 1842; Nuermberger, *Free Produce Movement*, 49–50.

69. Nuermberger, *Free Produce Movement*, 50–51, 117–119. While thorough, Nuermberger's lists of free-produce societies and stores in *The Free Produce Movement* are incomplete. For example, Sarah Pearson's long-running store (1844–1858) in

Hamorton, Pennsylvania, is missing from Nuermberger's list. Given the short life span of many of these associations and stores, such omissions are not surprising. For Pearson's store, see C. W. Heathcote, *A History of Chester County, Pennsylvania* (Harrisburg, Penn.: National Historical Association, 1932), 233.

70. Minutes, October 21, 1842, AFPA, HSP.

71. Nuermberger, *Free Produce Movement*, 50–52.

72. Levi Coffin, *Reminiscences of Levi Coffin, The Reputed President of the Underground Railroad* (Cincinnati, Ohio: Robert Clarke, 1880), 223–234; Walter Edgerton, *A History of the Separation in Indiana Yearly Meeting of Friends; Which Took Place in the Winter of 1842 and 1843, on the Anti-Slavery Question* (Cincinnati, Ohio: Achilles Pugh, 1856); Thomas E. Drake, *Quakers and Slavery in America* (New Haven, Conn.: Yale University Press, 1950), 164–165; Nuermberger, *Free Produce Movement*, 48–49; Ryan P. Jordan, *Slavery and the Meetinghouse: The Quakers and the Abolitionist Dilemma* (Bloomington: Indiana University Press, 2007), 46–58; Robertson, *Hearts Beating for Liberty*, 81–82; Thomas D. Hamm, David Dittmer, Chenda Fruchter, Ann Giordano, Janice Matthews, and Ellen Swain, "Moral Choices: Two Quaker Communities and the Abolitionist Movement," *Indiana Magazine of History* 87 (June 1991): 117–154.

73. Nuermberger, *Free Produce Movement*, 33–34; Jordan, *Slavery and the Meetinghouse*, 61.

74. Minutes, October 20, 1840, AFPA, HSP; *Liberator*, November 10, 1843.

75. Tolles, *Slavery and "The Woman Question,"* 57.

76. *Liberator*, February 19, 1847.

77. *Genius of Universal Emancipation*, October 1837.

78. *Liberator*, March 1, 1850.

79. Minutes, October 17, 1843, AFPA, HSP.

80. *Liberator*, March 5, 1847. The biblical reference is Matthew 23:24.

81. Elizabeth A. Pease to J. A. Collins, n.d.; Elizabeth Pease to Anne Warren Weston, June 24, 1841; Elizabeth Pease to unknown, February 24, 1842, all in Taylor, *British and American Abolitionists*, 140, 154, 169–170. William Bassett to Elizabeth Pease, April 25, 1842, ASC, BPL; Mehrota, "The British India Society," 139–142; Malcolm Chase, *Chartism: A New History* (Manchester: Manchester University Press, 2007), 158–160.

82. Drake, *Quakers and Slavery*, 172–173.

83. Anna Vaughan Kett, "Quaker Women, the Free Produce Movement and British Anti-Slavery Campaigns: The Free Labour Cotton Depot in Street, 1852–1858," (PhD diss., University of Brighton, 2012), 90, 107.

8. Bailing the Atlantic with a Spoon

1. Minutes, April 10, 1856, PFASS, HSP.

2. Lucretia Mott, "Diversities," *Liberty Bell*, January 1844.

3. Minutes, October 8, 1846, PFASS, HSP; Carol Faulkner, *Lucretia Mott's Heresy: Abolition and Women's Rights in Nineteenth-Century America* (Philadelphia: University of Pennsylvania Press, 2011), 113–114. Groups such as the Philadelphia Vigilance Committee provided food, shelter, and clothing to fugitive slaves.

4. Jean R. Soderlund, "Priorities and Powers: The Philadelphia Female Anti-Slavery Society," in *The Abolitionist Sisterhood: Women's Political Culture in Antebellum*

America, ed. Jean Fagan Yellin and John C. Van Horne (Ithaca, N.Y.: Cornell University Press, 1994), 72–73; Faulkner, *Lucretia Mott's Heresy*, 114.

5. Minutes, April 10, 1856, PFASS, HSP.

6. Samuel J. May to John Estlin, May 2, 1848, May Papers, BPL.

7. Thomas D. Hamm, *The Transformation of American Quakerism: Orthodox Friends, 1800–1907* (Bloomington: Indiana University Press, 1988), 20–35.

8. Christopher Densmore, "The Dilemma of Quaker Anti-Slavery: The Case of Farmington Quarterly Meeting, 1836–1910," *Quaker History* (1993): 86–87; Christopher Densmore, " 'Be Ye Therefore Perfect': Anti-Slavery and the Origins of the Yearly Meeting of Progressive Friends in Chester County, Pennsylvania," *Quaker History* 93 (Fall 2000): 28–46.

9. *An Address from the Farmington Quarterly Meeting of Friends, to its Members on Slavery* (1836), 5, 7; *Address to the Citizens of the United States of America on the Subject of Slavery* (New York, 1837); *Address of the Yearly Meeting of the Religious Society of Friends . . . to the Professors of Christianity in the United States on the Subject of Slavery* (New York: James Egbert, 1852); Densmore, " Dilemma of Quaker Anti-Slavery," 82–84; *Address of Farmington Quarterly Meeting (New York) to the Monthly Meetings Constituting It, and to the Members of the Same Generally* (Managers of the Free Produce Association of Friends of Ohio Yearly Meeting, 1850).

10. *A Brief Statement on the Rise and Progress of the Testimony of the Religious Society of Friends, against Slavery and the Slave Trade* (Philadelphia: Joseph and William Kite, 1843); Samuel Rhoads, *Considerations on the Use of the Productions of Slavery, Addressed to the Religious Society of Friends*, 2nd ed. (Philadelphia: Merrihew and Thompson, 1845), 27; Ruth Ketring Nuermberger, *The Free Produce Movement: A Quaker Protest against Slavery* (New York: AMS Press, 1942), 35–36.

11. See, e.g., *National Anti-Slavery Standard*, May 26, 1842.

12. Thomas E. Drake, *Quakers and Slavery in America* (New Haven, Conn.: Yale University Press, 1950), 172–173; Nuermberger, *Free Produce Movement*, 33.

13. William Still, *The Underground Railroad: A Record of the Facts, Authentic Narrative, Letters, &c.* (Philadelphia: Porter and Coates, 1871), 864–865; Josephine F. Pacheco, "Myrtilla Miner," in *Three Who Dared: Prudence Crandall, Margaret Douglass, Myrtilla Miner—Champions of Antebellum Black Education* (Westport, Conn.: Greenwood Press, 1984), 124–126.

14. *Constitution of the Free Produce Society of Pennsylvania* (Philadelphia: D. & S. Neal, [1827]; *The Friend*, May 29, 1830; April 27, 1833; and May 31, 1834; Edwin B. Bronner, *Sharing the Scriptures: The Bible Association of Friends in America, 1829–1879* (Philadelphia: Bible Association of Friends, 1979); Lucretia Mott to Phebe Post Willis, September 13, 1834, in *Selected Letters of Lucretia Coffin Mott*, ed. Beverly Wilson Palmer (Urbana: University of Illinois Press, 2002), 28; *Liberator*, June 2, 1837; Sarah Pennock Sellers, *David Sellers, Mary Pennock Sellers* (n.p., 1926), 45–46; Alex Derkin to Abraham L. Pennock, June 18, 1845, Civil War and Slavery Collection, Special Collections and University Archives, Grand Valley State University Libraries, Allendale, Michigan.

15. George W. Taylor, *Autobiography and Writings of George W. Taylor* (Philadelphia: n.p., 1891), 29–30, 39–43; Nuermberger, *Free Produce Movement* 83–84.

16. Philadelphia Free Produce Association of Friends, "To Our Fellow Members of the Religious Society of Friends," Quaker Broadsides, QC, HC.

17. Free Produce Association of Friends of Philadelphia Yearly Meeting, Minutes of the Board of Managers, April 17, 1846, Journals, Diaries, Etc. Collection, QC, HC; *Non-Slaveholder*, February 1846, 17, 23; May 1846, 65–69; July 1846, 97; October 1846, 153; May 1847, 97–102; October 1847, 222; April 1848, 75–79; Free Produce Association of Friends of New-York Yearly Meeting, Report of the Board of Managers, 1849, 1851, 1852, 1853, 1854, Friends Historical Library, Swarthmore College, Swarthmore, Penn.; Free Produce Association of New York Yearly Meeting, Circular, February 2, 1848, Friends Historical Library, Swarthmore College, Swarthmore, Penn.; Free Produce Association of Friends of Ohio Yearly Meeting, *Second Annual Report of the Board of Managers* (Mount Pleasant, Ohio: Enoch Harris 1851); Nuermberger, *Free Produce Movement*, 52–56; Free Produce Association of Friends of New England Yearly Meeting, Free Produce Meeting (c. 1850), Free Produce Meeting (c. 1851), Minutes of Free Produce Meeting, June 17, 1852, all in Quaker Broadsides, QC, HC. See also Nuermberger, *Free Produce Movement*, 35–39, 41–44, 52; Drake, *Quakers and Slavery*, 173–174.

18. Free Produce Association of Friends of Ohio Yearly Meeting, *The Plea of Necessity* (1851), 2; Free Produce Association of Friends of Ohio Yearly Meeting, *Considerations on Abstinence from the Use of the Products of Slave Labor* (1851); *Address from Farmington Quarterly Meeting*.

19. Hamm, *Transformation of American Quakerism*, 20–35; Charles Osborn, *Journal of That Faithful Servant of Christ: Charles Osborn* (Cincinnati: Achilles Pugh, 1854), 344. Edgerton as quoted in Hamm, *Transformation of American Quakerism*, 31; Thomas D. Hamm David Dittmer, Chenda Fruchter, Ann Giordano, Janice Mathews, and Ellen Swain, "Moral Choices: Two Indiana Communities and the Abolitionist Movement," *Indiana Magazine of History* 87 (June 1991): 145.

20. Bassett as quoted in Ryan P. Jordan, *Slavery and the Meetinghouse: The Quakers and the Abolitionist Dilemma* (Bloomington: Indiana University Press, 2007), 32–33.

21. Drake, *Quakers and Slavery*, 159; Christopher Clark, *The Communitarian Moment: The Radical Challenge of the Northampton Association* (Ithaca: Cornell University Press, 1995), 69–71; Jordan, *Slavery and the Meetinghouse*, 32–33; William Bassett, *Letter to a Member of the Society of Friends: In Reply to Objections against Joining Anti-Slavery Societies* (Boston: Isaac Knapp, 1837).

22. Christopher Clark, "A Mother and Her Daughters at the Northampton Community: New Evidence on Women in Utopia," *New England Quarterly* 75 (December 2002): 598; William Bassett to Elizabeth Pease, July 22, 1844, ASC, BPL. See also Clark, *Communitarian Moment*; Christopher Clark and Kerry W. Buckley, eds., *Letters from an American Utopia: The Stetson Family and the Northampton Association, 1843–1847* (Amherst: University of Massachusetts Press, 2004).

23. William Bassett to Elizabeth Pease, July 22, 1844, ASC, BPL; Clark, *Communitarian Moment*, 69–71. See also William Bassett, *Proceedings of the Society of Friends in the Case of William Bassett* (Worcester: Joseph S. Wall, 1840).

24. Clark, *Communitarian Moment*, 195.

25. *Non-Slaveholder*, May 1, 1850.

26. Minutes of New England Yearly Meeting, 1836–1847, June 1837, as quoted in Drake, *Quakers and Slavery*, 147.

27. Drake, *Quakers and Slavery*, 164.

28. *National Anti-Slavery Standard*, February 6, 1845.

29. Densmore, "'Be Ye Therefore Perfect,'" 34–35; Margaret S. Young, *The Memories and History of Ercildoun 1976*, (n.p., 1976), 16.

30. Thomas D. Hamm, "George F. White and Hicksite Opposition to the Abolitionist Movement," in *Quakers and Abolition*, ed. Brycchan Carey and Geoffrey Plank (Urbana: University of Illinois Press, 2014), 43.

31. *Correspondence between Oliver Johnson and George F. White, a Minister of the Society of Friends* (New York: Oliver Johnson, 1841); *Narrative of the Proceedings of the Monthly Meeting of New York, and Their Subsequent Confirmation by the Quarterly and Yearly Meetings, in the Case of Isaac T. Hopper* (New York, 1843); *National Anti-Slavery Standard*, March 25, 1841; Hamm, "George F. White"; Faulkner, *Lucretia Mott's Heresy*, 83–85, 120–121; Jordan, *Slavery and the Meetinghouse*, 99.

32. Densmore, "'Be Ye Therefore Perfect,'" 35–43; Densmore, "Dilemma of Quaker Anti-Slavery," 86–87.

33. Born in Chester County in 1816, Thorne was educated by Enoch Lewis. Thorne was a strict vegetarian. He was active in the Chester County Anti-Slavery Society, the Pennsylvania Anti-Slavery Society, and the American Anti-Slavery Society. In the 1840s, Thorne became involved in the Underground Railroad. He spearheaded efforts to build the People's Hall in Ercildoun. Thorne also helped organize the Society of Progressive Friends and helped build their Longwood meetinghouse. "J. Williams Thorne," T. Chalkley Matlack Notebooks, QC, HC; Mark E. Dixon, *The Hidden History of Chester County: Lost Tales from the Delaware and Brandywine Valleys* (Charleston, S.C.: History Press, 2011), 80–82.

34. Free Produce Association of Friends of Philadelphia Yearly Meeting, Minutes of the Board of Managers, April 17, 1846, AFPA, HSP.

35. Elihu Burritt to William Lloyd Garrison, September 8, 1846, in *British and American Abolitionists: An Episode in Transatlantic Understanding*, ed. Clare Taylor (Edinburgh: Edinburgh University Press, 1974), 287–288.

36. Elihu Burritt to George W. Taylor, September 29, 1846; Elihu Burritt to George W. Taylor, November 11, 1846; both Taylor Family Papers, QC, HC; Betty Fladeland, *Men and Brothers: Anglo-American Antislavery Cooperation* (Urbana: University of Illinois Press, 1972), 368–369; Peter Tolis, *Elihu Burritt: Crusade for Brotherhood* (Hamden, Conn.: Archon Books, 1968), 237–238; Elizabeth A. O'Donnell, "'There's Death in the Pot!': The British Free-Produce Movement and the Religious Society of Friends, with Particular Reference to the North-East of England," *Quaker Studies* 13 (March 2009): 189; Clare Midgley, *Women against Slavery: The British Campaigns, 1780–1870* (London: Routledge, 1992), 136.

37. Elihu Burritt to Gerrit Smith, October 6, 1856, in Merle Curti, *The Learned Blacksmith: The Letters and Journals of Elihu Burritt* (New York: Wilson-Erikson, 1937), 118, 125–126, 129–130; Tolis, *Elihu Burritt*, 238–244; Fladeland, *Men and Brothers*, 371; Louis Billington, "British Humanitarians and American Cotton, 1840–1860," *Journal of American Studies* 11, no. 3 (1977): 318–332.

38. R. J. M. Blackett, *Building an Antislavery Wall: Black Americans in the Atlantic Abolitionist Movement, 1830–1860* (Ithaca, N.Y.: Cornell University Press, 1983), 119–123, 143–145. Blackett argues, "The fact that black visitors were affiliated with one of the other wing of the movement was of little significance; what mattered was that their independent approach provided many British abolitionists with a 'practical' alternative."

39. Ibid., 119–123; Joel Schor, *Henry Highland Garnet: A Voice of Black Radicalism in the Nineteenth Century* (Westport, Conn.: Greenwood Press, 1977), 111–122; David E. Swift, *Black Prophets of Justice: Activist Clergy before the Civil War* (Baton Rouge: Louisiana State University Press, 1989), 251–258.

40. *Anti-Slavery Reporter*, January 1, 1846; Anna Vaughan Kett, "Quaker Women, the Free Produce Movement and British Anti-Slavery Campaigns: The Free Labour Cotton Depot in Street, 1852–1858" (PhD diss., University of Brighton, 2012), 85–88.

41. Benjamin Coates, *Cotton Cultivation in Africa: Suggestions on the Importance of the Cultivation of Cotton in Africa, in Reference to the Abolition of Slavery in the United States, through the Organization of an African Civilization Society* (Philadelphia: C. Sherman and Son, 1858); Swift, *Black Prophets of Justice*, 285–296; Schor, *Henry Highland Garnet*, 147–158; Carol Faulkner, "The Root of the Evil: Free Produce and Radical Antislavery, 1820–1860," *Journal of the Early Republic* 27 (2007): 399–403; Richard K. MacMaster, "Henry Highland Garnet and the African Civilization Society," *Journal of Presbyterian History* 48 (1970): 95–112. See also Emma J. Lapsansky-Werner and Margaret Hope Bacon, eds. *Back to Africa: Benjamin Coates and the Colonization Movement in America, 1848–1880* (Philadelphia: University of Pennsylvania, 2005).

42. *Weekly Anglo-African*, August 5, 1859.

43. Swift, *Black Prophets of Justice*, 285–296; Schor, *Henry Highland Garnet*, 147–158; Faulkner, "Root of the Evil," 399–403; Richard K. MacMaster, "Henry Highland Garnet and the African Civilization Society," *Journal of Presbyterian History* 48 (1970): 95–112. See also Werner-Lapsansky, *Back to Africa*.

44. James M. Day, *Jacob de Cordova: Land Merchant of Texas* (Waco, Texas: Texian Press, 1962), 141–142; Natalie Ornish, "De Cordova, Jacob Raphael," *Handbook of Texas Online*, http://www.tshaonline.org/handbook/online/articles/fde03.

45. *DeBow's Review and Industrial Resources*, June 1858.

46. *Saturday Review*, December 11, 1858.

47. Jacob de Cordova, *The Cultivation of Cotton in Texas* (London: J. King, 1858), 5, 15–19, 59.

48. Day, *Jacob de Cordova*, 141–142; Ornish, "De Cordova."

49. Laura Wood Roper, "Frederick Law Olmsted and the Western Texas Free-Soil Movement," *American Historical Review* 56 (October 1950): 58–64; Percy W. Bidwell, "The New England Emigrant Aid Company and English Cotton Supply Associations: Letters of Frederick L. Olmsted, 1857," *American Historical Review* 23 (October 1917): 114–118; Frederick Law Olmsted, *A Journey through Texas: A Saddle-Trip on the Southwestern Frontier*, ed. James Howard (Austin, Texas: Von Boeckmann-Jones Press, 1962).

50. Edward Atkinson, *Cheap Cotton by Free Labor* (Boston: A. Williams, 1861), 13–14, 24–25, 30–31.

51. Olmsted as quoted in Richard H. Abbott, *Cotton and Capital: Boston Businessmen and Antislavery Reform, 1854–1868* (Amherst: University of Massachusetts Press, 1991), 78.

52. John Andrew to Gustvaus Fox, November 27, 1861, in *The War of the Rebellion: A Compilation of the Official Records of the Union and Confederate Armies*, 128 vols. (Washington, D.C., 1880–1901), ser. 1, 15:412–413.

53. Abbott, *Cotton and Capital*, 77–82, 150–152; Ludwell H. Johnson, *Red River Campaign: Politics and Cotton in the Civil War* (Kent, Ohio: Kent State University Press,

1958), 7–9; Stephen Steinberg, *The Ethnic Myth: Race, Ethnicity, and Class in America* (Boston: Beacon Press, 1989), 189.

54. For Nathan Thomas's trip through the South, see Nathan Thomas to Samuel Rhoads, January 6, 1848; January 11, 1848; Nathan Thomas to George W. Taylor, January 25, 1848; February 2, 1848; February 7, 1848; March 12, 1848; March 24, 1848, all Taylor Family Papers, QC, HC.

55. *Citizen of the World* 1 (January 1855), 11.

56. Richard Carpenter to Richard Mott, December 5, 1850, Richard Mott Papers, QC, HC.

57. *Friends' Review* 7 (May 6, 1854): 533.

58. Edward E. Baptist, *The Half Has Never Been Told: Slavery and the Making of American Capitalism* (New York: Basic Books, 2014), 135–143, 350.

Conclusion

1. 2 Kings 4:38–41.

2. Walter Gratzer, *Terrors of the Table: The Curious History of Nutrition* (New York: Oxford University Press, 2005), 124–127.

3. Anna Richardson, *There Is Death in the Pot!* (London: C. Gilpin, c. 1850).

4. Clare Midgley, *Feminism and Empire: Women Activists in Imperial Britain* (London: Routledge, 2007), 63; Adam Hochschild, *Bury the Chains: Prophets and Rebels in the Fight to Free an Empire's Slaves* (New York: Houghton Mifflin, 2005), 193.

5. Donna McDaniel and Venessa Julye, *Fit for Freedom, Not for Friendship: Quakers, African Americans, and the Myth of Racial Justice* (Philadelphia: Quaker Press of Friends General Conference, 2009), 65; Ruth Ketring Nuermberger, *The Free Produce Movement: A Quaker Protest against Slavery* (New York: AMS Press, 1942), 115.

6. Elihu Burritt to George W. Taylor, September 29, 1846, Taylor Family Papers, QC, HC. Taylor's statement is penned as a note at the bottom of Burritt's letter and is dated, by Taylor, January 1, 1884.

7. Carol Faulkner, "The Root of the Evil: Free Produce and Radical Antislavery, 1820–1860," *Journal of the Early Republic* 27 (2007): 396–397.

8. *North Star*, June 23, 1848; Henry Richardson, *Revolution of the Spindles for the Overthrow of American Slavery* (n.p., c. 1848).

9. "Remarks of Alexander Crummell, 21 May 1849," in *The Black Abolitionist Papers*, 5 vols. (Chapel Hill: University of North Carolina Press, 1985), 1:149–150.

10. Nuermberger, *Free Produce Movement*, 114.

11. A substantial body of scholarship points to the connection between slavery and nineteenth-century capitalism. For an overview, see Seth Rockman, "Slavery and Capitalism," *Journal of the Civil War Era*, http://journalofthecivilwarera.com /forum-the-future-of-civil-war-era-studies/the-future-of-civil-war-era-studies -slavery-and-capitalism. For recent scholarship, see Edward E. Baptist, *The Half Has Never Been Told: Slavery and the Making of American Capitalism* (New York: Basic Books, 2014); Sven Beckert, *Empire of Cotton: A Global History* (New York: Alfred A. Knopf, 2014); Walter Johnson, *River of Dark Dreams: Slavery and Empire in the Cotton Kingdom* (Cambridge, Mass.: Harvard University Press, 2013); Joshua Rothman, *Flush Times and Fever Dreams: A Story of Capitalism and Slavery in the Age of Jackson* (Athens: Uni-

versity of Georgia Press, 2012); Craig Steven Wilder, *Ebony & Ivy: Race, Slavery, and the Troubled History of America's Universities* (New York: Bloomsbury Press, 2013).

12. See, e.g., Seth Rockman, *A Landscape of Industry: An Industrial History of the Blackstone Valley. A Project of the Worcester Historical Museum and the John H. Chaffee Blackstone River Valley National Heritage Corridor* (Lebanon, N.H.: University Press of New England, 2009), 110–131.

13. Thomas F. De Voe, *The Market Assistant, Containing a Brief Description of Every Article of Human Food Sold in the Public Markets of the Cities of New York, Boston, Philadelphia, and Brooklyn* (New York: Hurd and Houghton, 1867), 321–322.

14. Rockman, "Slavery and Capitalism," 5–6.

15. May to Estlin, May 2, 1848, May Papers, BPL.

16. Lawrence Glickman, *Buying Power: A History of Consumer Activism in America* (Chicago: University of Chicago Press, 2009), 88–89.

INDEX

abolitionist movement: abstention and, 39–40, 60–61, 62, 64, 123–34, 141–45, 169–70, 179–82, 187; free produce and, 1–3, 123–34, 141–45, 156–64, 166–67, 169–70, 179–82, 187; juveniles and, 115–22, 139–41; opposition to boycott within, 1–3, 10–11, 156–64, 166–67. *See also* antislavery movement

abolitionists: abstention and, 4–7, 8–9, 11, 36, 38, 60–61, 62, 64; free produce and, 1–3, 4–7, 8–9, 11, 166–67, 169–70, 183, 184, 187, 191; opposition to the boycott, 1–3, 9–10, 166–67, 170, 187, 190

abstention: boycott and, 195n1; free produce and, 73

Adam, William, 152, 154–55, 157–58, 159, 167

Africa, 29, 40, 42, 54, 65, 75, 80, 108; colonization and, 7, 8, 75, 80, 170, 182–83, 187, 191; cotton and, 182–83, 187; slave trade and, 22

African Americans, 78–81, 128; abstention and, 6–7, 81, 131–32, 179–82; activism, 64, 114–15, 131–32, 140, 156; colonization and, 80–81; community building, 79–81; free produce and, 6–7, 114–15, 131–32, 179–82; juvenile antislavery societies, 140; made "commercial commodities" by slave trade and slavery, 81; petitions, 78–79; publications, 79–81, 149, 191; racial equality, 78–81, 128. *See also* African Methodist Episcopal Church (Bethel); American Moral Reform Society; Annual Conventions for the Improvement of the Free People of Colour in the United States; Colored Female Free Produce Society; Colored Free Produce Society of Pennsylvania

African Civilization Society, 147, 182–83

African Methodist Episcopal Church (Bethel), 7, 80, 114, 115, 131, 132

Allen, Richard, 7, 79, 80, 114, 115, 131

Allen, William, 50

American Anti-Slavery Society, 108, 125, 127, 133, 139, 144, 148, 158

American Colonization Society, 75, 80–81, 88, 124, 125, 131

American Convention for Promoting the Abolition of Slavery and Improving the Condition of the African Race, 78

American Free Produce Association, 143–45, 146, 148–51, 154, 160, 161–68, 182; abolitionist movement and, 166; black abolitionists and, 7, 144; Quakers and, 2, 137, 144, 164–66, 172, 175; women and, 144, 159

American Moral Reform Society, 132

animals, 70

Annual Conventions for the Improvement of the Free People of Colour in the United States, 131–32

Anti-Corn Law League, 167–68. *See also* British India Society; Thompson, George

The Anti-Slavery Alphabet, 120–21. *See also* publications

Anti-Slavery Conventions of Women, 127–30, 142

antislavery fairs, 145

antislavery movement: abstention and, 39–40, 60–61, 62, 64, 123–34, 141–45, ; free produce and, 123–34, 141–45, 156–64, 166–67, 169–70, 179–82, 187; juveniles and, 115–22, 139–41; opposition to boycott within, 1–3, 10–11, 156–64, 166–67; parliamentary reform and, 41; women and 113–15. *See also* abolitionist movement

Association for Promoting the Abolition of Slavery, 137–38

9 781501 748493